STERLING-DOLLAR
DIPLOMACY

Oxford University Press, Amen House, London E.C.4

GLASGOW NEW YORK TORONTO MELBOURNE WELLINGTON
BOMBAY CALCUTTA MADRAS KARACHI CAPE TOWN IBADAN

Geoffrey Cumberlege, Publisher to the University

Harry Dexter White (*left*) and John Maynard Keynes

Photo by PIX

STERLING–DOLLAR DIPLOMACY

ANGLO-AMERICAN COLLABORATION
IN THE RECONSTRUCTION OF
MULTILATERAL TRADE

BY

RICHARD N. GARDNER

OXFORD
AT THE CLARENDON PRESS
1956

PRINTED IN GREAT BRITAIN

To

MY PARENTS

whose Love and Sacrifice

made this book possible

FOREWORD

THIS is a stimulating book on an important subject. The idea for it was conceived when Richard Gardner, then an American Rhodes Scholar at Oxford, came to me in search of an appropriate subject for doctoral research in his chosen field of international economics. Together we cast about for a topic which would fit Mr. Gardner's interests and skills. He was a lawyer primarily, already a member of the New York Bar, who had acquired a good grounding in economics. He was also an American in England, greatly interested in problems of Anglo-American relations. After some time we hit upon the idea that he should make a systematic examination of the interaction between public opinion in the two countries, on the one hand, and the course of their economic relations, on the other. This seemed a new field to explore. In the event, Mr. Gardner's work led him to an exhaustive study of the joint planning and drafting of certain vital institutions—the Bretton Woods organizations, the Anglo-American Loan Agreement, the International Trade Organization, and the General Agreement on Tariffs and Trade—and the fate of these institutions in the early post-war period. Thus this book comprises an authoritative review of an important piece of history, as well as a significant analysis of the interrelation between policy and opinion in international economic affairs.

The story so well told here seemed to me badly to need telling. I had in mind my own experience. I had taken an active part in the discussions of the drafts of the late Lord Keynes's Clearing Union and other documents relating to post-war plans, and subsequently I had watched the course of events from the periphery, but with inside knowledge. There had been a considerable momentum of enthusiasm for these plans at the centre. The British were struck by the adaptability of the Americans, and their readiness to look at many problems from points of view not their own and to modify their plans accordingly. It really seemed to me, and I think to many others concerned, that, despite serious differences, sufficient common ground of philosophy and policy and purpose had been achieved to make a great new era of economic co-operation possible after the war. One watched hopefully for big developments of worldwide significance.

Yet when I had slipped out of official employment as soon as the war was over, all seemed quite changed. These great purposes appeared to be lost to view. What had happened?

Was it that the new Labour Government took no interest in these vital questions? Yet its more important members had been in Mr. Churchill's coalition. Surely they had not overnight lost faith or their appreciation of the vital importance, even from a narrow British point of view, of economic co-operation with the Americans. Probably matters were still being pushed forward behind the scenes in ways of which, as an outsider, one knew nothing. But even more striking was the state of public opinion. I found even in well-informed circles the most dense ignorance about the purport of the plans, and, so it seemed, complete indifference about them. During the war much had naturally been secret, but now the plans, touching as they did Britain's most vital interests and her capacity for solvency, should be in the forefront of men's minds. But when I talked of these matters, I found superciliousness and incredulity. It was as though I was a traveller from distant lands telling tales that were frankly not believed. Keynes was exceedingly worried about this; he referred to the attitude of mind of the British public as one of 'invincible ignorance'; the expression seemed entirely just. Evidently the British authorities, preoccupied as they had naturally been with fighting the war, had not done a good job of education.

And what of the American side? We in Britain had some misgivings about the abrupt way in which Lend-Lease was terminated and about American attitudes at the Inaugural Meeting of the Fund and Bank. Had there been since Roosevelt's death a subtle shift in the balance of power as between different personalities which meant that the Americans had lost their adaptability and co-operative spirit? I could not know about these things. And then, what of American public opinion? Was there over there that same great gulf between inside opinion and outside opinion that was manifested in Britain?

This study contributes much to our understanding of these things. It confirms my view that on the English side too little effort was made to educate the public about what was afoot. This may have been due to the distractions of war; our civilian population was receiving V1 and V2 projectiles almost until the end. It may have been due to the reticence that is natural to the English, and to an unnecessary enlargement of the scope of what should be regarded as secret. Whatever the reason, however, there can be little doubt, in the light of Mr. Gardner's study, that this failure of education had a most serious effect.

The study also reveals certain points about the American attitude which I did not fully appreciate before. On that side there was plenty of publication, propaganda, education. The fault was that the hopes raised were too high. Not enough effort was made to explain the points of view and the problems of the British, and, indeed, of the other nations whose co-operation would be required. There was also the point of view that the United States should take a tactical advantage of the position created by Lend-Lease to wrench the British away from the policies to which they were otherwise addicted—in fine, to defeat British Imperialism. That is an approach quite different from that of collaboration. Instead of finding some common ground in which both partners believed—and there was really much common ground present—one tried to coerce one's partner into doing something that he really did not want to do. This book shows us how much we have suffered from this mistake.

All these things Mr. Gardner writes about with scholarship, good judgement, and a commendable objectivity. His position as an American writing an Oxford dissertation on such controversial matters was not an easy one. Yet he has managed to avoid special pleading on behalf of his own country or of his British hosts. Moreover, he has brought to his task that rare gift—a fine command of English prose style.

This book casts fresh light on recent events. As one who has been close to certain of them, I have been quite startled at some of Mr. Gardner's revelations. Yet it would be a pity if these revelations alone were the main matter that drew attention to the book. Its principal value, it seems to me, is as a study in the diplomatic relations between two democracies. By analysing some major difficulties in these relations it provides important lessons for the future. It is for this reason that Mr. Gardner's work should be read and pondered by everyone vitally concerned with the conduct of public affairs.

Mr. Gardner's story has an unhappy ending, but he carries it only to 1947. Since then matters have in some respects taken on a more cheerful aspect. Mr. Gardner finds that by 1947 the aim of multilateralism, which at the outset was common ground between the two countries, had been completely frustrated. In 1947 one might wonder whether the obstacles to its achievement were mainly transitional difficulties connected with the immediate aftermath of war, or whether the whole shape of things in the world today was inconsistent with the aim. The subsequent course of events should incline us to the former and more cheerful point of view. We have recently been making considerable progress towards the objective of multilateralism. But of course new troubles may blow up.

And therein lies the importance of this work. New troubles will call for new adjustments and new agreements. When nations have, as they will inevitably continue to have, somewhat different vital interests and different points of view, there is always difficulty in reaching agreements, and the intentions of the agreements may be somewhat differently interpreted by the parties to them. If it were not for this little bit of latitude, it would be even more difficult to reach agreements than it has so often proved to be. What is vitally important is that democratic leaders should regard it as their bounden duty to explain to their peoples what, to the best of their knowledge, the points of view and intentions and vital interests of the other partners are. Each nation must learn that the other nations naturally have different interests and points of view. The explanation of the other point of view should be done fairly and without malice, but must not understate the difference—otherwise the agreement will lead to frustration and mutual loss of confidence between the partners.

We have not only to think of co-operation between what we regard as members of the free world. We still cherish the hope, if we are optimistic, and it is right to be optimistic, that in due course and at long last there may be agreements on certain topics bringing the now divided world closer together. Then these problems will become very acute indeed. It will be absolutely incumbent upon responsible leaders to explain not only what they have in mind in appending their signatures to agreements, but also what, to the best of their understanding, the other parties to the agreements have in mind. If there can have been such grave and utter misunderstanding of the other point of view as between the two partners, the United States and Britain, locked in a close alliance during the war, what misunderstandings may there be in relation to agreements between the free democracies and the Communist powers! It is not only a question of the actual content of the commitments expressed by certain language in a given agreement, but of all the motives and intentions which govern the willingness of each party to sign such an agreement.

It is incumbent upon the leaders in each country to obtain a thorough understanding of what these are, and to explain them to their peoples in unvarnished terms. Much about the nature and scope of this problem may be learned by a careful study of Mr. Gardner's book. This is a matter of no little moment; indeed it is a matter of paramount and over-riding concern for us all.

R. F. HARROD

Christ Church, Oxford
January 1956

PREFACE

THIS, like most books, was inspired by a personal experience of the author. I was an American student in England some six years after the end of the Second World War. It was not a smooth period in Anglo-American relations. There was a good deal of uneasiness in Britain about American economic policies. There were even misgivings about the great effort of Anglo-American collaboration which had created the Bretton Woods organizations, the Anglo-American Financial Agreement, the Charter of the International Trade Organization, and the General Agreement on Tariffs and Trade. Hitherto I had rather taken for granted the soundness of this effort. But the intensity of the criticism impelled me to undertake a systematic study of the historical record. That study has now, some five years later, resulted in the present volume.

This introductory explanation may serve to warn the reader of what this book is and what it is not. It is not a book of economic theory in which one can find an original discussion of the principles of international trade. Still less is it a statistical analysis of the post-war pattern of international trade and payments. It is rather a book about the making of international economic policy and the shaping of institutions to implement that policy. It places special emphasis on the interaction between official policy and public opinion—particularly, on the difficult problem of explaining complex economic policies to a democratic electorate. Thus it is a hybrid work on the border-line of history, international relations, political science, and even international law. Perhaps it can best be described as 'a study in international economic diplomacy'.

For some time I have wanted to undertake such a study. Here is a field which has been somewhat neglected, partly, I suspect, because of our rather accidental classification of academic disciplines. Economists have only rarely attempted the writing of history; when doing so they have usually confined themselves to the history of 'pure' economic phenomena and avoided consideration of the political forces at work. Professional historians, for similar reasons of specialization, have been reluctant to analyse economic policies and events. Specialists in international relations and international law have also tended to neglect these subjects in their analysis of international institutions. Thus few studies have been undertaken in a fascinating and important field.

The present work represents one attempt to change this state of affairs. It is concerned with a sequence of historical events beginning with the drafting of the Atlantic Charter and ending finally with the decision of the United States Government to abandon the International Trade Organization. In the history of Anglo-American economic collaboration the period bounded by these two events forms something of an era. It was an era during which the United Nations embarked under Anglo-American leadership on the most ambitious programme of intergovernmental co-operation ever undertaken in the economic field. The aim of this programme was the reconstruction of 'multilateralism'—a system of international trade conducted along reasonably free and non-discriminatory lines.

The present work is a history of the multilateral goal and of the early life of the institutions which were to make it a reality—the International Monetary Fund and the International Bank for Reconstruction and Development; the Anglo-American Financial Agreement; the International Trade Organization; and the General Agreement on Tariffs and Trade. It seeks to answer three main questions: What exactly was the multilateral objective? What institutional devices were chosen to achieve it? Were the institutions well designed to promote the end in view?

Yet it would be misleading to present this work as a comprehensive account of the international economic institutions created after the Second World War. It is primarily a history of Anglo-American collaboration. Writing it has reinforced my belief in the critical importance of this collaboration for the prosperity and security of the free world. While Anglo-American collaboration by itself is hardly a sufficient condition for the achievement of these objectives, it certainly is a necessary one. Britain and the United States, the world's two largest trading nations and the centres of the world's two major currency areas, must strike a harmony in their economic policies if a workable international order is to be achieved. I chose to write this history mainly as a history of Anglo-American collaboration, not because I thought it would tell the complete story, but simply because I thought it would tell a coherent and important part of the story without which nothing else could be adequately understood.

I am bound to say in all honesty that on important aspects of this history others are better qualified than myself. I was not a participant in the Anglo-American negotiations and never knew Keynes, White, Vinson, or Morgenthau except as names in a newspaper headline. Yet there were several compelling reasons which emboldened me to the present effort. Although participants in the actual events still survived, most of them were prevented either by law or moral scruple from telling the full story themselves. If many were more familiar than I with certain aspects of the story, there were few, if any, who were well acquainted with all of it. Moreover, those who had been personally involved might find it difficult to tell the story without giving expression to individual or national prejudices. Finally— perhaps the most compelling point of all—nobody had in fact decided to make the attempt.

Serious difficulties were involved in writing this history of policy and opinion. With respect to policy, there was the problem of writing about controversial matters so closely after the event. Much official documentation had been published—the international agreements themselves, copious preparatory materials, and official statements of national positions. But much was also still unpublished. Except for newspaper accounts and one or two isolated memoirs, the public had not been given details of the planning within the two governments or of the negotiations between them which produced the final results.

This gap I was able to fill in part through the kindness of several persons who took an interest in my study. Professor Jacob Viner of Princeton, to whose writings I was already much in debt, granted me permission to use the collected papers of Harry Dexter White which Mrs. White had given to the Firestone Library after her husband's death. Professor Ross Pritchard of Tufts College was no less generous in making available some of the official papers of Will Clayton, about whom he was writing a study. These two major sources yielded official memoranda prepared within both Governments, records of meetings within the American Government, communications between the leading negotiators, and other equally valuable documents. With these as a beginning, with the help of certain other unpublished materials, and with the help of intensive interviews with actual participants in the events, I set about fitting together the pieces of the historical picture.

With respect to opinion as well as policy, the writing of this history presented problems. Here the difficulty was not a lack of materials, but a plethora. The events in which I was interested had stimulated a vast amount of discussion in daily newspapers, popular and scho-larly periodicals, books, and other published materials. I struck a particularly valuable mine of information in the newspaper clipping files of the Royal Institute of International Affairs, placed at my disposal by Miss Lois Simpson of that organization. This enabled me to make a systematic study of comment in leading newspapers published on both sides of the Atlantic. But that was only the begin-ning of the problem. From the mass of material it was necessary to distill the most significant expressions of opinion and to trace their development in time. Unfortunately, we have not yet devised wholly effective methods for such analysis. Consequently I had to write my history of opinion in a selective and almost impressionistic fashion, paraphrasing and quoting from those sources which seemed to me most important.

In writing this book I have been acutely conscious of the disability of all historians—that of maintaining a proper proportion between the facts as we know them to be today and the facts as they must have seemed to the actors at the time. 'History', as one historian has noted, 'is lived forward but is written in retrospect. We know the end before we consider the beginning and we can never wholly recapture what it was to know the beginning only.' I have sought to recapture the spirit of the years of which I have written and to judge the parti-cipants only in the light of what they actually knew or could have known at the time.

I must make one final point. This book discusses issues which have aroused considerable controversy. Some of them are still with us today. I have not been completely 'objective' in discussing them, if that word should be interpreted to mean the lack of a point of view on the desirability of multilateralism and on the means by which it can be achieved. I have aspired to 'objectivity' only in the sense of presenting national viewpoints as fully and fairly as possible and avoiding partisan pleading on behalf of my own country or of the country in which the study began. In short, the point of view of this work is designed to be neither 'pro-American' nor 'pro-British', but rather 'mid-Atlantic'.

Most books are based on an exchange of ideas, advice, and en-couragement. In this one the exchange has been very much in my favour. I owe a particularly large debt to the following persons on both sides of the Atlantic:

Professor John H. Williams, who first stimulated my interest in international economic relations when I was an undergraduate at Harvard.

Dean Eugene Rostow, Professor Myres McDougal, and Professor Harold D. Lasswell of the Yale Law School, who encouraged me to combine the study of international law with the study of international economics, and to pursue that combination at Oxford.

The Rhodes Scholarship Trust, whose benefaction enabled me to carry out this plan.

Roy Harrod, my Oxford superviser, whose *Life of John Maynard Keynes* inspired this book and whose wise and generous counsel guided it to completion.

Sir Donald MacDougall, who served as superviser during two terms of Mr. Harrod's absence, despite heavy commitments in Government service.

E. T. Williams, Warden of Rhodes House, and Professor Arthur Goodhart, Master of University College, who sustained me with helpful advice and encouragement throughout my Oxford career.

Dean Erwin Griswold and Associate Dean David Cavers of the Harvard Law School, who granted me a Teaching Fellowship in International Legal Studies during the academic year 1953–54, thus enabling me to complete my Oxford dissertation.

Mrs. S. G. Gurney, of Bayworth Corner, Boars Hill, Oxford, who gave me hospitality and moral support in the final stage of that effort.

Professor James Meade and Professor Agnes Headlam-Morley, my Oxford Examiners, who provided helpful suggestions for revising the Doctor of Philosophy dissertation into its present form.

Edward Bernstein of the International Monetary Fund and Richard Ford of G.A.T.T., who gave me much material on the history of those institutions.

Certain authorities who took special pains to read and advise on my preliminary drafts—Sir Frank Lee, Charles Kindleberger, Judd Polk, Bill Diebold, Emilio Collado, Harry Hawkins, John Leddy, George Bronz, and Winthrop Brown.

Mrs. Elizabeth Valkenier of the Council on Foreign Relations, who helped me in a final check of citations.

Mrs. Peter Steer, in Drayton St. Leonard, Oxford, and Mrs. Marcelle Jordan, in New York, who typed the manuscripts of the dissertation and book.

Coudert Brothers, and especially Alexis Coudert, whose kindness and generosity helped me through the final revision.

Last, but not least, the countless persons on both sides of the Atlantic in universities, journalism, and public life, who generously contributed ideas to the author. A complete listing of their names would be impractical and would, in some cases, violate express wishes for anonymity.

RICHARD N. GARDNER

New York City, N.Y.
February 1956

CONTENTS

Contents

LIST OF PLATES

The frontispiece is from a photograph by PIX
and plates 1–7 from photographs by 'WIDE WORLD PHOTOS'

For there are, in the present time, two opinions; not, as in former ages, the true and the false, but the outside and the inside; the opinion of the public voiced by the politicians and the newspapers, and the opinion of the politicians, the journalists, and the civil servants, upstairs and backstairs and behind-stairs, expressed in limited circles.

Those who live in limited circles and share the inside opinion pay both too much and too little attention to the outside opinion; too much, because, ready in words and promises to concede to it everything, they regard open opposition as absurdly futile; too little, because they believe that these words and promises are so certainly designed to change in due season, that it is pedantic, tiresome, and inappropriate to analyse their literal meaning and exact consequences. They know all this nearly as well as the critic, who wastes, in their view, his time and his emotions in exciting himself too much over what, on his own showing, cannot possibly happen. Nevertheless, what is said before the world, is still of deeper consequence than the subterranean breathings and well-informed whisperings, knowledge of which allows inside opinion to feel superior to outside opinion, even at the moment of bowing to it.

JOHN MAYNARD KEYNES

PART I

THE OBJECTIVE OF MULTILATERALISM

CHAPTER I

THE AMERICAN CHALLENGE

'LET there be no mistake about it. The policy put forward by the American Administration is revolutionary. It is a genuinely new conception of world order. It is an inspiring attempt to restate democracy in terms of the twentieth century situation, and to extend its meaning in the economic and social sphere.'

With these words *The Economist* in the midst of the Second World War described the 'challenge' in foreign economic policy presented by the words and actions of public figures on the other side of the Atlantic.[1] What inspired this enthusiastic British account of American post-war planning? Was it an accurate appraisal of the forces emerging to shape the foreign economic policy of the United States?

AN UNPROMISING LEGACY

Certainly there was very little in the history of the pre-war period to justify such an optimistic account of the role the United States was prepared to play in post-war economic affairs. The dominant tradition in this aspect of American policy had been a compound of economic isolation and economic nationalism. Before the mid-1930's the United States paid little attention to international economic problems; on the occasions when it was forced to do so it played a lone hand without much regard for the interests of other countries. The major features of this tradition are well known—the adoption of higher and higher protective tariffs; the insistence on repayment of the First World War debts; and the subordination of international to domestic recovery measures which disrupted the London Economic Conference of 1933.

Four factors may be cited as of particular importance in explaining this unpromising historical legacy. The first, plainly enough, was the tradition of American political isolation. In recent years it has been pointed out that the term 'isolation' is not entirely accurate as a description of American attitudes toward the rest of the world in the

---

[1] 'The American Challenge', cxliii (1942), p. 67.

B

early decades of the twentieth century; the sustained active interest in
South American and Far Eastern affairs would seem to confirm this
objection. But it is certainly true that, as regards the affairs of the
Old World, the posture of the United States was that of fairly consistent withdrawal. Since it was Europe, and Britain in particular,
which was the hub of the world's economy, the significance of that
posture for America's participation in international economic affairs
was clear enough. Having rejected membership in the League of
Nations, it was difficult for the United States to associate itself
closely with the League's official economic activities. At the same
time, the international activities of private finance were regarded
with deep suspicion. Thus American participation in international
economic affairs was inhibited even on the unofficial level.

A second factor in the American tradition of economic withdrawal
was the country's natural economic position. The United States was
a large continental land-mass, potentially self-sufficient in nearly all
branches of production. It had little need either to import large
quantities of goods from abroad or to look beyond its borders for
profitable investment outlets. These factors, of course, did not
preclude the possibility of deriving substantial benefits from international trade and investment carried on along the lines of comparative advantage. But they did make it much easier to forego such
benefits if other factors impelled the country to do so. In the years
before the Second World War foreign trade accounted for only
one-twentieth part of American national income. And while the
United States had once been a substantial importer of foreign
capital, it never adjusted to being a capital exporter on a comparable
scale.

A third obstacle to United States participation in international
economic co-operation—especially with Britain and other European
governments—was the devotion of a considerable body of American
opinion to the philosophy of *laissez-faire*. This may seem a rather
paradoxical statement. The most truly 'international' economic
system, surely, was one in which intervention by national governments was absent and comparative efficiencies, working through the
price mechanism, determined the allocation of world resources. The
answer to this objection, of course, was that the liberal system could
no longer be automatically achieved. After the havoc wrought by
two world wars and the Great Depression the reconstruction of a
liberal world economy was bound to require widespread government

intervention. Such an effort, especially if it involved active participation by the United States, would arouse determined opposition from the same American groups who opposed the extension of government activity in the domestic sphere.

The last and perhaps the most intractable factor inhibiting a hopeful American approach toward international economic affairs was the constitutional and political structure of the United States. Any country with a widely dispersed and heterogeneous population would find it difficult to form an integrated and consistent foreign economic policy. In the United States this natural difficulty was further aggravated by a political system which tended to subordinate national to local interests and, as a corollary of this, international considerations to considerations of a domestic character. The bargaining among sectional groups, so essential a part of the American legislative process, often produced unfortunate results when it came to matters affecting the relations of the United States with the rest of the world.

American tariff policy provided a notable example of this problem. Individual congressmen who held liberal views on the tariff question were often forced to give way to the protectionist demands of influential constituents. Congressmen from areas where the fear of foreign competition was great would support one another's restrictive proposals. In this way the natural protectionism of many American business men, especially those in industries making greater relative use of high-cost American labour, would be quickly transformed into national policy.

The same problem was present, to an even greater extent, in the field of agriculture. By the mid-1930's the most important American agricultural and mining interests, faced with such difficulties as overproduction, high labour costs, and uneconomic sources of supply, had abandoned the cause of liberal trade. The system of Congressional districting and of electing two Senators from each State regardless of population gave these interests a disproportionately large representation in the American Congress. The farm bloc was particularly well placed to press for greater protection against foreign foodstuffs and raw materials.

The forces of industrial and agricultural protection enjoyed an additional advantage on the eve of the Second World War. Although the early days of the New Deal had witnessed a striking growth in Executive power, the Congress was, to some extent, coming into its own again. National defence, aid to the Allies, and finally war itself brought a vast expansion in government expenditures. These expenditures could only be authorized by the legislature. Congress, with its critical power of the purse, was therefore in a strong position to influence American policy in the international economic field.

The four factors outlined above presented very considerable obstacles to the development by the United States of a positive foreign economic policy. What was the basis, then, of the American 'challenge' in international economic affairs?

THE POST-WAR PLANNERS

The nature of the American 'challenge' in foreign economic policy can best be understood against the general background of American post-war planning. There were three main centres of this activity. The first was in the Department of State under the direction of Secretary of State Cordell Hull and Under-Secretary of State Sumner Welles. The second was in the Treasury Department under Secretary of the Treasury Henry Morgenthau, Jr., and his deputy in charge of international financial problems, Harry Dexter White. The third was in the Board of Economic Warfare under Vice-President Henry A. Wallace.

The men who directed these various centres of post-war planning had numerous differences in outlook and policy. But they were all deeply influenced by three 'lessons' drawn from the unsuccessful efforts at peacemaking that followed the First World War. First, they remembered the fatal unpreparedness and confusion that bedevilled the American delegation at Paris. Thus they advocated detailed planning on post-war problems even during the war itself. Second, they were acutely conscious of the harm that had been done by the failure of the United States to join the League of Nations. Therefore, they wanted to base future American foreign policy on participation in a world organization. Finally, they recognized that a major reason for the breakdown of the last peace settlement lay in the inadequate handling of economic problems. Consequently, they placed great emphasis on economics in drawing blue-prints for a better world.

It is difficult to over-estimate the influence exerted by these 'lessons' from the past on the character of American post-war planning.

PLATE 1

Cordell Hull explains his foreign economic policy during 1943 Congressional hearings
on the reciprocal trade agreements programme

Plates 1–7 are from 'Wide World Photos'

To begin with, there was the idea that the post-war settlement should be planned in advance. A corps of specialists under Dr. Leo Pasvolsky, Hull's special adviser in charge of post-war planning, began drawing blue-prints of the post-war world as early as the autumn of 1939. Under-Secretary Welles, in paying tribute to the importance of this activity, explained that the President 'desired to be able later to reach in his basket and to find there whatever he needed in regard to post-war foreign policy and meanwhile wished to devote himself wholly to ways and means of winning the war'.[1]

This attempt to supplement the day-to-day making of policy with long-term planning by objective scholars was certainly an attractive idea. But such a division of functions might also be the cause of difficulty. If those charged with the conduct of the war did not share in the formulation of post-war objectives, they might adopt short-term policies inconsistent with the long-term plans. If the post-war planners had no share in the daily problems arising from the war, their planning might degenerate into abstract model-building remote from political and economic realities. The problem of reconciling principle and practice had confounded American leaders before. John Maynard Keynes had noted of Wilson's effort in 1919 that

when it came to practice, his ideas were nebulous and incomplete. He had no plan, no scheme, no constructive ideas whatever for clothing with the flesh of life the commandments which he had thundered from the White House. He could have preached a sermon on any of them or have addressed a stately prayer to the Almighty for their fulfilment, but he could not frame their concrete application to the actual state of Europe.[2]

Hull, unfortunately, was something like Wilson in this respect. During the war he persistently refused to consider the specific political and territorial issues which would have the greatest influence on the post-war settlement.[3] He had a most exaggerated notion of the efficacy of formal statements of general principle. In the weeks before Pearl Harbour, for example, he strove earnestly to get the signature of the Japanese Government to a declaration of economic and political principles, including a commitment to non-discrimination in commercial policy.[4] Such actions betrayed a certain insensitivity to the harsh environment of contemporary international relations.

[1] Harley A. Notter, *Post-War Foreign Policy Preparation 1939–1945* (Washington, 1949), p. 79.　　　　　　　[2] *Essays in Biography* (London, 1951), pp. 21–22.
[3] See Sumner Welles, *Seven Decisions That Shaped History* (New York, 1950), ch. 5.
[4] For the text of the declaration see Louise W. and Hajo Holborn, *War and Peace Aims of the United Nations*, vol. i, pp. 57–59.

There was a danger that the commendable emphasis on long-term planning might deteriorate into futile gestures of a similar kind.

The second assumption of the post-war planners was that the United States should participate in some kind of world organization. This idea was no less commendable than the first. But here again some pitfalls lurked. Some of the most influential American leaders seemed to think that such an organization would fundamentally alter the conduct of international relations and eliminate the need for intimate collaboration between countries with special economic and political ties. Hull had been deeply influenced by Wilson's idea that there should be 'no leagues or alliances or special covenants and understandings within the general and common family of the League of Nations'.[1] He, too, adopted a 'universal' approach to world order.[2] Like other leaders in post-war planning Hull rejected the notion that American interests might be uniquely linked with the political and economic position of the United Kingdom. He did not consider that successful reconstruction in the economic field would require closer collaboration with Britain than was possible with other nations of the world. Too much emphasis on Anglo-American collaboration, he believed, would interfere with the achievement of his 'universal' system. He urged his fellow Americans to avoid this danger by consulting 'with other interested nations *whenever* we consult with Britain'.[3]

This 'universal' approach to world order was a most difficult programme to apply in practice. Short of an effective system of world government—which Hull and his associates never advocated—the various nations would obviously need to form less than universal arrangements to further their political and economic interests. That influential Americans could have thought otherwise showed how far the United States had been sheltered from the harsh realities of international politics. The Foreign Minister of a European state would hardly have said of the post-war world, as Hull did, that 'there will no longer be need for spheres of influence, for alliances, for balance of power, or any other of the special arrangements through which, in the unhappy past, the nations strove to safeguard their security or to promote their interests'.[4] Nor is it likely that he would have

[1] Address opening the Fourth Liberty Loan Drive, reported in *The New York Times* (28 Sept. 1918).
[2] This was Hull's own description of his policy. See the *Memoirs of Cordell Hull*, vol. ii (New York, 1948), part eight.   [3] Italics supplied. Id., p. 1739.
[4] 'Memorandum on the Bases of the Foreign Policy of the United States', 1 Mar. 1944, Holborn, vol. ii, pp. 262–5.

described the basic assumptions of post-war planning in the same words as Harry White:

> It was expected that the early post-war would witness a degree of unity and good-will in international political relationships among the victorious allies never before reached in peace time. It was expected that the world would move rapidly . . . toward 'One World'. . . . No influential persons, as far as I remember, expressed the expectation or the fear that international relations would worsen during these years.[1]

Such naïvely optimistic assumptions about the post-war world naturally led to a neglect of less grandiose but more practical devices for the achievement of prosperity and peace.

There may have been another reason, to be sure, for the under-valuing of Anglo-American collaboration. Some of the most influential post-war planners were deeply suspicious of the United Kingdom. There was a good deal of bitterness about 'the Cliveden Set', 'colonialism', and the problem of India. Roosevelt himself expressed scepticism about Britain's capacity to take leadership in the building of a better world. Among some Administration leaders of left-wing persuasion there was a tendency to write Britain off as relatively unimportant and to place primary reliance in peace-making on Soviet-American relations. As Harry White put it:

> . . . The major task that confronts American diplomacy—*and the only task that has any real value in the major problems that confront us*—is to devise means whereby continued peace and friendly relations can be assured between the United States and Russia. Everything else in the field of international diplomacy pales into insignificance beside this major task. It matters little what our political relationships with England become or what happens in the Balkans or the Far East if the problems between the United States and Russia can be solved. Contrariwise, if we cannot discover ways to assure sincere friendship and military alliance between those two countries, the international political maneuvering in the Balkans, in the Far East and in Europe can only accentuate the fear of war, and if anything enhance the chances of major conflict.[2]

Scarcely less striking than the 'universal' approach of the post-war planners was their strong emphasis on the economic basis of a satisfactory world order. To a certain extent, such an emphasis was eminently desirable. One could hardly quarrel with the attempt to

---

[1] Rough draft (dated 19 May 1948) of a statement to be used in the introduction of proposed amendments to the Articles of Agreement of the International Monetary Fund, in *The Private Papers of Harry Dexter White* (hereafter cited as *White Papers*).

[2] Italics supplied. Untitled typescript dated 30 Nov. 1945, *White Papers*.

place the post-war settlement on a secure economic foundation. Still, it was necessary to maintain a proper proportion in the relative emphasis on economic and political planning. *The Economist* observed, not without concern, that the speeches of American leaders dwelt 'at much greater length and in much greater detail, on the side of post-war economic collaboration'.[1] Some of these statements carried the emphasis on economic policy rather far. Pasvolsky warned that unwillingness to abandon policies of economic warfare would constitute 'the *greatest* danger that can confront us after the war'.[2] Welles argued that 'one of the surest safeguards against war is the opportunity of all peoples to buy and sell on equal terms and without let or hindrance of a political character'.[3] In forwarding an early draft of his Stabilization Fund and Bank, White declared: 'Just as the failure to develop an effective League of Nations has made possible two devastating wars within one generation, so the absence of a high degree of economic collaboration among the leading nations will, during the coming decade, inevitably result in economic warfare that will be but the prelude and instigator of military warfare on an even vaster scale.'[4] The same theme was taken up by other American leaders. In the presence of this powerful *leitmotif* at least one observer became convinced that 'economic freedom for all is the basic American foreign policy for the prevention of war'.[5]

What was the explanation for such exaggerated emphasis on economic policy? To put it frankly, the Administration's programme for peace was much more clearly defined on the economic than on the political side. Moreover, the American people seemed more nearly ready to support measures of international co-operation in this particular area. The adoption of the Reciprocal Trade Agreements Act, the post-war planners recalled, had proved relatively easy compared with the repeal of neutrality legislation and the mobilization of public support for active measures against German aggression.

Still, the singular emphasis in the post-war planning was not just the result of political expediency. The principal planners shared a genuine belief in the critical importance of economic factors. 'If

[1] 'The American Challenge', p. 66.
[2] Italics supplied. Holborn, vol. i, p. 74.   [3] Id., pp. 29–30.
[4] Introductory section of undated typescript, 'Suggested Plan for a United Nations Stabilization Fund and a Bank for Reconstruction of the United and Associated Nations', in *White Papers*.
[5] Arthur Krock in *The New York Times* (27 May 1942).

goods can't cross borders, soldiers will' was a slogan well suited to the rationalist and materialist elements in the American intellectual heritage. The most faithful exponent of this view was Hull himself. As a Congressman during the First World War he became convinced that

unhampered trade dovetailed with peace; high tariffs, trade barriers, and unfair economic competition, with war. Though realizing that many other factors were involved, I reasoned that, if we could get a freer flow of trade —freer in the sense of fewer discriminations and obstructions—so that one country would not be deadly jealous of another and the living standards of all countries might rise, thereby eliminating the economic dissatisfaction that breeds war, we might have a reasonable chance of lasting peace.[1]

Hull was not content to state the truism that economic factors play an important role in international relations. He accorded them pride of place in his philosophy of world affairs. He had written to Secretary of State Lansing that 'the chief underlying cause' of the conflict which began in 1914 could be found 'in the strenuous trade conquests and bitter trade rivalry being conducted prior to the outbreak of the war'.[2] When Hull became Secretary of State this obsession with economics became an official part of American foreign policy. He insisted that his reciprocal trade agreements would be a major factor in achieving peace. To those who later objected that these agreements had not averted the Second World War he replied:

But it is a fact that war did not break out between the United States and any country with which we had been able to negotiate a trade agreement. It is also a fact that, with very few exceptions, the countries with which we signed trade agreements joined together in resisting the Axis. The political line-up followed the economic line-up.[3]

In reality, of course, the failure to conclude trade agreements with the Axis Powers was a symptom, not a cause, of the bad political relations that eventually led to war. Yet Hull's most enthusiastic disciples were so impressed with the efficacy of these agreements as a method of averting hostilities that as late as the

---

[1] Hull, *Memoirs*, vol. i, p. 81.
[2] Letter from Hull to Lansing, 16 Feb. 1916, National Archives, State Decimal File 1910–29, 600.0031/2, quoted in William R. Allen, 'The International Trade Philosophy of Cordell Hull, 1907–1933', *Am. Ec. Rev.*, xliii (1953), p. 107, n. 32.
[3] Hull, *Memoirs*, vol. i, p. 365.

winter of 1937–8 they were pressing for a trade agreement with Nazi
Germany:

> In the contribution which it could make towards the cause of peace a
> commercial agreement with Germany would merit, and might well receive,
> much approval by the American people. It is true that the argument has
> sometimes been advanced that such an agreement would tend to increase
> Germany's aggressiveness, and aid her to carry out her armament pro-
> gram, and ultimately to wage war. If this is true, then the basic philo-
> sophy of the trade agreements program is wrong. Would it not be more
> reasonable to expect that an agreement between Germany and the United
> States would be a factor making for peace? It would facilitate Germany's
> acquisition of raw materials; it would assist its export industries; it would
> be a proof to the German people that the democratic nations are not
> opposed to Germany's welfare; it would rob the Four-Year plan's drive
> toward an increased autarchy of some of its *raison d'être*.[1]

This memorandum was forwarded approvingly to Francis Sayre, then
Assistant Secretary of State for Economic Affairs, by Harry Hawkins,
Hull's principal adviser on the trade agreements programme. Hawkins specifically cited the argument that a German-American trade
agreement would be 'an important force making for world peace'.
This argument, like others made on behalf of the trade agreement,
seemed to him to be 'well taken'.[2]

How this sort of thinking was carried over into post-war planning
may be illustrated by the incident of the Russian loan. In March 1944
White brought forward a memorandum proposing a loan to the
Soviet Union of $5 billion on easy credit terms. His proposal did not
make the loan conditional on Soviet good behaviour or on the co-
operation of that Government in a satisfactory political settlement.
The mere giving to the Russians of reconstruction assistance would,
in his view, 'provide a sound basis for continued collaboration between the two governments in the post-war period'.[3] By January 1945
the idea had gained momentum and the size of the loan had been
increased to $10 billion. Morgenthau forwarded White's proposal to
President Roosevelt with a favourable recommendation for future
action. 'I am convinced', wrote Morgenthau, 'that if we were to
come forward now and present to the Russians a concrete plan to
aid them in the reconstruction period it would contribute a great

---

[1] Memorandum of Charles Darlington, 31 Dec. 1937, reprinted in U.S. Congress,
House of Representatives, Committee on Un-American Activities, *Soviet Espionage
within the United States Government*, 80th Cong., 2d Sess. (31 Dec. 1948), pp. 92–93.

[2] Memorandum from Hawkins to Sayre, 8 Jan. 1938, id., p. 96.

[3] Memorandum of White dated 7 Mar. 1944, *White Papers*.

deal towards ironing out many of the difficulties we have been having with respect to their problems and policies.'[1]

There may have been, to be sure, some reasonable arguments for expanding economic intercourse with Soviet Russia or Nazi Germany. But at the time of each of the episodes mentioned above, the country in question constituted the greatest potential threat to the security of the United States. Common sense should surely have rebelled against the simple notion that by assisting these countries economically they would necessarily become less belligerent and more co-operative. Although nations may occasionally be induced to co-operate by promises of future benefits, they are rarely induced to do so by the memory of benefits already received. That this fact was not more clearly recognized by some American leaders shows how much they exaggerated the efficacy of economic policies and how little they appreciated the political determinants of international relations. The most influential post-war planners seem to have persuaded themselves that the economic institutions established after the war could operate in a political vacuum, dispensing their resources without regard to the political policies of the recipients. Morgenthau was steadfastly to maintain this view in presenting the Bretton Woods agreements to the American Congress:

SENATOR FULBRIGHT.... It occurred to me that before the war we did business with such countries as Japan and Spain without any regard to political considerations. It does not seem to me that in the future we can isolate the economic from the political; and in stating several times that this must be done on an economic basis without regard to politics, that is not quite correct.

MR. MORGENTHAU. The discussion at Bretton Woods . . . the two American delegates that are sitting here at this committee table can either affirm or deny what happened—but the thought was—

THE CHAIRMAN [Senator Wagner]: I have just checked with Senator Tobey, and neither one of us heard any politics at all at Bretton Woods.[2]

MR. MORGENTHAU: The thought was that those countries could come to a world bank or a world fund and get their financial needs taken care of without having to sell their political souls . . . that is my conception of Bretton Woods. These are to be financial institutions run by financial people, financial experts, and the needs in a financial way of a country are to be taken care of wholly independent of the political connection. . . .[3]

[1] Morgenthau letter dated 10 Jan. 1945, forwarding White's memorandum of 1 Jan. 1945, id.

[2] The Senators, with all due respect, cannot have been very attentive members of the American delegation. The most important decisions at Bretton Woods, such as that on the size of national quotas, were largely determined by political bargaining.

[3] U.S. Congress, Senate, Committee on Banking and Currency, *Bretton Woods*

The impracticability of this idea in a world where the nation-state remained the dominant political unit should have been apparent to any one experienced in the conduct of international affairs.

We are now in a position to summarize the main characteristics of American policy toward the post-war world. It proceeded on the assumption that post-war planning should be carried on in advance; that the United States should base its foreign policy on membership in a world organization; and that the achievement of peace would require the adoption of appropriate policies in the economic field. These ideas were unexceptionable in themselves. Unfortunately, however, there was a tendency to press each of them too far. The resulting excesses we might describe as Legalism, Universalism, and Economism.[1] Such errors might lead to difficulty when the time came to implement the ambitious plans for prosperity and peace.

MULTILATERALISM AND MR. HULL

We must turn now from this general description of post-war planning to the specific nature of the 'challenge' put forward by the United States in the foreign economic field. The post-war planners were united in their determination to break completely with the legacy of economic nationalism and economic isolationism already described. They recognized that the United States, despite its comparative self-sufficiency, had a very great stake in the economic well-being of the rest of the world, not only because it needed foreign markets for the produce of its factories and farms, but because it needed a healthy environment on which to base its efforts at world peace. They considered that the United States, as the world's foremost economic power, should bear the primary responsibility for reconstructing a freely flowing system of international trade. Perhaps most important, they were prepared to devote a considerable amount of American wealth, influence, and energy toward the achievement

Agreements Act, Hearings on H.R. 3314, 79th Cong., 1st sess. (June 1945), pp. 14–15. In defending this approach against the objections of Senators Fulbright and Taft, Morgenthau said 'we have a right to assume as between nations there is going to be a new conception of dealings with one another'. Id., p. 15. This, of course, is precisely what no responsible maker of policy had a right to assume. These pages of the Hearings are worth a whole volume on the difference between the practical and the utopian approaches to the achievement of world order.

[1] For further discussion of the influence of these tendencies in American foreign policy see, respectively, George Kennan, *American Diplomacy 1900–1950* (London, 1952); Walter Lippman, *U.S. War Aims* (Boston, 1944); William Y. Elliott, *United States Foreign Policy* (New York, 1952).

of that end. Such a conjunction of power and idealism in economic affairs was entirely unprecedented in American history.

Perhaps the best short description of the Administration's basic objective in international economic affairs would be 'the reconstruction of a multilateral system of world trade'. For the purpose of this history we may define such a system as one in which barriers to trade and payments are reduced to moderate levels and made non-discriminatory in their application. This objective is obviously not the same as free trade. In monetary policy, for example, multilateralism does not require the complete elimination of all kinds of exchange control. It does, however, require the 'convertibility' of currencies. The residents of a country whose currency is convertible may not themselves have the right to convert their currency, but non-residents who hold that currency must have the right to do so. The same principle applies in commercial policy. Multilateralism does not mean the elimination, but only the reduction, of tariffs and other trade barriers. Any trade barriers remaining after this reduction, however, must be non-discriminatory in their application. Thus, while the residents of a country may not be able to purchase foreign goods on the same basis as they purchase goods from one another, any obstacles placed in the way of foreign purchases must apply in equal measure to all countries.[1]

The economic case for multilateralism is essentially the same as the familiar case for free trade. Multilateralism means fewer obstacles to the movement of goods and capital. Trade tends to flow in accordance with relative price considerations instead of being channelled in one direction or another by the need to strike a bilateral balance. Purchases can be made in the cheapest foreign market and sales in the most lucrative. Such a system promotes the international division of labour and encourages each country to specialize in the production of those things in which it enjoys the greatest comparative advantage.

Two important advantages may be claimed for this régime. First, the most is made at any given time of the world's existing stock of productive resources. Second, that stock of resources will be likely to increase over time more rapidly than under any alternative system. The latter result will occur because capital will be induced to flow to those parts of the world economy where it can make the greatest net

---

[1] This definition should probably be described as the *minimum* definition of multilateralism. As we shall see, the State and Treasury Departments early in the war went further and sought the elimination of direct controls such as quantitative restrictions and exchange controls on current transactions. See *infra*, pp. 20 and 76.

contribution to productivity. At the same time, productivity will be stimulated by competitive forces acting through the operation of the market mechanism. In this way multilateralism will tend to maximize the real income of the world as a whole.

To this broad generalization some qualifications must of course be made. Although free trade can be shown to maximize real income for the world as a whole, it may not do so for each of its constituent parts. Multilateralism can be shown to benefit everybody only if some mechanism exists for distributing the gains both within and between nations. Moreover, the greater efficiency in the use of resources made possible by multilateralism will be offset to the extent that the system causes the idleness of those resources. Multilateralism will maximize real income, therefore, only in conditions of economic expansion.

Even beyond these qualifications, multilateralism involves another difficulty. Several nations maintaining non-discriminatory trade barriers may decide to lower those barriers between themselves, without extending such benefits to the rest of the world. If they remove *all* the barriers between themselves and adopt common restrictions against other countries they will not have violated multilateral principles. But they may wish to stop short of this point. Can it be determined *a priori* that such a 'preferential system' is bad? Although this question has been the subject of much theoretical controversy, most economists would now agree that the answer is in the negative. Whether such a system increases or diminishes world income, they would say, depends on whether its 'trade-creating' effects offset its 'trade-diverting' ones. This depends, in turn, on the existing allocation of resources in the participating countries and on the extent to which specialization is possible between them.[1] As a practical matter, this test for promoting world income is unlikely to be passed by most preferential systems. For political reasons the reduction of trade barriers which takes place in such systems will probably do more to give the participating countries sheltered markets against the outside world than it does to stimulate vigorous competition between them. Thus, departures from non-discrimination, even if they are not evil in principle, will usually prove self-defeating when it comes to practice.

The case for multilateralism also has its non-economic aspects. The economic benefits of multilateralism can be said to promote, in a general way, the cause of world peace. Human beings whose

---

[1] See Jacob Viner, *The Customs Union Issue* (New York, 1950), pp. 41–55.

economic circumstances are improving will be less likely, everything else being equal, to challenge the internal or external order. It can be argued also that multilateralism, by insuring equal access to markets and raw materials, avoids the grievances felt by the victims of discrimination. Finally, as a very rough rule of thumb, it is probably true that the cause of peace is assisted by the reduction of government interference in international economic life.

But non-economic arguments for multilateralism deserve, like economic ones, the most careful qualification. To the extent that multilateralism increases inequality in income between or within nations, or causes serious fluctuations in incomes and employment, it may actually be a factor making for war. We may also doubt that discriminatory systems have frequently been the *bona fide* causes of aggression. Probably they cause little harm to political relations when the discrimination is small, uniform, and based on historical or regional ties. In general, as we have already suggested, undue attention to this aspect of the multilateral case places too great an emphasis on the economic causes of political conflict.

With this brief statement of the nature and purpose of a multilateralism we may return to the role of that idea in American postwar planning. At the outset, the independent character of the American Executive departments presents something of a problem. Although the post-war planners in the Department of State, the Department of the Treasury, the Board of Economic Warfare and other agencies all proclaimed multilateralism as their general goal, they did not place identical emphasis on the various means of promoting that objective. Cordell Hull, for example, was mainly interested in regulating the use of trade barriers. Harry White, while sharing this concern with commercial restrictions, put somewhat greater stress on the importance of economic expansion—as he put it, a high level of American business activity would 'do far more for our foreign trade than a complete wiping out of our tariff rates, or 100 trade treaties'.[1] Vice-President Wallace spoke out for a programme of international public works, including such ambitious projects as 'an international Tennessee Valley Authority' and 'a combined highway and airway from southern South America across the United States, Canada, and Alaska into Siberia and on to Europe, with feeder highways and airways from China, India, and the Middle East'.[2] Thus there was

---

[1] Untitled, undated typescript, apparently of a speech, in *White Papers*.
[2] Holborn, vol. i, p. 134.

no uniform 'American' view on the appropriate relation between the various elements of foreign economic policy.

Fortunately, however, our problem can be somewhat simplified. In the early war years with which we are now concerned, the primary responsibility for shaping American foreign economic policy rested with the Department of State. As we have already suggested, Hull's main interest was in the reduction of trade barriers. To be sure, considerable thought was also given to monetary stabilization, international investment, commodity agreements, and other matters. Some officials, like Herbert Feis, the Department's Economic Adviser, felt too much emphasis was being placed on the framing of fair trade principles which might prove of doubtful use in their practical application. Nevertheless, the Hull approach was clearly ascendant. It was developed by devoted subordinates of the Secretary such as Francis Sayre, the son-in-law of Woodrow Wilson, who became Assistant Secretary for Economic Affairs; Henry Grady, who later succeeded Sayre; and Harry Hawkins, a foreign service officer who took charge of the Division of Commercial Policy and Agreements. These men carried the major share of responsibility for working out the details of the multilateral approach.

Of the two main elements of multilateralism, it was non-discrimination to which the State Department gave pride of place. In this respect Hull and his associates were in the main stream of the American tradition. Non-discrimination was not simply a personal hobby of the Secretary of State; it was a doctrine approved generally within the American Administration and widely supported in the nation at large. Non-discrimination had been established as a basic element in American foreign policy at least as early as the Farewell Address of President Washington. 'The founder of his country' had advised his fellow-Americans, in their economic relations with the rest of the world, to 'hold an equal and impartial hand, neither seeking nor granting exclusive favors or preferences'.[1] This advice, it is true, had not been consistently followed, and the United States had clung to the conditional form of the most-favoured-nation clause, an ineffective practical basis for the policy of non-discrimination. But when, at the end of the First World War, a Republican Administration embraced the unconditional interpretation, the United States became the world's most vigorous champion of non-discriminatory trade.

---

[1] Farewell Address (17 Sept. 1796), reprinted in James D. Richardson, *A Compilation of the Messages and Papers of the Presidents* (New York, 1897), p. 215.

This campaign was endorsed by both political parties and by supporters of high as well as low tariffs. Well before the Second World War, therefore, equality of treatment had become firmly entrenched as a fundamental tenet of American policy.

What caused this strong American attachment to non-discrimination in trade? To begin with, the doctrine naturally recommended itself to a people who believed in the least possible interference with the free market mechanism. There was also, in the second decade of the twentieth century, a more practical factor. The First World War had hastened the transformation of the United States into a major exporter of mass-produced industrial products. These products were particularly vulnerable to the impact of tariff preferences and other forms of discrimination. The United States quickly recognized that its growing industrial efficiency might be progressively offset if American products were not guaranteed equal access to foreign markets.[1]

The American devotion to non-discrimination also had a political basis. The United States, just as Britain, had an interest in maintaining the balance of power. Its secure hemispheric position would be jeopardized by the rise of a European nation bent on adventures in the New World. Such a possibility, it seemed to some Americans, might be enhanced by the accelerating trend toward colonization and the development of exclusive economic concessions. Moreover, unless something were done to curb the tendency towards economic exclusion, the United States, itself reluctant to play an Imperial role, might be deprived of profitable opportunities for foreign trade and investment. It was largely considerations of this kind which led to John Hay's policy of the Open Door, and to Wilson's insistence, in the third of his Fourteen Points, on 'the removal so far as possible, of all economic barriers and the establishment of an equality of trade conditions among all nations consenting to the peace and associating themselves for its maintenance'. As Wilson explained it, this principle left 'every nation free to determine its own economic policy, except in one particular, that its policy must be the same for all other nations, and not be compounded of hostile discriminations between one nation and another'.[2]

The First World War did much to stimulate American concern

---

[1] See letter of William S. Culbertson, Acting Chairman of the Tariff Commission, to Secretary of State Hughes, 14 Dec. 1922, reprinted in Culbertson, *Reciprocity* (New York, 1937), pp. 246–51.

[2] Letter to Senator Hitchcock, quoted in Culbertson, *International Economic Policies* (New York, 1925), p. 295.

with the political importance of non-discrimination. An influential body of literature developed which cited unequal opportunity as one of the major causes of the conflict. Closed trade areas controlled by Imperial powers were held to deny other countries their natural rights to vital raw materials, markets, and investment outlets. The excluded countries, so the argument ran, not only felt aggrieved as a result of such discrimination; they were driven to obtain by force what they would otherwise have obtained by peaceful exchange. To some extent these same arguments might have been applied to high tariffs. But the protectionist revival in the United States was now in full swing. American exponents of equal access usually made an important distinction:

> Protection of the home market for the benefit of national industries is an expression of nationalism. Its object is to diversify a nation's economic life and to afford varied opportunities for the application of the genius of a people. It is in no sense aggressive. . . . Preference, on the other hand, is an expression of modern imperialism. In contrast with the policy of protection it is aggressive. In its extreme form . . . it seeks to extend to new areas . . . the control of the economic system of the country which happens to have the political power to impose the preferential conditions. . . . Excluded nations cannot be expected to accept the fiction of empire in justification of their exclusion from extensive areas of the earth's surface.[1]

The campaign against discrimination concentrated with particular intensity on preferential practices in the British Empire. This was hardly surprising in the light of American history. Every schoolboy had read of the special favours the American Colonies had been forced to grant to British commerce. Even after the Revolutionary War disputes had developed over British attempts to monopolize the trade of the West Indies. When the United States adopted the un-conditional form of the most-favoured-nation clause the Congress enacted a special provision authorizing the President to levy additional duties or even absolute prohibitions against the goods of any country which discriminated against the United States in favour of other 'foreign countries'. The term 'foreign countries' was defined to include 'any empire, country, dominion, colony or protectorate, or any sub-division or sub-divisions thereof (other than the United States or its Possessions) within which separate tariff rates or separate regulations are enforced'. This provision was aimed squarely at the preferences granted to Britain by its Colonies and Dominions and especially at the familiar argument that these preferences were not

---

[1] Culbertson, *International Economic Policies* (New York, 1925), pp. 185–6, 192.

discriminatory because they were in force between countries bound together by formal political ties.[1]

The climax of this campaign against Imperial Preference came with Hull's appointment as Secretary of State. American producers, beset by the Great Depression, were looking anxiously to foreign markets. In the midst of their difficulties they were met with the Ottawa Agreements, which not only increased the preferences granted to Britain by the Empire but inaugurated a comprehensive system of preferences in favour of the Empire by the United Kingdom. The Secretary of State, responding to the bitter complaints of American exporters, described these Agreements as 'the greatest injury, in a commercial way, that has been inflicted on this country since I have been in public life'.[2]

The hostility to the Ottawa Agreements on economic grounds was reinforced by political developments. The Axis Powers were devising economic policies to match their programmes of political expansion. Trade discrimination soon came to be regarded as the handmaiden of armed aggression. Hull began to emphasize that the principles of democratic foreign economic policy stood 'at the opposite pole from the predatory policies and the methods of totalitarians'.[3] It seemed particularly important to make sure that discriminatory policies were not practised by the democratic nations themselves. The Axis nations, after all, were justifying their aggression on the ground that they were 'have-nots' whom the older Imperial powers had cut off from essential raw materials. To some Americans this argument had a certain plausibility. The extension of Imperial Preference, they pointed out, had reduced the ability of countries outside the British Empire to earn foreign exchange for the purchase of Empire raw materials.[4] After the outbreak of the Second World War State Department spokesmen began to insist that no peace settlement 'would be valid or lasting unless it established fully and adequately the natural rights of all peoples to equal economic enjoyment. So long as any one government possesses a monopoly over natural

[1] Section 317 of the Tariff Act of 1922. For an idea of the origin of this provision see U.S. Tariff Commission, *Colonial Tariff Policies* (Washington, 1922).

[2] U.S. Congress, House, Committee on Ways and Means, *Extension of Reciprocal Trade Agreements Act*, Hearings on H.J. Res. 407, 76th Cong., 1st sess. (1940), vol. i, p. 38.

[3] *The Christian Science Monitor* (19 May 1941). For one of his most comprehensive statements of this philosophy, see *Economic Barriers to Peace* (New York, 1937).

[4] Hence the statement of Welles that 'Access to raw materials does not mean possession of a colony. It . . . comes in the end to access to the great buying markets of the world.' *Dept. of State Bull.*, vii (1942), p. 808.

resources or raw materials which are needed by all peoples, there can be no basis for a world order based on justice and peace.'[1] In this way, for the makers of American foreign policy, non-discrimination became a vital element in the moral armament of the democratic world.

Thus non-discrimination was a central element in the American 'challenge'. The second aspect of multilateralism—the reduction of trade barriers—also played an important part. Hull and his associates, like most Americans, were opposed to extensive government intervention in national economic life. It was natural that they should look with suspicion on government controls of all kinds. They drew a distinction, however, between various types of trade barriers. On the one hand, there were barriers which supplanted the free market entirely, like quantitative restrictions and exchange control. These were difficult to apply in a non-discriminatory fashion and involved all the major and political economic objections attendant upon discrimination. For this reason the State Department favoured their elimination. On the other hand, there were trade barriers, like tariffs, which made use of the free market mechanism. These might be objectionable if raised too high; but they were not regarded as evil in principle. The State Department favoured their retention in some measure to protect domestic producers.

In its emphasis on the elimination of direct controls, the State Department ran into considerable difficulty. The Roosevelt Administration, in its very early days, flirted with comprehensive programmes of planned economy. New Deal advisers such as Raymond Moley, George Peek, and Rexford Tugwell supported domestic recovery measures which involved resort to quantitative restrictions and bilateralism in foreign trade. It was only after many months of bitter struggle that Hull's liberal policy emerged triumphant. Only gradually did the New Deal abandon its early experiments and revert progressively to free market principles.[2]

There was, moreover, one important sector in which the reversion to orthodoxy did not occur. This was the field of agriculture. To alleviate the vast distress of the farm community the Administration enacted a system of production controls and price-support schemes for certain basic agricultural commodities. As a result of this legisla-

---

[1] Welles, *Dept. of State Bull.*, v (1941), p. 75.
[2] The struggles between Hull and the New Deal planners are poignantly described in Hull, *Memoirs*, vol. i.

tion American agricultural commodities were supported at prices well above those prevailing in the world market. The maintenance of this artificial two-price system had inevitable repercussions on American foreign trade policy. Section 22 of the Agricultural Adjustment Act authorized the President to employ import quotas whenever a commodity was being imported in such quantities as to interfere with the operation of any agricultural adjustment programme. Other provisions authorized the use of subsidies to facilitate the export of high-cost American products. By the beginning of the Second World War the price support system had been extended so far as to interfere considerably with Hull's programme for the elimination of direct controls.

The State Department was somewhat more successful in its policy with respect to tariffs. Once again, however, Hull's task was by no means easy. First he had to defeat the Al Smith–John Raskob element within the Democratic Party which had written its protectionist sympathies into the Party's platform in 1928. Then he had to cope inside the Roosevelt Administration with the influence of the Moley–Peek faction. Finally he had to contend with a Congress which, while considerably more sympathetic than its predecessors to the idea of tariff reduction, had no enthusiasm for a drastic programme which might complicate the problem of domestic recovery.

In the light of these obstacles Hull's successful sponsorship of the Reciprocal Trade Agreements Act in 1934 was a genuine achievement. Congress, for the first time in American history, delegated effective authority to the Executive for tariff-making. The President, it is true, had previously been authorized to raise or lower tariff rates, but he had been required to use his authority only to 'equalize the differences in the costs of production' between American and foreign goods. This provision proved administratively unworkable and negated the basic purpose of tariff reduction, which was, after all, the promotion of economically beneficial exchange based on differences in comparative costs.

The Reciprocal Trade Agreements Act was free from this irksome limitation. But it too had some defects as an instrument for more liberal trade. It was mainly designed to increase American exports, not to increase American imports. The primary purpose of the legislation, as stated in its preamble, was that of overcoming the industrial depression by 'expanding foreign markets for the products of the United States'. The President was authorized to enter into reciprocal trade agreements and to proclaim modifications in the American tariff resulting from those agreements only in order to promote this objective, and only when he found as a fact that 'existing duties or other import restrictions of the United States or any foreign country' were 'unduly burdening and restricting *the foreign trade of the United States*'.[1] The President could not, consistently with these provisions, carry out unilateral, across-the-board reductions in American tariff rates.

The Administration's public statements on the tariff issue conformed to this emphasis on selective, reciprocal, and moderate reduction. Hull assured his fellow Americans that the Act did not 'contemplate no tariffs, not even low tariffs, but a reasonable, moderate, decent level of tariffs, in lieu of existing rank and high rates and discriminations'.[2] When the Administration came to the Congress for renewal of the Act it placed its main emphasis on the extent to which the legislation had increased American exports. It promised, at the same time, that the reduction of tariffs would never be carried to a point where it caused serious injury to American producers.

In defence of the Department of State it may be said that no other approach could have succeeded in securing political support for a programme of tariff reduction. Unquestionably there is much in this argument. But the cautious emphasis of the Hull approach was not dictated by political considerations alone. The Secretary and his associates never faced the fact that an effective programme of trade liberalization would require major readjustments in the domestic economy. In view of its strong balance of payments position, the United States could not, short of large-scale loans, grants, or gold imports, significantly expand its exports without an equivalent increase in American imports. From a theoretical point of view, to be sure, an increase in the importation of particular commodities might not injure domestic producers if there was an equivalent increase in the total American consumption of those same products. In practice, however, this was not always likely to occur; important readjustments would certainly be required. The Administration's failure to explain this fact to the American people was not consistent with its persistent emphasis on tariff reduction as an instrument for the reconstruction of multilateral trade.

---

[1] Italics supplied.
[2] Department of State, *Press Releases* (6 May 1933), p. 314.

CONCLUSION

The general direction of American policy in the foreign economic field looked extremely encouraging to transatlantic observers at the outset of the Second World War. To a considerable extent, this appearance was not misleading. The post-war planners in the United States were determined to break with the unhappy legacy of economic isolationism and economic nationalism which had been inherited from the past. They were united in seeking the reconstruction of a multilateral trading system which could form the basis for prosperity and peace. Their planning toward this end reflected courage, generosity, and a large amount of genuine idealism.

At the same time, however, there were a number of grounds for concern. Administration leaders were making some bold promises to the rest of the world about the future shape of American policy. Yet the main elements in the unfavourable legacy had not entirely disappeared. It was by no means clear that the American spokesmen could deliver their promises in the face of such powerful tendencies toward isolationism, self-sufficiency, sectionalism, and *laissez-faire*. Moreover, in their dramatic reaction against the past, the post-war planners threatened to fall into new errors which we described for convenience as Legalism, Universalism, and Economism. These errors might cause grave difficulties if the revival of multilateralism became the object of Anglo-American economic collaboration.

CHAPTER II

THE BRITISH RESPONSE

How would the United Kingdom respond to the American 'challenge' in international economic affairs? In the early years of the Second World War the answer was still uncertain. There were powerful forces behind the idea of restoring a multilateral régime in close collaboration with the United States. But there were also powerful forces opposed to such a programme who advocated the widespread use of discriminatory and bilateral practices. Although public opinion on such a complex subject cannot be fitted neatly into separate categories, we must try now to indicate, in a rough kind of way, the major forces encouraging and hindering British participation in a multilateral régime.

THE FORCES FOR COLLABORATION

Perhaps the most striking fact to note at the outset is the comparative silence in official British circles on the economic programme put forward by the United States. Whitehall spoke much less frequently and in much less detail than Washington about the post-war revival of multilateral trade. By itself, this was no evidence that the British Government was ill-disposed toward the views expressed by American leaders. In part, the silence could be explained by the reluctance of British Ministers to 'think out loud' with the freedom enjoyed by their counterparts in the United States. There were also other reasons. British energies, unlike American, were almost wholly occupied with the problems of the war. There was little manpower to spare for speculations about the post-war settlement. Moreover, as we shall shortly observe, multilateralism remained a controversial public issue. British opinion was sharply divided on the merits of an open, non-discriminatory trading régime. Winston Churchill, the Prime Minister, felt strongly that questions of this kind should not be allowed to distract attention from the all-important problem of winning the war. It was mainly for these reasons that the public statements of British leaders provided so few clues to official thinking on the subject of multilateral trade.

Behind the non-committal façade of British policy, however, there were at least three important forces working for economic collaboration with the United States. The first was Britain's dependence on America for the achievement of her military, political, and economic objectives. Churchill was ever aware that Britain required American help, not only to win the war, but also to restore its strength in the post-war period. The same awareness had a profound influence on other members of the War Cabinet, particularly Anthony Eden, the Foreign Secretary, and Sir John Anderson, Lord President of the Council, who had general charge of home and economic policy. These British leaders fully recognized, as one unofficial source put it, that there was in America 'a strong correlation between sympathy for Britain and advocacy of trade liberation. If Great Britain disappoints Mr. Cordell Hull's supporters, she will be alienating those to whom she must look for assistance in the war and for collaboration in the peace.'[1] For this reason alone, if not for any other, they would go as far as possible to co-operate with the United States in its campaign for the revival of multilateral trade.

A second factor encouraging an affirmative response to the American challenge was Britain's favourable disposition toward the idea of international collaboration. In no country of the world, perhaps, had there been greater devotion to the League of Nations, or greater interest generally in international institutions. The principal British leaders were under the influence of the inter-war failures fully as much as their American counterparts. Some of them placed just as much emphasis on the need for a universal organization, particularly on one which would remove the economic causes of political unrest. The Labour Party formed a particularly important centre for planning of this kind; it proposed the establishment after the war of an international authority to eliminate imperialistic economic practices and raise living standards all over the world.[2] Some of its leaders in the coalition Government—Clement Attlee, Lord Privy Seal, Ernest Bevin, Minister of Labour, and Hugh Dalton, President of the Board of Trade—worked to embody such ideas in official policy. It was these men who provided the main response to the ambitious statements of economic objective that were thundering on the other side of the Atlantic. Attlee no less than Hull was insisting that after the war 'there must be equal access for all nations to markets and

[1] Editor, 'An End to Economic Nationalism', *The Banker*, lx (1941), pp. 174–81.
[2] *The Old World and The New Society* (London, 1942).

raw materials'.[1] Indeed, in their concern with the building of universal institutions and with the economic causes of war, some of the Labour Ministers threatened to lapse into the same errors already noted in American policy. Dalton, observing that Britain's post-war planning was progressing much faster on the economic than on the political side, declared that this was 'thoroughly healthy and I hope it will go on. In international discussions between the wars there was too much politics and too little economics.... One of the lessons we must learn is that in constructing post-war arrangements we must keep politics in a role in which primacy is given to economic endeavours and co-operation.'[2]

The third force working for economic collaboration with the United States was more directly related to the issue of multilateralism itself. This was the resurgence of the strong liberal economic tradition which had guided British policy during the greater part of the nineteenth century. In the seventy years between the repeal of the Corn Laws and the beginning of the First World War the United Kingdom had put no obstacles in the way of the free importation of goods from foreign countries. During this same time the Colonial Empire had been, with few exceptions, as open to foreign traders and investors as it had been to the traders and investors of the United Kingdom. The pound sterling, which financed the bulk of the world's trade, was freely convertible into other currencies at a fixed gold parity. Since Britain was the dominant country in international trade, its liberal policies were widely applied throughout the world as a whole. Commerce between nations flourished and the benefits promised by the classical economists were enjoyed to an unprecedented degree.

The interest of Britain in such a liberal system was obvious enough. It has been pointed out with sufficient frequency that the United Kingdom, a densely populated island with very limited resources, could be self-sufficient only at a tremendous cost. In the nineteenth century—and only somewhat less notably at the outset of the Second World War—Britain was greatly dependent on overseas supplies of foodstuffs and raw materials and on foreign markets for the output of its industrial plant. It had, moreover, an indirect stake in the development of free and prosperous international commerce, being at once a leading financier, carrier, and insurer of the trade of other nations.

Britain's interest in liberal trade had a political as well as an

---

[1] Holborn, vol. i, p. 672.
[2] 'First Place to Economics', *The Financial News* (23 Mar. 1944).

economic basis. As an island cut off from the rest of the world, the United Kingdom could not be a first-class political or military power. Its strong position depended on the uninterrupted flow of overseas supplies and on the maintenance of lines of communication with its overseas Empire. Moreover, Britain was a most successful practitioner of peaceful trade; it had an obvious interest in the maintenance of that particular form of international competition. If nations were denied access to markets or raw materials accessible to Britain, they might seek to obtain by force what they could not obtain by peaceful means. Britain's dedication to a free and open system of international commerce might serve as a safeguard against the envy or enmity of other nations. In the words of that shrewd analyst of Britain's interests, Sir Eyre Crowe: 'Second only to the ideal of independence, nations have always cherished the right of free intercourse and trade in the world's markets, and in proportion as England champions the principle of the largest measure of general freedom of commerce, she undoubtedly strengthens her hold on the interested friendship of other nations, at least to the extent of making them feel less apprehensive of naval supremacy in the hands of a free trade England than they would in the face of a predominant protectionist power.'[1]

These familiar arguments for liberal trade, which had reigned supreme until overwhelmed by the disasters of the inter-war period, were coming to the fore again in official planning for the post-war world. They had, to be sure, been formerly employed on behalf of free trade, which no longer found serious advocates in Government circles. But, as we indicated earlier, the economic and political arguments on behalf of free trade could be applied, with certain qualifications, to the system known as multilateral trade. In the early years of the war-time Government the reconstruction of such a régime became a major objective of British no less than of American planning. The British emphasis, of course, was rather more on the side of the lowering of trade barriers than on their non-discriminatory application. This followed naturally from the fact that liberal trade policy in Britain had meant no, not simply low and non-discriminatory, barriers to trade, and from the development of special economic ties between the members of the British Commonwealth. It followed also from Britain's urgent economic interests in the post-war period.

[1] 'Memorandum by Sir Eyre Crowe on the Present State of British Relations with France and Germany, January 1, 1907', in G. P. Gooch and H. Temperley (eds.), *British Documents on the Origins of the War 1898–1914* (London, 1928), vol. iii, p. 402.

British officials were preoccupied with the practical problem of achieving an increase in British exports at the end of the war sufficient to make up for the reduction in foreign exchange receipts caused by war-time losses of shipping and foreign investments. The magnitude of the necessary increase in exports was estimated in official circles at about 50 per cent. Such an increase would require not simply the absense of discrimination against British goods, but a very considerable lowering of barriers to world trade. In the words of the Chancellor of the Exchequer, Sir Kingsley Wood:

No nation's interest in the maximum growth and freedom of commerce will be as great as ours. We shall want to secure as large a volume of international commerce under conditions as free from restrictions as possible consistent with our commitments. Unless, in fact, we can effect a great move forward in our export trade, our relatively high standard of living must inevitably fall. We must never forget that we can only achieve this by providing our customers with the goods and commodities they want at prices they are willing to pay. . . .[1]

We have already mentioned some of the principal Ministers responsible for the liberal emphasis in British planning. But the problems of the war left these Ministers comparatively little time for detailed consideration of the issues of post-war economic policy. Planning in this field was directed by senior civil servants such as Richard N. V. Hopkins and Sir Percivale Liesching of the Treasury and Board of Trade, respectively, who were sympathetic to the development of a multilateral programme, and was carried out, in large part, by distinguished 'temporaries' who had come into the Government at the beginning of the war. In the latter category a particularly important role was played by the academic economists. Although they could not, in a formal sense, make decisions on high policy, they came to exercise, during the war years, a very considerable influence. Many had distinguished reputations which enabled them to speak with great authority; and their temporary positions in the Government service gave them a freedom of action they might have otherwise lacked. Their memoranda were debated back and forth in interdepartmental committees, reviewed by the senior civil servants, and finally forwarded to the Ministers themselves. The British response to the American challenge was thus profoundly influenced by their ideas.

The important role played by the academic economists greatly strengthened the forces working for the liberal revival in British

[1] 386 H.C. Deb. 818 (2 Feb. 1943).

economic policy. In their thinking on international trade the majority of Britain's leading economists remained loyal to the classical tradition. Two notable examples of the general tendency were Lionel Robbins and James Meade, who directed, in successive terms, the Economic Section of the War Cabinet Secretariat, and who made perhaps the most significant individual contributions to post-war planning on commercial policy. Before joining the Government Robbins and Meade had both written powerful defences of liberal trade.[1] Robbins had argued, no less emphatically than Cordell Hull, that to recommend a policy of autarchy in the existing state of world affairs was 'to recommend war as an instrument for making autarchy possible'.[2] And Meade, in drafting a blueprint for the government of world trade, had little difficulty in concluding that 'a free trade policy should be taken as the basis of the commercial policy of the International Organisation'.[3]

Thus on the side of commercial policy the academic economists in the Government were disposed to take a liberal line. The same was true, though less clearly at first, on the side of financial policy. Three academic economists of particular influence in the British Treasury were Hubert Henderson, Dennis Robertson, and John Maynard Keynes. Henderson was to remain profoundly sceptical of the practicability of achieving multilateralism in the post-war world. He was to prove more of a critic than an architect of the multilateral programme.[4] Robertson, on the other hand, was rather more constructive. He put a high value on the importance of reaching agreement with the United States on a programme of financial collaboration. The views of Keynes will be explored in detail at a later point.[5] Here we may note simply that his ideas on external policy were going through a period of transition. At one time he had held liberal views on international trade. During the Great Depression, when he became concerned with the problem of full employment, his position had begun to change. He despaired of gaining approval for policies of expansion on a world scale; he supported, as the only practical alternative, the use of autarkical measures to ensure domestic recovery. Now his views were changing again:

The autumn of 1941 was for Keynes a time of deep reflection and heart searching. . . . He was advised on every side that it would be needful to

[1] Robbins, *Economic Planning and International Order* (London, 1938); Meade, *The Economic Basis of a Durable Peace* (London, 1940).
[2] Robbins, p. 321.   [3] Meade, p. 76.
[4] See *infra* for a discussion of his views and those of other critics.
[5] See Chapter V.

maintain something like the war-time system, suitably modified, of tight controls, of blocked accounts and bilateral bargains. . . . Yet he revolted against all this. He, like the Americans, disliked reverting to the law of the jungle. His instincts were for international cooperation. If these instincts had been dormant in the years before the war, that was because such instincts seemed impracticable; the internationalists tended to be those who had not accepted Keynesian economics, and to hand international arrangements over to them would, in his judgment, be fatal. Until the world was converted to his views, one must aim at trying them out in Britain, even if this meant some insulation. But was the world changing now? . . . Perhaps the time was almost ripe to attempt to apply Keynesian thought on a world scale; that would be much better than doing so on a national scale only.[1]

Thus, at a critical time, a powerful force was added to the ranks of those who were sympathetic to the post-war reconstruction of multilateral trade.

THE CRITICS OF MULTILATERALISM

Within the British Government powerful forces were working for a favourable response to the American challenge. But opinion in Whitehall was by no means representative of the country as a whole. Outside the Government were powerful groups who opposed multilateralism in principle or who put so many qualifications on its reconstruction that their position amounted to the same thing. This opposition was not difficult to understand. The United Kingdom had tried the liberal alternative in both commercial and financial policy. After the First World War it had clung to free trade and the gold standard despite widespread defections by other countries. These traditional policies had been accompanied by mass unemployment and increasing pressure on the balance of payments. Henderson's was a minority voice within the Government, but he spoke for many outside when he wrote:

The history of the inter-war period provides no support for the view that we should attempt once again to reconstruct a war-shattered world on the basis of a freely working economic system, international credits, the reduction of trade barriers, and the outlawry of quantitative regulation. To attempt this would be not to learn from experience but to fly in its face. It would be to repeat the mistakes made last time in the name of avoiding them. It would be to invite the same failure, and the same disillusionment; the same economic chaos and the same shock to social and political stability; the same discredit for the international idea.[2]

[1] Roy F. Harrod, *The Life of John Maynard Keynes* (London, 1951), pp. 525–6.
[2] 'International Economic History of the Inter-War Period', a memorandum pre-

To put the matter bluntly, the inter-war misfortunes had destroyed the former faith in the efficacy of freely working market forces. The decline of this faith had been reflected in the decline of the Liberal Party. The Labour Party, which supplanted the Liberals as the second force in British politics, tended to identify the free market with mass unemployment and social injustice. The Conservatives, at the same time, were becoming increasingly responsive to demands for protection and exclusion on behalf of vested interests in industry and agriculture, for whom free trade had meant the loss of markets, falling profits, and even financial ruin. On neither Left nor Right, therefore, was there much enthusiasm for economic liberalism. On both sides there was less interest in efficiency than in security, less interest in the size of national income than in the nature of its distribution. It was not difficult to see the implication of these developments for British foreign economic policy:

We must . . . reconcile ourselves once and for all to the view that the days of *laissez-faire* and the unlimited division of labour are over; that every country—including Great Britain—plans and organises its production in the light of social and military needs, and that the regulation of this production by such 'trade barriers' as tariffs, quotas, and subsidies is a necessary and integral part of this policy.

This does not mean that the principle of the division of labour is in itself false, that world prosperity will not be enhanced by an abundant flow of international trade, or that Britain has not above all other countries a supreme interest in a revival of the free exchange of goods and services. What it does mean is that this exchange can no longer be left to the working of Adam Smith's 'invisible hand', but must be consciously and deliberately organized by those who are responsible for commercial policy.[1]

Thus very formidable opposition to the American challenge took shape on both extremes of the political spectrum. On the one side, British industry, which in earlier days had been a powerful supporter of liberal trade, had become much less confident about its ability to compete with producers in the United States and other more recently industrialized countries. It regarded with profound suspicion any attempts to modify the system of protection and Preference which had been erected in the wake of the Great Depression. When, for example, the British Government in 1937 began negotiations on an Anglo-American trade agreement, 150 members of the Parliamentary

pared 3 Dec. 1943 during Henderson's service in the British Treasury, reprinted in Henry Clay (ed.), *The Inter-War Years and Other Papers, a Selection from the Writings of Hubert Douglas Henderson* (Oxford, 1954), p. 245. [1] *The Times* (11 Jan. 1941).

Committee of the Empire Industries Association announced their 'emphatic objection to any action which would in any way interfere with the fuller development or even weaken the permanent effectiveness of our domestic and Imperial tariff system, or which would sacrifice home and Empire production for the sake of some illusory project for the revival of economic internationalism'.[1] A short time later the Federation of British Industries began to negotiate a comprehensive set of restrictive arrangements with the industrialists of Nazi Germany.[2] British business groups showed no signs of abandoning these policies in their planning for the post-war period. In notable contrast with their American counterparts, they urged the maintenance of widespread government controls and the development of more effective private agreements to control the movement of prices and the flow of trade.[3] The London Chamber of Commerce went so far as to suggest that international trade should be conducted permanently by a system of bilateral clearing,[4] and the Federation of British Industries declared:

It is easy to talk of Anglo-American co-operation, but we must be realistic and face the difficulties. . . . After the war we shall not be in the same favourable position as in the past. Instead of being a creditor, we shall be a debtor nation. . . . In such circumstances the view is widely held in industrial circles in this country that we must, at any rate for some considerable period, rely on a policy of directive imports, on the assumption that we only import from overseas countries those essential commodities for which such overseas countries are prepared to accept payment by the only means which will be open to us—i.e., by the export of our own products and such services as we can render. In effect, almost a system of barter, or, at any rate, a system of bilateral trade which will regulate our imports by our capacity to pay for them. This involves import and export controls, possibly by quota, preferential treatment of the imports of those countries which are prepared to assure us of the means of paying for them, and exchange control.[5]

---

[1] *The Times* (9 June 1937).
[2] The project was hastily terminated when the Germans marched into Prague. For the text of the agreement, see 345 H.C. Deb. 1107–9 (21 Mar. 1939).
[3] See Association of the British Chambers of Commerce, *Report of the Special Committee on Post-War Industrial Reconstruction* (London, 1942); London Chamber of Commerce, *Report on General Principles of a Post-War Economy* (London, 1942); and Federation of British Industries, *Reconstruction: A Report by the Federation of British Industries* (London, 1942). For a comparison of the views of British and American business groups, see the report on their trip to England of Eric Johnston and William Benton in *Life* (25 Oct. 1943); also Anonymous, 'The Post-War Exchange Regime', *The Banker*, lxiii (1942), p. 8.
[4] London Chamber of Commerce, op. cit., citing with approval Economic Reform Club, *Twentieth Century Economic System* (London, 1942).   [5] Op. cit.

The most obvious form of right-wing opposition to multilateralism came in the passionate defence of Imperial Preference. A considerable portion of British industry had become devoted to the Preference system, which provided shelter in Commonwealth markets and, so long as the Dominions did not become serious industrial rivals, no threat of competition at home. But Preference probably drew its widest support on non-economic grounds. To the people of a small island nation, confronted with increasingly powerful military and industrial rivals, the concept of membership in a vast Empire, knit together by intimate economic ties, naturally exerted a powerful appeal. This political aspect of Imperial Preference, though it had declined in importance in the inter-war period, was revived considerably by the Second World War. The members of the Commonwealth had stood together, and, for a time, virtually alone, against the German onslaught. Sentiment as well as self-interest, therefore, brought new support to the Ottawa idea.

The supporters of Imperial Preference found two strong spokesmen in the war-time Government. The first was L. S. Amery, Secretary of State for India, a veteran of the early campaigns for Imperial Preference fought under the leadership of Joseph Chamberlain. Amery was now Chairman of the Empire Industries Association and perhaps the most effective public spokesman for the Preference cause. The second spokesman for Preference was Lord Beaverbrook, Minister of Supply, the wealthy titan of the publishing world whose newspapers made a ritual of extolling the British Empire. Beaverbrook's close relations with the Prime Minister put him in a strong position to influence official policy. Churchill had not forgotten that when he was Chancellor of the Exchequer in 1925 Beaverbrook virtually alone among his friends had warned against the return to gold. He would be particularly sensitive to Beaverbrook's new warnings that Preference must not be sacrificed in any Anglo-American programme for reconstructing a liberal régime.

In discussing right-wing opposition to multilateralism we have so far concentrated on the attitude of industry. The influence of British agriculture was also considerable. The landowning classes, after all, had been traditionally protectionist, and the experience with free trade had done nothing to change their position. British agriculture had found it increasingly difficult to compete with cheap foreign supplies of grains and other foodstuffs; consequently, it had suffered a steady and serious decline. Although increasing reliance on overseas foodstuffs was economically justifiable, it did have grave implications for the national security. With the coming of the Second World War this consideration reinforced the supporters of agricultural protection. It proved necessary to achieve a large and rapid expansion in farm production. R. S. Hudson, the Minister of Agriculture, backed by the landed interests in the Conservative Party, urged that a large part of the expansion should be maintained after the war, even if it required substantial resort to subsidies, tariffs, and other devices. This was another factor obstructing a liberal approach to international trade.

For all these reasons the British right was profoundly sceptical of the American challenge. There was opposition also on the other end of the political spectrum. Here two main groups could be distinguished. The most extreme was composed of left-wing Socialists and miscellaneous radicals who advocated a thorough reordering of society in which capitalism would be replaced by centralized government planning of economic life. The members of this group, influenced by the writings of Marx and Lenin, feared the effects of capitalism in the international no less than in the domestic sphere. Its leading intellectuals, such as Harold Laski, G. D. H. Cole, and E. H. Carr, attacked liberal trade policy as a sure recipe for social injustice, depression, and even war.[1] In their view the competitive struggle for markets, raw materials, and investment outlets constituted one of the major causes of international conflict. This group was never, by itself, a very potent political force; but the ideas put forward by its major spokesmen sometimes found their way into the official statements of the Labour Party.[2]

A second group on the British left was of rather more political importance. Its opposition to multilateralism was based more on non-Socialist economic theory and Britain's inter-war experience. Industrial depression and balance of payments difficulties had focused attention on the workings of the free trade, gold standard system, which had so long been a part of British policy. This system, it was now widely understood, maintained international equilibrium through adjustments in domestic prices, interest rates, incomes, and

[1] One of their most influential books was Carr's *The Conditions of Peace* (London, 1942). In this stinging indictment of the capitalist system, Carr urged that 'we must cease to regard the mere removal of trade restrictions as an ideal—even as an impracticable ideal—and recognise that organised trading is an essential condition of the fulfilment of our purposes'. Id., p. 267.

[2] See, for example, *The International Post-war Settlement* (London, 1944), pp. 2–7, which held the elimination of capitalism essential both for social justice and world peace.

employment. External stability might therefore be achieved only at the cost of instability in the domestic economy. In the event of an American depression, for example, American prices would fall; this would stimulate British imports from the United States and retard British exports; Britain would lose gold until it experienced a similar deflation. At the same time, American interest rates would rise; capital would be drawn away from Britain to the United States until British interest rates were increased to a similar extent. Finally, the fall in American income and employment would reduce the American demand for British goods; this would reduce income and employment in Britain's export industries and eventually, through the operation of the 'multiplier' effect, income and employment throughout the country as a whole.

Keynes himself had probably made the most persuasive explanation of how the old-fashioned liberal trade system interfered with the requirements of domestic expansion. More than anyone else he had given to mercantilist doctrine a new respectability. Despairing of international solutions, he had urged his countrymen to remain 'as free as possible of interference from economic changes elsewhere, in order to make our own favourite experiments toward the ideal social republic of the future'.[1] Although he was turning away now from nationalistic solutions, his former writings had a continuing effect. A number of younger economists, taking up where Keynes left off, were investigating how domestic full employment and socialist reforms could be effectively insulated from foreign influence. A similar movement of opinion was taking place in left-wing political circles. By the outset of the Second World War, therefore, the Labour Party was considerably divided on the issue of liberal trade. Not simply exchange-rate flexibility, but exchange control, bilateralism, and state-trading had achieved a considerable vogue. This tendency would provide a further restraint on the British response to the American challenge.

THE CONDITIONED RESPONSE

Thus far we have concentrated on the irreconcilable opponents of the multilateral régime. In so doing we have engaged in exposition, not criticism. To refute with detailed argument the positions adopted toward multilateralism by the extremists of the left and right would unduly impede this historical study. That these positions were

[1] 'National Self-Sufficiency', *Yale Review*, xxii (1933), p. 769.

fundamentally unsuited to British interests is already suggested by our earlier observations. The policies of protection and Preference, for example, were already proving to be self-defeating, since they reduced British and Commonwealth exports to non-Commonwealth markets. They could bring benefits to selected segments of British industry and agriculture only at a considerable cost to the nation as a whole. The policies of bilateralism or autarchy, in a similar way, could protect stability and domestic reforms only at the cost of general impoverishment. Moreover, as Britain had already discovered, a country so greatly dependent on overseas supplies was not in a strong position when government bargaining replaced private arrangements as the primary method of international trade.

Yet the criticisms put forward on the left and right could not be entirely dismissed. Official planning could hardly afford to ignore such an influential constellation of attitudes, however misguided they might be. There were, moreover, some legitimate difficulties in developing a favourable response to the American challenge. Although the difficulties did not justify the negative approach of extremist criticism, they did justify some qualifications in the British response. These qualifications were raised increasingly in unofficial discussions and pondered quietly in Whitehall itself.

The first qualification involved the relationship between Britain and the Commonwealth. There was no justification, as we have indicated, for the doctrinaire devotion to the Preference system. But the United Kingdom had a strong stake in strengthening Commonwealth political and economic unity in an uncertain and insecure world. There were many unique aspects of this association which Britain had an interest in preserving. For example, the British Government always preceded its participation in international conferences by close consultation with other Commonwealth Governments. These consultations by no means produced a uniform Commonwealth point of view, but they made it possible for Commonwealth members to take one another's interests into account in putting forward their own views. In laying plans for the revival of multilateral trade the United Kingdom would insist upon continuing this practice. As for Imperial Preference, it was true that Britain's interests would not be served by the retention of the system as a whole. But there might be individual preferences of no great international significance—such as those granted to the British West Indies—whose elimination would work very severe hardship. In short, the British Government could not support any American programme which seemed to be aimed indiscriminately at weakening Commonwealth ties.

The second qualification derived from the concern with full employment and social welfare in the domestic sphere. The extremists' demands for complete insulation from world market forces were unrealistic, but it was not unreasonable to insist that any multilateral system should provide some safeguards against the spread from one country to another of industrial depression. Although moderate opinion considered the gains from multilateralism of sufficient importance to justify the frictional employment accompanying the adjustment of Britain's resources to changing patterns of international demand, it considered mass unemployment too high a price to pay. It was generally agreed that any future projects for the revival of multilateral trade would have to have an expansionist bias, with safeguards to protect the United Kingdom from fluctuations originating abroad. British opinion was particularly concerned with the danger of post-war depression in the United States. The British response to the American challenge would have to insist that some means be found to ensure that an American slump did not occur, or, failing this, that the United Kingdom and other countries be permitted to protect themselves against the spread of the slump to their own economies. If such safeguards could be devised it might yet be possible to reconcile the objectives of foreign and domestic economic policy.

The third qualification related to the balance of payments. Even before the war, it was becoming increasingly difficult for Britain to balance its accounts without liquidating foreign investments or drawing on gold and foreign exchange reserves. The war was aggravating this problem by causing further liquidation of reserves and investments. It would leave Britain at the end with a smaller income from invisible earnings. As we noted earlier, there would have to be a substantial increase in exports to make up for these losses. But now British exports were falling to a fraction of their pre-war level and Britain's productive capacity was being reduced by depreciation and aerial destruction.[1] How could the necessary increase in exports be achieved?

It was clear, to begin with, that post-war equilibrium could be only gradually restored. During the transition period Britain would have to

---

[1] A summary of the effect of the war on Britain's economic position is given in Chapter IX, *infra*.

have some means of making payments for imports while repairing its war damage and rebuilding its export trade. It would also need to restore its reserves to something like the pre-war level. This would mean substantial assistance from the United States. Without such assistance Britain could not participate in a system of multilateral trade.

Even beyond the transition period there might still be a balance of payments problem. In British eyes, this underlined the importance of a substantial reduction in the American tariff and the revival of American foreign lending. How far Britain participated in trade liberation would depend on how nearly balance of payments equilibrium was achieved. Since the United States was likely to run a large surplus, it would have to make a more than proportionate contribution to the lowering of trade barriers; Britain, in turn, if it continued to run a considerable deficit, could make only a small contribution. As Henderson put it:

The objective of securing a general lowering of trade barriers makes a strong appeal to us. None the less, this is not a matter on which we feel in a position to take a leading part. As we see it, the essential problem is to reconcile the aims of an expansion of international trade and equilibrium in the balance of payments. For this purpose what is chiefly needed is that those countries which are otherwise likely to have an unduly favourable balance of payments should be willing to do most to reduce import duties and to remove other impediments to imports. Countries which are likely to be faced with an adverse balance of payments should not be expected to respond in an equivalent degree. Indeed, it is only in so far as an expansion of their exports serves to bring their balance of payments toward equilibrium that measures likely to increase their bill for imports could be reconciled with ordinary prudence.[1]

In short, it could not be assumed that the universal resort to multilateral policies would in itself be sufficient to ensure equilibrium. For this reason, it was widely argued, Britain would have to remain free to achieve equilibrium by restrictive devices. To say this was not necessarily to depreciate the value of multilateral trade. But, in the words of Geoffrey Crowther, the editor of *The Economist*, it was 'no longer possible to believe, as it was in the Free Trade era, that imports automatically produce exports, that if bread is cast upon the waters in the form of purchases from overseas it will return in due season in the form of orders from abroad'.[2] This was yet another ground for caution in responding to the American challenge.

[1] 'Great Britain's Post-war Commercial Policy', memorandum of 6 Jan. 1943, in Clay (ed.), pp. 272–3.   [2] 'Anglo-American Pitfalls', *For. Aff.*, xx (1941), p. 14.

CONCLUSION

The American challenge in foreign economic affairs evoked a mixed and uncertain response in the United Kingdom. In government circles there was a distinct revival in the liberal economic philosophy that had marked British policy in the nineteenth century. But outside Whitehall there were powerful forces working in the opposite direction. There were pressures on the right for protection and Preference; and on the left for autarkical measures to insulate domestic programmes of planning and control. Even moderate opinion had considerable misgivings about British participation in a multilateral régime.

Official planning on post-war economic policy was inevitably influenced by these facts. Out of regard for public opinion as well as for British interests the response to the American challenge would have to be qualified in three major respects. First, it would have to take account of the historic ties between Britain and other members of the Commonwealth. Second, it would have to take account of the need to protect the British economy against the kind of violent fluctuations that had marked the inter-war period. Third, it would have to take account of the need to maintain equilibrium in the balance of payments.

To put it another way, British officials charged with preparing an agenda for Anglo-American economic collaboration had to ask a number of questions. Would the United States, in its emphasis on non-discrimination, refrain from interfering with useful economic ties between the Commonwealth countries? Would it take steps to maintain reasonably full employment, or, failing that, provide some mechanism for easing the impact on other countries in the event of an American slump? Would it assist the United Kingdom in restoring equilibrium in its balance of payments? With respect to the latter question, would it provide financial aid for British reconstruction? In the longer run, would it reduce barriers to imports and undertake foreign investment in sufficient magnitude to bring about equilibrium? These were a considerable list of questions to put to the American Government. But unless affirmative answers were received on all of them, it would not be possible to participate fully in the ambitious programme for multilateral trade.

CHAPTER III

THE ATLANTIC CHARTER

OUR preliminary survey of American and British foreign economic policy has indicated that powerful forces in both countries were working for the reconstruction of multilateral trade. But we have also noted substantial differences between the two countries, not only on the specific means by which multilateralism was to be achieved, but also on the precise meaning of that elusive term. Clearly no common programme could be successfully worked out until the participants agreed on precisely where it was they wanted to go.

During the early years of the Second World War the United States and Britain made two major attempts to define their common objectives in the international economic field. The first occurred in the Atlantic Conference held in August 1941. Here, in the fourth and fifth paragraphs of the Atlantic Charter, the two governments drafted a definition of multilateralism to guide their subsequent efforts at post-war reconstruction. To understand this definition and its relation to Anglo-American policy we must return to the scene of the Atlantic Conference.

THE SETTING OF THE ATLANTIC CONFERENCE

The famous conference between Roosevelt and Churchill interests us here because it produced an important statement of economic objectives. But we would do well to recall that the Atlantic Charter was, as one leading history puts it, 'a by-product of the conference rather than its primary objective'.[1] President Roosevelt first suggested the meeting because he wanted to exchange views with the British Prime Minister on Lend-Lease and other questions relating to the war. Churchill, for his part, had little desire to discuss post-war issues and was chiefly concerned with improving the desperate military position of Britain. In accepting the suggestion for a conference with the American President he saw an excellent opportunity to associate the United States more closely in the European war and to present a united Anglo-American front in the face of Japanese aggression.

[1] William L. Langer and S. Everett Gleason, *The Undeclared War* (New York, 1953), p. 677.

The decision to seek a joint statement of Anglo-American war aims appears to have been made by Roosevelt early in the summer of 1941. Political rather than economic problems were uppermost in the President's mind. He believed that an authoritative declaration of the principles for which the Allies were fighting might 'hold out hope to the enslaved peoples of the world'.[1] He also considered that a declaration of this kind would have a beneficial effect on domestic opinion. At the time of the Atlantic Conference, it should be remembered, the United States was still neutral. The American public had been brought by exceptional efforts to support the enactment of Lend-Lease, but it seemed reluctant to endorse additional measures which involved the risk of direct participation in the war. To rally support for such measures Roosevelt felt he needed dramatic evidence that Britain was fighting for the same principles of freedom and justice that had been affirmed as the objectives of the United States. No doubt he remembered the unfortunate experience of Woodrow Wilson, who had drafted a unilateral statement of American war aims during the First World War in ignorance of the secret treaties already concluded between America's allies.

Roosevelt's conception of a joint statement did not include any very detailed definition of economic objectives. As a rule he took little interest in discussions of economic principles, and this was no exception. He was mainly concerned with reaching Anglo-American agreement on political questions such as self-determination, disarmament, and freedom of the seas. As far as issues of post-war economic policy were concerned, he would be satisfied with a general statement—for example, that the nations of the world should have equal opportunity to enjoy the world's resources and should work together to improve their living standards. As we have seen, however, the President's attitude in this regard was not shared by the State Department and certain other branches of his Administration. It was to be expected that Cordell Hull would press the President to seek more specific commitments in the economic field.

This natural tendency was reinforced by an event that occurred in Washington shortly before the Atlantic Conference. In the midst of negotiations on the Mutual Aid (Lend-Lease) Agreement Keynes shocked American officials by making a strong statement about Britain's post-war economic policies. He declared that the British Government would find itself beset by such grave economic

[1] Sumner Welles, *Where Are We Heading?* (London, 1947), p. 6.

difficulties at the end of the war that it would be forced to resort to bilateral arrangements and other forms of outright discrimination against the United States.[1] This statement made a profound impression. It prompted Hawkins, who represented the State Department in these negotiations, to draw up a new draft of the Mutual Aid Agreement which prohibited any form of discrimination by Britain in the post-war period.[2] It also set in motion a process by which similar prohibitions found their way into the draft of the joint statement which Under-Secretary of State Welles, at the behest of Roosevelt, was preparing for the Atlantic Conference.[3] In this way detailed issues of economic policy seeped into the preparations for a conference whose primary concern was with the military problems of the war and the political problems of the post-war settlement.

THE FIRST DEFINITION OF MULTILATERALISM

The Atlantic Conference began on 9 August 1941, when Roosevelt and Churchill met at a secret ocean rendezvous in Placentia Bay, Newfoundland. The President was accompanied by Welles, representing the Department of State, and Harry Hopkins, his trusted personal adviser. Churchill was assisted by Sir Alexander Cadogan of the Foreign Office and later by Beaverbrook, at this time Minister of Supply, who arrived on the scene by air.

At a preliminary meeting on the first day Welles suggested to Cadogan the drafting of a joint declaration and placed particular emphasis on the economic issues involved. Welles cited the attitude that had been expressed in Washington by Keynes, remarking that an element in British opinion seemed to be 'directing its energies towards the resumption or continuation by Great Britain after the war of exactly the kind of system which had proved so fatal during the past generation'. He advanced the hope that Cadogan recognized 'the need, when the time came for world reconstruction to be undertaken, of the freest possible economic interchange without discriminations, without exchange controls, without economic preferences utilized for political purposes and without all of the manifold economic barriers which had in my judgment been so clearly responsible for the present world collapse'. Cadogan expressed

---

[1] For a description of Keynes's warnings and the American reaction see Harrod, p. 513, and E. F. Penrose, *Economic Planning for the Peace* (Princeton, 1953), pp. 14–15.

[2] For the text of the revised draft, see *infra*, p. 56.

[3] Langer and Gleason, p. 679, citing *Berle Diary* (MS.) (17 July 1941) and memorandum of the Division of Commercial Treaties (4 Aug. 1941).

general sympathy with Welles's remarks but was not prepared to pursue the matter further until the question of the joint statement was taken up by the two leaders themselves.[1]

On the evening of 9 August Roosevelt dined with Churchill and proposed that they draft a joint declaration 'laying down certain broad principles which should guide our policies along the same road'.[2] The Prime Minister responded eagerly and by noon of the following day, with a speed suggesting anticipation of the President's proposal, produced a five-point draft which formed the basis of the final declaration. 'Considering all the tales of my reactionary, Old World outlook, and the pain this is said to have caused the President, I am glad that it should be on record that the substance and spirit of what came to be called the "Atlantic Charter" was in its first draft a British production cast in my own words.'[3] But the Prime Minister, having heard of Welles's strong representations to Cadogan, was anxious to avoid an untimely controversy. His draft on economic matters was deliberately vague:

Fourth, they will strive to bring about a fair and equitable distribution of essential produce, not only within their territorial boundaries, but between the nations of the world.[4]

For Welles this formulation was unacceptable. He was determined to execute the precise commitment which was sought by Hull and the officials in the State Department's Commercial Policy Division. He was also personally convinced of the ineffectiveness of the Churchill draft, which he found 'reminiscent of the pious hopes expressed in a thousand and one economic conferences that "a fair and equitable international distribution of commodities" would come into being, during the very years when tariffs were being built up in the United States, and when every variety of discriminatory trade barrier was being erected in an increasingly autarchic world'.[5] Since it was his responsibility to redraft the British version on behalf of the United States, he seized the opportunity to spell out a precise commitment:

Fourth, they will strive to promote mutually advantageous economic relations between them through the elimination of any discrimination in either the United States of America or in the United Kingdom against the importation of any product originating in the other country; and they will

---

[1] Memorandum of conversation between Welles and Cadogan (9 Aug. 1941), cited in Langer and Gleason, pp. 681–2.
[2] Winston S. Churchill, *The Grand Alliance* (London, 1950), p. 385.
[3] Id., p. 386.   [4] Ibid.   [5] Welles, p. 7.

endeavour to further the enjoyment by all peoples of access on equal terms to the markets and to the raw materials which are needed for their economic prosperity.[1]

The phrases before the semicolon in Welles's draft were virtually identical to those of the revised text of Article Seven of the Mutual Aid Agreement which Hawkins and his associates in the Commercial Policy Division had drafted in response to the alarming statements by Keynes.[2] To Roosevelt, they read too much like the text of a detailed trade agreement and seemed out of place in what was intended to be a lofty statement of general purpose. He told Welles it would be better 'to limit the scope of the entire declaration to principles, rather than include therein references to immediate issues'. For this reason he struck out the words before the semicolon; but he retained their general import by inserting the words 'without discrimination' in the passage that followed, so that the section now provided for 'access without discrimination and on equal terms'. In Welles's view this retained the 'essential point' of the excised section. Welles re-wrote his draft of the Charter once more, incorporating the suggestions of the President, and in this form it was discussed on the morning of 11 August by Churchill and Roosevelt, assisted by Welles, Hopkins, and Cadogan.[3]

Churchill immediately noted the revised wording of his fourth paragraph. He asked whether the phrase 'without discrimination' would be held to proscribe the Ottawa Agreements. If so, it would be his duty as Prime Minister to submit the text not only to his own Government but to the Governments of the Dominions, and, he added, 'I should have little hope that it would be accepted'.[4] Welles acknowledged the difficulty, but called attention to the words 'endeavour to further', which he said negated the suggestion of an immediate contractual obligation. Roosevelt added that the question was of importance 'as a means of assurance to the German and Italian peoples that the British and the United States Governments desired to offer them, after the war, fair and equal opportunity of an economic character'.[5] With this objective the Prime Minister expressed his personal sympathy, but he repeated that at least a week would be required to seek the necessary approval.

---

[1] Welles, p. 8.   [2] See *infra*, p. 56.   [3] Welles, pp. 9–10.
[4] Churchill, p. 387. Robert E. Sherwood, in *Roosevelt and Hopkins* (New York, 1948, vol. i), p. 360, credits Beaverbrook, who had arrived at the Conference by this time, with persuading the Prime Minister that he had no authority to accept the American draft as it then stood.   [5] Welles, p. 13.

At this point the President's advisers gave divided counsel. Hopkins, who was concerned more with the importance of reaching speedy agreement on the joint declaration than with specific questions of commercial policy, suggested that Cadogan and Welles be asked to work out a compromise draft of the controversial provision. 'It was inconceivable', he declared, 'that the issuance of the joint declaration should be held up by a matter of this kind.'[1] Welles, however, was adamant:

I said that in my own judgment further modification of that article would destroy completely any value in that portion of the proposed declaration. I said it was not a question of phraseology, but that it was a vital principle which was involved. I said that if the British and the United States governments could not agree to do everything within their power to further after the termination of the present war, a restoration of free and liberal trade policies, they might as well throw in the sponge and realize that one of the greatest factors in creating the present tragic situation in the world was going to be permitted to continue unchecked in the postwar world. . . . I said . . . that it seemed to be imperative that we try to agree now upon the policy of constructive sanity in world economics as a fundamental factor in the creation of a new and better world and that except through an agreement upon such a policy by our two governments there would be no hindrance whatsoever to the continuation later of the present German policies of utilizing trade and financial policies in order to achieve political ends.[2]

This forceful presentation of the State Department's views appears to have provoked the British Prime Minister. 'I could not help mentioning the British experience in adhering to Free Trade for eighty years in the face of ever-mounting American tariffs. . . . All we got in reciprocation was successive doses of American protection.'[3] At these observations, Churchill recalls, Welles looked 'a little taken aback'.[4] The Prime Minister then proposed amendments to the American draft—strike out 'without discrimination', substitute 'trade' for 'markets', and, most important, insert the saving clause 'with due respect for existing obligations'. The President, evidently impressed, asked Churchill to undertake the job of drafting the article in acceptable terms.

At the close of this discussion Churchill cabled to the War Cabinet in London a text of the Charter and some of his own comments. On the economic question he remarked:

The fourth condition would evidently have to be amended to safeguard our obligations contracted in Ottawa and not prejudice the future of

---

[1] Ibid.   [2] Id., pp. 13–14.   [3] Churchill, p. 387.   [4] Ibid.

Imperial Preference. This might fall into its place after the war in a general economic settlement, with decisive lowering of tariffs and trade barriers throughout the world. But we cannot settle it now. For the sake of speedy agreement I have little doubt he [Roosevelt] will accept our amendments.[1]

On the last point the Prime Minister's judgement proved to be correct. The cable was hardly sent when Welles made a brave but fruitless effort to carry out the State Department's wishes. He warned the President that to remove the phrase 'without discrimination' and to add the saving clause 'with due respect for existing obligations' would leave intact the Ottawa Agreements and cause the article to be 'gravely weakened'. He begged the President to ask Churchill to 'cut corners' and accept the American draft without consulting the Dominions.[2] Roosevelt rejected this advice. He wanted publication of the joint declaration to coincide with announcement of the Atlantic Conference and agreed with Hopkins that the commercial policy issue was not important enough to stand in the way. Thus, shortly before the next meeting to discuss Churchill's compromise text, he wrote to Welles: 'Time being of the essence I think I can stand on my own former formula—to wit: access to raw materials. This omits entirely the other subject which is the only one in conflict: discrimination in trade.'[3] The note suggests how little understanding the President had of the State Department's economic doctrines, since Department spokesmen had repeatedly held that a system of discriminatory import tariffs such as the Ottawa Agreements was inconsistent with the principle of equal access to raw materials.[4] One might almost conclude that even apart from the saving clause about 'existing obligations' the President did not consider Imperial Preference and other commercial policy issues to be affected by a promise to provide equal access 'to the raw materials of the world'.[5]

The President's decision to accept Churchill's amendments removed further impediments to agreement on the fourth paragraph. On the morning of 12 August Roosevelt and Churchill met over the final draft of the Atlantic Charter. The controversial paragraph now expressed the desire of the two countries 'with due respect for their existing obligations, to further the enjoyment by all States, great or small, victor or vanquished, of access, on equal terms, to the trade and to the raw materials of the world which are needed for their

---

[1] Churchill, p. 391.   [2] Welles, p. 15.
[3] Id., p. 16.   [4] See p. 19, *supra.*
[5] In any case, the final draft of the Charter specified equal access to *trade* as well as raw materials.

economic prosperity'. Since the previous meeting Churchill had received a message from the War Cabinet suggesting qualifications to the fourth paragraph beyond those which he had already made, but the Prime Minister did not press them when the President expressed a preference for the wording of Churchill's own amendments. The misgivings of the War Cabinet apparently included both the Preference issue and the issue of protection generally, since the Prime Minister found it necessary to cable back: 'Phrase about "respect for existing obligations" safeguards our relations with Dominions. We could not see how competition of cheap labour would come in as all countries preserve the right of retaining or imposing national tariffs as they think fit pending better solutions.'[1]

In addition to suggesting amendments to the fourth paragraph the War Cabinet proposed a fifth, which expressed in more affirmative terms the objectives of economic betterment and social justice— objectives which occupied such a conspicuous place in British post-war planning:

Fifth, they desire to bring about the fullest collaboration between all nations in the economic field with the object of assuring, for all, improved labour standards, economic development and social security.

With the ready acceptance of this new paragraph by the President the drafting of the first definition of Anglo-American post-war economic objectives was finally complete.

THE ATLANTIC CHARTER IN ANGLO-AMERICAN OPINION

The text of the Atlantic Charter was released to the public on 14 August 1941 in a communiqué which announced that the President and the Prime Minister had met at sea to discuss the problem of war supply and the wider implications of Axis aggression. The joint declaration itself was presented simply as a statement of 'certain common principles in the national policies of their respective countries on which they base their hopes for a better future for the world'.[2]

The cautious tone of these phrases reflected the concern of both Roosevelt and Churchill to avoid the appearance of having made firm commitments on behalf of their respective governments. The President knew that any formal instrument in the nature of a treaty

---

[1] Churchill, p. 397.
[2] For the text of the communiqué and a comprehensive report of the Conference see *The New York Times* (15 Aug. 1941).

would probably require Congressional approval; he feared the reaction of Congress to any document which looked like an Anglo-American military alliance against the Axis powers. Roosevelt's anxiety was fully justified, for even with its cautious introduction the Charter was bitterly assailed by isolationist Congressmen. Administration supporters had to give assurances that the document constituted only 'a general statement of policy' and involved 'no moral obligation of any sort during or after the war'.[1]

The Prime Minister was faced with a similar problem. Just as Roosevelt feared the domestic political repercussions of a formal association with the Allied powers, so did Churchill fear the divisive internal controversies that might accompany specific engagements about the future of the British Empire. In reporting to the British people, therefore, he emphasized that the Charter was not a declaration of 'final and formal peace aims' but only 'a simple, rough-and-ready war-time statement of the goal towards which the British Commonwealth and the United States mean to make their way'.[2] Similarly, in his presentation to Parliament, he sought to convey the impression that the Charter imposed no new commitments but simply affirmed principles which had 'long been familiar to the British and American democracies'.[3]

As might be expected, however, qualifications of this kind made less impression on the public mind than the eight bold paragraphs of the Charter themselves. In Britain the reference to 'the final destruction of Nazi tyranny' and 'a wider and permanent system of general security' were welcomed as heralding the end of American isolation. Although British opinion evinced some disappointment that a more definite commitment of military support was not included, the Charter served to encourage hopes that the United States would eventually enter the European war.[4]

The American public set even greater store by the document. Because it provided not only for 'equal access' to raw materials but also for the 'self-determination' of subject peoples, it was hailed as a significant anti-Imperialist manifesto. One historian captures what was the American mood when he describes the effect of the Charter as 'cosmic and historic', adding: 'The British learned that when you state a moral principle, you are stuck with it, no matter how many fingers you have kept crossed at the moment. . . . Even the qualifying

[1] 87 *Cong. Rec.* 7209 (19 Aug. 1941).   [2] *The New York Times* (25 Aug. 1941).
[3] 374 H.C. Deb. 67 (9 Sept. 1941).   [4] *The New York Times* (15 Aug. 1941).

phrase about "existing obligations" became inconsequential under the superior weight of the new responsibilities firmly if not formally assumed.'[1] When the text of the Charter was released it was described triumphantly by Hull as a 'statement of basic principles and fundamental ideas which are universal in their practical application'.[2] Other government spokesmen saw in the Charter the promise of a new order of international relationships. Welles exclaimed:

> The age of imperialism is ended. The right of all peoples to their freedom must be recognized. . . . The principles of the Atlantic Charter must be guaranteed to the world as a whole—in all oceans and in all continents.[3]

Particular enthusiasm was displayed in the United States over the Charter's economic clauses. Administration spokesmen held out the fourth and fifth paragraphs as a victory for the principles of foreign economic policy which the United States had been advocating in recent years. Welles was quite specific in his interpretation: 'The Atlantic declaration means that every nation has a right to expect that its legitimate trade will not be diverted and throttled by towering tariffs, preferences, discriminations or narrow bilateral practices.'[4] He suggested that the pledge to economic good-neighbourliness would mainly require changes in the policies of other countries, since the principles of the Atlantic Charter had already become a part of the foreign economic policy of the United States:

> Most fortunately we have already done much to put our own house in order. So long as we adhere to and persistently implement the principles and policies which made possible the enactment of the Trade Agreements Act, the United States will not furnish, as it did in the last war, an excuse for trade-destroying and trade-diverting practises.[5]

British leaders spoke less often and less specifically than their American counterparts about the economic clauses of the Atlantic Charter. In explaining the fourth and fifth paragraphs to the British public, the Prime Minister remarked simply that 'instead of trying to ruin German trade by all kinds of additional trade barriers and hindrances, as was the mood of 1917, we have definitely adopted the view that it is not in the interests of the world and of our two countries that any large nation should be unprosperous or shut out from the means of making a decent living for itself and its people by its industry and enterprise'.[6] Nothing was said about specific issues

---

[1] Sherwood, pp. 440–1. [2] *The New York Times* (15 Aug. 1941).
[3] Id. (31 May 1942). [4] Id. (8 Oct. 1941).
[5] Ibid. [6] Id. (25 Aug. 1941).

in British trade and financial policy which might provoke differences in the War Cabinet. Indeed, the scepticism with which many business leaders as well as left-wing Socialists regarded the restoration of multilateralism made it dangerous to try to spell out the implications of the Charter's economic clauses in any great detail. The silence maintained on this score caused one British commentator to complain that 'the implications of our acceptance of the principle of equal access are hardly anywhere yet being taken seriously in this country'.[1]

This last remark was probably something of an over-statement. Despite the silence from Whitehall, the British press was quick to see the far-reaching significance of the Charter's economic clauses. *The Times* spoke for the large majority, declaring: 'Equal opportunity for all is a principle which must be written large in our international, as well as in our national, programme of reconstruction.'[2] The Editor of *The Banker* noted approvingly that the Charter forecast 'an integrated world economy and not a series of independent and mutually exclusive systems'.[3] The *News Chronicle* remarked with satisfaction that 'the considerable number of people in this country who are already planning our post-war trade in terms of barter, bilateralism, trade zones, clearings, exchange control, and by the concepts of the "between wars" era must begin at once to recast their ideas'.[4] And *The Economist* declared:

> The Atlantic Declaration . . . is . . . a statement in the most general terms, of the joint and several need of all nations to re-establish the equality of trading opportunity upon which the prosperity and progress of the world have depended in the past; and, more specifically, it is a repudiation of the considerations of power which have elevated self-sufficiency from being a *sauve qui peut* expedient to be a principle of national policy.[5]

If any reservations were heard, they were not so much to the general objective as to the specific means designed to achieve it. *The Times* issued a warning:

> The negative conception of the removal of trade barriers is not enough. It may be doubted whether equal access to raw materials . . . will suffice . . . to bring about that revival of international trade which Great Britain, above all countries, ardently desires. During the troubled interval between the two wars purchasers were rarely if ever excluded from markets in which

---

[1] Oscar Hobson, 'Point Four—Do We Mean It?', *News Chronicle* (25 Sept. 1941).
[2] (18 Aug. 1941).   [3] 'An End to Economic Nationalism', lx (1941), p. 174.
[4] (15 Aug. 1941).   [5] 'Freedom to Trade', cxli (1941), p. 221.

they could afford to buy. The crux of the problem was the drying up of purchasing power, of production brought to a standstill and men kept in idleness, not because there was no demand for their products, but because there was apparently no method known to orthodox finance of bridging the gap between consumer and producer. This is the barrier which must be broken down.[1]

As statements of an ultimate objective, therefore, the economic clauses of the Atlantic Charter were widely approved on both sides of the Atlantic. But one untidy and insistent detail intruded in this broader picture: the question of Imperial Preference. Immediately following publication of the Charter, Secretary Hull was asked whether the phrase 'with due respect for existing obligations' meant the continuation of the Ottawa Agreements.[2] Although Welles believed that the phrase was inserted 'solely to take care of what it was hoped would be merely temporary impediments to the more far-reaching commitment originally envisaged',[3] Hull regarded it as of greater importance. He did not say so publicly at the time, but he felt that the saving clause 'deprived the article of virtually all significance', since it meant that the preferential system would be retained.[4] Discouraged and resentful, he regarded the concession to the Prime Minister as a serious betrayal of State Department purposes. Indeed, he felt so strongly on this score that some weeks later he proposed adding to the fourth paragraph an unqualified commitment for the elimination of Preference. Only when Ambassador Winant reported the misgivings of Churchill about the reception such a proposal would have from the War Cabinet and from the Dominion Governments was the Secretary prevailed upon to abandon his project.[5]

The statement by Secretary Hull that the saving clause of paragraph four 'deprived the article of virtually all significance' was striking evidence of his passionate concern with the Ottawa Agreements. In the light of history, it may be thought to show a certain lack of perspective. These agreements were, after all, only one of many forms of discrimination which the promise of 'equal access' was designed to proscribe. Moreover, the statement seems to concede a greater exception for the Ottawa Agreements than is required by the language of the Atlantic Charter. The saving clause provided only that '*due* respect' should be accorded to '*existing* obligations'. The preferential agreements in existence between the Dominions ran

---

[1] (18 Aug. 1941).   [2] *The New York Times* (15 Aug. 1941).
[3] Welles, *The Time for Decision* (New York, 1944), p. 176.
[4] Hull, *Memoirs*, vol. ii, pp. 975–6.   [5] Langer and Gleason, p. 680.

only for a specific term of years and could be terminated at any time by mutual consent. Accordingly the qualifying phrase did not make Imperial Preference a permanent exception to the principle of equal access; it merely permitted a short-run exception to avoid violation of the temporary preferential agreements then in force.

This was, in fact, the general interpretation given—and given approvingly—during public discussion in the United Kingdom. Most of the major periodicals minimized the saving clause and stated flatly that the Ottawa Agreements stood in contradiction to the objective stated in the fourth paragraph of the Charter.[1] In the words of the *Financial News*: 'It is true that all this is subject to the qualifying clause, "with due respect for existing obligations". But the implication is surely, that when those obligations conflict with the spirit of the new Anglo-American agreement, they will be amended at the earliest possible moment.'[2]

CONCLUSION

The Atlantic Charter embodied the first agreed statement of the post-war economic objectives of Britain and the United States. This fact alone may be considered sufficient to justify its place in the annals of modern history. But perhaps there will be an objection to this view. It may be argued that the economic clauses of the Charter were drafted in such general terms as to be virtually meaningless, that 'access on equal terms' was an abstraction designed to obscure specific Anglo-American differences, and that the abortive attempt to resolve the Preference issue provided proof that beneath the sonorous phrases there lay no real agreement on ultimate objective.

The answer to this objection may be stated in both negative and affirmative terms. In the first place, as the Prime Minister himself declared, the Charter 'does not try to explain how the broad principles proclaimed by it are to be applied to each and every case. . . . It would not be wise for us, at this moment, to be drawn into laborious discussions on how it is to fit all the manifold problems with which we shall be faced after the war.'[3] In August 1941 the United States had not entered the war; it was impossible to determine how the war would be won—even whether it would be won at all. The leaders of the two great Western nations had met primarily to reach

---

[1] See, for example, 'Freedom to Trade', *The Economist*, cxli (1941), p. 221; Financial Editor, *The Manchester Guardian* (15 Aug. 1941); Editor, *The Banker*, lxi (1941), pp. 188–9.　　　[2] (15 Aug. 1941).　　　[3] 374 H.C. Deb. 68 (9 Sept. 1941).

a broad understanding on resistance to Nazi aggression. This had, for reasons already described, brought them to consideration of the kind of world which might eventuate if such resistance were successful. A meeting devoted to these ends was not the proper occasion for discussing specific issues of financial and commercial policy—subjects with which the two leaders had neither the time nor the competence to deal. One may even regret that an issue like Imperial Preference was raised in direct form and that the controversy about it became such a celebrated part of the history of the Atlantic Conference.

There is also a more affirmative case for the Charter's economic clauses. Despite their generality, they contained clear enough markers to direct the foreign policies of the two governments. The promise of equal access to trade and raw materials meant as a very minimum the avoidance both of exclusive economic blocs and the use of totalitarian trade practices for political ends. The promise of international collaboration for economic advancement meant that the United States and Britain, through appropriate bilateral or multilateral institutions, would work together to improve the living standards and economic security of their own and other friendly peoples. In view of the history of the inter-war period, the significance of these two promises was not inconsiderable. It remained to be seen, however, whether and under what circumstances they would both be kept.

CHAPTER IV

ARTICLE SEVEN

THE United States and Britain made a second major attempt to define their post-war economic objectives in the Mutual Aid Agreement signed on 23 February 1942. The primary object of the Agreement was to lay down certain principles governing the provision of Lend-Lease supplies; but Article Seven, dealing with the eventual terms of Lend-Lease settlement, stimulated a further exchange of views on post-war trade policy. This Article went well beyond the hastily drafted economic clauses of the Atlantic Charter. It required eight months of intermittent negotiation and emerged in final form as a binding international commitment which defined the multilateral objective in some detail. Its terms were subsequently incorporated in the Mutual Aid Agreements concluded by the United States with other Lend-Lease recipients. In this way Article Seven became the basic legal framework for post-war planning in the economic field.

THE QUESTION OF 'CONSIDERATION'

'The existence of the great war debts is a menace to financial stability everywhere. . . . We shall never be able to move again, unless we can free our limbs from these paper shackles. A general bonfire is so great a necessity that unless we can make it an orderly and good-tempered affair in which no serious injustice is done to anyone, it will, when it comes at last, grow into a conflagration that may destroy much else as well.'

Keynes wrote these prophetic words in the aftermath of the First World War.[1] Unfortunately, they had gone unheeded. The European Allies had sought to collect huge reparations from a defeated Germany. They had been required, in turn, to service large war debts owing to the United States. The result had been economic dislocation, eventual default, and an enduring legacy of bitterness and ill will.

The British and American Governments were determined now to avoid a repetition of this experience. There was little difficulty in agreeing that the defeated nations should not be asked to pay huge

[1] *The Economic Consequences of the Peace* (New York, 1920), pp. 279–80.

reparations. But avoidance of war debts between the Allied powers posed a more difficult problem. Thanks to some ingenious New Deal lawyers, Lend-Lease had been devised just in time to avoid exhaustion of Britain's reserves of gold and dollars, which had been brought to the vanishing-point by the 'cash and carry' system.[1] Still, a nation for whom neutrality still seemed a practical possibility naturally regarded Lend-Lease more as a generous measure on behalf of one belligerent than as an instrument necessary to its own survival. Most Americans (and most of their representatives in Congress) thought the United States should be repaid for Lend-Lease supplies, either by cash settlements or by the granting of military bases and raw materials concessions.[2]

The Administration was reluctant to jeopardize the enactment of the Lend-Lease bill by making a frontal attack on the repayment question. Consequently the bill left the whole matter unresolved. It authorized the President to 'sell, transfer title to, exchange, lease, lend, or otherwise dispose of' any 'defense article' to any country whose defence he deemed 'vital to the defense of the United States'. It gave him broad discretion to determine the conditions of the Lend-Lease settlement. But—and this was a very important qualification—the terms of that settlement were to contain some 'benefit to the United States'—a 'payment or repayment in kind or property, or any other direct or indirect benefit which the President deems satisfactory'.[3]

This arrangement had the effect of removing the decision on Lend-Lease repayment from the jurisdiction of the American Congress. But the matter was still subject to Congressional influence. For the power to appropriate public funds was lodged in Congress by the Constitution. From the very beginning the price of Congressional co-operation in appropriating Lend-Lease funds was the assurance that the President would require some 'benefit' in return for Lend-Lease beyond the defence of the United States by the military action of other countries. Accordingly, the President and his advisers had to find a 'benefit' which they could hold out as the 'consideration' for Lend-Lease assistance. What they hit upon was

---

[1] British reserves were down to $12 million in the spring of 1941. *Statistical Material Presented During the Washington Negotiations*, Cmd. 6706 of 1945, p. 5.

[2] Witness the results of a public opinion poll taken in Feb. 1942, where 84 per cent. of those interviewed expressed the opinion that Britain should repay the United States for Lend-Lease aid; 9 per cent. thought Britain should not repay; 7 per cent. gave qualified answers or expressed no opinion. Eugene Staley, 'The Economic Implications of Lend-Lease', *Am. Ec. Rev.*, xxxiii (Supp., 1943), p. 367, n. 4.

[3] Section 3. 55 Stat. (Part 1) 31 (1941).

the promise by Britain and other aid recipients to co-operate in the post-war reconstruction of multilateral trade.

This decision was not determined by domestic political considerations alone. The leaders of the Administration genuinely believed that they would enhance the prospects for multilateralism by exacting specific commitments from the Allies on post-war trade policy. To get such commitments seemed both a shrewd exercise of 'bargaining power' and a logical arrangement suggested by the history of the recent past. After all, it was argued, the attempt of the United States to collect 'war debts' after the First World War had provided a major obstacle to achievement of the multilateral objective. It seemed only reasonable that if the American Government now promised to remove that obstacle the beneficiaries should promise to support the objective itself.

Thus it happened that formal undertakings on post-war trade policy were inserted in the Mutual Aid Agreement concluded with Britain and the other Lend-Lease recipients. Whether these undertakings would really promote the cause they were designed to serve is a question which future events would have to answer.

THE SECOND DEFINITION OF MULTILATERALISM

The historic Anglo-American negotiations on Article Seven began with the visit of Keynes to Washington in the summer of 1941. As we have already noted, his blunt warning about Britain's post-war trade policy spurred the American negotiators to define the 'consideration' for Lend-Lease in precise and unambiguous terms. On 28 July Keynes was handed a draft of Article Seven containing the same strict commitment to non-discrimination that Welles was to press without success two weeks later in the Atlantic Conference:

The terms and conditions upon which the United Kingdom receives defense aid from the United States of America and the benefits to be received by the United States of America in return therefor, as finally determined, shall be such as not to burden commerce between the two countries but to promote mutually advantageous economic relations between them and the betterment of world-wide economic relations: they shall provide against discrimination in either the United States of America or the United Kingdom against the importation of any product originating in either country; and they shall provide for the formulation of measures for the achievement of these ends.[1]

[1] Harley A. Notter, *Postwar Foreign Policy Preparation 1939–1945* (Washington, 1949), App. 8, p. 463.

Although this draft left no doubt that Britain would have to forswear Imperial Preference and other forms of discrimination against the United States, it said nothing at all about the essential counterparts in American policy—the lowering of tariffs and the avoidance of a serious post-war depression. Accordingly, Keynes found its provisions unacceptable—he even referred to them as the 'lunatic proposals of Mr. Hull'.[1] The negotiations reached an impasse, and Keynes returned home without agreement on Article Seven. Although this did not mean any interruption in Lend-Lease supplies, it did mean that the British were still without the vital American commitment to make a generous settlement of the Lend-Lease account. Nevertheless, it was deemed untimely to pursue the matter further. In September Ambassador Winant informed the State Department that the British were absorbed in urgent war problems and asked that further negotiations on the Article be postponed.

In the meantime, E. F. Penrose, economic adviser to Ambassador Winant, had been called to Washington to receive from the State Department an account of the issues which were standing in the way of Anglo-American agreement. In these conversations, and in later talks in London with Keynes and others, Penrose probed the major grounds of British resistance to Article Seven. He found that British reservations fell under the two major heads already described. In the first place, there was concern with the balance of payments problem which would face Britain in the post-war transition period. In Keynes's view the full seriousness of this problem was not appreciated in Washington. Here Penrose did not find it possible to be very reassuring. Personally, he felt that Lend-Lease should be made retroactive, so that Britain could be reimbursed for the sizeable expenditures made in the United States before the programme had begun. But he could not cite any specific plans under way in the American Administration for implementing this view. Nor could he hold out any hope that such a plan would have the slightest chance of Congressional approval.[2]

On the second main ground of British anxiety—the fear of an American slump—Penrose sought to be more reassuring. The idea was widespread in Whitehall that the State Department was entirely absorbed with the reduction of trade barriers and was blind to the importance of complementary measures to maintain high levels of

[1] Harrod, p. 512.   [2] Penrose, pp. 16–17.

employment and economic activity. This idea Penrose rejected in emphatic terms:

I did my best to impress on Mr. Keynes and other government economists that the desire for freer and for non-discriminatory trade in the State Department should not be written off as the product of a nineteenth century laissez-faire attitude toward economic affairs, untouched by recent economic thought and experience. It was true that Secretary Hull and Harry Hawkins had a particular concern with trade, but this arose from the Secretary's leading role in that field for many years and Hawkins' position at the head of the division concerned with trade matters. In conversations in Washington both Acheson and Hawkins showed themselves progressive in outlook and under no illusion that freer trade alone was a panacea for all economic ills.[1]

These arguments may have helped to allay British fears. But it was unlikely that the resistance to Article Seven would be overcome without more concrete evidence of American concern with the goal of economic expansion.

During the autumn hiatus developments occurred on both sides of the Atlantic which enhanced the possibility of agreement. On the British side an important factor appears to have been the evolution of Keynes's thinking. Here one can only speculate on the major influences at work. Keynes delved more deeply into projects such as his Clearing Union, which could form the basis of a multilateral system. He also pondered the consequences of a possible trade war with the United States. The likelihood of such a conflict in the event of discriminatory practices by the United Kingdom had been impressed upon him during one of his conversations in Washington. Hawkins had said in no uncertain terms that the United States had its own exponents of economic nationalism and that in a trade war between the two countries the United States would inevitably triumph. This was a strong argument, Keynes saw, for attempting a more constructive approach to the problem.[2]

On the other side of the Atlantic a more flexible attitude toward Article Seven was also emerging. After informal negotiations with Lord Halifax, the British Ambassador in Washington, and Redvers Opie, economic advisor to the British Embassy, the State Department produced a new, and, as it turned out, final draft of the Article. This contained the same preface as the State Department's July draft but continued instead with the following language:

To that end, they shall include provision for agreed action by the United States of America and the United Kingdom, open to participation by all

[1] Penrose, p. 18.　　　　[2] Harrod, p. 513.

other countries of like mind, directed to the expansion, by appropriate international and domestic measures, of production, employment, and the exchange and consumption of goods, which are the material foundations of the liberty and welfare of all peoples; to the elimination of all forms of discriminatory treatment in international commerce, and to the reduction of tariffs and other trade barriers; and, in general, to the attainment of all the economic objectives set forth in the Joint Declaration made on August 14, 1941, by the President of the United States of America and the Prime Minister of the United Kingdom.

At an early convenient date, conversations shall be begun between the two Governments with a view to determining, in the light of governing economic conditions, the best means of attaining the above-stated objectives by their own agreed action and of seeking the agreed action of other like-minded Governments.[1]

About this draft, which awaited British approval in the closing weeks of 1941, two observations must be made. First, the new wording represented a notable attempt to meet the major grounds of British anxiety already described. The terms of settlement were to provide, not directly for a régime of non-discrimination, but rather for 'agreed action ... directed to' this end—action to be determined 'in the light of governing economic conditions'. Moreover, the elimination of discrimination was no longer formulated as the only aim of joint action, but was balanced by an equally important end—'the expansion ... of production, employment, and the exchange and consumption of goods'.

This much is fairly obvious. But the revised draft of Article Seven was significant in a second respect. The 'consideration' clause of the Article now contained mutually interdependent obligations. The promise to move towards the elimination of discrimination, for example, depended on the promise to promote economic expansion. Failure on the part of the American Government to combat a slump would therefore release the British Government from its obligation to remove discrimination. Moreover, the elimination of discrimination was to occur in step with the 'reduction of tariffs and other trade barriers'. Thus if the United States determined to pursue a protectionist policy, it could not demand that Britain eliminate 'discriminatory treatment'.

In short, the whole character of Article Seven had been subtly changed. The July draft, by providing for mutual undertakings of non-discrimination, had put the greater burden of practical implementation on the shoulders of the United Kingdom, since no appreciable discrimination was being practised by the United States. This greater burden had been justified on the grounds that the obligations

[1] *Dept. of State Bull.*, vi (1942), p. 192.

undertaken by Britain were the 'consideration' for the promise of a generous Lend-Lease settlement on the part of the United States. But with the revisions of late autumn an effective mutuality had been brought about within the 'consideration' section itself—the British undertakings on economic policy were payment for similar American undertakings of equal value. Was it necessary to continue to suggest that they were also payment for the promise of a generous Lend-Lease settlement? Were not the American undertakings on tariffs and economic expansion adequate 'consideration' for British promises to embrace a multilateral régime?

These questions apparently were answered in the negative. The link between the promises on trade policy and the terms of the Lend-Lease settlement was retained—even after the entry of the United States into the Second World War. In retrospect this may seem rather surprising. Administration leaders probably felt that the American public would continue to demand a *quid pro quo* for the provision of Lend-Lease beyond the co-operation of the recipients in a common war effort. Perhaps, too, some British leaders feared that the exchange of promises about post-war economic co-operation could not command public support on its own merits but needed the additional argument that it was required as an inducement to a favourable settlement of Lend-Lease. The most likely explanation of all is that the negotiations begun before Pearl Harbour to put a 'consideration' in the Mutual Aid Agreement simply drifted along on their own momentum.

In any case, when approval of Article Seven was finally sought at the highest political level, the linking of Britain's post-war policy obligations to the terms of the Lend-Lease settlement provided a major source of difficulty. What particularly concerned the members of the British Cabinet was the commitment to eliminate 'discriminatory treatment'. This, the American negotiators had explained in unmistakable terms, definitely meant the elimination of Imperial Preference.[1] Some members of the Cabinet, such as Beaverbrook and Amery, were opposed to the elimination of Preference in any circumstances. The majority did not take such an uncompromising view, but shrank from approving any agreement which seemed to make the dismantling of Commonwealth economic arrangements the 'price' of Lend-Lease aid. As Penrose recalls:

Early in February [1942] Ambassador Winant spent a week-end at Chequers with the Prime Minister. Returning, he described the ministerial

---

[1] See *infra*, p. 66, for more detailed discussion of this point.

position to me as follows: some three-quarters of the Cabinet were opposed to having any reference to trade preferences in the Lend-Lease agreement. Of these, a few were out-and-out supporters of Empire preference on principle but others, including Mr. Churchill, did not believe that preferences served any useful purpose and were ready to begin discussions immediately, outside the scope of the Lend-Lease negotiations, on preferences, tariffs and other postwar questions of economic policy. They objected, however, to carrying on such discussions within the framework of the Lend-Lease negotiations, on the ground that the association of these two subjects gave the impression that Empire ties would be bartered away or sold in exchange for goods which Britain needed to wage the war.[1]

As the British Cabinet hung back from final agreement on Article Seven, the State Department became increasingly restive. When Churchill visited Washington in December 1941, shortly after America's entry into the war, Hull pressed Roosevelt and Halifax to take up Article Seven with the Prime Minister. The British Ambassador pleaded that Churchill was absorbed with war matters, but Hull replied 'that it was very important from our viewpoint that some action be taken without delay, for the reason that another Lend-Lease appropriation bill would come up in Congress in January and we would be called upon to explain why Britain delayed signing the proposed agreement'.[2] The Secretary himself brought the matter to Churchill's attention during a dinner at the White House on 12 January. But the Prime Minister was resolute in refusing to agree to the inclusion of any provision calling for the elimination of Preference in the pending Lend-Lease agreement.[3]

Having made no headway on Article Seven during Churchill's visit in December, Hull at last succeeded in enlisting the intervention of Roosevelt himself. Early in February the President, at Hull's suggestion, cabled the Prime Minister requesting speedy affirmative action by the British on the Article Seven draft. This intervention came at a time of grave British reversals culminating in the fall of Singapore—the event Churchill later described as 'the worst disaster and largest capitulation of British history'.[4] The Prime Minister cabled back that in the opinion of his Cabinet it would be a serious mistake to associate a promise to eliminate Preference with the provision of Lend-Lease aid—particularly at such an unfortunate moment in the war. An arrangement of this kind would provoke unpleasant debates in Parliament and enable enemy propagandists to say that

[1] Penrose, p. 24.   [2] Hull, vol. ii, p. 1152.   [3] Id., p. 1153.
[4] Churchill, *The Hinge of Fate* (London, 1951), p. 81.

the United States was capitalizing on British adversity to seize control of the British Empire.[1]

Roosevelt replied to this message in sympathetic and imaginative terms. Sherwood has paraphrased his words as follows:

He [Roosevelt] told Churchill, 'I understand something of the nice relationships which are required by your constitution for dealings between your Home Government and the Dominions.' He said that nothing could be further from his mind than an attempt to use Lend-Lease as a trading weapon over the principle of imperial preference. He urged that there be 'bold, forthright and comprehensive discussions looking forward to the construction of what you so aptly call "a free, fertile economic policy for the postwar world"'. He expressed the belief that developments 'which neither of us dreams of will be subjects of the most serious consideration in the not-too-distant future. So nothing should be excluded from the discussions.'[2]

There was also another statement of the President's which proved of particular significance to the Prime Minister. As Churchill later declared, the President provided 'a definite assurance that we were no more committed to the abolition of Imperial Preference, than the American Government were committed to the abolition of their high protective tariffs'.[3] On the basis of this and the President's other statements, the Cabinet was won over. In Washington, on 23 February 1942, the revised draft of Article Seven was finally signed.

THE ANGLO-AMERICAN REACTION

The Anglo-American response to the publication of Article Seven was similar to that which greeted the publication of the Atlantic Charter. With only a few exceptions, comment was generally favourable. At the same time, there was some difference in emphasis on the constituent parts of the Article and considerable disparity in the weight attached to the Article as a whole.

The favourable comment which the Mutual Aid Agreement evoked in the United States was mainly inspired by its promise of a liberal international trading system. There was no noticeable surprise that such a commitment should have been included in the document. And the fact that Britain and the United States had reached broad agreement on post-war economic matters received more attention than all the rest of its provisions put together.[4]

[1] Sherwood, pp. 506–7.   [2] Id., p. 507.
[3] The full text of the Prime Minister's statement is given *infra*, p. 65.
[4] See, for example, James Reston, 'Pact with Britain Sets Freer Trade as Basis of Peace', *The New York Times* (25 Feb. 1942).

In explaining Article Seven to the public, Administration spokes-men put rather more emphasis on non-discrimination and the reduc-tion of trade barriers than on the additional goal of economic expansion. There was also a tendency, evident in discussion of the Atlantic Charter, to equate the commitments included in the Article with the policies already being applied by the United States. Hull, for example, declared that Article Seven was implementing the promise of the Atlantic Charter that post-war economic relations would be based 'on the principles and objectives which have been tirelessly advocated by our Government on all appropriate occasions in recent years'.[1]

The Mutual Aid Agreement was well received in the United King-dom mainly because it offered hope of a Lend-Lease settlement which would avoid the repetition of the unhappy experience with war debts after the First World War. Although certain business groups entered qualifications to the non-discriminatory and anti-protec-tionist flavour of Article Seven,[2] most public discussion took a line similar to that of *The Economist*, which, while expressing surprise that commitments on post-war trade policy should have been inclu-ded in a Lend-Lease agreement, stated nevertheless that the terms of the Article 'admirably combine a statement of the objectives with a realisation that they cannot be attained overnight'.[3] Most of the favourable comments concentrated on the objective of economic ex-pansion rather than on that of lower trade barriers. *The Times* con-sidered the agreement 'a great step forward', explaining:

> The common economic policy to which the two Governments are thus committed opens up the prospect of a world in which the two greatest industrial and commercial nations, in co-operation with other countries will work together to promote the prosperity for all instead of competing for selfish advantages. Once the expansion of production and consumption and of employment is accepted as the overriding objective of policy, all other obstacles—finance, tariffs, discriminatory arrangements—become comparatively unimportant and lose most of their power for mischief.[4]

No less notable than these differences in emphasis were the differences in the weight which public opinion in the two countries accorded to Article Seven as a whole. The British Government made little effort to impress upon the British public the significance of its new commitment. Indeed, it said hardly anything about Article

---

[1] *Dept. State Bull.*, vi (1942), p. 479.
[2] See, for example, *The Times* (5 June 1942).
[3] 'Lend-Lease Terms', cxlii (1942), p. 281.   [4] (25 Feb. 1942).

Seven at all. In the United States, on the other hand, a vigorous
campaign was launched to convince the public that the Article contained a valuable *quid pro quo* for the provision of Lend-Lease.
Roosevelt told Congress that two of the direct benefits the United
States was getting in return for Lend-Lease were the defence of the
United States and reverse Lend-Lease, adding that the 'third direct
benefit received in return for our aid is an understanding with Britain
(and prospectively with others of our allies) as to the shape of future
commercial and financial policy'.[1] Welles declared that the exchange
of promises between the United States and its allies in the Mutual
Aid Agreements might become 'the nucleus of a United Nations
organization for the relief and economic reconstruction of the post-
war world'[2] and later noted more generally that the 'future prosperity
and peace of the world, and of the United States, depend vitally on
the good faith and the thoroughness with which we and they together carry out those promises'.[3] Another American Government
official went so far as to describe Article Seven as 'virtually a Magna
Carta for postwar economic collaboration'.[4] In the wake of government statements of this kind, unofficial publicists began to attach
considerable significance to Article Seven. As one of them put it:
'The master Lend-Lease agreement is a solemn contract signed for
the United States government with the approval of Congress and
signed by other nations because of definite advantages to be received
in return for definite services rendered. If this solemn agreement in
section 7 regarding trade barriers is not good, nothing else in international relationships can be trusted.'[5]

A PROBLEM OF INTERPRETATION

No further discussion of Article Seven would be required at this
point were it not for one particular detail that has provided a persistent source of controversy. Did the Article commit the United Kingdom to the elimination of Imperial Preference? In the years that
followed the signing of Article Seven the members of Churchill's
war-time government were frequently accused of having bartered
Preference away in return for Lend-Lease aid. Naturally enough,

---

[1] *A Report on the First Year of Lend-Lease Operations* (11 Mar. 1942), Holborn,
vol. i, p. 78.
[2] Id., p. 96.   [3] Id., p. 117.
[4] Lynn R. Edminster (member of the U.S. Tariff Commission), 'International Trade
and Postwar Reconstruction', *Am. Ec. Rev.*, xxxiii (Supp., 1943), pp. 303–4.
[5] Otto T. Mallery, 'A Practical Approach to a World Trade Board', *Annals Am. Ac.
of Pol. and Soc. Sci.*, ccxxxiv (1944), p. 84.

they sought to minimize the commitment that had been undertaken. Probably the most famous statement was made by Churchill himself on 21 April 1944 when he told the House of Commons

how strictly I have during my stewardship, safeguarded the structure of Imperial Preference, which has arisen out of the controversies and the achievements of the last forty years, against any danger of being swept away in the tumult of this war. . . . [I]n February, 1942, when the United States was our closest ally, I did not agree to Article 7 of the Mutual Aid Agreement without having previously obtained from the President a definite assurance that we were no more committed to the abolition of Imperial Preference, than the American Government were committed to the abolition of their high protective tariffs. The discussions as to how a greater volume of trade and a more harmonious flow of trade can be created in the immediate post-war years, in agreement ,leave us, so far as action is concerned, perfectly free. How could it be otherwise, when Parliament itself would not only have to debate the matters, but would have to legislate upon them, when they were brought before it?[1]

Statements of this kind appear to have encouraged the view that Article Seven did not really provide for the elimination of Imperial Preference and that the American Government had consented to grant some sort of special exemption for the Preference system. Shortly after the Prime Minister's first statement Sir John Anderson, then Chancellor of the Exchequer, told the financial and commercial leaders of the City of London: 'Under Article VII of the Mutual Aid Agreement . . . we agreed to work for the elimination of all forms of discrimination in international commerce. The only qualification was concerned with imperial preferences.'[2] Some months later, when discussing the 'Proposals for an International Conference on Trade and Employment' worked out by American and British negotiators,[3] Anderson declared:

SIR JOHN ANDERSON. I find in this document a very unpleasant and challenging reiteration of the new word 'elimination'. That has not appeared in any document of this kind before in this relation.

MR. DALTON. Article 7.

SIR JOHN ANDERSON. I do not think elimination of preference comes in there.

THE PRESIDENT OF THE BOARD OF TRADE [Sir Stafford Cripps]. The elimination of discriminatory practices.

SIR JOHN ANDERSON. Yes, the elimination of discriminatory practices, but it was left rather at large how far Imperial Preference between a group of

[1] 399 H.C. Deb. 579–80 (21 Apr. 1944). For a subsequent statement by Churchill to the same effect see 417 H.C. Deb. 723 (13 Dec. 1945).

[2] Speech at the Mansion House, London (4 Oct. 1944), Holborn, vol. ii, p. 521.

[3] See Chapter VIII, *infra*.

nations, bound together by special ties, could in this connection be so treated.[1]

These statements by Anderson are hard to reconcile with the manifest intention of the drafters of Article Seven. There can be little doubt that the State Department officials intended 'discriminatory treatment' to embrace Imperial Preference and made this clear to their British counterparts. The purpose of using the more inclusive term was to embrace other forms of discriminatory treatment along with preferences—discriminatory internal taxes, discriminatory exchange restrictions, and the like. Another purpose may have been to avoid the difficulties for the British Government which specific mention of preferences might have entailed. As Hull has written:

> We informed British Ambassador Halifax that we had expressed Article VII in general terms so as to avoid specific reference to preferential arrangements, which reference might cause political embarrassment to the British Government. We added that all such arrangements were included within the scope of our general provisions and that, if the agreement were published and we were asked to explain what did fall within the term, we proposed to say it was all-inclusive.[2]

The suggestion that preferences occupied a specially reserved position seems equally improbable when Article Seven is interpreted in the light of its major purpose. The Article was designed to chart the way in general terms toward the agreed objective of multilateral trade. Given this objective it is difficult to justify a privileged position for tariff preferences, which divert trade and distort the market mechanism in much the same way as other forms of discrimination. Article Seven could hardly have granted preferences a special exemption consistently with Roosevelt's desire for 'bold, forthright and comprehensive discussions' from which 'nothing should be excluded'.[3]

Thus the interpretation of Article Seven suggested in the Anderson statements must be rejected. But what of Churchill's declaration that 'we were no more committed to the abolition of Imperial Preference, than the American Government were committed to the abolition of their high protective tariffs'? What of his remark that 'so far as action is concerned' the provisions of Article Seven left the British Government 'perfectly free'? These statements are in a

[1] 417 H.C. Deb. 453 (13 Dec. 1945).   [2] Hull, vol. ii, p. 1152.
[3] See p. 62, *supra*. It should also be noted that at the time Article Seven was signed British commentators took it for granted that the 'elimination of discriminatory treatment' included the elimination of Imperial Preference. See, for example, 'Lend-Lease Terms', *The Economist*, cxlii (1942), p. 281.

different category. Unlike those of Anderson, they do not assert that Article Seven distinguished between preferences and other forms of discrimination. They merely express the truism that neither the Prime Minister nor the President, nor any of their subordinate Ministers, has the power to legislate for their respective governments. They only emphasize that Article Seven was a commitment to work toward certain long-term goals and not a commitment to make immediate changes in trade policies.

Thus the statement that Britain was not committed to action with respect to preferences was technically accurate. But this was true of action with respect to other obstacles to multilateral trade as well. For this reason the form of Churchill's statement must be regarded as somewhat misleading. A more comprehensive exposition of the legal position would be the following, drafted by a Congressional committee considering appropriations for Lend-Lease:

Article VII . . . does not reduce tariff barriers, nor remove discrimina-tions, nor set up machinery to secure an expansion of employment, produc-tion and consumption. It does, however, bind the signatories to confer together, with all other countries of like mind, to determine the best means of attaining the economic objective which it sets forth. Those conversations will concern all the subjects dealt with in Article VII, without limitation or exception. The results of negotiations undertaken in accordance with this provision are then to be referred for action to the proper constitutional authority in each of the countries concerned.[1]

Somewhat less formal, but no less accurate, was this statement given to Congress by Dean Acheson:

Now, in this agreement what [the President] has tried to do is to stop a tendency which might very easily develop of having a series of closed economies, closed against us and against one another, and to say to the other countries, 'You must agree to sit down with us and work out an arrangement which will have the effect of increasing the whole volume of production in the world, of consumption and employment and reducing the barriers of trade and doing away with discrimination.' And they agree that they will do that. *They are not holding out any of their special arrange-ments as being sacred or being protected from these negotiations.*[2]

In the light of the history and purpose of Article Seven this emphasis on its all-inclusive character seems entirely justified.

---

[1] U.S. Congress, House, Committee on Foreign Affairs, *Report on the Extension of Lend-Lease*, House Rept. no. 188, 78th Cong., 1st sess. (Washington, 1943).

[2] Italics supplied. U.S. Congress, House, Committee on Foreign Affairs, *Extension of Lend-Lease*, Hearings on H.R. 1501, 78th Cong., 1st sess. (Jan.–Feb. 1943), p. 109.

CONCLUSION

Agreement on Article Seven of the Mutual Aid Agreement represented a second important step in the definition of the post-war
economic objectives of the United States and Britain. It had not
been achieved without considerable difficulty. Because of their concern with domestic full employment and the post-war reconstruction
problem the British negotiators had resisted a firm commitment to
multilateral principles. Their resistance had been finally overcome by
making economic expansion a companion goal of post-war policy
and by relating the pursuit of non-discrimination to 'governing
economic conditions'. British acceptance of Article Seven was also
hampered by the linking of commitments on post-war economic
policy (notably the elimination of Imperial Preference) to the promise
of a generous Lend-Lease settlement. This link had been forged at
the behest of the American Government, which believed that it
would help overcome domestic political opposition to Lend-Lease
and would further the cause of multilateralism itself. Whether the
American view was justified on either of these grounds is a question
to which we shall subsequently have occasion to return.

Despite attendant difficulties, agreement on Article Seven was
significant in reaffirming the decision of the two governments to
collaborate in the reconstruction of the world economy along multilateral lines. The air was soon filled with hopeful reports of bold
planning to implement this objective. In his fifth quarterly report on
Lend-Lease Roosevelt forecast the development of 'a series of agreements and recommendations for legislation, in the field of commercial policy, of money and finance, international investment and
reconstruction'.[1] British spokesmen, responding to American initiative, were quick to announce the support of their government. As
one of them put it: 'There is no scheme for the maintenance of international peace and of financial stability in the post-war world so bold
or far-reaching that we are not prepared to consider it with the
utmost goodwill, or in which, if agreement can be reached, we are
not prepared to take our full share of responsibility—heavy though
it may be.'[2] By the beginning of 1943 the British Government had
joined the American in announcing specific topics for the economic
agenda.[3] The definition of the objective had been accomplished: the
hour of planning was now at hand.

[1] (11 June 1942), Holborn, vol. i, p. 93.
[2] Harcourt Johnston, Secretary of the Department of Overseas Trade, *The Sunday
Times* (19 July 1942).   [3] Sir Kingsley Wood, 386 H.C. Deb. 825 (2 Feb. 1943).

PART II

PLANNING FOR MULTILATERALISM

CHAPTER V

PLANNING FOR FINANCIAL COLLABORATION

THE drafting of an agreed definition of multilateralism was but the prelude to a second and more difficult stage of Anglo-American collaboration—that of devising the specific means by which the objective could be achieved. Fortunately, planning for post-war economic collaboration was well advanced in both countries by the time Article Seven was finally signed. Particular progress had been made in the financial field. Indeed, two highly placed economists working independently on either side of the Atlantic had already produced detailed blue-prints of a mechanism for international monetary co-operation.

KEYNES, WHITE, AND HISTORY

In origin and basic purpose the British and American financial plans were remarkably similar. The principal author of each was a former academic economist with a special interest in problems of monetary policy. Both plans were framed in the light of the monetary difficulties which had disrupted international trade in the inter-war period. Both were designed to facilitate the achievement of balance of payments equilibrium in an international environment of multi-lateral trade and in domestic conditions of full employment. They differed in their emphasis on these objectives according to the philosophies of their authors and the national interests of the two countries.

The White Plan

The American plan for post-war financial collaboration originated in the United States Treasury and particularly in the mind of Harry Dexter White. These facts had a decisive influence on the future course of Anglo-American economic collaboration. We would do well to consider for a moment how it was they came about.

By the time the United States entered the Second World War its great executive departments were engaged in a major struggle over their respective responsibilities for the planning of post-war foreign economic policy. By virtue of its jurisdiction in the general field of foreign affairs, the Department of State might have been expected to assume the dominant role. Indeed, a vast amount of planning on foreign economic policy was taking place under the direction of Cordell Hull's special adviser on post-war planning, Dr. Leo Pasvolsky. But other departments were advancing claims in this field as well—among them, the Board of Economic Warfare, the Department of Commerce, and the Department of Agriculture. The most serious challenge of all came from the Treasury Department itself.

In the ensuing struggle for control of foreign economic planning the State Department was hampered by the lack of thoroughly close relations between Roosevelt and Cordell Hull. Roosevelt considered Hull rather hidebound and conservative; he came to depend on others to carry responsibilities in the international field. On economic matters Henry Morgenthau, Jr., the Secretary of the Treasury, was the obvious choice. Morgenthau appeared to have a 'New Deal' outlook. His Department contained some of the ablest young exponents of that philosophy. Besides, he and Roosevelt had practically grown up together as neighbours in New York's Dutchess County. When Morgenthau came to see the President he brought with him not only a congenial outlook but the unparalleled advantage of a lifelong personal association.

Thus it happened that the State Department had to share with the Treasury the primary responsibility for the planning of post-war foreign economic policy. The State Department took charge of planning on commercial policy—planning that led eventually to the drafting of the Charter of the International Trade Organization and the General Agreement on Tariffs and Trade. The Treasury took charge of planning on financial policy—planning that led eventually to the creation of the International Monetary Fund and the International Bank for Reconstruction and Development. The co-ordination of planning in the financial and commercial fields, obviously a vital necessity, was persistently hampered by defective liaison between the two Departments. This condition was only somewhat ameliorated by the development of a system of inter-departmental committees to discuss the general problems of foreign economic policy.[1]

---

[1] A description of the machinery for co-ordinating the planning of foreign economic policy between the various departments can be found in Notter, op. cit.

From the very outset, therefore, the American Treasury assumed the dominant role in the planning of post-war international financial policy. The supreme position of Harry White was rather more difficult to explain. He was widely considered to be a difficult personality —aggressive, irascible, and with a remorseless drive for power. His general unpopularity might have provided an obstacle to the realization of his personal ambitions. But he was an indefatigable worker and his quick and active mind soon made a profound impression on Secretary Morgenthau. His rise in the Treasury was meteoric. He arrived in Washington in the early 1930's from the campus of an obscure college in the American mid-west. Within a few years he became one of the principal Treasury technicians responsible for the operation of the American Stabilization Fund and the Tripartite Stabilization Agreement. He assumed a leading role in the drafting of an abortive plan for an Inter-American Bank. Even before Pearl Harbour his thoughts were turning to questions of post-war financial policy. By the end of 1941 he had produced, probably on his own initiative, an outline of the plan that was subsequently to bear his name. In December of that year Morgenthau put him in full charge of Treasury planning on post-war international financial policy.

Unfortunately, there is now some difficulty in evaluating White's historical role. Recent charges have coloured his reputation with a sinister ambiguity. It has been asserted on the highest authority that while working in the Treasury White was a 'Communist spy' who helped to smuggle secret documents to the Soviet Union.[1] Since complete evidence for this charge has not been made public, we do not know precisely how far White was subject to Communist discipline. So far no evidence has appeared to disprove the traditional assumption that White put forward his financial plans in the sincere belief that they would further the interests of the United States. It should also be remembered that in drafting these plans White had a number of brilliant associates whose loyalty has not been questioned. For these reasons we must discuss the plans on their merits, even though we can hardly forget the cloud that has since enveloped their principal author.

The main objectives of the Treasury's post-war financial planning were stated in the detailed blue-print which White and his assistants

---

[1] Speech by Attorney-General Herbert Brownell, *The New York Times* (7 Nov. 1953).

brought forth early in 1942. This bore the title 'Suggested Plan for a United Nations Stabilization Fund and a Bank for Reconstruction of the United and Associated Nations'.[1] It aimed 'to prevent the disruption of foreign exchanges and the collapse of monetary and credit systems; to assure the restoration of foreign trade; and to supply the huge volume of capital that will be needed virtually throughout the world for reconstruction, for relief, and for economic recovery'. The two institutions whose creation was proposed were designed 'to carry on effective work as soon as the war is over. It would be ill-advised, if not possibly dangerous, to leave ourselves at the end of the war unprepared for the stupendous task of world-wide economic reconstruction.'

The programme set out in this early plan was bold and idealistic. It called for a notable departure from powerful traditions of political isolation and financial orthodoxy which still had a strong hold on American opinion. The Fund and Bank were to be the principal agencies for the post-war conduct of international finance. Their membership was to be open to all of the United and Associated Nations. They were to become genuine institutions of international government, serving the needs of their members without regard to national political considerations. The Stabilization Fund was to have total resources of at least $5 billion, made up of contributions from member countries in gold, local currencies, and government securities. These resources were to be available for short-term lending to members in temporary balance of payments difficulties. In return for this additional source of international liquidity members would be required to part with a considerable measure of economic sovereignty. In specific terms, they would have to surrender the right to vary their exchange rates; abolish all forms of exchange control; and submit to Fund supervision over domestic economic policies.

The Bank plan was even more ambitious. The Bank was to have a capital stock of $10 billion, half paid in immediately by members in the form of gold and local currency. It was 'designed chiefly to supply the huge volume of capital to the United and Associated Nations that will be needed for reconstruction, for relief, and for

---

[1] The *White Papers* contain three very early drafts of a plan for a Fund and Bank. The undated typescript bearing the title quoted in the text appears to be the first of these. This is followed by a typescript dated Mar. 1942 and a mimeographed draft dated Apr. 1942. These second and third drafts are virtually identical; the first draft contains several significant differences from the other two. The following citations to the 'first draft' of the Fund and Bank plans refer to this undated typescript.

economic recovery'. It was designed also to eliminate world-wide
fluctuations of a financial origin and reduce the likelihood, intensity,
and duration of world-wide depressions; to stabilize the prices of
essential raw materials; and more generally to raise the productivity
and living standards of its members. It was specifically empowered to
buy and sell gold and securities of participating governments, to dis-
count and rediscount bills and acceptances, to issue notes, and to
make long-term loans at very low rates of interest.

In the beginning, therefore, Treasury planning for financial collaboration dealt equally with the problem of monetary stabilization
and with the problem of post-war recovery and reconstruction. But
as time went on the latter problem came to be overshadowed by preoccupation with the former. The inter-departmental committee on
financial planning established in the spring of 1942 devoted itself
mainly to developing the Stabilization Fund.[1] Work on the Bank
plan began to languish. Without equivalent progress on the urgent
tasks of reconstruction, discussion of the technical problems of
monetary stabilization occurred in an increasingly unrealistic atmosphere. Indeed, White was warned by representatives in other executive departments that his Stabilization Fund assumed the solution of
all the world's major post-war economic problems.[2] The planners in
the Department of State who were more aware of the need to devise
a prior and separate solution to the general reconstruction problem
were inhibited by the Treasury's jurisdictional supremacy.[3] White and
his assistants remained the chief architects of post-war international
financial policy and continued to devote their main attention to the
long-term problem of monetary stabilization.

White's great emphasis on the problem of monetary stabilization

[1] Two committees were actually in existence, a Cabinet-level committee and a sub-
committee known as the 'American Technical Committee', the latter consisting of
technicians from the Treasury, the Department of State, the Department of Commerce,
the Board of Governors of the Federal Reserve System, the Securities and Exchange
Commission, and the Foreign Economic Administration. The Technical Committee
met under White's chairmanship and was mainly responsible for the development of
the financial plans.

[2] This objection was raised by such members of the Technical Committee as Alvin
Hansen and Benjamin Cohen of the Department of State and E. A. Goldenweiser of
the Federal Reserve System.

[3] John Parke Young and other technicians in the Department of State produced a
plan which made special provision for the prior solution of the major tasks of economic
reconstruction. The Young plan called for the creation of an International Bank with a
special reconstruction and rehabilitation fund to be administered on different principles from those used in the Bank's long-term operations. A copy of this plan can be
found in the *White Papers*.

was not a personal foible; it reflected the general Treasury attitude born in the experience of the inter-war period. Treasury planning was profoundly influenced by the symptoms of economic disorder which had followed the last armistice—the wild currency fluctuations, the speculative capital movements, the bank failures. White and his colleagues identified these developments with the onset of the Great Depression. They also identified an illiberal international monetary policy with the onset of the Second World War. For in the hands of Nazi Germany exchange control and exchange discrimination had become the handmaidens of military aggression. Accordingly, the Treasury planners considered the elimination of such practices one of the primary tasks of post-war reconstruction.

But it would be a mistake to suggest that Treasury planning was confined to these rather negative objectives. Morgenthau, White, and their subordinates were not believers in *laissez-faire*; they shared the belief of most New Deal planners that government had an important responsibility for the successful direction of economic life. To some extent they were under the influence of the new formulations of Keynesian economics.[1] They sought to make finance the servant, not the master, of human desires—in the international no less than in the domestic sphere. In their view the events of the 1920's and early 1930's had discredited private finance. They considered government control of financial policy the key to the objectives of high employment and economic welfare. Morgenthau's dominant objective as Secretary of the Treasury was—in his own words—'to move the financial center of the world from London and Wall Street to the United States Treasury, and to create a new concept between nations in international finance'.[2] He wanted to erect new institutions which would be 'instrumentalities of sovereign governments and not of private financial interests'[3]—in short, 'to drive . . . the usurious money lenders from the temple of international finance'.[4] Thus the primary aim of the Treasury planners was not to restore a régime of private enterprise but to create a climate of world expansion consistent with the social and economic objectives of the New Deal.

---

[1] This is not to say that either Morgenthau or White ever studied Keynes's *General Theory* in detail, but the ideas of the *General Theory* certainly exerted a major influence in their intellectual *milieu*.
[2] Letter to President Truman quoted in *The New York Herald-Tribune* (31 Mar. 1946).   [3] Ibid.
[4] Address of Morgenthau at the final session of the Bretton Woods Conference (22 July 1944), U.S. Department of State, *Proceedings and Documents of the United*

By the spring of 1943, however, the expansionist bias of the Treasury's post-war financial plans had been considerably reduced. Domestic political factors had begun to exercise a restraining influence. The Democratic party lost considerable ground in the Congressional elections of 1942; the balance of power on economic issues was shifting to a conservative coalition of Republicans and Southern Democrats. Within the Administration itself some unrepentant New Dealers were being ousted by more conservative leaders recruited from the ranks of finance and industry. White considered himself a shrewd judge of the political mood; rather than risk rejection he would cut his plans to an acceptable pattern. The more ambitious aspects of the Bank plan were gradually eliminated, in particular the function of contra-cyclical lending in the event of world depression. The project itself was held in abeyance. In April 1943 only the plan for a Stabilization Fund was released for publication— and even it now contained substantial compromises with the demands of national sovereignty.[1] There was a growing danger that the Treasury's financial programme might not form an adequate basis for reaching a compromise with British opinion.

The Keynes plan

To Keynes as well as White the Second World War brought a unique opportunity to apply a long-standing interest in international monetary problems. When, with the coming of the war, he was called from Cambridge into government service, he brought a combination of theoretical training and practical experience which could not be matched by any other living economist.

In the summer of 1940 Keynes moved into an office in the Treasury and began a new career as adviser to the Chancellor of the Exchequer. Since he was not a civil servant and drew no salary, his position was rather anomalous. But his very independence from formal ties enabled him to exert a profound influence. Characteristically, he wanted to make his views known right away on a wide variety of current problems. Soon the regular Treasury officials were receiving his unsolicited memoranda on matters over which they had hitherto exercised a largely exclusive jurisdiction.

Nations Monetary and Financial Conference, Bretton Woods, New Hampshire, July 1–22, 1944, vol. ii (Washington, 1948), p. 1227.
[1] Some examples of these compromises are given *infra*.

It was not long before Keynes turned his attention to devising a mechanism of international finance which might facilitate Britain's participation in a multilateral régime. This was the International Clearing Union, which eventually achieved the status of a Cabinet paper and became the basis for inter-departmental discussion. At first it was 'regarded as impractical, a sketch of something one might achieve in a world not realised. . . . But in the course of discussion, comment and re-drafting, gradually, over a period of many months, by an imperceptible process, it came to be regarded as the main Treasury plan.'[1]

The major purposes of the Clearing Union were essentially the same as those of the Stabilization Fund. As the Chancellor of the Exchequer explained:

We want a system in which blocked balances and bilateral clearances would be unnecessary. We want an orderly and agreed method of determining the value of national currency units, to eliminate unilateral action and the danger which it involves that each nation will seek to restore its competitive position by exchange depreciation. Above all, we want to free the international monetary system from those arbitrary, unpredictable and undesirable influences which have operated in the past as a result of large-scale speculative movements of capital. We want to secure an economic policy agreed between the nations and an international monetary system which will be the instrument of that policy. This means that if any one Government were tempted to move too far either in an inflationary or a deflationary direction, it would be subject to the check of consultations with the other Governments, and it would be part of the agreed policy to take measures for correcting tendencies to dis-equilibrium in the balance of payments of each separate country. Our long-term policy must ensure that countries which conduct their affairs with prudence need not be afraid that they will be prevented from meeting their international liabilities by causes outside their own control.[2]

The last sentence was the key to the British approach. The most important purpose of the Clearing Union was to resolve the dilemma between internal and external financial stability which had posed such difficult problems in the inter-war period. The gold standard had assured stability in the external value of sterling; but it had deprived the British Government of effective control over domestic monetary and fiscal policy. In the inter-war period it had been accompanied by the spread of deflationary forces from one country to

---

[1] Harrod, p. 528.   [2] 386 H.C. Deb. 826 (2 Feb. 1943).

another, falling prices and incomes, and mass unemployment. What was needed was some way to combine a policy of stability in the exchanges with a policy of domestic expansion—in Keynes's own words—to 'obtain the advantages, without the disadvantages, of an international gold currency'.[1] The Clearing Union was designed to provide such a way. If it worked successfully it would substitute 'an expansionist, in place of a contractionist, pressure on world trade'.[2]

The outline of the Keynes plan was essentially simple. The Clearing Union would make large overdraft facilities available to its members, facilities related to their pre-war share of world trade. According to the tentative formula suggested in the plan, overdraft facilities to the United Nations and their dependencies would amount to some $26 billion.[3] Since no limits were set on the value of individual credit balances, the Union provided a complete clearing mechanism.[4] Surpluses and deficits in the balance of payments of member countries would be reflected in credits and debits on the books of the Union, expressed in 'bancor', an international unit of account. With these vast reserves of liquidity at their disposal, members would be able to eliminate all exchange restrictions on current account, maintain stability in their exchange rates, and pursue policies of domestic expansion without fear of the consequences on their foreign balance.

The structure of the Clearing Union reflected the preoccupation of Keynes and other British planners with the importance of domestic expansion. The large overdraft facilities would certainly go far to assure the members that policies of domestic expansion would not be inhibited by deficits in their balance of payments. Thus it might effectively guard against the spread of unemployment. But did it make equally sure that the pursuit of inflationary policies in member countries would not be a persistent cause of disequilibrium? Here, as we shall soon see, the plan may have been less satisfactory. It assumed that deflation rather than inflation would be the main source of danger in the post-war period. There was little recognition of the possibility that other causes besides the failure to maintain full employment could produce balance of payments disequilibria. As the plan put it, 'there is great force in the contention that, if active employment and ample purchasing power can be sustained in

---

[1] U.K. Treasury, *Proposals for an International Clearing Union* (London, 1943), Section V, Para. 20.   [2] Section IV, Para. 10.

[3] For the basis of this calculation, see Joan Robinson, 'The International Currency Proposals', *Ec. Journ.*, liii (1943), p. 161.

[4] This point is discussed in greater detail *infra*.

the main centres of world trade, the problem of surpluses and un-
wanted exports will largely disappear'.[1] This bias in an inflationary
direction might well provide difficulty when the Keynes plan was
presented to the United States.

THE TWO PLANS AS INSTRUMENTS OF MULTILATERALISM

Both the Stabilization Fund and the Clearing Union were principally designed to assist the nations of the world to deal with financial
crises of relatively short-term origin. They aimed to promote a system
of multilateral payments in which external equilibrium could be
maintained at levels of domestic full employment. To this end each
provided its members with additional international liquidity—
liquidity that would provide a protective cushion against temporary
economic disturbances and make unnecessary the resort to illiberal
internal or external policies.

The success of any plans designed to achieve these purposes
depended upon three basic conditions. The first was progress toward
solving the deeper political and economic difficulties that threatened
to beset the post-war world. The second was the provision of liquidity
in such volume and on such terms as to give complete confidence to
members that they could abandon resort to restrictive economic
practices. The third was the creation of a suitable mechanism of
adjustment by which temporary disequilibrating factors could be
dealt with and equilibrium restored in the balance of payments. Our
next task will be to determine whether and to what extent these three
conditions were satisfied by the White and Keynes plans.[2]

The transitional issue

The successful transition to approximate political and economic
equilibrium after the war was the first prerequisite of an effective
Stabilization Fund or Clearing Union.[3] The political point was obvious enough. The institutions were to operate, as it were, in a
political vacuum—dispensing resources according to technical economic criteria and without regard to the political character of their members. This was implicit in the very earliest drafts of the Stabilization

[1] Section IV, Para. 18.
[2] Unless otherwise indicated, the following analysis of the Keynes and White plans
is based on the published drafts of April 1943.
[3] It may be thought inapt to describe this as only a 'transitional' problem, since the
achievement of political and economic equilibrium had long-term aspects. But at this
point it is the particular problem of the *restoration* of equilibrium in the transition
period that we wish to emphasize.

Fund. Similarly, the Clearing Union was expressly designed to have a 'purely technical and non-political character'.[1] One of its greatest merits was supposed to be

> its 'anonymous' or 'impersonal' quality. No particular member States have to engage their own resources as such to the support of other particular States or of any of the international projects or policies adopted. They have only to agree in general that, if they find themselves with surplus resources which for the time being they do not themselves wish to employ, these resources may go into the general pool and be put to work on approved purposes. . . . We have here a genuine organ of truly international government.[2]

This was an admirably idealistic aspect of the White and Keynes plans. But perhaps there was a danger in pushing ahead with plans fixed to this assumption before the post-war political climate could be foreseen with greater certainty. The White and Keynes plans were conceived in the very earliest days of the war and were published in the spring of 1943. This was before any comparable advances had been made in framing the post-war political order. Was it really wise to accord primacy to planning on the economic side—particularly to the rather technical problem of monetary stabilization?

There were certain arguments, it is true, for seeking early agreement on monetary matters. By giving evidence that constructive solutions would be found to the world's post-war economic problems, the plans might provide a helpful stimulus to the allied cause.[3] Agreement on the plans might only prove possible in the midst of the close working war-time alliance.[4] Moreover, all projects for post-war organization were interdependent—a beginning had to be made somewhere.[5]

---

[1] Section I (*f*). [2] Section IX, Para. 40.

[3] In forwarding to Roosevelt an early draft of the Stabilization Fund and Bank Morgenthau declared: 'I am convinced that the launching of such a plan at this time has tremendous strategic as well as economic bearing. It seems to me that the time is ripe to dramatize our international economic objectives in terms of action which people everywhere will recognize as practical, powerful and inspiring.' Memorandum (16 May 1942), *White Papers*. The next year Morgenthau told a joint meeting of House and Senate committees concerned with foreign affairs and economic policy that 'a plan for international monetary co-operation can be a factor in winning the war'. (5 Apr. 1943), *Documents on American Foreign Relations*, vol. v, p. 649. Reading these statements in retrospect one has the feeling that the point was rather over-emphasized.

[4] In the words of the Keynes plan: 'It may be doubted whether a comprehensive scheme will ever in fact be worked out, unless it can come into existence through a single act of creation made possible by the unity and purpose and energy of hope for better things to come, springing from the victory of the United Nations, when they have attained it, over immediate evil.' Section I, Para. 3.

[5] The Preface to the Keynes plan explained that it was convenient to give finance priority 'because some general conclusions have to be reached under this head before much progress can be made with other topics'. It also made the point that the transition out of reconstruction into the long-term period 'cannot be wisely effected unless we know into what we are moving'.

G

Although something could be said for all of these arguments, still more could be said for the other side. No agreement on monetary matters could make any significant contribution to world peace without equivalent solutions in the deeper areas of possible conflict. Without an entirely new world political order which eliminated the need for special alliances and traditional power politics, the basic assumption underlying the Keynes and White plans would be destroyed. Nations would not be willing to allow the free use of their financial contributions by monetary institutions with world-wide membership. The 'impersonal' and 'anonymous' character of the institutions would become not an asset but a liability. If the monetary plans were launched with detailed provisions on such matters they would quickly break down. Their failure would only add to the difficulties of promoting really effective international organization.

The dependence of the monetary plans on the assumption of equilibrium was just as apparent on the economic as on the political side. The Stabilization Fund and the Clearing Union were both designed to deal with disturbances to economic equilibrium of a short-term nature—typically, the periodic industrial fluctuations and exchange crises which beset the world in the inter-war period. They provided only a mechanism of exchange clearing, not a mechanism for dealing with the problems of long-term investment or with those of relief and reconstruction. If the long-term economic problems were not solved outside the monetary organizations, the limits of their resources would soon be reached; they would fall into a lop-sided position; the clearing mechanism would quickly break down.

Indeed, both plans acknowledged, either implicitly or explicitly, their dependence on the assumption of economic equilibrium. One of the purposes of the Stabilization Fund was to 'shorten the periods and lessen the degree of disequilibrium in the international balance of payments of member countries'.[1] Given its definitely limited resources the Fund could not hope to do this unless the deeper disequilibrating forces were dealt with by outside agencies. Moreover, the Fund was to sell foreign exchange only where members needed assistance to 'meet an adverse balance of payments on current account'.[2] The needs of the members for reconstruction and for long-term capital assistance were to be met by the companion institution,

---

[1] Section I, Para. 2. U.S. Treasury, *Preliminary Draft Outline of a Proposal for an International Stabilization Fund of the United and Associated Nations* (Washington, 1943). [2] Section III, Para. 3 (a).

the Bank of the United and Associated Nations. Similar limitations were expressed in the plan for the International Clearing Union. It was emphasized that the Union was not 'to assume the burden of long-term lending which is the proper task of some other institution'.[1] The Keynes plan also declared: 'Obviously, it [the Clearing Union] does not by itself provide any long-term solution against a continuing disequilibrium . . . the purpose of the overdraft facilities is mainly to give time for adjustments. . . .'[2]

The most urgent threat to the assumption of economic equilibrium lay in the large-scale disequilibrium which was likely to exist at the end of the Second World War. The war was causing widespread physical destruction; perhaps even more important, it was disrupting the pre-war pattern of international trade. An ambitious programme of reconstruction would be needed to repair productive facilities and build a new trade pattern in which equilibrium could be restored. Unfortunately, the magnitude of this effort might be underestimated in the preoccupation with monetary stabilization. There was a danger of forgetting the limitations of the long-term plans as instruments of transitional finance.

The danger was already becoming apparent in the United States. There was a regrettable tendency to bracket the Fund and Bank together and to assert that both would 'provide a large part of the capital needed for reconstruction'.[3] Great emphasis was placed upon putting the institutions into operation 'as soon as the war is over'.[4] It was pointed out that 'international currency stability is essential to reconstruction in the post-war period'.[5] This proposition was true enough on its face; but just how was the Fund to operate in the transition period? Was it to make its facilities available as in normal times? If so, how could it ensure that they were not employed for other than short-term stabilization purposes? The repeated insistence on the importance of the Fund's role in the transition might encourage the view that it was not simply designed for monetary stabilization but was designed to assist in the broader tasks of reconstruction as well.

[1] Preface to *Proposals for an International Clearing Union.*
[2] Section IV, Para. 16.
[3] White, 'Postwar Currency Stabilization', *Am. Ec. Rev.*, xxxiii (Supp., 1943), p. 387.
[4] 'Suggested Plan for a United Nations Stabilization Fund and a Bank for Reconstruction of the United and Associated Nations' (undated typescript), *White Papers.*
[5] Morgenthau before the joint meeting of the Congressional committees (5 Apr. 1943), *D.A.F.R.*, vol. v, p. 649.

There was one respect, indeed, in which the Fund made an express attempt to deal with the reconstruction problem. This was with regard to the large sterling balances that were being accumulated in London to the account of members of the sterling area and certain other countries.[1] The growth of these balances reflected Britain's large deficit in current war-time trade and its considerable military expenditures for the defence of its far-flung Empire. A large part of the balances could be considered analogous to the paper credits accumulating to the account of the United States under the system of Lend-Lease. Like Lend-Lease, they were extraordinary transactions growing out of the war effort; they had eventually to be dealt with in a similar way. Obviously, a satisfactory method of dealing with the inter-allied war debts was one of the major tasks of the transition period.

The Treasury planners were concerned with the problem of the sterling balances from the very beginning. They sought to solve it through the mechanism of the Stabilization Fund.[2] The Fund was to buy up these balances from the creditor nations, reselling part of them over a period of years both to the creditors and to the nations whose obligations they were. Thus the Fund, the creditors, and the debtors would each bear a part of the burden. This was an admirable attempt to reach a general solution of the war debt problem. But was it wise to attempt to achieve this purpose by means of the Stabilization Fund? The Fund was an instrument for the conduct of normal finance. Its resources were limited. If it were burdened with the large sterling debts at the beginning of its operations, it might not be able to carry out those operations successfully. And if the problem of the sterling balances were finally removed from the jurisdiction of the Fund, would it be handled by some other institution? Was this mixing up of the stabilization with the reconstruction problem conducive to encouraging a separate attack on the reconstruction problem itself?

The answer to this question was already being suggested by the evolution of the plans for an International Bank. In its original form, the Bank was almost entirely directed at the problem of reconstruction. It was 'designed chiefly to supply the huge volume of capital to the United and Associated Nations that will be needed for recon-

---

[1] The problem of the sterling balances is discussed in greater detail in Chapter IX *infra*.

[2] Section III, Para. 9.

struction, for relief, and for economic recovery'.[1] The destruction caused by the war was expected to be 'stupendous'.[2] In the post-war reconstruction period there would be an 'unprecedented' demand for capital.[3] 'To supply this capital at rates of interest low enough with a period of repayment long enough to give the borrowing country reasonable hope of being able to repay the loan, is the prime task and justification of a Bank of the character described in this report.'[4]

In this original version the Bank was given prodigious resources to carry out its task. Its capital stock of $10 billion may seem inadequate in retrospect, but it was an impressive sum in terms of the existing price level.[5] Moreover, a large part of this capital was to be immediately paid in and available for use. Most important, the Bank could, with its broad powers to issue notes and securities, make available resources many times as large as its subscribed capital.

Unfortunately, the Bank's authority as an instrument of post-war reconstruction was subsequently reduced. The objective of economic development was given an equal claim on its resources.[6] Its lending powers were scaled down. And the entire project was withheld from publication. Thus no basis was left for the assumption that the Stabilization Fund would operate in the requisite environment of economic equilibrium.

An equivalent difficulty existed with the Keynes plan. Its role in the transition period was also ambiguous. On the one hand, it appeared to be intended only for purposes of short-term stabilization. On the other hand, it aimed at 'starting off every country after the war with a stock of reserves appropriate to its position in world commerce, so that without undue anxiety it can set its house in order during the transitional period to full peace-time conditions'.[7] Moreover, its facilities were to be 'of particular importance in the transitional period after the war, as soon as the initial shortages of supply have been overcome. Many countries will find a difficulty in paying for their imports, and will need time and resources before they can

---

[1] First draft of the Bank plan.
[2] Ibid.   [3] Ibid.   [4] Ibid.
[5] One might double the $10 billion figure to get an idea of the real value which the resources of the Bank seemed to have at the time.
[6] In the title of the original Bank draft the word 'development' did not even appear. It was added in the later drafts of Mar. and Apr. 1942. By the end of 1943 the development functions had become as important as those of reconstruction.
[7] Section I (*e*).

establish a readjustment.'[1] The Clearing Union might or might not be supplemented by an International Development Board; it might or might not open overdraft facilities in favour of other bodies concerned with post-war relief, rehabilitation, and reconstruction.[2] And the means of restraining its expansionist influence in the event of an immediate post-war inflation was by no means clear:

> A reconciliation of these divergent purposes is not easily found until we know more than is known at present about the means to be adopted to finance post-war relief and reconstruction. If the intention is to provide resources on liberal and comprehensive lines outside the resources made available by the Clearing Union and additional to them, it might be better for such specific aid to take the place of the proposed overdrafts during the 'relief' period of (say) two years. . . . Nevertheless, the immediate establishment of the Clearing Union would not be incompatible with provisional arrangements. . . . Overdraft quotas might be allowed on a reduced scale during the transition period. . . . If, on the other hand, relief from outside sources looks like being inadequate from the outset, the overdraft quotas may be even more necessary at the outset than later on.[3]

It appeared, therefore, that the Keynes plan was designed to provide substantial reconstruction aid if such aid were not otherwise made available. The very size of its overdraft facilities encouraged this idea. Its reference to a '"relief" period of (say) two years' reflected an inadequate appreciation of the profound character of the reconstruction problem.[4] Like its American counterpart, the Clearing Union was not designed to encourage that separate attack on the transitional problem which was essential to its successful operation.

The liquidity issue

The second essential condition for the success of the monetary plans was that they should adequately fulfil their functions as providers of international liquidity. For unless the Stabilization Fund and Clearing Union made resources available of sufficient size and on sufficiently liberal conditions, their members could not be expected to give up exchange controls and freedom to vary their exchange

---

[1] Section IV, Para. 15.   [2] Section IX.
[3] Section X, Para. 42.

[4] Keynes wrote to Jacob Viner: 'Everyone seems to be assuming, without sufficient reason, that the United States is going to run after the war an enormous credit balance after having allowed for long-term capital movements. I regard this as quite uncertain.' *Letter to Viner, June 9, 1943.* Of course, it may be argued that Keynes was referring here to the period *after* reconstruction. Even so, he appears to have underestimated the magnitude of the reconstruction problem itself.

rates. One of the major differences between the Keynes and White plans lay in the degree of emphasis they placed on the importance of this function.

The first and most obvious contrast was in the amount of resources which the two plans made available. While the total resources of the Stabilization Fund were limited to $5 billion, the overdraft facilities of the Clearing Union amounted to $26 billion. Even these figures did not indicate the full measure of the difference. The resources of the Stabilization Fund consisted of contributions from member countries. Its quotas represented the maximum liability of members as well as their maximum drawing rights. Thus, for example, the maximum amount of credits the United States could be asked to supply was limited to its contribution of about $2 billion. The Clearing Union, on the other hand, was based on the overdraft principle. The quotas allotted to member countries imposed a limit only on their total drawing rights, not on the total liability they might be called upon to bear. The amount of unrequited American exports that could be financed in this way was limited only by the total drawing rights of other countries—about $23 billion. Thus while the Fund was an imperfect clearing mechanism, in which the total demand for dollars might exceed the capacity of the Fund to supply them, the Clearing Union constituted a closed system in which the concentration of demand upon the currency of any one member could provide no threat to the institution as long as the debtors were within their maximum drawings. There was still another point. The total resources of the Fund were definitely limited by the original contributions; they could only be increased by making a direct approach to the member governments. The overdraft facilities of the Clearing Union could be varied by the management of the Union in the light of changing conditions of world demand. This provided an additional assurance that an adequate amount of liquidity would be made available to the member nations.

Hardly less important than the total amount of liquidity offered by the two institutions were the conditions of its availability. The White plan was not entirely clear on this point. It placed no direct restraints on the use of its resources. But the Stabilization Fund was empowered to sell currency to its members only under certain conditions. One of these was that the members required assistance to meet an adverse balance of payments on current account.[1] Another was that when

[1] Section III, Para. 3 (a).

'a member country is exhausting its quota more rapidly than is war-ranted in the judgment of the Board of Directors, the Board may place such conditions upon additional sales of foreign exchange to that country as it deems to be in the general interest of the Fund'.[1] The phrasing of the Fund's provisions suggested that it would be 'active' rather than 'passive' in its operation—it would exercise dis-cretion in dealing with requests for financial aid rather than make such aid automatically available.[2] This conditional nature of Fund assistance was probably implicit in its basic structure. Because it was an imperfect clearing mechanism, its holdings of any one currency were liable to be exhausted by an over-liberal exercise of its members' drawing rights. The Clearing Union, on the other hand, had no such reason for restricting access to its overdraft facilities. Indeed, the automatic availability of the overdraft facilities was considered an essential feature by the British planners. As Keynes wrote an Ameri-can friend, no international monetary organization could work if it were 'too grand-motherly'.[3] Or, as Dennis Robertson put it, when a country wished assistance 'there must be no question of its cheque being returned to it as non-acceptable'.[4]

If that feature of the Plan were to be removed, then I do not say—I certainly do not say—the whole house would crumble to the ground; but I do say it would have to be explored again very carefully with a lamp, in order to determine which of its chambers would remain safe for our con-fident habitation.[5]

Unless Anglo-American agreement could be reached on this point there could be little hope for the effective operation of any stabiliza-tion plan.

The adjustment issue

The third major requirement for the success of the monetary plans was an adequate mechanism of adjustment. As we have seen, the international liquidity supplied by the plans was not for the purpose of long-term financing; it was designed only to provide temporary relief while measures were taken to restore equilibrium. These measures could take three main forms—exchange restrictions,

---

[1] Section III, Para. 3 (d).
[2] The other aspect of 'passivity'—whether the Fund could engage in exchange operations on its own initiative—need not concern us here.
[3] *Letter to Viner, October 17, 1943.*
[4] Address to the Boards of Directors of the Federal Reserve Banks, Chicago, Ill. (28 Aug. 1943), reprinted as 'The Post-War Monetary Plans', *Ec. Jour.*, liii (1943), p. 360.   [5] Ibid.

changes in exchange rates, and internal changes in prices and incomes.[1]

It was scarcely to be expected that resort to exchange controls would be the normal method of adjustment embodied in the Keynes and White plans. One of the major objectives of both plans was to produce a system of multilateral clearing in which widespread resort to exchange controls would be unnecessary. Indeed, both plans prohibited the use of exchange controls on current transactions. It should be noted, however, that the published version of the White Plan was rather less strict on the subject of exchange controls than were its earlier versions. In the original version, members were obliged to abandon all exchange restrictions within six months after joining the Fund or after the cessation of hostilities, whichever was later.[2] In the published version, members were required to abandon restrictions only on current transactions and only when they decided that conditions permitted them to do so.[3] The published version did provide, however, that members could not impose any new restrictions without the approval of the Fund and that the Fund might recommend that members remove their existing controls.[4] Thus neither the White nor the Keynes plan envisaged that exchange controls would provide the normal method of adjustment.

Since another objective of both plans was to promote exchange stability, it was equally unlikely that the normal method of adjustment would be found in frequent changes in exchange rates. Both plans required a considerable surrender of national freedom in this field. The Stabilization Fund was empowered to fix the exchange rates of its members, and changes in these rates could only occur when necessary to correct a 'fundamental disequilibrium'.[5] Since changes even for this purpose had to receive the approval of four-fifths of the member votes, the possibility of frequent adjustments was closely circumscribed.[6]

The Clearing Union placed scarcely less emphasis on exchange rate stability. Members were required to agree among themselves on the initial values of their currencies in terms of bancor; they could alter

---

[1] Changes in commercial policy constitute another method of short-term adjustment. But from the point of view of exposition it is preferable to exclude detailed consideration of this method from our analysis of the monetary plans.

[2] First draft of the Fund plan.

[3] Section VI, Para. 2.   [4] Ibid.   [5] Section III, Para. 2.

[6] It should be noted that under the proposed voting formula the United States was allotted over one-quarter of the votes, and thus could 'veto' any proposed change in exchange rates.

these values without permission only when faced with a persistent deficit—and then only to the extent of 5 per cent.[1] During the early years, the Union was enjoined to give special consideration to requests for exchange rate changes on grounds of unforeseen circumstances.[2] But it is clear that such changes were to be an infrequent occurrence. Keynes himself declared that exchange fluctuation as a means of adjustment was 'nothing like as fashionable as it used to be'.[3] Therefore, he believed, any international monetary organization should aim at 'as great stability as possible . . . exchange depreciation is not at all a good way of balancing trade unless the lack of balance is due to a particular cause. This particular cause is the movement of efficiency wages in one country out of step with what it is in others.'[4] If this criterion were followed, exchange rate changes would not occur except at relatively infrequent intervals.

Thus both exchange controls and exchange rate variations were ruled out as the typical method of restoring balance of payments equilibrium. The only method remaining was that of the domestic adjustment of prices and incomes. The great advantage of the gold standard had been that it assured the making of these adjustments without any formal restriction of national sovereignty. An intergovernmental organization did not enjoy this advantage: if it was to ensure the making of internal adjustments, it would have to place direct limitations on sovereign power. Its constitution would have to ensure deflation in the case of the debtor nations and inflation in the case of the creditors.[5] The central problem in the White and Keynes plans lay in their provisions on this score.

In view of the strong creditor position of the United States, the White Plan might have been expected to make provision for one-sided adjustment by the debtor nations. But the Treasury planners were too thoroughly imbued with the expansionist philosophy to give their plan a deliberate deflationary bias. The Stabilization Fund seemed to envisage roughly comparable adjustments on the part of both creditors and debtors. In its original form it made a remarkably bold attempt to ensure that these adjustments were actually made. Members were obliged 'not to adopt any monetary banking measure promoting either serious inflation or serious deflation without the

---

[1] This was not merely the maximum allowed on any one occasion; it was the maximum for all time. Section II, Paras. 6 (3) and 8 (a).

[2] Section II, Para. 6 (3).   [3] *Letter to Viner, June 9, 1943.*   [4] Ibid.

[5] Or, if it is preferred, *dis*inflation in the case of the debtors and *re*flation in the case of the creditors.

consent of a majority of member votes of the Fund'.[1] In a subsequent draft this was altered to read: 'Not to adopt any monetary or general price measure or policy, the effect of which, in the opinion of a majority of the member votes, would be to bring about sooner or later a serious disequilibrium in the balance of payments, if four-fifths of the member votes of the Fund submit to the country in question their disapproval of the adoption of the measure.'[2] White conceded that acceptance of this provision might prove politically difficult, but he insisted that it was 'important to the successful functioning of the Stabilization Fund'.[3]

By the time the Stabilization Fund was ready for publication, this important provision had been considerably weakened. The published version provided only that members should 'give consideration to the views of the Fund on any existing or proposed monetary or economic policy, the effect of which would be to bring about sooner or later a serious disequilibrium in the balance of payments of other countries'.[4] The Fund no longer had any authority to demand internal adjustments. But even now the emphasis on internal adjustments was not inconsiderable. There was still this specific reference to domestic policies, albeit in somewhat weakened form. Moreover, the total amount of drawing rights was relatively limited—a member could not put off internal adjustments for any great length of time. Finally, if a debtor country wished to draw more than half of its quota in two years, or more than the full amount of its quota thereafter, it could receive additional resources only if it received approval of four-fifths of the member votes, and only if it agreed 'to adopt and carry out measures recommended by the Fund designed to correct the disequilibrium in the country's balance of payments'.[5]

The sanctions on creditor countries were hardly less significant. If the Fund's holdings of a country's currency dropped below 15 per cent. of that country's quota, the Fund was required to render a report to the country outlining the causes of the disequilibrium and the measures which were required to bring it to an end.[6] If it became

---

[1] First draft of the Fund plan.
[2] Subsequent draft dated March 1942.
[3] First draft of the Fund plan.
[4] Section VI, Para. 5.
[5] Section III, Para. 3 (b) (i). There was an alternative provision that permitted the debtor country to overdraw its quota if the Fund believed that its balance of payments difficulties would be shortly corrected.
[6] Section III, Para. 6. This was the original 'scarce-currency' clause. It does not appear in the early drafts of the spring of 1942. According to E. M. Bernstein it was

evident that the demand for the currency of the creditor country
would soon exhaust the Fund's holdings of its currency, the Fund
was required to ration the scarce currency among the members
demanding it and to propose means of equating the anticipated demand and supply for the currency. The possibility that creditor
countries might not only be the object of special Fund recommendations but might have their currencies rationed as well indicated that
the responsibility for curing disequilibria would not rest on the
debtor countries alone.

The provisions for internal adjustment were not quite so clear nor
so symmetrical in the Keynes plan. The Clearing Union began with a
definite injunction against interference with domestic policies—an injunction that was obviously designed to safeguard the unfettered right
of Britain and other nations to pursue policies of domestic expansion:

There should be the least possible interference with internal national
policies and the plan should not wander from the international terrain.
Since such policies may have important repercussions on international
relations they cannot be left out of account. Nevertheless, in the realm of
internal policy, the authority of the governing board of the proposed
institution should be limited to recomendations, or at most, to imposing
conditions for more extended enjoyment of the facilities which the institution offers.[1]

The Keynes plan also stated that one of its major purposes was to
'discourage creditor countries from having unused large liquid
balances which ought to be devoted to some positive purpose. . . . In
recognizing that the creditor as well as the debtor may be responsible
for a want of balance, the proposed institution would be breaking
new ground'.[2]

These general observations at the outset of the Keynes plan were
reflected in its specific provisions. On the side of internal adjustments
by debtor nations, the plan dealt with a very light touch. Debtor
countries could draw upon their very liberal overdraft facilities without restraint (except for a very small interest charge) until half of
these facilities had been exhausted. At this point the Union could
require a country to deposit collateral, depreciate its currency, control outward capital movements, or surrender gold or other liquid
reserves in reduction of its debit balance.[3] It could also 'recommend

inserted by White in the summer of that year to correct what White considered a
'logical flaw' in the Fund mechanism—that the rights of members to purchase a
particular currency might exceed the Fund's ability to supply that currency.

[1] Preface to the *Proposals for an International Clearing Union*.
[2] Ibid.　　　　　　　　　　　　　　　[3] Section II, Para. 6 (8) (b).

to the Government of the member State any internal measures affecting its domestic economy which may appear to be appropriate to
restore the equilibrium of its international balance'.[1] After exhausting
three-quarters of its balance a debtor nation could be declared in
default. In practice these provisions would enable debtor nations to
run balance of payments deficits equivalent to several billions of
dollars annually before being called sharply to account.

What adjustments were required on the side of the creditors?
There would be no formal sanctions against a creditor (except for
the same interest charge required of debtors) until its credit balance
exceeded half its quota. Then it would be required to discuss with the
Union measures to restore equilibrium in its balance of payments,
including measures to expand domestic credit and domestic demand,
appreciation of its currency, reduction in its tariff and in other dis-
couragements to imports, and the making of international development loans.[2] On its face, therefore, the Keynes plan seemed to contain equally balanced obligations. But this equivalence was illusory:
the creditor nations would be subjected to pressure by the very fact
of their mounting credit balances—balances which signified the shipment of unrequited exports. A creditor would be forced to make
adjustments in order to reduce the proportion of its national production that was being given away to other nations.[3] There was no limit
to the liability that might be assumed by the creditor in this way,
except the total overdraft facilities of all the other nations. The United
States, for example, might have to part with $23 billion or more in
unrequited exports.[4]

Until debtor nations exhausted one-half or perhaps three-quarters
of their overdraft facilities, therefore, virtually the whole responsibility for adjustment would be placed upon the creditor countries.
This was not considered an inequitable or undesirable result. The
creditor nations, the plan stated, would still have the same means of
reducing their unrequited exports that existed in the absence of the
Clearing Union. They could import gold, make short and long-term

---

[1] Ibid.   [2] Section II, Para. 6 (9).
[3] The expression 'given away' may be thought too extreme, since in theory the
creditor country might draw upon its accumulated credit balance in the future. But
see the argument set out *infra*. In earlier drafts of the Keynes plan the sanctions
on creditor countries were even greater, since provision was made for the periodic
cancellation of credit and debit balances.
[4] The total quotas of the members of the United Nations minus the United States
quota. The total American liability would be even greater if the Clearing Union
exercised its powers to increase the original overdraft facilities.

loans, or increase their purchases of goods and services from abroad. The difference was that in the absence of the Clearing Union the exports of the creditor country would be automatically curtailed once these measures of receiving payment for them had been exhausted.

Thus, the effect of the Clearing Union is to give the creditor country a choice between the voluntary curtailment of its exports to the same extent that they would have been involuntarily curtailed in the absence of the Clearing Union, or, alternatively, of allowing its exports to continue and accumulating the excess receipts in the form of bancor balances for the time being. Unless the removal of a factor causing the involuntary reduction of exports is reckoned a disadvantage, a creditor country incurs no burden but is, on the contrary, relieved, by being offered the additional option of receiving payment for its exports through the accumulation of a bancor balance. . . . *If, therefore, a member State asks what governs the maximum liability which it incurs by entering the system, the answer is that this lies entirely within its own control. . . .*[1]

This was an ingenious formulation of the adjustment problem. But it had one fatal flaw which made the Keynes plan an inadequate basis for Anglo-American negotiations. It assumed that the only threat to equilibrium lay in the danger of unemployment and deflation in the creditor countries. What if the disequilibrium were caused by inflation in the debtor countries—by the attempt of these countries to live consistently beyond their means? Then a creditor like the United States might run a persistent surplus that was *not* within its own power to control—or, more precisely, a surplus that it could control only by engaging in even more violent inflation than the debtor countries themselves. The encouragement of such policies would not serve the long-term interests of either creditors or debtors, much less promote the maintenance of a multilateral régime.

This, in outline, was the way the Keynes and White plans satisfied the three basic conditions for successful monetary stabilization. The implications for Anglo-American financial collaboration were now clear. The gulf between the British and Americans on the question of creditor-debtor adjustment was very great. If it were not bridged to their mutual satisfaction, greater reliance would have to be placed on the very devices which the plans were supposed to eliminate—namely, frequent exchange rate depreciation and exchange control. The two plans were also far apart on the total amount of liquidity to be made

---

[1] Italics supplied. Section III, Paras. 8–9.

available and the conditions of its availability. Most important, perhaps, they revealed little appreciation of the magnitude of the transition problem and of the need for attacking it with separate measures.

In view of these facts, would it be wise to proceed at once to negotiation of a detailed instrument of financial collaboration? Would it not be better to concentrate first on informal arrangements designed to cope with reconstruction itself? The case for this latter course was greatly reinforced by the reaction which now greeted the publication of the plans on the two sides of the Atlantic.

THE TWO PLANS IN ANGLO-AMERICAN OPINION

If there was any doubt that there were major differences between the British and American publics on the subject of external financial policy it was removed after publication of the Keynes and White plans in April 1943. In each country the foreign plan was widely criticized, and considerable opposition even developed to both plans. The device of releasing the plans before seeking an Anglo-American compromise helped to inflame the natural differences. In both countries there was a regrettable tendency, despite official disclaimers, to regard the plans as rival national programmes. Thus comment tended to concentrate on the points of difference between the plans, and their important points of similarity were very often ignored.

In the United Kingdom considerable scepticism was expressed about the White plan. The provisions for gold subscriptions and for the fixing of exchange rates in terms of gold encouraged widespread fears that it involved 'a full return to the gold standard'.[1] The irreconcilable opponents of multilateralism were able to evoke all the baleful associations of the inter-war years. Robert Boothby, a Conservative M.P. who employed arguments of Left and Right with equal dexterity, warned his colleagues that the White plan

. . . will be the end. The end of all our hopes of an expansionist policy, and of social advance. It will be the end of the Beveridge Plan, of improved education, of housing reconstruction, the end of the new Britain we are fighting to rebuild. It will lead again to world depression, to chaos, and, ultimately, to war.[2]

The same note was echoed by the Beaverbrook press:

[I]t should be clearly stated that this country is not going back to gold.

[1] F. W. Pethick-Lawrence, 389 H.C. Deb. 666 (12 May 1943).
[2] Id., col. 702.

Thirteen years ago Britain shook the gold dust off her feet, and the change began in our fortunes. Clinging on to gold meant restriction and unemployment among our people. Any move to put us back on gold will result in disaster to those who attempt it.[1]

One financial journalist reported widespread opposition to putting the American Treasury in a position 'to veto any decision to change the value of sterling' and described Parliamentary opinion as profoundly pessimistic about the prospects for any sort of Anglo-American compromise:

'Some quarters are likely to go so far as to oppose both currency plans on the ground that it would be preferable to have two international systems, a dollar bloc and a sterling bloc. It is argued that conditions, interests, and mentality within the two groups differ fundamentally, and that for this reason any attempt to lump them together is foredoomed to failure.[2]

These, of course, were unusually hostile comments. On the whole, British discussion of the White plan was more moderate. Keynes promoted the cause of understanding considerably when he stressed the essential similarity between the two plans during the debate on financial collaboration in the House of Lords.[3] Nevertheless, even journals such as *The Times* and *The Economist* found considerable fault with the White plan, not simply on the ground that it allowed too little national freedom over exchange rates but on the grounds that its resources were too limited, that its sanctions against creditor nations were inadequate, and that other of its provisions threatened to interfere unduly with the internal policies of debtor nations.[4] *The Manchester Guardian* stated flatly that 'no British Government could accept anything remotely like these proposals and remain in power beyond the first post-war election'.[5] The prevailing concern with domestic expansion was so strong that some commentators doubted if even the Clearing Union would provide adequate safeguards for a policy of full employment. *The Times* went so far as to declare that the Keynes plan placed 'the onus on the wrong shoulder' because while 'obdurate debtors are called to account, the only penalty im-

---

[1] The *Daily Express* (3 Feb. 1944).
[2] Paul Einzig, 'Parliamentary Opinion Stiffening Against White Plan', *The Financial News* (12 May 1943).
[3] 127 H.L. Deb. 521–63.
[4] See, for example, *The Times* (8 Apr. 1943), *The Economist*, cxlv (1943), p. 261.
[5] (24 Aug. 1943).

posed on obdurate creditors is an interest charge on credit balances exceeding the agreed quota'!¹

On the other side of the Atlantic the prospects for a compromise were not much more hopeful. If the White plan spelled financial orthodoxy and deflation to the British critics, the Keynes plan spelled reckless experimentation and inflation to the American. Part of the difficulty was due to the widespread suspicion with which Keynesian ideas were still regarded in the United States. *The New York Times* reminded its readers that Keynes had been 'an antagonist of stability of foreign exchange rates and . . . a champion of currency devaluation and credit expansion'.² The novel features of the plan itself confirmed the suspicions that were felt about its author. In the opinion of *The Wall Street Journal* the Clearing Union was 'a machine for the regimentation of the world'.³ A small Iowa newspaper summed up the recurrent American fear that the clever British were preparing to do in Uncle Sam. 'If we are big enough suckers to swallow the Keynes plan', it exclaimed, 'we shall be swindled out of everything we have left from the war—and we shall deserve to be swindled.'⁴ One conservative economic expert described the suggestion for taxing credit balances as 'utterly grotesque'.⁵ Similar difficulty was caused by the proposal to replace gold with bancor as the principal means of international settlement:

> The British plan . . . contains something different. . . . The credit balance —the difference between what the United States, for example, sold and what it bought—does not go into the American Treasury or domestic pockets. . . . If you have a persistent balance of trade you don't get your money.⁶

Indeed, it appeared as if any international monetary plan would face considerable difficulty. To begin with, there were the isolationists, who could be counted upon to oppose any diminution of American freedom in the economic or political field. Some of them opposed both plans simply because they opposed joining any sort of international organization at all. Others objected specifically to depriving the United States of its unfettered right to dispense foreign

---

¹ (8 Aug. 1943). For a comprehensive statement of the view that both the Keynes and White plans provided insufficient safeguards for domestic expansion, see E. F. Schumacher *et al.*, 'New Plans for International Trade', *O.I.S.B.*, v (Supp., 1943).
² (30 Mar. 1943).   ³ (13 Apr. 1943).
⁴ The Council Bluffs, Iowa *Nonpareil*, quoted in the *Evening Standard* (16 Apr. 1943).
⁵ Benjamin Anderson, *The Postwar Stabilization of Foreign Exchange* (May, 1943), p. 26.   ⁶ The *Chicago Daily News* (28 June 1943).

assistance at its own will and pleasure.[1] Still others feared that the organization might interfere with America's power to control its domestic economic affairs. As one newspaper reminded its readers: 'An old-fashioned document called the Constitution gives to Congress alone the power to regulate the value of money.'[2]

Isolationist forces alone, however, were not enough to doom the prospects for collaboration. A considerable majority of the American people were now convinced of the necessity for full participation in international organizations to promote peace and prosperity after the war. Rather more serious was the opposition to both plans from political conservatives and exponents of financial orthodoxy. The White as well as the Keynes plan appeared to contain too many novel and untried devices. Public opinion seemed to be retreating from the ideas of government intervention, cheap money, and deficit spending which had played an important part in animating the original Fund and Bank plans. By the summer of 1943 a large majority of the American press had expressed misgivings about the White plan. The opposition was led by leaders of the New York financial community who had been the persistent antagonists of the American Treasury. The Guaranty Trust Company called both plans 'dangerous' on the grounds that they would 'enable nations to buy merchandise without being able to pay for it' and would 'substitute fallible human judgment and discretion for the impersonal action of the markets in regulating balances of international payments and foreign exchange rates'.[3] Particular criticism was levelled at the suggestion that nations might have free access to a central stock of resources without regard to their credit worthiness. In the words of the American Bankers Association,

... a system of quotas or shares in a pool which gives debtor countries the impression that they have a right to credits up to some amount is unsound in principle, and raises hopes that cannot be realized. Such a system would encourage the impression that credits received may not have to be liquidated, and would invite abuses of the facilities.[4]

What system was conservative financial opinion prepared to accept? There was considerable support in some circles for the old gold stan-

---

[1] This was not a misgiving of extremists only. After all, it was entirely unprecedented for the United States in time of peace to put large financial resources at the disposal of an international economic organization.

[2] The *Chicago Daily News* (8 Apr. 1943).

[3] 'Plans for World Currency Stabilization', *The Guaranty Survey*, xxiii (1943), p. 4.

[4] American Bankers Association, Economic Policy Committee, *The Place of the United States in the Post-War Economy* (New York, Sept. 1943), pp. 14–15.

dard. Both *The New York Times* and *The New York Herald-Tribune* urged this solution as the only way to insure against reckless policies of credit expansion by national governments. The *Times* declared:

> If . . . each nation were fully convinced that it would best serve its own interest by maintaining the integrity of its currency unit, no elaborate arrangements or clearing houses would be needed. Every nation, rich or poor, is free to stabilize its own currency system with respect to gold . . . provided that it abstains from domestic credit expansion and inflation. The gold standard was, without any international agreements, the most satisfactory international standard that has ever been devised. . . . It is often said that the gold standard 'failed'. The truth is that governments sabotaged it deliberately, because it interfered with the nationalistic 'planning' that governments preferred to stability of exchange rates.[1]

The statement by one of America's most influential newspapers that the gold standard was 'the most satisfactory international standard that has ever been devised' suggested the measure of the gulf that existed between opinion in the two countries.

There may be a danger, however, of over-emphasizing the adverse nature of the American reaction. It was true that a majority of the American newspapers opposed the plans; but so had they opposed the President of the United States in his campaigns for that office in three previous elections. On none of those occasions had they proved a reliable guide to the mood of the general public. Even after the 1942 elections, the Democratic Administration was still able to get its way with Congress on foreign, if not always on domestic, affairs. It was by no means clear that approval could not be achieved for the White plan or for some variant thereof. It was possible, however, that the plan might have to be hedged about with sufficient safeguards to neutralize the opposition of conservative financial and political opinion. The American reaction served notice on the American planners that they might have to explore this possibility. It was in this sense that it provided a poor augury for the eventual achievement of an Anglo-American compromise.

CONCLUSION

Planning for multilateralism had proceeded swiftly on the financial side. By the spring of 1943 the British and American Governments each had published a tentative monetary plan to avert the currency disorders, exchange controls, and economic fluctuations which had

[1] (30 Mar. 1943). See also *The New York Herald-Tribune* (1 Oct. 1943).

beset the nations in the inter-war period. These plans were strikingly similar both in their origin and in their fundamental purpose. But there were several grounds for misgiving. In the increasing preoccupation with the monetary problem there was a danger of forgetting that neither plan could work satisfactorily without the prior solution of the political and economic problems that would arise in the transition from war to peace. Moreover, the plans were far apart on such central problems of international monetary stabilization as the provision of liquidity and the allocation of responsibility for adjustment between creditor and debtor nations.

The public discussions of the two plans reinforced the impression that a large gulf separated British and American opinion on external financial policy. British critics attacked the American plan—and sometimes both plans—on the grounds that they possessed too great a resemblance to the gold standard and threatened to interfere unduly with an expansionist domestic policy. American critics attacked the plans for precisely the opposite reasons. In these circumstances, one authority was moved to observe:

> The main question about the British and American currency plans . . . is whether we are prepared, on either side, to adopt them in our present divided state of thinking. Any solution acceptable to both nations will have to involve some fairly drastic compromising of national attitudes. Whether this can be achieved by a formal plan, at one stroke, and with all the elaboration of an international governing body with votes and quotas, is one of the chief problems. . . . Whatever plan is followed, the essential prerequisites for its success are a completely separate plan for handling the problems of transition from war to peace and a thorough-going British-American understanding.[1]

Whether an attempt to gain early acceptance for some kind of detailed monetary compromise would help or hinder the prospects for achieving a separate plan for reconstruction and a genuine Anglo-American understanding was a matter that remained to be seen.

[1] John H. Williams, 'Currency Stabilization: American and British Attitudes', *For. Aff.*, xxii (1944), p. 247.

CHAPTER VI

PLANNING FOR COMMERCIAL COLLABORATION

THE publication of the White and Keynes plans in the spring of 1943 indicated that planning for post-war financial collaboration was far advanced. But an effective multilateral régime could not be created by planning on the financial side alone; it would have to be based on equivalent measures in the field of commercial policy. As we have seen, an adequate mechanism of adjustment—either by internal correctives or exchange fluctuations—was an essential element in a monetary plan designed to facilitate multilateral payments. Neither of these devices could have its intended effect on a country's balance of payments unless other countries were restrained in their use of commercial restrictions. Thus collaboration in the control of trade barriers was obviously a necessary supplement to collaboration in the financial field.

THE CONCEPTION OF I.T.O.

Although the fact was not widely publicized at the time, both the White and Keynes plans had early counterparts in the field of commercial policy. In the United States, as might be expected, the subject received particularly intensive consideration. For nearly three decades Cordell Hull had dreamt of drafting a comprehensive code to govern the conduct of world trade. At last this dream was becoming a reality. The main responsibility for bringing it to life now devolved upon the State Department's Division of Commercial Policy under Harry Hawkins and the inter-departmental committees set up to co-ordinate the post-war planning of the various branches of the Administration.[1]

The main assumptions behind this activity were summed up in a memorandum prepared by one of the inter-departmental committees:

A great expansion in the volume of international trade after the war will be essential to the attainment of full and effective employment in the United States and elsewhere, to the preservation of private enterprise, and to the success of an international security system to prevent future wars.

[1] For details on the organization of post-war commercial policy planning in the United States see Notter, op. cit.

In order to create conditions favorable to the fullest possible expansion of international trade, on a non-discriminatory basis, it will be necessary for nations to turn away from the trade-restricting and trade-diverting practises of the inter-war period and to cooperate in bringing about a reduction of the barriers to trade erected by governments during that period. International trade cannot be developed to an adequate extent unless excessive tariffs, quantitative restrictions on imports and exports, exchange controls, and other government devices to limit trade are substantially reduced or eliminated. Moreover, if this is not done, there may be a further strengthening of the tendency, already strong in many countries before the war, to eliminate private enterprise from international trade in favor of rigid control by the state.[1]

In short, the achievement of America's political and economic objectives depended upon the achievement of a large volume of international trade, which in turn depended on a comprehensive programme for the reduction of trade barriers. The memorandum continued:

The only nation capable of taking the initiative in promoting a world-wide movement toward the relaxation of trade barriers is the United States. Because of its relatively great economic strength, its favorable balance of payments position, and the importance of its market to the well-being of the rest of the world, the influence of the United States on world commercial policies far surpasses that of any other nation. While the cooperation of the United Kingdom will be essential to the success of any broad program to reduce trade barriers, the prospective post-war position of the United Kingdom is such that its cooperation can be obtained only if it is assured that strong leadership will be furnished by the United States.[2]

Thus it was recognized that the United States had a major responsibility for assuring the success of its commercial policy programme. It was also maintained that the programme should be inaugurated 'as soon as possible—preferably before the end of the war',[3] in order to capitalize on the co-operative spirit that existed between the allies. The major element in the programme would be the negotiation 'among as many nations as possible' of 'a multilateral convention on commercial policy'.[4] The convention would embody agreement on such obstacles to multilateral trade as tariffs, preferences, quantitative restrictions, subsidies, and state-trading. By this method it was hoped that swift progress could be made in the direction of a multi-lateral régime.

[1] 'Summary of the Interim Report of the Special Committee on Relaxation of Trade Barriers' (18 Dec. 1943), id., App. 45, p. 622.
[2] Ibid.   [3] Ibid.   [4] Ibid.

This, in outline, was the nature of the American programme. In the United Kingdom, planning was taking place along strikingly similar lines. Even as Keynes was developing his plans for a Clearing Union, James Meade in the Economic Section of the War Cabinet Secretariat was drafting a complementary plan on commercial policy. This came to be known as the Commercial Union. Meade developed his plan in conjunction with officials in the Board of Trade. By 1943 the Commercial Union had reached a stage in which it was being considered as a possible basis for international negotiations.

In its main outline the Commercial Union looked very much like the multilateral convention on commercial policy which was being developed on the other side of the Atlantic. The plan put great emphasis upon the political and economic importance of liberal trade policies. It called for the drafting of a convention which would reduce tariffs and put a severe curb on direct controls. It provided for an international body which would have the power to interpret this convention and settle disputes between member nations. As Penrose recalls, 'it covered most of the main points of what was to become, about five years later, subject to ratification, the International Trade Charter'.[1]

THE 'SEMINAR' ON COMMERCIAL COLLABORATION

It was now an auspicious moment for instituting Anglo-American negotiations. Early in 1943 Winant suggested to Eden that the American and British experts working in this field might come together for informal talks. Eden responded sympathetically and plans for a meeting were discussed in greater detail between Penrose, Winant's economic adviser; Hugh Dalton, the President of the Board of Trade; and Richard Law, Minister of State. Dalton and Law were strong supporters of Meade's Commercial Union and were anxious to explore the subject with the appropriate American authorities. It was finally agreed that a British mission headed by Law should visit Washington in September 1943 to discuss post-war economic problems, including problems of commercial policy.

The Washington talks on commercial policy brought together the architects of the Commercial Union, on the one hand, and of the proposed 'multilateral convention on commercial policy', on the other. The principal British participants were Sir Percivale Liesching, the senior civil servant responsible for the Commercial Union in the

---

[1] Op. cit., pp. 94–95.

Board of Trade; Meade, the principal author of the plan; and Robbins, then head of the Economic Section of the War Cabinet Secretariat. The American participants included Myron C. Taylor, head of the United States delegation, Acheson, Hawkins, and a scattering of experts not only from the State Department but from other interested Government agencies. The talks were entirely exploratory—in the spirit of a university seminar rather than of a formal international conference. As the official American summary put it, 'no attempt was made to reach definite conclusions but rather to prepare an orderly agenda for further study by each of the respective Governments and for possible further informal joint conversations'.[1]

The British and American participants in these conversations found themselves in agreement[2] on the need for a multilateral convention on commercial policy, supplemented by an international trade organization which could interpret the convention, investigate complaints, and settle differences between members. The experts on both sides considered that the rules of the convention should be made as precise as possible. They discussed a large number of subjects which might be embraced in the convention—not simply governmental obstacles to trade but international commodity agreements, cartels, and the co-ordination of measures to promote high levels of employment. We shall not attempt to summarize all the matters discussed in these conversations. Instead we shall confine our attention to three issues which occupied the centre of the stage in these and all subsequent negotiations—the relation between employment and trade policy; the elimination of quantitative restrictions; and the reduction of tariffs and the elimination of preferences.

The employment issue

The important relation between employment policy and the achievement of multilateral trade was now widely appreciated on both sides of the Atlantic. It was clear that no plan for the revival of multilateralism could work in the face of the violent fluctuations of the trade cycle that had characterized the inter-war period. Both the British and American experts in the 1943 discussions agreed on the need to supplement co-operative action in the field of trade barriers

[1] 'Memorandum Concerning the Washington Meeting Between British and American Economic Experts with Reference to Article VII of the Mutual Aid Agreements', Notter, App. 30, p. 562.

[2] Since these were only informal exploratory discussions this term should not be thought to imply a commitment of any kind.

with co-operative action to maintain high levels of income and employment.

Within this general framework there were, of course, differences of emphasis—differences not only between the British, on the one hand, and the Americans, on the other, but differences within their respective delegations. There was, for example, the influential study of the Department of Commerce which emphasized the impact of fluctuations in American income and employment on the level of American imports and foreign investment, and hence on economic conditions in the rest of the world.[1] This study expressed the conviction of some Administration planners that the maintenance of high and stable levels of American income and employment was a pre-condition of progress toward the liberalization of international trade. Hawkins and some of his colleagues in the State Department put the emphasis rather differently. Although they acknowledged that employment policies had important implications for the liberalization of trade, they tended to place more weight on the contribution that trade liberalization could make to the maintenance of high levels of employment. They were more inclined to regard trade restrictions as a cause of the Great Depression than the other way round. Accordingly they may have failed to appreciate the scepticism with which some British observers regarded plans for the removal of trade barriers that were unaccompanied by safeguards against the recurrence of an American slump.

In discussing the relation between employment and trade policy the British experts were probably closer to the views of the Department of Commerce than to those of the Department of State. In short, they put more emphasis on the contribution that the maintenance of high levels of employment could make to the liberalization of trade than on the contribution that the reduction of trade barriers could make to employment. Nevertheless, the differences that emerged in the discussions did not prove to be very great. Although Churchill's coalition Government accorded considerable importance to the maintenance of high levels of employment, its leaders stopped well short of the far-reaching interventionist programme advocated by the British left-wing. As indicated in the White Paper published in 1944,[2] it planned to maintain full employment by relying on monetary and fiscal policy rather than on comprehensive planning and direct

---

[1] *The United States in the World Economy* (Washington, 1943).
[2] Cmd. 6527.

controls. Meade and Robbins were working on the White paper at the time of the Washington talks and they brought its flexible, moderate approach to the discussions of international employment policy.

In this field, therefore, the British and American experts found themselves in agreement on a number of general principles. They agreed that measures for the maintenance of employment should be taken in both the international and the domestic sphere. On the domestic side, nations should seek to maintain high levels of employment by measures appropriate to their political and economic institutions. These measures should be supplemented by action on the part of international agencies such as the institutions concerned with monetary stabilization and international investment, the organization concerned with commodity policy, and the international trade organization itself. Co-ordination of domestic and international measures to promote employment should be carried out by an Advisory Economic Staff, which might be part of the organization concerned with trade and employment policy or part of a general co-ordinating body established by the United Nations in the economic field. Among other things, the Staff might determine whether particular nations were pursuing policies designed to promote full employment internationally or policies involving the 'export' of unemployment.

Beyond these generalities the experts did not find it possible to go. Both the British and American representatives recognized the difficulty of utilizing international measures for the promotion of employment in the existing imperfect state of the world's political organization. Accordingly, they left detailed planning on this subject to be taken up at a later date.

The issue of quantitative restrictions

Another problem of considerable concern to both the British and American experts was that of quantitative restrictions. There was solid agreement that such restrictions represented a particularly injurious form of trade barrier. It was agreed that direct physical controls caused a more violent disruption of the natural pattern of international trade than tariffs and other restrictions operating by means of the price mechanism. It was also agreed that they were far more difficult to reconcile with multilateral principles, since there was no satisfactory method of assuring their non-discriminatory application.

For all these reasons both the British and American experts agreed that quantitative restrictions should be abolished. There were to be no exceptions to this rule—not even for infant industries, for agriculture, or for industries considered essential to the national security. There was, however, one exception of particular importance for the future of commercial collaboration between the two countries. The experts agreed that quantitative restrictions should be permitted for the purpose of safeguarding the balance of payments.

This exception, it should be noted, was closely circumscribed. Quantitative restrictions to safeguard the balance of payments were to be subject to approval by the international organization. This approval would be required in advance in the case of drastic action cutting imports below their level in a previous representative period. Nations maintaining such restrictions for more than two or three years would be obliged to consult with the international organization with a view to their early removal. Finally, restrictions employed to safeguard the balance of payments were to be non-discriminatory as between countries. No exceptions were made with reference to this latter principle. The British and American experts seemed equally determined to subject quantitative restrictions to the strictest kind of international control.

The tariff-preference issue

Probably the most controversial issue in these early discussions was that concerning the reduction of tariffs and the elimination of tariff preferences. In Article Seven of the Mutual Aid Agreement the British and American Governments had promised to undertake agreed action directed to the 'reduction' of tariffs and the 'elimination' of all forms of discriminatory treatment—including tariff preferences. But this formula indicated only the final result. By what methods were tariffs to be reduced and preferences eliminated? How much reduction in the one would be required to accomplish elimination of the other? These specific questions lay at the heart of the Anglo-American conversations.

The American position on this issue has already been described. On the one hand, the Department of State, and, to a somewhat lesser extent, other branches of the Administration, were determined to achieve the elimination of the Imperial Preference system. They considered preferences an unjustifiable interference with American export trade, a major departure from the principle of non-discrimination, and a menace to world prosperity and world peace. Tariffs applied in a non-discriminatory fashion by means of the unconditional most-favoured-nation clause they did not consider to be in the same category. During the Washington talks the American representatives emphasized that the United States could not contemplate substantial future tariff reductions unless it received firm assurances that the Preference system would be brought to an end.

The British representatives took a rather different view of the problem. They placed far less emphasis on the distinction between tariffs and preferences. Their main concern was to achieve agreement on some formula that would ensure a drastic levelling of both kinds of trade barriers. Although they might be willing to concede in principle that Article Seven envisaged a situation in which preferences were abolished, they did not believe that this objective could be achieved merely by the kind of selective tariff reduction that had been accomplished under the Reciprocal Trade Agreements Act. Their position has been summarized by Penrose as follows:

In numerous personal conversations with leading officials since Article VII of the Mutual Aid Agreement had been signed, it had been made unmistakeably clear to me that the method of bilateral negotiations was not regarded by the British as an adequate means for reducing trade barriers immediately after the war, and that tariff reductions under bilateral trade agreements would not be accepted as a full discharge of the obligations arising out of Article VII to reduce trade barriers. It followed that the United Kingdom would not agree to the abolition, although they would agree to the reduction, of preferences in return merely for reciprocal reductions of tariffs under the Reciprocal Trade Agreements Act. . . . British spokesmen did not deny the obligation to abolish discriminations under certain conditions. But they repeatedly declared, at first privately and later during negotiations, that they would abolish preferences only in return for a heavy all-round and not a 'selective' reduction of tariffs and other trade barriers. Though they have not stated to this day, so far as I am aware, what in their opinion the extent of such a reduction would have to be, my impression at an early stage was that it would have to be much more than 50 per cent. of the pre-war height of all tariffs.[1]

During the Washington conversations the British experts emphasized the importance of reaching agreement on measures of tariff reduction so drastic as to make possible the elimination of discriminatory treatment envisaged in Article Seven. They proposed that all tariffs should be reduced by an agreed percentage, subject to

[1] Op. cit., pp. 92–93.

a minimum *ad valorem* level, and subject at the same time to a maximum *ad valorem* level above which they would not be permitted to go. The Americans foresaw very grave difficulties in gaining Congressional approval for any plan embodying a ceiling on tariff levels and, indeed, for any across-the-board formula at all. Nevertheless, they agreed in principle that if an acceptable tariff-reducing formula could be worked out it would provide the best method of achieving the objectives of Article Seven.

CONCLUSION

The informal exploratory talks between the British and American experts in the autumn of 1943 revealed a wide measure of agreement on the broad outlines of commercial collaboration. There was a remarkable degree of unanimity, for example, on the interdependence of trade and employment policy, on the need for eliminating quantitative restrictions, and on the desirability of finding an automatic tariff-reducing formula to facilitate the achievement of the 'substantial' reduction of tariffs and the 'elimination' of discriminatory treatment called for in Article Seven. Moreover, the British and American representatives were agreed on the need for some form of international trade organization that could interpret the code of multilateral principles and settle disputes between members.

All these developments offered real hope that a compromise plan of commercial collaboration could eventually be achieved. But the difficulties were by no means over. So far the talks had been held only at the expert level. The fully multilateral programme had still to receive the approval of the responsible political authorities in the two countries and, eventually, of public opinion at large. Moreover, the talks had only been on the level of general principle. The experts had agreed that the future undertakings on commercial policy should be made as precise as possible. It remained to be seen whether the wide area of Anglo-American agreement could be maintained when the general principles were reduced to more specific obligations.

CHAPTER VII

THE COMPROMISE ON FINANCIAL COLLABORATION

IT is time to turn our attention once again to the development of planning on the financial side. The publication of the White and Keynes plans in the spring of 1943 stimulated efforts to draft an acceptable compromise. Now ideas were advanced by other countries, such as Canada, France, and the Soviet Union. For obvious reasons, however, the crucial decisions continued to be made in bilateral negotiations between Britain and the United States. These two were bound to be the dominant members of the new international financial system. Equally important, they were the main sources of the expert man-power needed to devise that system and make it work.

The Law mission which came to Washington in September 1943 included Keynes and other British financial experts. The financial negotiations which then took place produced a compromise of the Keynes and White plans which was presented to the public in April 1944 as the *Joint Statement by Experts on the Establishment of an International Monetary Fund*. The key provisions of this document were embodied, with only minor changes, in the Articles of Agreement of the International Monetary Fund adopted in July 1944 by the United Nations Conference at Bretton Woods, New Hampshire.

Separate action was also taken, if somewhat more slowly, on the American proposal for an International Bank. The Bank plan was published in November 1943. But it met with little response from the British Government until a few weeks before the Bretton Woods Conference. Then, at a preliminary meeting at Atlantic City, New Jersey, Keynes enthusiastically took up the subject. Sufficient progress was made toward Anglo-American agreement to permit the successful consideration of the Bank by the delegates at the Bretton Woods Conference.

Such, in brief outline, was the sequence of events that led to the drafting of the Articles of Agreement of the International Monetary Fund and the International Bank for Reconstruction and Development. Let us turn now to the critical Anglo-American negotiations which determined the basic character of these institutions.

DRAFTING THE FINANCIAL COMPROMISE

In view of the largely personal authorship of the British and American financial plans it was only natural that the main responsibility for drafting the compromise should fall upon Keynes and White themselves. We can hardly proceed with our analysis of that compromise without making a few observations about the fascinating relationship between these two men.

What powerful and contradictory forces were at work in this association! The sources of friction were obvious enough. Both were proud, sensitive, and self-confident to the point of arrogance. Not much else did they have in common. White was an ambitious middle-class boy who had made good; Keynes an urbane product of cultured academic stock. The first set little store by social conventions; the second was the product of a society where manners were the mark of a man. One bore a deep resentment of the advantages that heredity could bestow; the other possessed the well-bred Englishman's easy self-confidence. Veterans of the Anglo-American negotiations recall how, in the midst of some controversy, White would address Keynes as 'your Royal Highness', sitting back with an ironic smile to watch the latter's ill-disguised irritation. It was certainly a wonder that these two could get along together at all.

Yet they did get along—and even came to regard one another with respect and admiration. Although Keynes often found White rude and truculent, he had to testify to his energy and persistence. Moreover, White was one of the staunchest supporters of international co-operation in the American Administration, and certainly one of the most sympathetic to Keynesian ideas. It would have been folly for Keynes to antagonize such an important ally. As for White— well, to be truthful—he secretly worshipped Keynes. The author of the *Economic Consequences of the Peace* and the *Treatise on Money* had been his idol ever since student days. What a satisfaction it must have given White to negotiate on equal terms with the great man himself! Well might one veteran of these negotiations remark: 'The happiest moment in the life of Harry White came when he could call Keynes by his first name.'

With the help of recollections from eye-witnesses we can reconstruct the encounters of these men. In the conduct of negotiations they were not unlike two vain and rather jealous economics professors striving to impress a university seminar. See them sitting together at the head of a long table, the other members of the British and American delegations on either side. Occasionally interventions were made by these other delegates; but it was Keynes and White who led the discussion, controlling its subject-matter and setting its tone. 'Well, Harry', Keynes would say, 'what shall it be to-day—passivity, exchange stability, or the role of gold?' With this informal beginning the two of them would exchange observations on some theoretical issue. Occasionally bitterness would creep in. Keynes would take White out of his depth; White would feel, but not admit, his intellectual inferiority; he would say something to remind Keynes that he, not Keynes, represented the stronger party in the negotiations. There would be angry words; papers would be thrown on the floor; one of them would stalk out of the room. The other negotiators would stay to patch up the quarrel. The next day the same procedure would be repeated. Eventually a tentative agreement would be reached, which could be submitted to the respective Governments for approval. In this way, slowly, almost imperceptibly, there emerged the terms of the financial compromise.

We must now determine of what major elements this compromise was composed. Our discussion will proceed under the three major heads discussed earlier—the liquidity issue, the adjustment issue, and the transitional issue.

The liquidity issue

We have already noted the substantial differences between the United States and Britain on the size and availability of international liquidity. The Keynes plan called for overdraft facilities of at least $26 billion, in which the potential American liability might be as much as $23 billion. This was entirely unacceptable to the American negotiators. They informed their British counterparts at an early stage that the United States could support an international monetary authority only if it were based on the contributory principle and if the American contribution were limited to $2 or $3 billion.[1] Congress, they explained, would never accept the notion of virtually unlimited liability. Indeed, a clearing mechanism based on a system of overdrafts might be held to violate the exclusive constitutional authority of Congress to authorize federal expenditures. For these reasons the overdraft principle which constituted such a vital part of the Keynes

[1] John Parke Young, 'Developing Plans for an International Monetary Fund and a World Bank', *Dept. State Bull.*, xxiii (1950), p. 778.

plan had finally to be abandoned. In return, the Americans agreed to a slight enlargement of the contributions contemplated in the White plan, and at Bretton Woods final agreement was reached on a Fund with resources of $8·8 billion, with an American contribution of $3·175 billion.

Thus at the outset the total amount of liquidity to be made available by the new institution was fixed at a much lower limit than that sought by the British negotiators. Once this struggle had been lost Keynes devoted his efforts to assuring that the smaller resources would be automatically available. Since the total drawing rights were so rigidly circumscribed it was more important than ever that the new international institution should not become 'too grand-motherly'. The British position on this matter was quite firm: 'Our view has been very strongly that if countries are to be given sufficient confidence they must be able to rely in all normal circumstances on drawing a substantial part of their quota without policing or facing unforeseen obstacles.'[1]

As we noted earlier, the White plan had not embodied this principle of unconditional access to the Fund's resources. Even the limitations it had laid down were regarded by many Americans as inadequate. It was no wonder, therefore, that the American representatives should now take the line that 'discretion on the part of the Fund was essential if the Fund's resources were to be conserved for the purposes for which the Fund was established and if the Fund were to be influential in promoting what it considered to be appropriate financial policies'.[2] When Keynes left Washington in October 1943 he acknowledged that the Anglo-American differences on this subject constituted 'one of the matters on which we have not yet reached final accommodation'.[3]

The compromise finally worked out on this issue was embodied in the Articles of Agreement adopted at the Bretton Woods conference. Some of the wording seemed to reflect a victory for the British view. It was stated flatly that a country 'shall be entitled' to buy currency from the Fund provided only that the member 'desiring to purchase the currency represents that it is presently needed for making in that currency payments which are consistent with the provisions' of the Fund Agreement.[4] On its face this provision appeared to suggest that

[1] Keynes, *Letter to Viner, October 17, 1943.*   [2] Young, op. cit., p. 783.
[3] *Letter to Viner, supra.*
[4] Article V, Section 3 (a). This was subject, of course, to the quantitative limitations on the drawings that could be made in any given year, the limitation on drawing

the right to draw on Fund resources was virtually unqualified and that the Fund could not look behind the representations of its members. But there were other provisions that seemed to incorporate the American position. The Fund could limit the access of a member to its resources when it was of the opinion that the member was using those resources in a manner contrary to the purposes of the Fund.[1] To this extent the Fund could adopt an 'active' rather than a 'passive' role in considering requests for financial aid. Indeed, this appeared to be necessary if the Fund were to fulfil one of its major purposes—'to shorten the duration and lessen the degree of disequilibrium in the international balances of payments of members'.[2] One could not be sure from the wording of the Articles themselves whether the British or the American view on this subject would finally prevail.

The adjustment issue

We noted earlier that a second condition of success for any compromise plan was agreement on a mechanism for maintaining equilibrium in the balance of payments. The need to reach a settlement on this score was increased by the decision to put firm limits on the total amount of available liquidity. For now there would be less time during which balance of payments adjustments could be deferred.

Once he had been forced to give up the expansionist features of the Clearing Union, Keynes began to seek an alternative safeguard for policies of domestic expansion. He was forced to take a second look at the possibilities of exchange variation. Accordingly, in the summer and autumn of 1943, the British position on the subject began to change. In place of the relative fixity provided in the Clearing Union plan, the British now asked a large measure of national freedom to make exchange rate adjustments. To Viner, who had criticized the degree of exchange rigidity in both plans, Keynes now wrote: 'On this point we in London have come round entirely to your point of view. With some difficulty, we have persuaded White to come a long way to meet us. I hope you will find the new formula acceptable. My own feeling now is that it goes far enough.'[3]

The 'new formula' involved a considerable alteration in the philosophy of the monetary plans. Members were still only entitled to make exchange rate changes which, in the words of the White

a currency that had been declared scarce by the Fund, and several other exceptional qualifications that need not concern us here.   [1] Article V, Section 5.
[2] Article I (vi).   [3] *Letter to Viner, supra.*

plan, were necessary to correct a 'fundamental disequilibrium'. But the Fund was now required to concur in any change proposed by a member—no matter how large—provided the change could be shown to satisfy that criterion. If a change was less than 10 per cent. from the original par value, the Fund was given no power to object at all. Perhaps most important, it could not object to a change in an exchange rate on the grounds of the 'domestic social or political policies of the member proposing the change'.[1] Keynes believed this phrase would insulate policies of domestic expansion from foreign deflationary pressures. But the price of such an accomplishment may have been the impairment of the exchange stability that was one of the original objectives of the Keynes and White plans. For by dosing itself with domestic inflation any country could get into 'fundamental disequilibrium' and thus become entitled to vary its rate of exchange.

As if to justify these fears the new reliance on exchange flexibility was accompanied by a considerable decrease in the emphasis on internal correctives. The White plan had once contained a strong provision authorizing the Fund to require changes in the domestic policies of its members. In its original form this provision had been considered impractical; it had been substantially modified when the plan was prepared for publication. But the British representatives would not accept even the modified reference to internal correctives contained in the published version. Such a provision, they feared, might be used as a basis for interference in Britain's policies of internal expansion. In the end, the entire provision was removed. Thus disappeared one of the last clear acknowledgements of the domestic responsibilities of debtor countries.

At Bretton Woods the American delegation did succeed to some extent in repairing this omission. The Fund was given the right at any time to communicate its view to members 'on any matter arising under this Agreement'.[2] Moreover, it could by a two-thirds vote issue a public report to a particular member 'regarding its monetary or economic conditions and developments which directly tend to produce a serious disequilibrium in the international balance of payments . . .'.[3] This new provision made it clear that the saving clause on domestic policy inserted among the provisions on exchange

---

[1] Article IV, Section 5 (*f*).
[2] Article XII, Section 8. This section did not appear in the *Joint Statement*.
[3] Ibid.

depreciation did not make the domestic policies of Fund members entirely immune from criticism. It remained to be seen, however, whether this fact would be equally understood on both sides of the Atlantic.

The problem of increasing the burden of adjustment on creditor nations was hardly less important to the British representatives than that of reducing the burden of adjustment on the debtors. With the abandonment of the overdraft principle an important sanction on the creditors had been removed. Could some other sanction be found? Keynes had been sceptical of White's 'scare-currency' provision. 'Over here we find this feature of S.F. rather obscure. Are you clear how it would work? Do you think that it is a satisfactory way out?'[1] As the negotiations progressed, however, he began to see great possibilities in the clause. If discrimination were authorized in time of dollar scarcity, he reasoned, the United States would be under great pressure to avoid the development of such a situation.

No wonder that Keynes eagerly grasped the American offer to expand the 'scarce-currency' clause. As it finally appeared, the clause not only empowered the Fund to ration its supply of the scarce currency but authorized members 'temporarily to impose limitations on the freedom of exchange operations in the scarce currency'.[2] In determining the nature of these limitations each member was to have 'complete jurisdiction'.[3] With these additions yet another safeguard was erected against the dangers of deflationary pressure from abroad. At the same time, an important measure of responsibility for maintaining balance of payments equilibrium appeared to have been placed on the creditor nations.

Did the 'scarce-currency' clause really provide an effective mechanism of adjustment? The answer was by no means clear. In the first place, controls against the scarce currency were authorized only in the event that 'the demand for a member's currency seriously threatens the Fund's ability to supply that currency . . .'.[4] Suppose a general scarcity developed outside the Fund, while at the same time the Fund had ample resources of the scarce currency. This could occur if for some reason the Fund were restricting its lending operations.[5] In such a case members might not be permitted to employ

---

[1] Keynes, *Letter to Viner, June 9, 1943.*   [2] Article VII, Section 3 (*b*).
[3] Ibid.   [4] Article VII, Section 3 (*a*).
[5] As, for example, in the transition period, when the Fund could not be sure that members needed its resources for uses consistent with the purposes of the Fund. See Chapter XV, *infra.* There was also the technical possibility of a shortage outside but

the 'scarce-currency' controls; they might have to rely entirely on exchange rate fluctuations to protect themselves in the face of deflationary pressure from abroad. In the second place, even assuming that a currency became scarce inside as well as outside the Fund, would the spread of direct controls against its exports really force the creditor country to make adjustments? The creditor might consider that the causes of the scarcity lay not in its own policies but in faulty policies of the debtors. The version of the 'scarce-currency' clause finally adopted at Bretton Woods contained no implication of special creditor responsibility in such a situation. Indeed, there was notably absent from the Articles the specific provision contained in the White Plan directing the Fund to issue a report *to the creditor country* with recommendations for restoring equilibrium.[1] Absent also was the provision instructing members in such a situation to 'give immediate and careful attention to recommendations made by the Fund'.[2] The disappearance of these provisions suggested that the United States Government was no longer willing to accept even that measure of creditor responsibility which had been contained in the published version of the White plan a year before.

The transitional issue

As we noted earlier, one of the basic requirements for the success of any compromise plan for financial collaboration was a comprehensive attack on the post-war reconstruction problem. Unfortunately, with the passage of time, this problem came to be increasingly excluded from the Anglo-American negotiations.

The development of the Bank plan provided a case in point. We have already seen how the resources it could devote to reconstruction were drastically reduced by discussions within the American Government. Now further modifications of a conservative nature were made as the result of the Anglo-American negotiations. For quite some time the British expressed little interest in having a Bank at all. Only in the discussions preliminary to Bretton Woods at Atlantic City, New Jersey, did their attitude begin to change. Keynes suddenly became impressed with the potentialities of the Bank. Even so, the British approach was still extremely cautious. They were particularly anxious to restrict the scope of the Bank's direct lending operations.

not inside the Fund in the event of a sudden and severe American slump. In such a situation members might be short of dollars and yet be unable to draw dollars from the Fund because of the quantitative limits on annual drawings set by the Fund Articles.   [1] Stabilization Fund, Section III, Para. 6.   [2] Ibid.

The reason for this was not hard to find. Britain did not expect to ask the Bank for financial aid; at the same time, its financial position was too precarious to enable it to make a large contribution for loans to other countries. Accordingly, the British representatives sought assurances that the Bank would not engage in any large amount of direct lending and that only a small part of its capital would be called up at all.[1] The American negotiators had to agree that the Bank 'should primarily be concerned with aiding and encouraging the provision of private funds for international investment by means of guarantees. The greater part of the capital should not be called up for use by the Bank in making loans but should be set aside in the form of subscriptions as a reserve for meeting the Bank's obligations of guaranteed loans.'[2]

These conservative features were embodied in the Articles of Agreement of the International Bank for Reconstruction and Development that were agreed upon at Bretton Woods. Although the Bank was empowered to make loans from its original resources as well as to guarantee private loans and to raise new capital by issuing securities, the provisions concerning the payment of member subscriptions indicated that its role as an independent lender would be closely limited. Of the Bank's authorized capital of $10 billion, only 20 per cent. was immediately subject to call, and only 2 per cent. had to be paid over in gold or U.S. dollars.[3] Moreover, the maximum amount of the Bank's loans and guarantees, previously fixed at a multiple of the Bank's total capital, was now limited to 100 per cent. of that capital.[4] Finally, the Bank was enjoined to pursue a cautious lending policy, paying due regard to the capacity of borrowers to service their obligations.[5] Thanks to modifications of this kind, the Bank was now a respectable and conservative financial institution. At the same time, the original function of the Bank as a generous provider of reconstruction aid had been rather obscured. In view of this fact it was perhaps unfortunate that the first Article of the Bank still proclaimed that one of the institution's major functions would be to facilitate reconstruction 'including the restoration of economies destroyed or disrupted by war'.[6]

[1] British note of 20 Apr. 1944, commenting on the American Bank draft of 24 Nov. 1943, *White Papers*.
[2] U.S. note of 23 May 1944, replying to British note of 20 Apr. 1944, ibid.
[3] Article II, Sections 5 and 7.
[4] Article III, Section 3.   [5] Article III, Section 4 (v).
[6] Article I (i). The Bank was also still supposed to 'assist in bringing about a smooth transition from a wartime to a peacetime economy'. Article I (v).

The Fund's role in the transition period was also circumscribed in the course of the Anglo-American negotiations. Both the Stabilization Fund and Clearing Union had been intended to assume some functions in the transition period. The White plan, for example, had included a specific provision for the liquidation of the accumulated sterling balances. However well intentioned, this provision involved a dangerous 'mixing-up' of the transitional and long-term financial problems. The nature of the danger soon became apparent. The British quickly rejected the idea of burdening the Fund with the handling of the balances. They considered that the relatively modest resources now agreed upon should not be taxed with the job of liquidating the war-time indebtedness.[1] Thus, at an early point in the Anglo-American negotiations, the provision on the balances was removed. When some of the large sterling creditors tried to reverse this decision at Bretton Woods, the British and American Governments joined ranks in opposition. Keynes declared that 'the settlement of these debts must be . . . a matter between those directly concerned'.[2] An American spokesman added reassuringly that although the Fund could not 'deal directly with indebtedness arising out of the war . . . its operations will facilitate the development of an environment . . . in which the problem of war-time indebtedness can be amicably settled by the countries directly concerned'.[3] Thus the problem was omitted from the Fund's operations, while no other satisfactory method of settlement was found.

The failure to supplement the post-war financial plans by adequate measures to deal with the reconstruction problem caused increasing concern to the British negotiators. Keynes wrote:

We are naturally beginning to give close attention to what arrangements we can best make to meet our external payments in the immediate post-war period of uncertain duration which provisionally we think of as being (say) three years. This will be a period of demobilization and changeover to peacetime production, when abnormal British Government expenditures . . . will remain on a large scale, whereas British exports cannot yet be raised to their full post-war volume. In these circumstances our balance of payments on current account can only come to something like equilibrium rather gradually.

[1] It should be noted that the size of the balances had grown considerably since the American proposal for handling them in the Fund had first been made.
[2] U.S. Department of State, *Proceedings and Documents of the United Nations Monetary and Financial Conference, Bretton Woods, New Hampshire, July 1–22, 1944*, vol. ii, p. 1168.   [3] Ibid.

It seems to us to be virtually certain that our accumulating deficit during this period will arise in conditions and reach an order of magnitude that are outside the true scope of the new institution. Indeed, the institution might find its future usefulness and strength greatly impaired if it were to attempt to handle such problems.

The conditions will be a sequel to the war and the deficiency will in fact be a delayed instalment of the costs of the war and should be handled as a part of the war-time finance and not regarded as belonging to a subsequent peace-time régime. But this being so it is most important that there should be no misunderstanding between us as to how we contemplate handling our problem in this period.[1]

This was a powerful appeal for devising a separate programme of transitional finance. Until such a programme existed, Britain would need to have greater freedom to depart from the principles of multi-lateral trade. To this end Keynes proposed to insert in the Fund a new section on 'Transitional Arrangements':

We have not yet any cut and dried plan and are not likely to be in a position to have one much in advance of putting it into operation. Owing to this uncertainty we have to retain a somewhat wider latitude of action than may actually be required in practice. . . .

This transitional clause as we intend it would allow us not only to maintain sterling area arrangements and payments agreements with other countries of general character now in force but to adapt and extend these as for example by concluding payments agreements with any part of the sterling area with which we could not reach an alternative satisfactory arrangement. It would also allow us to make new inter-governmental or inter-Central Bank credit or clearing arrangements on the model for example, of the recent Belgo-Dutch agreement or of our own Anglo-French agreement.[2]

The British proposals on 'Transitional Arrangements' found their way with little alteration into the Articles of Agreement of the International Monetary Fund that were finally adopted at Bretton Woods. It was agreed that the Fund was 'not intended to provide facilities for relief or reconstruction or to deal with international indebtedness arising out of the war'.[3] It was also agreed that members would be free to 'maintain and adapt to changing circumstances . . . restrictions on payments and transfers for current international transactions'.[4] Members would be obliged in employing these restrictions to pay

---

[1] Keynes, *Letter to White, December 18, 1943, White Papers.*
[2] Ibid.   [3] Article XIV, Section 1.
[4] Article XIV, Section 2. Only members whose territories had been occupied by the enemy would be permitted to introduce *new* restrictions.

continuous regard to the purposes of the Fund, and also to withdraw the restrictions as soon as they were able. But they were put under no direct pressure to remove their restrictions for at least five years after the beginning of the Fund's operations. After that time, they were obliged to consult with the Fund as to the further retention of their restrictions.[1] Even then, the Fund could propose the removal of a member's restrictions only 'in exceptional circumstances'.[2] In effect, the members of the Fund were given freedom to depart from multilateral payments practices for what might turn out to be an indefinite period.

Now we can see the essential nature of the financial compromise that emerged from the Anglo-American negotiations. The settlement embodied the American desire for a smaller amount of financial resources, although the conditions of access to those resources were still obscure. At the same time, references to internal correctives were almost entirely eliminated and much greater emphasis was placed on exchange rate flexibility. The 'scarce-currency' clause was reinforced by permitting members to employ exchange restrictions against the scarce currency, but it was not clear that the implications of this clause in terms of creditor country responsibility were understood by the British and Americans in the same way. Finally, provisions for handling the reconstruction problem were removed from the monetary institution, with a corresponding increase in the freedom of members to maintain exchange restrictions in a transition period of indefinite duration.

In view of these developments, did the Fund and Bank provide a secure foundation for Anglo-American collaboration? Did they embody any genuine consensus on the means by which multilateralism could be restored? These questions would soon be answered by the debate on the Bretton Woods agreements which was now beginning to unfold on both sides of the Atlantic.

THE BRITISH DEBATE

With the final drafting of the financial compromise the time had come for a major political decision on the part of the British Government. Up to this point the Anglo-American negotiations had resulted only in general statements about ultimate objectives. Now they had

---

[1] In the original U.K. draft on 'Transitional Arrangements' members were obliged to consult with the Fund after only three years. This shorter period was included in the *Joint Statement* but apparently was considered insufficient at Bretton Woods.
[2] Article XIV, Section 4.

produced specific institutions which Britain was expected to join. Parliament would want to be consulted. The financial compromise would become the subject of a nation-wide political debate.[1]

Second thoughts on multilateralism

The time for decision was not propitious. In mid-1944 British opinion seemed to be hardening against multilateral ideas. Extremists on both sides were gaining in influence. On the one hand, a small but vocal group of left-wing economists expounded a foreign trade philosophy to match their programme of comprehensive planning in the domestic sphere. Many of their more liberal colleagues who might have published articles in defence of multilateralism were restrained from doing so by their positions in the Government service. To a large extent, therefore, these critics held the field alone. They expressed opposition to any international monetary plan that might subject the British economy to external influences, particularly to economic fluctuations in the United States. What they wanted was a financial plan that would 'permit single countries to maintain full employment irrespective of the consequences of this policy on the balance of their international payments'.[2] The Anglo-American financial compromise did not appear to satisfy this condition. In its place they proposed the use of quantitative restrictions and state trading. They urged that bilateral clearing and bulk-purchase agreements be concluded with those countries of the Commonwealth and Western Europe which were also dedicated to comprehensive programmes of domestic planning. In short, they dreamed of a bloc of planned economies insulated as far as possible against economic blasts from the free-enterprise world outside.[3]

These critics wielded considerable influence in academic circles. But politically their weight was probably less than that of the opponents of multilateralism at the other end of the spectrum. Here were the financial interests of the City of London, the industrial leaders who feared foreign competition, the old-fashioned propagandists of

---

[1] The British debate on the financial compromise can be regarded as lasting from the publication of the *Joint Statement* in Apr. 1944 to Parliamentary approval of the Bretton Woods agreements in Dec. 1945. Most of the material in this section is drawn from the early stages of the debate; in its final stages the Bretton Woods debate became part of the debate on the Anglo-American Financial Agreement discussed in Chapter XII.

[2] Thomas Balogh, 'International Aspects of Full Employment', in *Economics of Full Employment* (Oxford, 1944), p. 159.

[3] For leading expositions of this view, see Balogh, op. cit., and E. F. Schumacher, *Export Policy and Full Employment*, Fabian Research Ser. No. 77 (London, 1944).

the Empire. Opposition of this kind caused increasing concern to American observers. In the spring of 1944 Ambassador Winant cabled to Washington that

a majority of the directors of the Bank of England are opposed to the Bretton Woods program. . . . It is argued by those in opposition that if the plan is adopted financial control will leave London and sterling exchange will be replaced by dollar exchange. Right Wing Conservatives such as Amery . . . who represents Imperial thinking in the Cabinet, are disturbed by this argument.[1]

Winant added that the Prime Minister was under heavy pressure from these critics and was reluctant to make a decision on the compromise monetary proposals.

Still more unfavourable as an augury for financial collaboration were developments taking place in what had been relatively moderate opinion. Earlier in the war the choice had been between multilateralism and bilateralism, and nearly all but the extremists had been willing to choose the former. Now there was a tendency to look for a middle way—a method by which Britain could enjoy the advantages of multilateralism without its attendant risks. The search for such an alternative was stimulated by the growing anxiety about the future direction of American policy. Would the Americans maintain full employment? Would they make available a sufficient supply of dollars either by reducing tariffs or by investing more abroad? As *The Manchester Guardian* put it: 'Should Britain join a free world system of payments which will work only if 130 million Americans play the game? Or should we seek shelter against American instability by building up our own planned trade and currency system and a fortified sterling area?'[2]

There were now many who were prepared to support the second approach. *The Economist* and *The Times* in particular lent their influence to this alternative. Each ran a series of articles describing how the benefits of multilateralism might be achieved among a group of countries by means of bulk-purchase agreements, quantitative import controls, and a system of planned discrimination against American goods—in short, a system not very different from that recommended by the left-wing economists.[3] This *The Economist* called the 'less-than-

[1] Telegram from Winant to the Secretary of State (Washington), 12 Apr. 1944, *White Papers*.   [2] (2 Jan. 1945).
[3] See 'The Principles of Trade', *The Economist*, cxlvi (1944), pp. 4–5, 32–34, 64–65, 94–95, 136–7, 169–70, 204–5, 232–3; 'World Monetary Policies', *The Times* (21, 22, and 23 Aug. 1944).

universal, the less-than-fully-multilateral, the less-than-completely-orthodox alternative'.[1] Both *The Times* and *The Economist* appeared to accord complete primacy to domestic over foreign economic objectives. Like the critics of the left wing, *The Economist* seemed now to believe that domestic expansion should be pursued without regard to the consequences for the foreign balance. It recognized the dangers in this attitude, but professed to see no other alternative:

> May there not be occasions when a country's international trade difficulties are due to mistakes in its policies, and can best be corrected by compelling it to set its internal house in order? May there not be times when an insistence on expansion may merely lead to inflation? There may be substance in these doubts; but they run counter to the economic philosophy which is the deliberate choice of the present generation.[2]

Perhaps the best evidence of the hostile trend in British opinion was the House of Commons debate which followed publication of the *Joint Statement* in the spring of 1944.[3] All the participants were cautious or critical on one or more aspects of the monetary plan. They complained that it would tie sterling too closely to gold; that it made inadequate provision for adjustments by creditor countries; that it would prejudice the maintenance of war-time controls in the sterling area; and that it precluded resort to devices of commercial policy such as Imperial Preference, quantitative restrictions, and bulk purchase. There was no effective defence of the plan from any quarter. Even the members who spoke on its behalf were quick to recite its deficiencies. They emphasized that the Government was only asking approval of the plan as a basis for further discussions. In the opinion of an American Embassy official 'the outstanding psychology of the debate seemed to be, first, the fear that a post-war slump in the United States is inevitable and second, the fear that the United States does not allow Britain and other countries to adopt the necessary measures of self-defence and that, consequently, the United States will drag the whole world with her down into the abyss'.[4]

The financial compromise: British version

In the midst of this widespread criticism virtually the only whole-hearted endorsement of the financial compromise came from Keynes himself. In presenting the *Joint Statement* to the House of Lords he

---

[1] 'The Principles of Trade', cxlvi (1944), p. 137.   [2] Ibid.
[3] 399 H.C. Deb. 1935–2046 (10 May 1944).
[4] Cable sent by Casaday to the Secretaries of State and Treasury (13 May 1944).

spoke out for a fully multilateral system in which sterling could once more be generally convertible. He reproved those whose thinking was running along more restrictive lines:

> To suppose that a system of bilateral and barter agreements, with no one who owns sterling knowing just what he can do with it—to suppose that this is the best way of encouraging the Dominions to centre their financial systems on London, seems to me pretty near frenzy. As a technique of little Englandism, adopted as a last resort when all else has failed us, with this small country driven to autarchy, keeping to itself in a harsh and un-friendly world, it might make more sense. But those who talk this way, in the expectation that the rest of the Commonwealth will throw in their lot on these lines and cut their free commercial relations with the rest of the world, can have very little idea of how this Empire has grown or by what means it can be sustained.[1]

To stem the unfavourable tide of British opinion it was necessary to put the best possible face on the Anglo-American financial com-promise. Keynes placed great emphasis on the matter of liquidity. He acknowledged that the resources of the Fund were not so large as those that would have been made available by the Clearing Union. But, he pointed out, they were still considerable; they would provide a good deal of security in time of need.

> Our own share . . . is £325,000,000, a sum which may easily double, or more than double, the reserves which we shall otherwise hold at the end of the transitional period. The separate quotas of the rest of the sterling area will make a substantial addition to this. Who is so confident of the future that he will wish to throw away so comfortable a supplementary aid in time of trouble?[2]

By counting Britain's quota as part of its reserves Keynes appeared to be suggesting that the Fund's resources would be automatically available. Did he have the support of the Americans for this view? Apparently he thought so. As he had written a few months earlier: 'It was a very great concession on their part, to come round to our view of the Fund as a reserve of resources, entirely passive, except in the more extreme contingencies where countries were running towards the limit of their facilities in one direction or another.'[3]

A second advantage which Keynes claimed for the compromise

[1] 131 H.L. Deb. 840 (23 May 1944).   [2] Id. at col. 841.
[3] Memorandum written by Keynes upon return from the Anglo-American negotia-tions held in the autumn of 1943, quoted in Harrod, p. 570.

monetary plan was the 'scarce-currency' clause. This clause, he had
written the Chancellor of the Exchequer,

puts the creditor country on the spot so acutely that in the view of us all, the
creditor country simply cannot afford to let such a situation arise. . . . If the
Americans really live up to their present proposals it will be the U.S.A. and
not the rest of us which will get into real trouble, if U.S.A. develops a favourable balance of payments which is not adequately disposed of by foreign
lending or in some way.[1]

In short, the primary responsibility for a scarcity of dollars had been
placed on the United States. He made the same assertion to the
House of Lords:

The Americans, who are the most likely to be affected by this, have, of
their own free will and honest purpose, offered us a far-reaching formula of
protection against a recurrence of the main cause of deflation during the
inter-war years, namely, the draining of reserves out of the rest of the world
to pay a country which was obstinately borrowing and exporting on a scale
immensely greater than it was lending and importing. Under clause VI of
the plan a country engages itself, in effect, to prevent such a situation from
arising again, by promising, should it fail, to release other countries from
any obligation to take its exports, or, if taken, to pay for them. I cannot
imagine that this sanction would ever be allowed to come into effect. If by
no other means than by lending, the creditor country will always have to
find a way to square the account on imperative grounds of its own self-
interest.[2]

Encouraged by this interpretation, financial journalists were soon
claiming that the 'scarce-currency' clause 'places on the United States
the responsibility of radically modifying her pre-war trade policy'.[3]

Once he had established the responsibility of the United States for
maintaining equilibrium, Keynes turned to the question of 'whether,
in return, we are surrendering anything which is vital for the ordering
of our domestic affairs . . .'.[4] He reminded his audience that during
the inter-war years he had been an untiring advocate of flexible exchanges, cheap money, and domestic expansion. 'I hope your lord-
ships will trust me not to have turned my back on all I have fought
for.'[5] Far from involving a return to the gold standard, he declared,
the new monetary plan was 'the exact opposite of it'.[6]

In fact, the plan introduces in this respect an epoch-making innovation
in an international instrument, the object of which is to lay down sound

[1] Memorandum of 16 Oct. 1943, quoted in Harrod, p. 571.
[2] 131 H.L. Deb. 842 (23 May 1944).
[3] Oscar Hobson in the *News Chronicle* (4 Aug. 1944).
[4] 131 H.L. Deb. 844 (23 May 1944).   [5] Ibid.   [6] Id. at col. 845.

and orthodox principles, for instead of maintaining the principle that the internal value of a national currency should conform to a prescribed de jure external value, it provides that its external value should be altered if necessary so as to conform to whatever de facto internal value results from domestic policies, which themselves shall be immune from criticism by the Fund.[1]

This appeared to mean that adjustments by debtor nations were to be made by changes in their exchange rates rather than by internal correctives. Is this what the Americans had understood? What authority did Keynes have for stating that domestic policies would be 'immune from criticism'? The Fund Articles provided only that the Fund could not object to a request to depreciate on the grounds of a member's domestic policy; they did not preclude the Fund from observing that a change in domestic policy would make possible the elimination of exchange controls. Moreover, the Articles expressly authorized the Fund to issue reports on the domestic policies of member Governments.[2] There was a danger that British opinion might be badly misled about these facts. Indeed, *The Manchester Guardian* now believed that the Fund management 'will not be allowed to criticize our domestic policy or ask us to change it'.[3] And the *Financial Times* thought that under the compromise plan 'a member country is perfectly free to follow any economic policy it chooses'.[4]

On the question of the transition period Keynes felt able to provide equally comforting assurances. He stressed that the resources of the Fund were 'not intended as daily food for us or any other country to live upon during the reconstruction or afterwards. Provision for that belongs to another chapter of international co-operation, upon which we shall embark shortly unless you discourage us unduly about this one'.[5] In short, the monetary plan was to be followed by a new measure of Anglo-American collaboration to solve Britain's post-war difficulties. Until these difficulties were overcome the British Government remained free to maintain all the necessary economic defences. As Keynes explained,

it is clearly recognized and agreed that, during the post-war transition period of uncertain duration, we are entitled to retain any of those war-time restrictions, and special arrangements with the sterling area and others which are helpful to us, without being open to the charge of acting contrary to any general engagements into which we have entered. Having this assurance, we can make our plans for the most difficult days which will follow

[1] Ibid.
[2] Of course this latter provision was inserted at Bretton Woods after the statement made by Keynes above.   [3] City Editor (24 Apr. 1944).
[4] (22 Apr. 1944).   [5] 131 H.L. Deb. 841–2 (23 May 1944).

the war, knowing where we stand and without risk of giving grounds of offence.[1]

On this matter Lord Keynes was supported by the official British explanation of the *Joint Statement*, which declared that although the Fund might make representations that the time had come for the withdrawal of restrictions, no member was 'committed as to any fixed date for this final removal'. On the contrary, every country was 'entitled to use its own judgment as to when it is strong enough to undertake the free convertibility of its currency . . .'.[2]

There was one last element in the catalogue of assurances that British opinion was demanding about the financial compromise. Suppose Britain accepted the plan—would it be bound in any way in the field of commercial policy? The question was put forward with particular insistency by *The Times*, which was now in the forefront of the advocates of discriminatory and restrictive practices. By way of answer the Chancellor of the Exchequer gave his assurance that 'there is nothing in the plan which will prevent us from entering into reciprocal trade agreements with other countries or groups of countries . . .'.[3] Keynes himself expressed the same view.[4] This apparently meant that the British Government considered itself free to employ bilateralism and discrimination in commercial policy at the same time that it was bound by multilateral undertakings in the financial field. Where, in all this discussion, was the recognition of Britain's solemn obligations under Article Seven? The main lines of Britain's trade policy did not appear, after all, to have been finally determined.

The general character of the British debate was now apparent. It was summed up in a front-page headline in the *Financial News*: 'Sir John Anderson on Monetary Plan—Designed to Aid our Full Employment Policy—Return to Gold not Involved—Way Open for Reciprocal Pacts with Other Countries.'[5] British opinion, still undecided on the feasibility of multilateral trade, had been assured that the financial compromise would not foreclose the issue. As the *Observer* noted, 'The Monetary Fund plan would not cut across special currency arrangements within the sterling area; it would not tie us to gold; and it would not put internal monetary policy at the mercy of the balance of payments position.'[6] In the words of *The*

---

[1] 131 H.L. Deb. 841–2 (23 May 1944), col. 839.
[2] U.K. Treasury, *Joint Statement by Experts on the Establishment of an International Monetary Fund*, Cmd. 6519 of 1944.
[3] Sir John Anderson, 339 H.C. Deb. 2045 (10 May 1944).
[4] Letter to *The Times* (20 May 1944).   [5] (11 May 1944).   [6] (7 May 1944).

Manchester Guardian: 'We are free to maintain exchange control, free to do away with gold except as an accounting device, free to vary our exchange rate, and free to discriminate against the goods of any country which is declared an under-importer.'[1] This emphasis on negative safeguards might facilitate the acceptance of the plan in the United Kingdom. One wondered, however, whether it could provide a sound basis for future Anglo-American financial collaboration.

THE AMERICAN DEBATE

While Britain hung back from ratifying the financial compromise, the American Government pressed eagerly forward. In January 1945 President Roosevelt forwarded to Congress the Articles of Agreement of the Fund and Bank with an appeal for their speedy approval. The American Treasury set in motion a powerful publicity campaign to win support for the two institutions. There was need for its best efforts. The results of Bretton Woods were too technical to arouse widespread public interest. At the same time, opposition to the plans —to the Fund in particular—had already begun to crystallize. This opposition was not broadly based; as we noted earlier, it was provided mainly by a strange alliance of mid-western isolationists and eastern bankers, who opposed the plans for somewhat different reasons. But in the long period between the publication of the monetary plans and the presentation of the Bretton Woods agreements to Congress these groups had been able to agree on several common lines of attack. As the time for decision drew near they provided the Administration with increasing difficulty.

The attack on Bretton Woods

The first major line of attack on the Bretton Woods agreements came on the troublesome question of international liquidity.[2] The critics objected to any plan that would put American resources at the disposal of an international organization in which the United States possessed only minority control. They were particularly hostile to the suggestion that those resources might be freely available without regard to the credit-worthiness or the economic policies of borrowing countries. Robert A. Taft, the conservative Republican

---

[1] (27 Apr. 1944).

[2] In the following discussion we shall concentrate on the criticisms directed against the Fund, since these raised the most critical issues for Anglo-American financial collaboration. By the end of the Bretton Woods debate all but the most implacable critics were willing to accept the Bank.

Senator from Ohio, took the position that the United States was 'putting . . . all the valuable money in the Fund'. Since the United States had only one-third of the voting power, participation in the Fund would mean 'pouring money down a rat hole'.[1] Utah's Senator Elbert Thomas was even more emphatic in expressing contempt for the idea of an international pool of currencies. Brandishing a fistful of foreign moneys during the Senate debate, he challenged any one of his colleagues to 'go downtown in Washington and get his shoes shined with this whole bunch of bills'.[2] The attitude of the banking community was expressed in rather more sophisticated fashion. Its representatives complained that the Fund's liquidity provisions were a derogation of 'sound business principles'. In the private financial world, they explained, the lender himself determined whether and under what conditions to make a loan. In the Fund, on the other hand, 'we should be handing over to an international body the power to determine the destination, time, and use of our money'. In short, the United States would be abandoning, without receiving anything in return, a vital part of its economic bargaining power.[3]

During the Congressional hearings the critics and the defenders of the Fund Agreement had some heated exchanges on this question:

MR. WHITE. And if you say that we are not in control in the sense that we should be in a position to ram down the throats of every other country whatever the opinion of the United States should be, I say that is not in the Fund Agreement, and I say that the representatives of this country at Bretton Woods would be the first to insist that it should not be. After all, the Fund Agreement provides for an international institution, not machinery to impose our views on others.

SENATOR TAFT. I think it is outrageous, because I think in this case this is a question of creditors and debtors. . . . And in this case we are giving our money to a board which is controlled by the debtors, the very fellows who are going to borrow. . . . I do not think anybody has ever proposed to give away American money as this Fund proposes to give it away, to people who themselves will control its disposition.[4]

Allied with the fear that the U.S. Government would have no control over its contribution to the Fund was the fear that the con-

---

[1] 91 *Cong. Rec.* 7573 (16 July 1945).

[2] Ibid. For details on this colourful interlude see 'Senators Wave Greek Drachmas to Show "Minescule" Billions', *The New York Herald-Tribune* (17 July 1945).

[3] American Bankers Association, *Practical International Financial Organization* (1 Feb. 1945).

[4] U.S. Congress, Senate, Committee on Banking and Currency, *Bretton Woods Agreements Act*, Hearings on H.R. 3314, 79th Cong., 1st sess. (June 1945), pp. 125–6.

tribution would achieve none of the intended objectives. Senator Taft complained that he and his fellow-citizens would be 'spending the $6 billion' on the Fund and Bank but 'would not get anything for our money'.[1] In his view the Fund's provisions on exchange rates and exchange restrictions were so loose as to be virtually meaningless. What was there to prevent Fund members from helping themselves to the Fund's resources without taking any step in the direction of multilateral payments? Taft cited Keynes's speech to the House of Lords as evidence that 'so far as the British are concerned they do not propose to change one exchange restriction, one trade restriction, or one sterling area, or anything else in the present machinery they have built up to assure complete discrimination in favor of British trade'.[2] Animated by similar fears, *The New York Times* urged that instead of contributing to an international fund the United States should make 'moderate gold loans' on a bilateral basis in return for 'reforms' such as the abolition of exchange controls and quantitative import restrictions. The loans should be made 'so far as possible . . . by our private investors, who, through their representatives, would be in a much better position diplomatically to insist on sound policies within the borrowing nation than our Government would be'.[3]

In the opinion of the critics, therefore, the Fund was seriously deficient in the responsibilities it placed on debtor nations. What of the responsibilities it placed on the creditors? These were regarded as greatly excessive. Randolph Burgess, President of the American Bankers Association, called the scarce-currency clause 'an abomination of the wicked' because it put 'the whole burden of responsibility on the creditor'.[4] Senator Taft—who considered that 'no international body should have any jurisdiction over the domestic policies of the United States'[5]—regarded the provision as a dangerous threat to American sovereignty. Some of his colleagues even wondered if it did not violate the American Constitution:

SENATOR MILLIKIN. You have developed that when you get to a short dollar position then foreign countries have control over our exports.

MR. HART [*a witness opposing the Bretton Woods agreements*]. Right.

SENATOR MILLIKIN. Well, that is control over our commerce.

MR. HART. Certainly.

SENATOR MILLIKIN. The Constitution lodges that power in Congress.

MR. HART. Certainly.

---

[1] 92 *Cong. Rec.* 7624 (24 Apr. 1946).   [2] 91 *Cong. Rec.* 7572 (16 July 1945).
[3] (1 July 1944).   [4] Senate Hearings, p. 475.   [5] Id., p. 371.

SENATOR MILLIKIN. It might be all right to delegate that to somebody within the United States, to some official organism of this country. It seems to me a very large question is raised when we talk about delegating it to an international body where we have a minority interest.[1]

Thus the Fund's liquidity provisions and its mechanism for adjustment were both subjected to serious criticism. The most powerful attack of all, however, was directed at the inadequacy of the Bretton Woods plans in the post-war transition period. During this period most Fund members would need to rely on exchange controls to maintain equilibrium in their balance of payments. What scope would there be for normal stabilization operations? 'It makes no sense', the critics argued, 'for countries to have both exchange control and access to the Fund. . . . If you are controlling your balance of payments by exchange control you cannot have a deficit, except as a deliberate act of borrowing, and the Fund is not for that purpose.'[2] The Fund could not work effectively until the major reconstruction problems—particularly those of Britain—had been solved. It was premature to adopt the Fund before this solution was even in sight:

The worst bargain we could make, but unfortunately as matters now stand perhaps the easiest, would be to adopt promptly the Bretton Woods agreements in toto but be left with the discriminatory trade and exchange practices and without the bases for genuine co-operative efforts. The essential question is whether we should delay the fund and in the interval find a solution to the British problem or whether we should adopt the fund in the hope that we will understand clearly that a solution of that problem must be found, outside the fund but by methods that are consistent with it. I am afraid, human nature being what it is, that if we leave the matter in the latter way we will not do the job. Our only hope of success is to face the problem squarely now.[3]

This anxiety about the transitional problems of the United Kingdom produced the only constructive alternative to the Bretton Woods agreements: the 'key currency' proposal. It was advanced initially by Professor John H. Williams of Harvard University[4] and was given wider publicity by representatives of the New York financial community such as Winthrop Aldrich and Leon Fraser.[5] In

[1] Senate Hearings, at pp. 377–8.   [2] John H. Williams in Senate Hearings, p. 348.
[3] Williams, 'The Bretton Woods Agreements', Address before the American Academy of Political Science (4 Apr. 1945), reprinted in Senate Hearings, pp. 319–25.
[4] Also Vice-President of the Federal Reserve Bank of New York. Some of his most important articles in favour of the 'key currency' approach are reprinted in *Postwar Monetary Plans* (3rd ed., Oxford, 1949).
[5] Chairman of the Board of the Chase National Bank and President of the First National Bank of New York, respectively.

specific terms it called for a large loan or grant to meet the transitional needs of the United Kingdom, a thorough-going solution to the problem of the sterling balances, and a bilateral stabilization agreement linking the pound and the dollar. The latter would take the lines of the Tripartite Agreement of 1936, except that it would be strengthened to insure co-operation on internal financial policies. Other countries would be invited to join the Anglo-American arrangement as progress was made in reconstruction and the financial problems of the post-war period could be more clearly seen. In short, the 'key currency' approach was designed to achieve the same objectives as the Fund. It was 'less ambitious only in the sense that it is less extensive and more ambitious in the degree of co-operation contemplated'.[1]

The 'key currency' approach provided a valuable reminder that the achievement of multilateralism depended on close Anglo-American collaboration and on the prior solution of Britain's transitional problems. But in its original form it may have understated the need for having a general forum for international economic collaboration. An exclusively Anglo-American arrangement might have conflicted with the demands of other nations to be heard on the subject of monetary policy. It would certainly have conflicted with the desire of the American people for a more general and all-inclusive form of collaboration. In the closing phases of the Bretton Woods debate some of the exponents of the 'key currency' approach appeared to recognize this fact; they urged that their approach should be considered not as an alternative but as a supplement to the Bretton Woods programme.[2] Unfortunately, the breach between Wall Street and the Treasury was so great that no compromise was now possible. As we shall see, the Treasury summarily rejected the 'key currency' proposal and stood firmly on the adequacy of the Bretton Woods institutions in the post-war reconstruction period.

The financial compromise: American version

These major lines of attack had now to be countered by the American Administration. What strategy was to be employed? At first White was prepared to make no concessions. Let the critics complain, for example, that America could not control the Fund's operations; he would admit the fact and take a firm stand on the Fund's international character. But other Administration figures

[1] Williams, 'Currency Stabilization: The Keynes and White Plans', *For. Aff.*, xxi (1943), p. 657.
[2] Williams, 'The Bretton Woods Agreements', Senate Hearings, pp. 319–25.

regarded this approach as impractical. More conservative tactics would have to be used. The Congress would be given assurances that the Fund would operate in accordance with the national interests of the United States.

These assurances were provided in part by the terms of the Bretton Woods Agreements Act. This legislation constituted a major departure from the original conception of a Fund and Bank managed by impartial financial experts rather than representatives of national governments. It subordinated the American Executive Directors to a National Advisory Council on International Monetary and Financial Problems—a Cabinet-level committee chaired by the Secretary of the Treasury and composed of the heads of the interested departments of the American Government. It required the American Director on the Fund to have the Council's approval before voting on any matter on which his approval was necessary under the Fund Articles. It also required him to have the Council's approval before voting for a waiver of the conditions on Fund lending or a declaration that the dollar was a scarce currency. The Director was also enjoined to seek an interpretation by the Fund that its resources could be used only for current monetary stabilization operations and not for 'relief, reconstruction . . . or to meet a large or sustained outflow of capital . . .'.[1] Although similar language was already in the Fund Articles, this put additional pressure on American representatives to oppose the British view that the Fund's lending operations were virtually automatic.

The Bretton Woods Agreements Act was not the only assurance given by the Administration that restrictions would be placed on the use that was made of the Fund's resources. In testimony before Congressional Committees Administration spokesmen specifically rejected the suggestion that the Fund's resources would be automatically available. White declared that the Fund was not mainly designed 'to provide additional exchange resources. Primarily, the Fund is the means for establishing and maintaining stability, order and freedom in exchange transactions'.[2] Thus there could be no thought of unconditional drawing rights. In the words of an official Treasury pamphlet, 'a country's right to assistance from the Fund is contingent upon its adoption of policies in harmony with the purposes of the Fund'.[3] These statements appeased some of the critics, but others

[1] Section 13. 59 Stat. 517 (1945).
[2] 'The Monetary Fund: Some Criticisms Examined', *For. Aff.*, xxiii (1945), pp. 209–10.
[3] U.S. Treasury, *Questions and Answers on the Fund and Bank* (Washington, 1945), p. 8.

PLATE 2

Above: Henry Morgenthau, jr. (*centre*) meets with (*left to right*) Senators Warren Austin, Alben Barkley, and Arthur Vandenberg. *Below*: Morgenthau explains the Fund and Bank plans to the House Banking and Currency Committee

were still concerned about the express provision that a Fund member 'shall be entitled' to purchase currency provided only that the member 'represents that it is presently needed for making in that currency payments which are consistent with the provisions' of the Fund Agreement. A battle royal soon developed about divergent interpretations of this provision:

MR. ACHESON. . . . That does not mean that anyone has a right to walk into this fund and withdraw 25 per cent a year. Nothing could be further from the truth than that concept. It is only if amounts are presently needed for making payments in the currency of the country that he has any right to come in at all.

SENATOR TAFT. That is not what the English says. The English says only that he has to represent that. It doesn't give the board any power to question his representation, and the board has no power to question his representation, Mr. Acheson. And that is the construction and the only reasonable construction to put on the language.

. . . .

MR. ACHESON. There is no idea whatever that a person walks in and goes through the empty formality of saying 'I need this presently to make a payment', and no one can look into it. That would be too childishly absurd.

SENATOR TAFT. Well, Mr. Acheson, it is childishly absurd. It is the whole basis on which this whole thing has been negotiated with these countries.

MR. ACHESON. I assure you that that is not so.[1]

These assurances that the Fund's resources would not be made unconditionally available were matched by equally firm assurances that the Fund would bring tangible benefits in the field of multilateral trade. The Treasury stated without qualification that the establishment of the Fund 'would permit 44 countries to an international agreement to maintain stable exchange rates and to remove exchange controls'.[2] On the subject of exchange stability, White declared that under the Fund Articles 'whatever changes are made in exchange rates will be made solely for the purpose of correcting a balance of payments which cannot be satisfactorily corrected in any

[1] Senate Hearings, p. 45. Similar assurances of a most unambiguous kind were given before the Banking and Currency Committee of the House of Representatives: 'The Committee has been assured, both by the delegates participating in the Bretton Woods Conference, and by bankers and experts in international finance who have studied the documents of the Conference, that the fund's management will have ample power to control the use of its resources and that there is no unqualified right to credits from the Fund. . . . In the words of a prominent banker who testified before the committee, *the quotas are in the nature of a line of credit extended by a bank to its customers, the use of which is circumscribed by safeguards and subject to continual scrutiny.*' Italics supplied. *Participation of the United States in the International Monetary Fund and International Bank for Reconstruction and Development*, H. Rept. No. 629, pp. 52–53.

[2] U.S. Treasury, *Questions and Answers*, p. 10.

other way . . .'.[1] This appeared to mean that internal correctives, not exchange depreciation, would be the normal method of adjustment—an interpretation rather different from the one given by Keynes to British critics. On the subject of exchange control, Acheson promised that the Bank and Fund in and of themselves 'would eliminate the use of some of the most flagrant devices for discriminating against the trade of the United States by other countries'.[2] And an Assistant Secretary of the Treasury went so far as to declare that with the establishment of the Fund *all* restrictions on current transactions would be 'quickly removed in the countries which have not been devastated by the enemy'.[3]

Thus the Administration encouraged the belief that the Bretton Woods agreements would achieve exchange stability and a speedy elimination of exchange restrictions. It was taken for granted that the swift removal of financial controls would be matched by equivalent progress on the commercial side. Congress was certainly not prepared to accept the view that Fund members would be free to replace controls over the transfer of payments with controls over the transfer of goods. Indeed, it felt strongly enough on this score to insert a special provision in the Bretton Woods Agreements Act[4] emphasizing that the financial obligations contained in the Fund Agreement would have to be supplemented by equivalent obligations in the field of commercial policy. Administration spokesmen were no less emphatic. Clayton declared that

the success of the Bretton Woods arrangement . . . depends more on the eventual elimination of trade discriminations and the reduction of trade barriers than any other single thing. The evil practices which Bretton Woods is supposed to correct grew out of the existence of trade discriminations and excessive trade barriers, and these must be corrected; otherwise, any beneficial effect which Bretton Woods might have will be transitory and costly.[5]

Obviously the Administration was placing great emphasis upon the role of the Fund in reforming the economic policies of other countries. It did not put equivalent emphasis on the need for adjustment in American policies. The arguments employed on behalf of the Bretton Woods institutions suggested that they would be valuable mainly as a stimulant to American exports. Morgenthau promised a

[1] 'The Monetary Fund: Some Criticisms Examined', *For. Aff.*, xxiii (1945), p. 199.
[2] 'Statement on Postwar International Economic Problems to a Sub-committee of the Committee on Postwar Economic Policy and Planning of the House of Representatives', *Dept. State Bull.*, xi (1944), p. 656.
[3] John Pehle, *Yale L.J.*, lv (1946), p. 1127.   [4] Section 14.
[5] Letter to Bernard Baruch (26 Mar. 1945), *Clayton Papers*.

group of Detroit industrial leaders that if the Bretton Woods agreements were adopted world trade would be 'freed from restrictive exchange controls and depreciating exchange rates' and the American automobile industry could 'look forward to a standing export market for more than a million cars a year'.[1] The Congress of Industrial Organizations was encouraged to believe that the Fund and Bank would create 5 million additional jobs for American workers.[2] Amid all this discussion little was said about the implications of Bretton Woods for an increase in American imports.

There was still, however, the 'scarce-currency' clause. Did this not establish America's responsibility for reforming its import policy in unmistakable terms? With obvious relish Taft confronted White with Keynes's statement that the clause placed upon the shoulders of the United States the main burden for correcting a disequilibrium in the balance of payments. After reading Keynes's remarks into the record, he asked: 'Now, does that state substantially the results? Do you think it states the result of this conference?'[3] White replied: 'I dislike very much to criticize anything that Lord Keynes has said, because I have a very high regard for his integrity and ability and understanding of the subject. . . . However, I would not have written it that way.'[4] How, then, would he interpret the provision? His answer was already a matter of record:

Very definitely this country assumes no moral responsibility for a scarcity of dollars. The technical representatives of the United States have made it clear to other countries in a number of memoranda that a scarcity of dollars cannot be accepted as evidence of our responsibility for the distortion of the balance of payments. I quote from such a memorandum: 'It should not be overlooked that the disequilibrium in the balance of payments cannot be manifested as a problem peculiar to one country. Whenever the supply of a member country's currency is scarce this scarcity is likely to be accompanied by excessive supplies of the currencies of other countries. In such cases the responsibility for the correction of the maladjustment is not a unilateral one. It will be the duty of the Fund to make a report not only to the country whose currency is scarce but also to the member countries who are exhausting or are using the resources of the Fund in a manner which is not consistent with the purposes of the Fund.'[5]

Now the critics of the Fund had been given assurances on all but one of the major grounds of misgiving. The last, however, proved the

---

[1] *The New York Herald-Tribune* (27 Feb. 1945).
[2] Statement of the Congress of Industrial Organizations, reported in *The New York Times* (4 Feb. 1945).   [3] Senate Hearings, p. 170.   [4] Ibid.
[5] 'The Monetary Fund: Some Criticisms Examined', *For. Aff.*, xxiii (1945), p. 205.

most difficult to deal with. Was it not true that the Bretton Woods institutions were unsuited to deal with the problems of the transition period? Would it not be better to approach these problems in a more modest way by informal arrangements between Britain and the United States?

The Administration made no concessions to objections of this kind. It contended, first of all, that an exclusive system of Anglo-American collaboration would not be desirable. On its face this argument was plausible enough. But in its eagerness to answer the 'key currency' critics the Administration may have overstressed the point. At times it seemed oblivious of the unique role of Britain in the world economy and of the critical importance of Anglo-American collaboration. White, for example, entirely ignored the point that the pound sterling and the dollar were the 'key currencies' in international trade. Instead, he simply noted that the exports and imports of the two countries accounted for less than one-quarter of the world's total and asked: 'Is it of no importance to achieve currency stability in the countries carrying on nearly 75 per cent of world trade among themselves?'[1] Following a similar line, Morgenthau warned against 'a dictatorship of the world's finances by the two countries' and added that 'the problems considered at Bretton Woods are international problems, common to all countries, that can be dealt with only through broad international co-operation'.[2]

This last statement reflected a familiar confusion of thought. A general, all-inclusive international organization might be useful for dealing with some international problems; but others might be dealt with more effectively by nuclear arrangements among the nations principally concerned. The emphasis on Universalism threatened to obscure the fact that an intimate form of Anglo-American collaboration was an essential condition to the revival of multilateral trade. An illustration of this danger could be found in the words of the *New York Times* correspondent who wrote that 'the whole postwar international structure is based upon the concept of multilateralism if not universalism . . . to limit such an important part of the total economic structure as currency stabilization to a few countries would be dramatically opposed to that principle'.[3]

To defend against the 'key currency' critics the Administration found it necessary not only to deprecate the unique importance of

[1] *For. Aff.*, xxiii (1945), p. 206.
[2] 'Bretton Woods and International Co-operation', id., p. 192.
[3] John Crider (18 Feb. 1945).

Anglo-American collaboration but to rebut the suggestion that the Fund and Bank would be helpless instruments in the transition period. Indeed, it had to put great emphasis on the role of the Bretton Woods institutions as instruments of reconstruction. White's deputy, Edward M. Bernstein, declared flatly that if the Fund were not put into operation immediately 'the hope for international monetary cooperation would have to be entirely abandoned. The Fund is essential during the period of transition.'[1] Encouraged by such statements, the Senate Banking and Currency Committee declared that 'the transition may be the time when the Fund is most needed'.[2] On the floor of the Senate a leading Administration supporter warned against the proposal to postpone the Fund's operations, insisting that 'the time to stabilize economic conditions is when they need stabilizing. The time to start to regulate the world's monetary system and assist in the world's reconstruction is now, not after we have returned to normalcy.'[3]

These assertions simply ignored the fact that the successful operation of the Fund depended upon the prior achievement of economic equilibrium. They could be justified, if at all, only by showing that a separate plan was being devised to deal with the reconstruction problem—the plan belonging, as Keynes had promised, 'to another chapter of international co-operation, upon which we shall embark shortly if you do not discourage us unduly about this one'.[4] Was there such a plan? If there was, the Administration denied it. It made no acknowledgement that measures additional to Bretton Woods might be needed. It expected the reconstruction problem to be solved by the International Bank, supplemented by existing measures for relief and a small amount of conventional financing.[5] The proposal for special reconstruction aid to Britain was represented as the undesirable alternative to acceptance of the Fund and Bank. As White explained:

A loan to Britain to enable her to establish exchange stability and freedom from exchange control will not of itself help significantly with Britain's problem, or with the world's problem of establishing a sound postwar pattern of international payments. Such a loan might burden Britain with a dollar debt while making no real contribution towards balancing Britain's

[1] 'A Practical International Monetary Policy', *Am. Ec. Rev.*, xxxiv (1944), p. 784.
[2] *Participation of the United States in the International Monetary Fund and the International Bank for Reconstruction and Development*, Report to Accompany H.R. 3314, 79th Cong., 1st sess., S. Rept. 452 (1945), vol. i, p. 20.
[3] Senator Downey, 91 *Cong. Rec.* 7689–90 (18 July 1945).
[4] 131 H.L. Deb. 841–2 (23 May 1944).   [5] See Chapter IX, *infra*.

international payments. *On the other hand*, the Fund and Bank, by providing for expanding world trade and investment, would be of real help in establishing a sound postwar pattern of international payments and would contribute substantially to prosperity in this country and abroad.[1]

In the final stages of the Bretton Woods debate a number of Congressmen, concerned by the arguments of the 'key currency' critics, asked for more definite assurances about the adequacy of the Fund and Bank in the transition period. They made it clear that Congress would not be sympathetic to another request for large-scale aid.

MR. WOLCOTT. . . . What I am getting at is, are there any other plans that contemplate our rehabilitating Europe or Asia or contributing to the economic rehabilitation of other countries out of the Treasury of the United States? You know what I mean when I say 'out of the Treasury'; I mean direct loans.

MR. ACHESON. So far as I know, there are not.[2]

By assurances of this kind the Congress was encouraged to believe that after passage of the Fund and Bank no additional appropriations would be needed to solve the world's major reconstruction problems.

Congress 'takes a chance'

The Administration had now provided assurances on all the major grounds of misgiving which threatened to impede the passage of the Bretton Woods institutions. How much these assurances influenced the final outcome is by no means clear. When it voted on the Bretton Woods agreements Congress was not mainly concerned with technical economic considerations. The climax of the debate coincided with the end of the Second World War. The United Nations Charter had just been signed at San Francisco; a new era seemed to be dawning. Issues of monetary and financial policy were easily confused with other issues—regionalism and universalism, war and peace, isolationism and internationalism. There was a natural temptation to exploit the temporary enthusiasm for international co-operation and to claim all good things for the Bank and Fund:

MR. SMITH. Do you believe the adoption of the fund proposal, Mr. White, would be a fine thing for the United States?

MR. WHITE. I definitely do, Mr. Smith.

MR. SMITH. Do you believe it would contribute to world peace?

---

[1] Italics supplied. 'The Monetary Fund: Some Criticisms Examined', *For. Aff.*, xxiii (1945), p. 203. Although White insisted that the creation of the Bretton Woods institutions would make special assistance to Britain unnecessary he did not reach the same conclusion with respect to the Soviet Union. See p. 10, *supra*.

[2] U.S. Congress, House, Committee on Banking and Currency, *Bretton Woods Agreements Act*, Hearings on H.R. 2211, 79th Cong., 1st sess. (Mar.–Apr. 1945), vol. i, p. 242.

MR. WHITE. I certainly do.

MR. SMITH. Do you believe that it would create confidence among industrialists to go ahead and plan for the future?

MR. WHITE. I should think it would be a great help in that direction.

MR. SMITH. Do you believe it would create employment and bring prosperity?

MR. WHITE. I do.

. . . .

MR. SMITH. Do you think that we must have this fund?

MR. WHITE. I think we would make a very serious error if we do not have it. I think history will look back and indict those who fail to vote the approval of the Bretton Woods proposals in the same way that we now look back and indict certain groups in 1921 who prevented our adherence to an international organization designed for the purpose of preventing wars.[1]

This last argument made opposition exceedingly difficult. Like White, Morgenthau cast all those who had reservations about Bretton Woods in the role of wilful isolationists and claimed that if the United States failed to ratify the Bretton Woods agreements other countries would be 'convinced that the American people either do not desire to co-operate or that they do not know how to achieve co-operation'.[2] A particularly blunt use of this weapon was made in a pamphlet issued by a private group of artists and writers whom the Treasury had enlisted on the side of the Bretton Woods agreements: 'Less trouble, and less expensive, than building a bomb shelter would be a letter or wire to your Senators and Representatives urging ratification of Bretton Woods. We suggest it, we urge it, as both the privilege and duty of every American citizen who is fed up with war. . . .'[3] The link between Bretton Woods and peace was emphasized most strongly of all by White himself:

MR. PATMAN. . . . Dr. White, if we had adopted something like the Bretton Woods agreements back in the early twenties, and it had worked as you expect this to work, would that have had any effect in preventing the war that we are in now?

MR. WHITE. I think it would very definitely have made a considerable contribution to checking the war and possibly might even have prevented it. A great many of the devices which Germany and Japan utilized would have been illegal in the international sphere, had those countries been participating members. . . .[4]

[1] House Hearings, vol. i, p. 155.
[2] 'Bretton Woods and International Co-operation', *For. Aff.*, xxiii (1945), p. 184.
[3] Writer's War Board, 'Recipe for World War III', reprinted in House Hearings, vol. ii, p. 1331.   [4] House Hearings, vol. i, p. 139.

However exaggerated these arguments may seem in retrospect, they paid rich dividends at the time. The Fund and Bank moved through the Congress on soaring hopes for a better world. There was a good bit of full-blown Senatorial oratory, such as that of Senator Downey, who said he was casting his vote 'to engage American wealth, energy, and our national honor in this epic, pioneering, world-wide movement, the Bretton Woods Agreement'.[1] There were also more sober appeals to idealism, such as Senator Fulbright's answer to the cautious objections of an opposition witness:

> The movements you have suggested are the traditional movements that were utilized in the past 20 to 25 years. There is a general feeling not only in the financial but in the political field that we have tried that system and look at the trouble we are in. Now you are suggesting the traditional way. It is tried . . . there is a feeling that we must do something a little different. . . . There is a tendency to say we must take a chance.[2]

This feeling that 'we must take a chance'—that however imperfect, the Bretton Woods institutions must be tried—played a decisive part in winning final approval. It divided the Republicans against themselves, winning over traditional isolationists like Senator Tobey and leaving the fight against the agreements to irreconcilables like Senator Taft:

SENATOR TOBEY. We have a world that is prostrate. If we are going to live in it ourselves we have got to make some effort to get it back on its feet. There has to be an element of faith, an element of confidence somewhere. That is what we are trying to do here. We can afford to take some chances. I am willing to do it. The risks are small compared to the benefits that will come from this. The world is in extremis. We have got to do something.

SENATOR TAFT. Well, I say that is baloney. It will ruin this country, that kind of doctrine. Every cent we give away must come from the American working man.[3]

By mid-July 1945 the struggle was over. Senator Taft had been effectively isolated from a majority of his own party. Most Republicans had come out in favour of the Fund and Bank. So had the nation's major farm, labour, and civic groups. A number of business and financial spokesmen had endorsed the institutions; those who had been hostile modified their opposition. The Bretton Woods Agreements Act passed the House of Representatives by an over-

---

[1] 91 *Cong. Rec.* 7690 (18 July 1945).
[2] Senate Hearings, p. 314.   [3] Id., p. 37.

whelming majority. In the Senate a last-minute effort to postpone
the Fund was defeated by a vote of 52–31. On 18 July 1945 the
Senate passed the legislation authorizing American participation in
both institutions. The American Congress had decided to 'take a
chance' on Bretton Woods.

CONCLUSION

The British and American Governments had succeeded in drafting
a compromise that appeared to dispose of the major issues dividing
them in the financial policy field. This compromise had been embodied in the two institutions whose charters were completed at
Bretton Woods—the International Monetary Fund and the International Bank for Reconstruction and Development. But the elaboration of detailed rules was by itself no guarantee of Anglo-American
collaboration; the rules would work only if they reflected a genuine
consensus between the two countries on the means by which multilateral payments might be achieved.

As it turned out, the debate on the Bretton Woods agreements
revealed striking differences on some of the major issues. The British
appeared to regard the International Monetary Fund as an automatic
source of credit; the Americans seemed to consider it as a conditional
provider of financial aid. The British emphasized their freedom to
maintain equilibrium by depreciation and exchange control, placing
on creditor countries the main burden of adjustment; the Americans
looked forward to the early achievement of free and stable exchanges,
specifically rejecting the suggesting of any one-sided responsibility
on the United States. Most disquieting of all, the British considered
their adherence to multilateral principles contingent upon bold new
measures of transitional aid; the Americans claimed that the Bretton
Woods institutions would meet Britain's post-war needs and that no
additional measures would be required. Without a meeting of minds
on these matters, it was hard to see how the two institutions could be
made to work.

The magnitude of the difficulty may be appreciated by recapitulat-
ing the situation as it stood in mid-1945. Although the American
Congress had approved the Bretton Woods plans, the British Government still held back. In the absence of adequate measures to bridge
the transitional difficulties, the Bretton Woods programme was regarded with considerable scepticism in the United Kingdom. As *The
Economist* explained:

Public opinion in this country on the subject of Bretton Woods can be divided into three sections. There is one small section, not very heavily represented outside official circles, which likes the Agreement for its own sake. There is another small but very vocal section which will not have it at any price, regardless of the consequences of rejection. The great majority would seem to be in the position of being very doubtful about the wisdom or practicability of the schemes for the Fund and Bank, but conscious of the fact that they are intended to form only a part of a much wider scheme of international economic reconstruction. This being so, it is only common prudence to wait and see what the rest of the structure looks like and whether it is worth paying what may be a heavy price for it. In particular, British action must necessarily wait upon American; Congress must speak before Parliament, for the simple reason that the great unknown in the whole situation is how far the United States is prepared to go in restoring a workable international system.[1]

British acceptance of the financial compromise, in short, depended on the extent to which the United States made new sacrifices to solve the British problem. Did the Bretton Woods debate encourage the hope that these sacrifices would be forthcoming? The answer, unhappily, was in the negative. Professor Williams, the exponent of the 'key currency' approach, was moved to observe:

I sometimes wonder whether the main effect of the Bretton Woods debate has not been to shift the emphasis from the concrete problem, on the solution of which the success of the Bretton Woods agreement must depend, to more formal and abstract solutions which will give us a comfortable feeling of cooperation without the actuality. Perhaps the most unfortunate aspect of the discussion has been that in the heat of debate these two approaches have come to be regarded as alternatives, whereas what we need in the end is both. Some of the Bretton Woods delegates have made disparaging remarks about any form of direct aid to England, and the trend of the hearings . . . has been such as to suggest that if the Bretton Woods agreements are adopted, there will be no direct aid—at any rate not in the form of lend-lease or in the form of a credit on terms which England could afford to accept.[2]

This was the precarious state of Anglo-American financial collaboration as the post-war transition period drew near.

[1] cxlvii (1944), p. 471.
[2] 'The Bretton Woods Agreements', Senate Hearings, p. 324.

CHAPTER VIII

THE COMPROMISE ON COMMERCIAL COLLABORATION

THE months following the visit of the Richard Law mission to Washington in the autumn of 1943 had seen rapid progress in drafting a financial compromise. Events did not move so swiftly in the field of commercial policy. This was no fault of the United States Government, which devoted increasing attention to the subjects that had been discussed in the Anglo-American commercial policy talks. It was on the other side of the Atlantic that progress struck a serious snag. After the Law mission returned from Washington, an official summary of the commercial policy talks was circulated to the interested Ministers. It produced a mixed reaction. Some Ministers supported further discussions with the Americans—among them, Anderson, Eden, Dalton, and Law. Others, however, were extremely critical. Amery objected to any compromise on the subject of Imperial Preference, while Hudson feared the implications of the multilateral programme for policies of agricultural protection. Beyond the opposition of these traditional critics, there were increasing misgivings from those concerned with the post-war balance of payments. 'Grave concern is felt here', an official of the American Embassy reported, 'regarding the absence as yet of any specific measures to fill the gap between the end of Lend-Lease and the re-establishment of British export trade, and such absence makes prohibitions of quantitative controls appear to be an ideal which is remote and academic.'[1] All these factors delayed the resumption of the Anglo-American talks until the beginning of 1945. It was not till then that work began again on the drafting of a commercial compromise.

NEGOTIATING THE COMMERCIAL COMPROMISE

The compromise on commercial policy was worked out in two separate stages. First, there were informal talks in London during the first half of 1945 between officials of the American Embassy and representatives of the Board of Trade. Second, there were commercial policy negotiations in Washington beginning in September 1945

---

[1] Telegram from Bucknell to the Secretary of State (13 May 1944), *White Papers*.

and culminating in the publication of the 'Proposals for Consideration by an International Conference on Trade and Employment'.[1] Although the latter negotiations occurred after the surrender of Japan and as part of broader negotiations on Britain's transitional problem, they may properly be considered as part of the war-time planning for post-war commercial collaboration. For they followed the general pattern established in 1943 and drew heavily upon the preparatory work done in London earlier in the year.

Unfortunately, the circumstances attending the publication of the 'Proposals' were not designed to make these facts clear. Publication of the document was delayed to coincide with publication of the Anglo-American Financial Agreement, so that the American Government could claim the 'Proposals' as one of the benefits received in return for the loan to Britain and the writing-off of Lend-Lease. Moreover, the British Government was unwilling for reasons of domestic politics to appear as co-sponsor of the 'Proposals'. Instead, it simply stated that it was 'in full agreement on all important points in these proposals and accepts them as a basis for international discussions; and it will, in common with the United States Government, use its best endeavours to bring such discussions to a successful conclusion, in the light of views expressed by other countries'.[2]

The implications of the decision to present the 'Proposals' as an American document and to link them with the granting of financial aid will be discussed in a later chapter. Here we shall be concerned only with the main lines of the commercial compromise itself—in particular, with the three central issues we discussed in connexion with the 1943 talks.

The employment issue

The 'Proposals for Consideration by an International Conference on Trade and Employment' consisted of two parts—'Proposals Concerning Employment' and 'Proposals Concerning an International Trade Organization'. The separate and equal status of the employment provisions indicated the importance which the subject was accorded in the Anglo-American negotiations. The provisions them-

---

[1] These were published by the U.S. Department of State as part of a more inclusive document, *Proposals for the Expansion of World Trade and Employment*, Dept. of State Pub. 2411 (Washington, 1945). The term 'Proposals' when used in the text refers only to the principles agreed to in the Anglo-American negotiations.

[2] *Anglo-American Financial and Commercial Agreements*, Dept. of State Pub. 2439 (Washington, 1945), p. 3.

selves reflected a large measure of agreement between the two countries
on the importance of coupling the reduction of trade barriers with
complementary measures in the employment field. It was stated
that the attainment and maintenance of 'approximately full employment' by the major industrial and trading nations was 'essential to
the expansion of international trade' and 'to the full realization of
the objectives of all liberal international agreements'. On the other
hand, it was also stated that domestic programmes to expand employment 'should be consistent with realization of the purposes of
liberal international agreements and compatible with the economic
well-being of other nations'. Beyond these general principles, several
'undertakings' were envisaged in the employment field. Each country
would agree to 'take action designed to achieve and maintain full
employment within its own jurisdiction, through measures appropriate to its political and economic institutions'. It would also agree
not to 'seek to maintain employment through measures which are
likely to create unemployment in other countries or which are incompatible with international undertakings designed to promote an
expanding volume of international trade and investment in accordance with comparative efficiencies of production'. Finally, it would
agree to participate, under the aegis of the United Nations Economic
and Social Council, in the collection, analysis, and exchange of information on employment problems; to consult regularly on the
subject; and to participate in special conferences in case of a threat of
widespread unemployment.[1]

Taken together, these provisions on employment were among the
least satisfactory of the provisions in the Anglo-American compromise. Yet they probably embodied the highest level of agreement
that could be achieved between the two Governments. Certainly they
went as far as the United States negotiators dared to go. After all,
the American Congress had rejected the specific 'full-employment'
commitments in the Full Employment Act of 1945. From the point
of view of the United Kingdom, on the other hand, the provisions on
employment probably represented the very minimum that could be
accepted. British opinion was now profoundly impressed with the
need for action in this field. It could hardly be expected to look with
approval on plans for a trade charter that did not contain employment commitments of some kind. But there was a more basic reason
why the employment provisions in the 'Proposals' were vague and

---

[1] 'Proposals Concerning Employment', *Proposals*, pp. 9–10.

loosely drawn. The truth of the matter was that neither Government had any well-developed views on how the employment problem could usefully be handled in any international agreement.

The issue of quantitative restrictions

In the 1943 commercial policy talks the British and American negotiators had agreed on the principle that quantitative restrictions should be prohibited. They had also agreed on a major exception to this principle—that such restrictions might be employed to safeguard the balance of payments. The 'Proposals' now included both the principle and the exception, stating that quantitative restrictions could be used 'as an aid to the restoration of equilibrium in the balance of payments'. Detailed criteria to govern the use of these restrictions were to be agreed upon at a later date.

Meanwhile certain general principles were laid down. Quantitative restrictions would be permitted during a post-war transition period of unspecified duration. During this time they were to be governed by principles that would 'promote the maximum development of multilateral trade' and that 'in no event would be more restrictive of such trade' than the principles applicable to the use of financial restrictions under the transitional provisions of the Articles of Agreement of the International Monetary Fund. The length of the transition period was to be determined by a procedure analogous to that provided in the transitional provisions of the Fund Articles. After the transition period, restrictions were to be non-discriminatory, except when this rule 'would have the effect of preventing a member from utilizing inconvertible currencies for buying needed imports'.[1]

These provisions were sufficiently general to accommodate very different views on the proper scope of quantitative restrictions under the balance of payments exception. What, for example, would be the nature of the criteria of balance of payments difficulties to be later agreed upon? The United States was of the opinion that quotas should be employed only 'to prevent the aggravation of a seriously adverse balance-of-payment position'.[2] The British would probably want greater freedom than this. At the same time, the permission to discriminate in order to use inconvertible currencies—without any fixed time limit—represented a considerable departure from the rule

---

[1] 'Proposals Concerning an International Trade Organization', Chapter III, Section C, *Proposals*, pp. 13–15.

[2] 'Summary of the Interim Report of the Special Committee on Relaxation of Trade Barriers' (8 Dec. 1943), reprinted as App. 45, Notter, p. 622.

of non-discrimination that had been envisaged in 1943. It was likely that the Americans would seek to achieve a narrower definition of this exception.

In general the provisions covering the use of quantitative restrictions for balance of payments purposes seemed to contemplate a code of behaviour no less strict than that provided in the Fund Agreement with respect to exchange controls. This appeared to be the barest minimum that would satisfy the American Government. Considerable domestic criticism had greeted the relatively loose transitional provisions of the Fund, and it was likely that at a future date the American Government would seek to apply more stringent rules in the commercial field. For Britain, on the other hand, the formula appeared to strain domestic opinion to the breaking point. The British debate on the Bretton Woods plans had revealed a strong desire to maintain a freer hand in commercial policy than the Fund Agreement permitted on the financial side. The existing Anglo-American consensus might be seriously jeopardized if an effort were made to spell out in greater detail the terms of the balance of payments exception.

To complicate matters further, another troublesome exception to the general ban on quantitative restrictions emerged from the 1945 negotiations. In the informal conversations two years earlier no special let-out had been envisaged on behalf of agricultural producers. But in both countries agriculture had greatly expanded during the war years; it was hardly practicable to expect that this sector of the two economies could be placed suddenly at the mercy of world market forces. The American Administration was now committed to price-support programmes for certain basic agricultural products. Since these programmes involved maintaining domestic prices above world market levels, their effective operation required restrictions against lower-cost foreign production. This fact, as we have seen, was already recognized in the Agricultural Adjustment Act, which authorized the President to employ quantitative restrictions on agricultural imports to protect certain domestic price-support programmes. Accordingly, when the question of quantitative restrictions was reached in the 1945 negotiations, the United States Department of Agriculture insisted on a provision authorizing the use of such restrictions. The result was a special exception permitting countries to impose quantitative restrictions on agricultural imports not only in conformity with international commodity agreements but also when necessary to the enforcement of national price-support schemes.[1]

Fortunately for the cause of multilateralism this exception was surrounded with a number of significant limitations. Import quotas on agricultural commodities were permitted only where necessary to the enforcement of domestic programmes which restricted the output or marketing of like products or provided for the disposal of temporary surpluses. Quotas employed in conjunction with domestic restrictions were not to operate in such a way 'as would reduce imports relatively to domestic production as compared with the proportion prevailing in a previous representative period, account being taken in so far as practicable of any special factors which may have affected or which may be affecting the trade in the product concerned'.[2] An important check was thus achieved on the resurgent forces of agricultural protection. It remained to be seen, however, whether this check could be permanently maintained.

The tariff-preference issue

The subject of tariffs and preferences was perhaps the most critical issue in the Anglo-American negotiations. We noted that in the 1943 discussions the representatives of both countries favoured the adoption of an automatic method of reducing tariffs according to a pre-arranged formula, provided such a formula could be worked out to their mutual satisfaction. The British had indicated that such an approach was essential if they were to participate wholeheartedly in a convention eliminating preferences and prohibiting other forms of discrimination. The increasing scepticism of British opinion toward multilateralism in the period after the 1943 talks only reinforced this view. More than ever the responsible officials in Whitehall sought an acceptable formula that would insure a drastic levelling of American tariffs. As Penrose puts it: 'In 1945 the British negotiators pressed the advantages of such an approach even more vigorously than they had done in 1943. They considered that the success of the whole venture depended on its adoption and were more emphatic than ever on the inadequacy of the machinery of bilateral trade pacts to give effect to the obligations in Article VII of the Lend-Lease agreement.'[3]

---

[1] Chapter III, Section C, 1, e.   [2] Ibid.
[3] Op. cit., p. 106. Penrose was a leading participant in the preliminary negotiations on the 'Proposals' in London during the early months of 1945.

On this subject, however, events in Washington had been tending in another direction. Although the American experts had agreed in principle on the desirability of an across-the-board method of tariff reduction, they found increasing opposition to this plan at higher levels in the Administration. In the closing months of 1944 a proposal for automatic reduction by prearranged formula was still included in American drafts of a convention on commercial policy. In the winter of 1944–45, however, this proposal was finally rejected, on the grounds that it could not possibly prove acceptable to the American Congress. When it came to the decisive test the Administration's promises of a bold foreign economic programme were quickly dissipated by the hard domestic political realities.

The impact of this event on the development of British commercial policy can hardly be overestimated. Once again the words of Penrose tell the story:

> The final rejection in Washington of any attempt at a bold handling of tariff reduction by a single stroke was a great disappointment to Whitehall. A leading official told Mr. Hawkins and me that the abandonment of this approach would end all his hopes of achievement. . . . Without this he believed that the British would go into any other approach with no heart and without expectation that much would come of it.[1]

In place of the across-the-board method of tariff reduction the American Administration decided to retain the traditional system of bilateral bargaining for the selective reduction of individual tariff rates. It planned only one major departure from recent practice. Instead of entering into bilateral negotiations separately with a number of countries, the American Government was prepared to negotiate for tariff reductions at a large conference in which many pairs of bilateral negotiations could be carried on simultaneously. This 'multilateral-bilateral' method of negotiation would enable participating countries to make reductions not just on the basis of concessions offered to them directly but on the basis of concessions gained indirectly through the operation of the unconditional most-favoured-nation clause. The Anglo-American commercial compromise of 1945 was drafted on the basis of this approach.

Although the discussions of 1945 now occurred in the context of selective rather than across-the-board tariff reductions, the American Government was no less firm on the subject of the elimination of Imperial Preference. Cordell Hull had retired from the Department

[1] Id., p. 107.

of State, but his vigorous attitude on preferences was still shared by a large number of American officials—in particular, by Will Clayton, the new Assistant Secretary of State for Economic Affairs, who had charge of the American side of the commercial policy negotiations in Washington.[1] Clayton felt strongly that Britain had been committed to the elimination of Imperial Preference by Article Seven of the Mutual Aid Agreement; now he sought unequivocal recognition of this fact in the 'Proposals'. The British negotiators did not object to this demand on the level of principle. But in view of the American rejection of the across-the-board method of tariff reduction they had very great doubts that sufficient concessions would ever be offered in practice to justify the elimination of Imperial Preference. According to Penrose, who was in a position to know the British view on this score, 'there was never at any time even a remote chance that preferences would be abolished in return merely for a group of bilateral agreements to reduce tariffs on selected commodities'.[2]

The formula eventually adopted in the 'Proposals' maintained the general commitment contained in Article Seven but left the final terms of the tariff-preference settlement rather obscure:

> In the light of the principles set forth in Article VII of the Mutual Aid Agreements, members should enter into arrangements for the substantial reduction of tariffs and for the elimination of tariff preferences, action for the elimination of tariff preferences being taken in conjunction with adequate measures for the substantial reduction of barriers to world trade, as part of the mutually advantageous arrangements contemplated in this document.[3]

Certain aspects of this formula should be particularly noted. On the one hand, the United States secured specific recognition that 'preferences' were to be eliminated. This reinforced the language of Article Seven, which had used the more inclusive term 'discriminatory treatment'. On the other hand, the United Kingdom secured a number of major qualifications—it was committed only to 'enter into arrangements for' certain action—there was no question, therefore, of the immediate abandonment of the Preference system. Elimination of preferences was to take place only in conjunction with 'adequate measures' for the 'substantial reduction'—not just of tariffs—but of

---

[1] Details of Clayton's views on foreign economic policy are given in Chapter X, *infra*.   [2] Op. cit., p. 102.

[3] 'Proposals Concerning an International Trade Organization', Chapter III, Section B, 1.

all 'barriers to world trade'. Moreover, the final settlement was to be 'mutually advantageous'. Thus the 'Proposals' embodied a formula which took account of all the major British reservations.

In addition to this general commitment, the 'Proposals' contained more specific provisions on the tariff-preference issue. First, existing agreements with the Dominions were not to stand in the way of action with respect to tariff preferences. Second, reductions in tariffs were automatically to reduce or eliminate margins of preference. Third—and perhaps most important—margins of preference were in no cases to be increased and no new preferences were to be introduced. In the view of the Americans, these three commitments would serve to confine and eventually to eliminate the Imperial Preference system.

One final aspect of the tariff-preference compromise was of considerable importance. The Americans succeeded in including a provision for an escape clause similar to the one which they had begun to insert in their reciprocal trade agreements during the war.[1] In the words of the 'Proposals', this clause would be inserted in undertakings 'with regard to tariffs' and would permit countries to take 'temporary action to prevent sudden and widespread injury to the producers concerned'.[2] From the wording of this provision it was doubtful that the escape clause could also be invoked on behalf of producers hurt by the reduction of tariff preferences.[3] If this were the case, the provision would represent a further recognition of the American position that there was a fundamental distinction between the two kinds of trade barriers.

THE ANGLO-AMERICAN REACTION

The main outlines of an Anglo-American compromise on commercial policy were now embodied in the 'Proposals' of 1945. The wide measure of agreement that had been achieved on these difficult issues provided a good augury for the future of collaboration between the two countries. But to this general statement there would have to be one important qualification. On several critically important matters major differences had arisen. These differences stemmed less, perhaps, from genuine differences of view between the negotiators themselves than from political difficulties on both sides of the Atlantic.

---

[1] The origin of the American escape clause is discussed *infra*, p. 159.
[2] Chapter III, Section B, 3.
[3] I.e., producers in the country *receiving* the preference whose margin had been reduced.

The differences might be overcome in time if the two Governments could establish an intimate form of collaboration and proceed in a manner that would not inflame domestic opinion. Unfortunately, the American Government appeared to believe that commitments on controversial matters of commercial policy should be spelled out in great detail in formal international instruments. This approach would produce lengthy written agreements which might give the appearance of a consensus between the two countries but which would make no contribution toward reconciling their fundamental differences. Indeed, the attempt to draft detailed statements of principles might even produce a hardening of positions and set back the prospects for a long-term settlement. The dangers inherent in this method were already becoming apparent in the discussions of the tariff-preference issue on both sides of the Atlantic.

The commercial compromise: British version

The Bretton Woods debate had provided strong indications that British opinion, even if it could be brought to favour participation in the Fund and Bank, would demand a larger measure of freedom to depart from multilateralism on the commercial side. There was no blinking the fact that increased support had emerged for bilateral and discriminatory policies. One symptom of the trend was the revival of sentiment in favour of Imperial Preference. As we noted earlier, the years just preceding the Second World War had witnessed a certain disenchantment with the working of the arrangements made at Ottawa. There was a general willingness to contract the Preference system provided that suitable concessions in other markets could be secured in return. During the war, however, this attitude seemed to lose ground. It was no longer clear that British opinion would sanction—under any foreseeable circumstances—a radical change in the Imperial Preference system.

In this revival of sentiment for Imperial Preference at least three factors seem to have been at work. First, there was the growing preoccupation with the problem of the post-war balance of payments, which, it was argued, the elimination of Imperial Preference would only aggravate. Second, there was the linking of Preference elimination with the receipt of American aid, which roused against multilateralism the powerful sentiment of national pride. Finally, there was the resurgence of Imperial sentiment as the result of the war. How this factor influenced moderate thinking on the Preference issue is illustrated by the following passage, written by a scholar who had shown little previous interest in maintaining the Ottawa system:

[I]n the fateful summer of 1940 ... when I was myself at sea, I heard over the wireless that a British tanker had been torpedoed and its crew of West Indian sailors wiped out by fire. This was at a time when the Neutrality Act still kept American ships away from our dangerous waters. I remember thinking, 'This news rather changes ideas about Imperial Preference. I have always discussed it as a problem of international economic policy, but now I see that it is also a problem of our own brotherly affection and duty. West Indians are our comrades in war. Can we deny them our comradeship in peace. If they offer us their very lives, can we refuse them an extra penny or two of preference on their sugar?'[1]

How all these factors were working to revive Preference sentiment was revealed in the House of Commons debate on Empire and Commonwealth Unity in the spring of 1944. A remarkable sympathy was expressed for the Ottawa system on both sides of the House. Although the Labour Party had shown little interest during the pre-war years in fostering Imperial ties, it was none other than Emanuel Shinwell, a left-wing Socialist, who began the debate by moving that 'the United Kingdom should do its utmost by close co-operation and regard for the different points of view of the nations of the Commonwealth to preserve in time of peace the unity of purpose and sentiment which has held them together in time of war'.[2] What this meant in economic terms was indicated by another leading Labour figure, the President of the Board of Trade. Dalton had taken a sympathetic view of the commercial policy negotiations with the United States, but he dispelled any notion that he regarded Imperial Preference as a minor matter that could be lightly bargained away. 'I think it is generally agreed in all parts of the House', he said, 'that Imperial Preference has been of quite definite value both to us and the Dominions.'[3] Observing the widespread support for Imperial Preference among representatives of both major parties *The Economist* concluded that 'there is no chance that the British Parliament would consent to the abolition of the system of Imperial Preference save possibly as part of a very large reconstruction of international trade involving concessions of other countries far larger than any that are yet in prospect'.[4]

[1] W. K. Hancock, *Empire in the Changing World* (New York, 1943), pp. 103–4.
[2] 399 H.C. Deb. 390 (20 Apr. 1944).
[3] Id., col. 481.   [4] cxlvi (1944), p. 564.

The publication of the 'Proposals' at the end of 1945 did not find any lessening of interest in the defence of the Preference system. The prospects for elimination of Preference had, if anything, become less favourable. The influence of the Beaverbrook faction was more powerful in Conservative Party councils—indeed, the official Conservative manifesto in the election campaign of 1945 had urged 'the closest possible concert' with other parts of the Commonwealth including 'mutually advantageous arrangements . . . to foster Imperial trade'.[1] The Labour Government which took office unexpectedly in July was wary of any removal of trade controls that might complicate its reconstruction plans. For the most part, discussions of post-war trade policy occurred as if no commitment in Article Seven had ever existed. The *Observer* even went so far as to remark: 'Soviet Russia is committed to State-trading; the United States to non-discriminatory private trading; Britain to discriminatory bilateralism, of which the Ottawa system is the outstanding example.'[2]

In these circumstances the publication of the tariff-preference formula contained in the 'Proposals' could not be expected to have a very favourable reception. The debate on the Anglo-American Financial Agreement in December 1945 indicated that Parliament would not permit the elimination or even the substantial reduction of Imperial Preference—at least not in return for any counter-concessions that the United States was likely to make. Moreover, the suggestion that tariffs and preferences constituted different orders of 'evil' in international trade aroused widespread resentment among commentators on all sides. Lord Croft, a traditional supporter of Imperial Preference, was so incensed by the 'Proposals' that he was moved to describe them as 'the Boston Tea Party in reverse' and 'an interference with the freedom of our own country to manage its own affairs, an interference that I regard as unparalleled in the history of the world'.[3] But what was really surprising were the objections expressed from another quarter. Lord Lindsay of Birker spoke for many of his Socialist colleagues when he declared:

I am not a friend or an adherent of Colonial preference. That no doubt is a dreadful thing to confess, but it is true that I am not. But it perhaps makes it all the more emphatic when I say that when I heard Americans making snooty remarks about that poor little preference of ours, I thought it was the limit, and I still think so. . . .[4]

---

[1] *Mr. Churchill's Declaration of Policy to the Electors* (London, 1945).
[2] 'World Trade Talks May Be Abandoned' (5 Aug. 1945).
[3] 138 H.L. Deb. 754 (17 Dec. 1945).   [4] Id., cols. 838–9.

The central provision in the 'Proposals' concerning the tariff-preference issue was that which pledged the countries to negotiate for the 'reduction' of tariffs and the 'elimination' of preferences. The United States regarded the distinction between 'reduction' and 'elimination' as fundamental and considered it a major accomplishment to have embodied it once more in a formal agreement with the United Kingdom. But it was precisely this distinction that was considered inadmissible by a large number of Parliamentary spokesmen. Oliver Lyttleton complained, for example, that the wording of the 'Proposals' was 'unfortunate' because it would lead the ordinary reader to suppose that 'we might find ourselves in a situation where tariffs were reduced and Imperial Preferences eliminated. That is a situation in which we should not get . . . '.[1] To quiet misgivings on this score Sir Stafford Cripps, the new President of the Board of Trade, cited the qualifications that had been inserted by the British negotiators and gave assurances that the British Government was 'absolutely at liberty' to attach to the elimination of preferences whatever conditions it pleased.[2] He emphasized that if a British negotiator were asked by the Americans to eliminate a preference he could say 'I cannot do it unless you reduce your tariffs by 100 per cent.'[3] Lord Pakenham, introducing the 'Proposals' in the House of Lords, took a similar line. He reminded his colleagues that at the English Bar a barrister could 'never refuse a brief' but could 'mark it with an impossible fee'. In the case of preferences, he said, 'an almost prohibitive fee might be imposed'.[4] Perhaps the most comprehensive statement of the British attitude on the tariff-preference formula was given by Churchill, now Leader of the Opposition:

Some have said that the United States might make what looked like a substantial reduction of tariffs already so high as to be prohibitive, and that then, although those tariffs still remain an effective barrier against our exports to America, we should be obliged to abandon or reduce our present preference. I could not agree with that view. On this side of the House we reserve the unlimited right of free judgment upon the issue as it appears, when definite, concrete proposals are put before us. *It is, therefore, in my view, quite untrue to say that we are at this time being committed by the Government to any abandonment of Imperial Preference and still less to its elimination.* Of course, if we find ourselves in the presence of proposals to effect a vast sweeping reduction of tariffs and trade barriers and restrictions all over the world of a character to give great exporting power to this

---

[1] 417 H.C. Deb. 577–8 (13 Dec. 1945). [2] Id., col. 492.
[3] Id., cols. 489–90. [4] 138 H.L. Deb. 744 (17 Dec. 1945).

island . . . if we are faced with that, then, undoubtedly we should have to do justice. . . . *I cannot see that there is the slightest justification for suggesting that we are compromised and fettered in any way in respect of Imperial Preference.*[1]

It was evident from these comments that British opinion was not prepared to eliminate Imperial Preference except in return for a very substantial *quid pro quo*—in Churchill's words—'a vast sweeping reduction of tariffs and trade barriers and restrictions all over the world'. The prospects for such a development would depend very largely on the post-war trade policy that was already emerging on the other side of the Atlantic.

The commercial compromise: American version

The winter of 1944–45 was an important period in the evolution of the post-war commercial policy of the United States. Some particularly important decisions were taken with respect to the problem of tariff reduction. As we noted earlier, the Administration rejected the idea of an across-the-board reduction according to a prearranged formula and decided instead to negotiate with other nations within the framework of the Reciprocal Trade Agreements Act. To bolster its leadership in the direction of more liberal trade policies it requested Congress to grant additional authority to reduce tariffs to 50 per cent. of their existing levels.[2]

For a number of reasons this plan was not likely to result in the kind of widespread tariff reduction which British opinion regarded as the essential condition for the elimination of Imperial Preference. To begin with, even if reductions were made to the full extent of the new authority, many American tariff rates would remain at prohibitive levels. More important than this quantitative limitation was the broad philosophy of the Reciprocal Trade Agreements Act. This Act, as we noted earlier, was designed to increase American exports.[3] In coming to Congress for periodic renewals of the legislation the Administration was usually required to demonstrate that the trade agreements made under its authority had facilitated an expansion of American exports at least equivalent to the expansion of imports from other countries. It was also required to show that no domestic industry had been seriously injured. During the war the Administra-

---

[1] Italics supplied. 417 H.C. Deb. 723–4 (17 Dec. 1945).

[2] The 1934 Act had empowered the President to reduce tariffs to 50 per cent. of the then existing levels; this authority had been exhausted on a wide range of duties.

[3] See p. 21, *supra*, and the excerpts from the Act there quoted.

tion had devised an escape clause to remove Congressional anxieties in the latter regard. This clause permitted parties to trade agreements to withdraw concessions which resulted in serious injury to domestic producers.[1] Thus—even when reinforced by the additional grant of authority—the Reciprocal Trade Agreements Act could facilitate only limited and selective reductions in the American tariff.

These inhibiting factors were strengthened by the assurances which the Administration gave to Congress in seeking the additional powers to reduce tariffs in the spring of 1945. In order to persuade Congress to grant these powers, the Administration found it necessary to promise that all future trade agreements would contain an escape clause designed to protect domestic producers.[2] President Truman gave an undertaking that the new authority would not be used to endanger any segments of American industry, agriculture, or labour.[3] Edward R. Stettinius, the new Secretary of State, provided additional assurances that it would

work no fundamental change in the principle of the existing law, nor will it change in any way the administration of the law as it was established by the Congress in 1934. It was the intention of the Congress in the original law that trade agreements should be employed to expand our foreign trade by a process of hard-headed and business-like bargaining. The Act has been administered in strict accord with this purpose and it will continue to be administered in that way.[4]

These statements did not provide a hopeful augury for the achievement of the ambitious plans for the revival of multilateral trade. Could not the Administration have taken a bolder line? Did not the circumstances of 1945 offer a unique opportunity for a liberal reform in American commercial policy? The war had brought great prosperity to American agriculture and industry; there was little immediate prospect of competition from foreign producers; there was the general war-time disposition to make sacrifices for a better post-war world. All this is true; but it is easy in retrospect to underestimate the difficulties. Without a conservative approach to tariff reduction

[1] The escape clause was first inserted in the trade agreement with Mexico in 1942.

[2] See the explicit reference to this undertaking in U.S. Congress, House, Committee on Ways and Means, *Foreign Trade Agreements*, Report to Accompany H.R. 3242, H.Rept., 594, 79th Cong., 1st sess. (1945), p. 9.

[3] U.S. Congress, Senate, Committee on Finance, *1945 Extension of the Reciprocal Trade Agreements Act*, Hearings on H.R. 3240, 79th Cong., 1st sess. (May–June 1945), p. 7.

[4] U.S. Congress, House, Committee on Ways and Means, *1945 Extension of the Reciprocal Trade Agreements Act*, Hearings on H.R. 2652 superseded by H.R. 3240, 79th Cong., 1st sess. (Apr.–May 1945), p. 10.

the Administration might have obtained nothing at all. A number of influential business and labour groups, not to mention the majority of Republican Congressmen, opposed even the additional grant of tariff-reducing authority; indeed, this authority was removed from the legislation by the Senate Finance Committee and was only restored when the legislation reached the Senate floor. The difficult struggle to secure renewal of the Act in its amended form suggests that nothing very much more ambitious could have been achieved.

If there is one aspect of the Administration's policy that can be criticized it is not its conservative line on tariff reduction but its over-optimistic view of the contribution to multilateralism that the available reduction would be able to make. Clayton appeared to believe that the Administration's new power to reduce tariffs was so significant that it would bring about a radical alteration in Britain's foreign economic policy. He made much of this point in defending the Trade Agreements Act before the American Congress:

SENATOR MCMAHON. England, of course, is operating with sterling blocs. Is it your opinion we would be able to break through that system if we adopted this Act?

MR. CLAYTON. I think that if we had this Act and the Bretton Woods instruments steps can be taken that will, within a reasonable time, change that whole picture.[1]

On the subject of Imperial Preference Clayton also maintained a confident line—even in the face of disturbing statements from across the Atlantic:

MR. KNUDSON. My attention has been called to a statement made by Mr. Churchill that they would no more change the Imperial Preferences than we would abolish the tariff. How about that?

MR. CLAYTON. Well, wise men often change their minds.[2]

The net impression left by this and other testimony was that the new tariff-reducing authority might induce the United Kingdom to liquidate the Imperial Preference system. This was a comforting assumption. It would be unfortunate, however, if it failed to stand up on the day of reckoning.

CONCLUSION

The United States and Britain had now reached a compromise on commercial as well as financial policy. This compromise was

[1] Senate Hearings, p. 38.   [2] House Hearings, p. 37.

embodied in the 'Proposals for Consideration by an International Conference on Trade and Employment' published in November 1945. In this document the two Governments expressed their agreement on a number of controversial issues. Among these were the relation of trade and employment policy, the regulation of quantitative restrictions, and the reduction of tariffs and the elimination of preferences.

For the most part the formulae in the 'Proposals' were well suited to the degree of consensus that existed between the two Governments. But in at least one case—that of tariffs and preferences—the United States had sought to achieve a degree of precision greater than the degree of underlying agreement. Developments during 1945 indicated that there were very different interpretations of this formula on the two sides of the Atlantic. Moreover, the formula had already caused a widespread reaction against the 'Proposals' in British opinion.

But it was not yet time to become concerned with these problems of long-term policy. The transition to multilateralism had still to be negotiated. It is to this critical matter that we must now turn.

PART III

THE TRANSITION TO MULTILATERALISM

PART IV

THE TRANSMISSION OF
VULTERALISM

CHAPTER IX

THE RISE AND FALL OF WAR-TIME COLLABORATION

NATIONAL policy is rarely influenced as much by impressive blue-prints for future action as by daily expedients contrived to cope with current problems. The course of Anglo-American economic relations at the end of the Second World War provides an excellent illustration of this fact. Looking back from our present vantage point we can see that the measures adopted to bridge the transition from war to peace did more to influence the quest for multilateralism than all the planning in advance of permanent institutions for post-war collaboration. Our history would be incomplete, therefore, if it did not attempt to tell the story of the post-war transition period. This story properly begins with the system of war-time economic collaboration, the early planning for the post-war transition, and the disintegration of collaboration that accompanied the sudden end of the Second World War.

THE SYSTEM OF WAR-TIME ECONOMIC COLLABORATION

Less than a year after the Japanese attack on Pearl Harbour *The Economist* observed with satisfaction that the British and American leaders had 'gone further to co-ordinate the nations' two war efforts and two economies than ever previously in the history of any international alliance'.[1] This was scarcely an overstatement. An impressive pyramid of collaboration had been constructed, beginning with Churchill's visit to Washington in December 1941. At the top of the pyramid were the Combined Chiefs of Staff working out joint military strategy under the general direction of the President and the Prime Minister. Next came the combined boards implementing the programme of the Combined Chiefs in the vital fields of war supply—the Combined Munitions Assignment Board, the Combined Raw Materials Board, and the Combined Shipping Adjustment Board.[2] These boards did not involve the surrender of national decision-making to

[1] 'The End of Isolation', cxliii (1942), p. 666.
[2] Later supplemented by the Combined Food Board and the Combined Production and Resources Board.

a supra-national authority; they sought rather to achieve a concert of policies by associating national representatives in close and flexible working arrangements. In the words of an official British history,

the British-American alliance did not provide itself with any formal organ of supreme control. This was not a matter of accident but of conscious decision. . . . The War Cabinet showed itself positively alarmed by rumours coming from Washington to the effect that the Americans wished too pedantically to copy inter-Allied constitution-making of the past. In fact, the rumours were without foundation. The Americans were no more anxious than the British to jeopardise the flexible and natural growth of British-American co-operation by clamping upon it a political directorate of excessive formality.[1]

Although these arrangements grew with little fanfare, leaders in both countries came to regard them not only as indispensable measures for winning the war but as important institutions for winning the peace. An American newspaper correspondent noted early in 1942 that 'the higher one goes in the ranks of the Administration the more talk one finds of this war-time machinery forming the basis of some kind of solid, practical economic collaboration for peace'.[2] Assistant Secretary of State Adolph A. Berle devoted a major foreign policy address to the need for maintaining the war-time machinery in the transition period; by way of warning he recalled 'the breaking of all ranks which took place in 1918'—an error which caused victory to be 'literally frittered away'.[3] Churchill went perhaps the farthest of all in his Harvard speech of 1943 when he cautioned against the dismantling of Anglo-American war-time collaboration before the projected universal organizations had time to prove themselves:

It would be a most foolish and improvident act on the part of our two governments, or either of them, to break up this smooth running and immensely powerful machinery the moment the war is over; but for our own safety, as well as for the security of the rest of the world, we are bound to keep it working and in running order after the war . . . not only till we have set up some world arrangement to keep the peace but until we know that it is an arrangement which will readily give us that protection we must have from danger and aggression—a protection we have already had to seek across two vast world wars.[4]

[1] W. K. Hancock and M. M. Gowing, *British War Economy* (London, 1949), p. 402.
[2] James Reston, 'Economic Unity, for War and After, Started', *The New York Times* (8 Feb. 1942).
[3] (15 Oct. 1942), *Dept. of State Bull.*, v (1942), p. 831.
[4] (6 Sept. 1943), British Information Services, *British Speeches of the Day*, No. 7 (Sept. 1943), p. 1.

Of particular interest for our present study is the way in which the Anglo-American war-time machinery involved the pooling of military and economic resources. The importance of traditional boundaries might for this purpose almost be said to have disappeared: armaments, shipping, and raw materials were dispatched to their most efficient uses regardless of their national origin.[1] This system of war supply implied an equivalent system of financial accounting. Roosevelt seemed to be looking forward to such a system when he declared: 'No nation will grow rich through the war effort of its allies. The money costs of the war will fall according to the rule of equality of sacrifice.'[2] Thus there could be no ground for indebtedness between the Allies as long as each contributed its utmost to the common military effort.

This method of financial accounting, unfortunately, was not carried out in practice. One of the most notable lapses occurred in the system of war-time economic collaboration between the members of the sterling area. Here was a case where dangers as well as benefits lurked in the familiar British tendency to 'muddle through' with existing institutions when circumstances cried for new ones. The war did, it is true, bring changes to the sterling area's system of financial control. Its members replaced their informal practices with more formal undertakings better suited to the emergency. The foreign exchange earnings of residents of the overseas sterling area, formerly banked in London as a matter of convenience, were now subjected to compulsory appropriation by the several governments and deposited in London for common use in a central pool. Although these governments were still permitted to draw needed foreign exchange upon request, they undertook in the interest of the common war effort to draw only such exchange as was necessary to cover essential requirements. But these changes in the system of financial control were not accompanied by changes in the system of keeping accounts. Contributions and withdrawals from the central pool of foreign exchange

[1] There were, it must be admitted, occasional exceptions. See William A. Brown and Redvers Opie, *American Foreign Assistance* (Washington, 1953), p. 60.

[2] *Fifth Report to Congress on Lend-Lease Operations* (June 1942), pp. 22–23. It should be noted that the President thought equality of sacrifice would be attained if each nation devoted 'roughly the same fraction of its national production' to the war. At the time *The Economist* thought this formula 'might work well enough' between Britain and the United States but might work hardship on poorer countries, such as the Republic of China. It is a measure of the changes that have occurred in estimates of the economic strength of Britain and the United States that such a formula for the allocation of defence burdens should be regarded a decade later as placing a disproportionate strain on Britain's greatly inferior national resources.

continued, as in peace-time, to give rise to changes in the sterling balances held to the account of the governments of the overseas sterling area. The value of these balances rose accordingly from £856 million at the end of 1941 to a total of £2,723 million in mid-1945.[1]

There was a twofold explanation for this staggering increase in the sterling balances. In the first place, as a result of voluntary restraint and war-time controls over shipping and supply, most of the overseas sterling countries became net dollar earners and found themselves making large contributions to the central reserve. In the second place, the United Kingdom balance of current payments with the rest of the sterling area became heavily adverse. This was due to its inability to maintain the normal flow of peace-time exports, to its heavy import of sterling area foodstuffs and raw materials, and to its large expenditures on behalf of British armies in sterling countries such as India and Egypt.

Given the principle of equality of sacrifice, changes in the war-time balances of the sterling area countries should not have resulted in the accumulation by Britain of such a heavy burden of post-war debt. Some of the items in the accumulating indebtedness were particularly hard to justify—for example, the purchase from Egyptians of goods and services for the defence of their own country, and the expensive provisioning of the Indian Army during its campaigns upon foreign soil.[2] The injustice of these and other claims aroused considerable attention within the British Government—notably on the part of the Prime Minister and his personal adviser, Lord Cherwell. Yet when it came to action, the British Government did little more than utter desultory and ineffective pleas for reasonableness on the part of its creditors.[3] It consistently rejected attempts by the United States and

---

[1] The sterling balances of non-sterling area countries rose from £443 million to £632 million during the same period, bringing the total amount of sterling indebtedness of Britain at the end of the war to £3,355 million. *Statistical Material Presented During the Washington Negotiations*, Cmd. 6706 of 1945, p. 11. Although for convenience we have confined our discussion to the sterling area's system of financial accounting, the main points apply with equal force to the accumulation of sterling balances by the non-sterling countries.

[2] The prices paid for these goods and services were also greatly inflated. In 1944 the wholesale price indexes for Egypt and India stood at 311 and 302 compared with 171 in the United Kingdom, relative to the first six months of 1939. League of Nations, *Monthly Bulletin of Statistics* (Apr. 1945), p. 121.

[3] See, for example, the remarks of Anderson at the Mansion House, London (4 Oct. 1944), that Britain's creditors 'must be reasonable and not seek to treat war debts on the footing of ordinary commercial obligations'. Holborn, vol. ii, pp. 522–3.

other countries to treat the sterling debts as a matter of international concern.[1]

How are we to account for this apparently short-sighted behaviour on the part of the British Government? The answer must be sought in an analysis of several forces at work in the shaping of British policy. One of these may be conveniently described as the Bank of England view—the attitude that a banker must, at any cost, make good on his solemn obligations. The officials who held this view put a commendable emphasis on the importance of maintaining respect for British honour and British credit, but they certainly underestimated the nation's precarious financial position and the dangers that a huge volume of sterling indebtedness would hold for other aspects of British policy. A second factor shaping British policy might be described as the Board of Trade approach—the attitude that the sterling balances would prove useful as a fillip to Britain's post-war export trade. Those who took this line were too preoccupied with the fear of post-war unemployment to recognize the threat the balances posed to balance of payments equilibrium. Even Keynes, who scorned the Bank of England argument against a large scaling-down of the sterling balances, succumbed for a time to the Board of Trade approach.

A third force shaping British policy, harder to contend with, was ultimately decisive. This was the consideration that preoccupied the leaders of the Foreign, Commonwealth Relations, and Colonial Offices. In general terms, the argument ran somewhat as follows: The principle of equal sacrifice was all very well, but it could only be applied where there was equal national interest in the war effort. Such an assumption was clearly inappropriate in the cases of the largest sterling creditors. Eire, for example, never even became a belligerent. India entered the war through the action of a British official rather than of a popularly elected Indian Parliament. The strength of Egypt's interest in the Allied cause was also questionable. Any attempt to cast doubts upon the validity of the sterling debts during the course of the war risked serious defection from the very peoples whose co-operation seemed most precarious and most essential.

Here was a frankly political argument for an unwise economic policy. Its strongest specific justification lay in the problem of India.

---

[1] As in the negotiations on the International Monetary Fund. See Chapters V and VII, *supra*.

The peaceful and gradual evolution of the Indian people to self-government within the Commonwealth was a central objective of the British Government. Indian opinion was adamant on the subject of the sterling balances. Having been debtors of Britain for so long, the Indians were determined to take advantage of the change in their country's external economic fortunes and demand repayment in full from the United Kingdom. Their case, like that of other sterling creditors, seemed to be strengthened by the plausible argument that could be made on welfare grounds. India was a poor country which would desperately need large-scale British investment to help raise its living standards at the end of the war. But was this argument really valid? The poverty of various sterling creditors may have been a good reason for initiating a careful programme of development generally; it was not a good reason for creating a large and irrationally distributed block of sterling holdings that would jeopardize the solvency of the central banker. Nevertheless, the welfare argument continued to be made, strengthening the hand of those who opposed a bold solution to the problem of the balances out of regard for the precarious state of Anglo-Indian political relations.

These, in brief outline, were the main reasons why nothing was done to alter the sterling area's system of financial accounting. What of the system employed between Britain and the United States? This compared favourably with that employed between the countries of sterling area. The record may be regarded as particularly good in the light of the fact that America and Britain were not bound, as were most of the sterling countries, by formal political ties. In the course of the war the United States supplied without charge some $30 billion of Lend-Lease materials to members of the British Commonwealth, of which nearly $27 billion went to Britain, and received some $6 billion of 'reverse Lend-Lease' articles in return. Compared with previous war-time arrangements between allies, Lend-Lease certainly seemed to merit Churchill's commendation as 'the most unsordid act in history'.

Yet even these arrangements did violence to that philosophy of pooled resources which underlay the operation of the Combined Boards. The failure was particularly serious in view of the linking of Lend-Lease with commitments on post-war economic policy. A basic assumption behind Article Seven was that the Lend-Lease system, by applying the principle of 'equality of sacrifice', would facilitate the revival of multilateralism at the end of the war. This assumption was undermined wherever the operation of Lend-Lease fell short of the ideal.

Unfortunately, Anglo-American financial accounting was no more free from political problems than the financial accounting of the sterling area. The administrators of Lend-Lease in the United States were continually on the defensive before domestic criticism. Much of this criticism came from groups who regarded Lend-Lease as another New Deal instrument for deficit spending and government control. Much of it came from isolationists and other groups who opposed the giving of such large assistance to foreign countries. The truth of the matter was that many Americans did not share the prevalent British view that Hitler was an equal threat to the survival of both countries, that America's entry into the European war was inevitable, and that in the days before Pearl Harbour Britain had been defending America as well as itself. In short, 'equality of sacrifice' was never entirely accepted as the basis of Anglo-American war finance for one of the same reasons that it was not accepted among the sterling area countries themselves.

The first problem in the operation of Lend-Lease was the basic one of whether or not payment would eventually be demanded for articles consumed in the war. The Lend-Lease Act, it may be recalled, had been deliberately vague on this point.[1] Once the United States entered the war, full acceptance of the pooling concept should have prompted a declaration that no bill would ever be tendered for the provision of war supplies. In fact, abortive attempts were made to do this. In a letter transmitting to Congress his *Eleventh Report on Lend-Lease Operations* Roosevelt declared that 'the United States wants no new war debts to jeopardize the coming peace. Victory and a secure peace are the only coin in which we can be repaid.' Yet a short time after their publication these statements were bluntly repudiated. The President told a press conference that the controversial sentences contained some truth, but that other countries would be expected to repay for the receipt of Lend-Lease supplies as far as they could— though not necessarily in dollars.[2] This was the last time during the course of the war that the Administration sought to make a direct approach to the repayment question. Accordingly the United Kingdom and other countries had no assurance in planning their post-war

---

[1] See Chapter IV, *supra*.
[2] 'President Asserts World Will Repay', *The New York Times* (8 Sept. 1943), and 'Roosevelt Revises Lend-Lease Letter', id. (15 Sept. 1943).

trade policies that they would be entirely free from the burden of war debts owing to the United States.

Why did the Administration hesitate to clarify the repayment question? In the first place, leading figures in the State and Treasury departments were reluctant to surrender the 'bargaining power' which forgiveness of Lend-Lease might give them in persuading the United Kingdom to embrace a policy of multilateral trade. Second, there was the attitude of Congress. After the conservative trend of the Congressional elections of 1942, the annual appropriations for Lend-Lease were subject to increasing scrutiny. Many Republicans were already convinced that Lend-Lease had become a tremendous 'give-away'; some Southern Democrats took a hardly less critical view. Even the Administration's main Congressional supporters were asking greater safeguards for American interests. Walter F. George, chairman of the Senate Foreign Relations Committee, had already expressed the view that the United States should receive raw materials in payment for Lend-Lease at the end of the war.[1] The same suggestion was now made by the influential War Investigating Committee under the chairmanship of Senator Harry S. Truman.[2] In the House of Representatives, the Colmer Committee was soon to urge repayment of Lend-Lease in 'rights to control of raw materials, bases, aviation rights, sites and buildings for embassies, and other tangible and intangible assets'.[3] Thus it was doubtful that the President, without making a supreme effort, could gain the necessary support for complete forgiveness of the Lend-Lease account.

The United States accordingly kept a strict accounting of Lend-Lease supplies sent to the various allied governments and of the reverse Lend-Lease received in return. These accounts were published periodically and received wide publicity. The questionable validity of such accounts, due both to disparities in price levels and to certain logical difficulties in 'charging' for Lend-Lease supplies employed at the front,[4] received little public attention. Moreover, the American

[1] Senator George originally favoured an amendment to the Lend-Lease Act requiring the Executive to get a 'lien' over the rubber and tin of the British Empire.

[2] 'Truman Group Asks Pay for Lend-Lease Aid', *The New York Times* (7 Nov. 1943).

[3] U.S. Congress, House, Special Committee on Postwar Economic Policy and Planning, *Economic Reconstruction in Europe*, H. Rept. no. 1205, 79th Cong., 1st sess. (12 Nov. 1945).

[4] To take one example: if British soldiers storm an enemy position in American-made tanks, should Britain be charged for the tanks or should the United States be charged for the services of the crew? See Eugene Staley, 'The Economic Implications of Lend-Lease', *Am. Ec. Rev.*, xxxiii (Supp., 1943), p. 362.

Government continued to refer to the programme as 'Lend-Lease', a title which suggested ultimate repayment (unlike the term 'Mutual Aid' employed in Britain). It was hardly surprising, therefore, that public opinion polls at the end as well as the beginning of the war should reveal that a substantial majority of the American people both desired and expected repayment from Britain for Lend-Lease aid.[1] After reviewing the mistakes of the First World War and the current confusion surrounding the conduct of Lend-Lease, one observer was moved to warn: 'Unless the formalities of Lend-Lease are brought into line fairly soon with our own assertions accepting full partnership in this war, we may accumulate a war debts problem and the same sort of thing may happen again. . . .'[2]

In the matter of repayment, therefore, Lend-Lease was not handled in complete conformity with the ideal of 'equality of sacrifice'. The same was true with respect to its day-to-day administration. Provided each of the allies was making its maximum effort and was devoting its resources to their most efficient uses, questions about the composition of a country's exports or the level of its gold reserves should have been largely irrelevant. Yet Anglo-American war-time finance was continually plagued by these matters. American exporters were concerned lest Lend-Lease assistance should be used by Britain in commercial competition with the United States. To allay these fears Britain had to issue the Eden White Paper in September 1941, promising not to permit any export of Lend-Lease goods, articles made with Lend-Lease goods, or even 'substantially similar' articles. Throughout the war the American Government, under considerable pressure from export interests, sought to ensure the strict administration of this undertaking. As a result, British businessmen complained bitterly that Lend-Lease was destroying Britain's export trade. While British exports were being mainly curtailed for other reasons, it is

---

[1] A Gallup Poll taken in the late summer of 1945 showed that 65 per cent. of Americans interviewed believed that Britain would repay either in whole or in part for Lend-Lease goods received during the war; only 13 per cent. believed that Britain would not repay; 22 per cent. expressed no opinion. At the same time, 83 per cent. of those interviewed expressed the view that Britain *should* repay the United States in some way for Lend-Lease material. 'United States Public Opposes Writing Off of Lend-Lease', the *Chicago Daily News* (28 Sept. 1945). Commenting on this poll the *Wall Street Journal* (8 Oct. 1945) found the results 'not particularly surprising, for if the term Lend-Lease on its face indicates anything, obviously it indicates an arrangement under which goods and services are lent and leased'. The *Journal* concluded that the main cause of public misunderstanding had been the failure of the Administration to be more specific as to the nature of the war-time aid, 'particularly after we entered the war and lend-lease took on a multilateral character'.

[2] Staley, p. 366.

likely that the commitments in the Eden White Paper, despite subsequent modifications, did aggravate the decline which brought them
by the end of the war to one-third of their pre-war volume. If some
kind of agreement about the re-export of Lend-Lease goods had to be
made to appease the American business community, it should at least
have been accompanied by an American guarantee to assist Britain
pending the restoration of her exports after the war. Here again, the
operation of Lend-Lease did not lay a proper foundation for multilateral policies in the post-war period.

Another source of difficulty in the administration of Lend-Lease
occurred with respect to the British gold and dollar reserves. A year
before the war they had exceeded $4 billion. By the time Britain
began receiving Lend-Lease shipments they had been virtually exhausted. If the philosophy of 'equality of sacrifice' had been literally
applied, there should have been no objection to a moderate increase
in these reserves—in fact, a grant-in-aid might have been positively
required in order to make such 'equality' effective. Yet until the very
last months of the war the American Government exerted continuous
pressure to keep British reserves to a figure not greatly in excess of $1
billion. This principle of 'scraping the barrel' as a condition of
eligibility for Lend-Lease materials was prompted in part by the
Administration's fear of Congress. But it was prompted also by the
same concern with 'bargaining power' that we have already noted on
the part of some Administration officials. For the lower the level at
which British war-time reserves were kept, the greater would be
the British dependence on American post-war assistance. And the
greater that dependence, it was argued, the greater would be the
chances of gaining acceptance for American views on multilateral
trade.

The issue of the gold and dollar reserves came to a head in the
winter of 1943-4. In December 1943 Morgenthau and White made
strong representations that these reserves had grown too high and
that Britain would now have to pay in cash for some of the goods
being supplied on Lend-Lease account. When British officials pleaded
the need to maintain adequate reserves for the post-war period,
Morgenthau assured them that Britain's post-war needs would be
met by special measures at a later date. Sir David Waley, the British
Treasury representative, took a dim view of this approach, remarking
that Britain could not afford to deplete its dollar balances in reliance
on 'a promise that the American Government could make available

through one means or another substantial sums after the war'.[1] A few months later Churchill himself entered the controversy. With some vigour he declared that 'the suggestion of reducing our dollar balances, which constitute our sole liquid reserves, to one billion dollars would really not be consistent either with equal treatment of Allies or with any conception of equal sacrifice or pooling of resources'.[2] Nevertheless, it was not until the Second Quebec Conference that the American Government conceded that British reserves should be permitted to rise much in excess of this figure. Here the administration of Lend-Lease clearly aggravated British fears that their reserves would prove too small to provide an adequate margin of safety against the uncertainties inherent in a multilateral régime.[3]

Perhaps the most important respect in which the operation of Lend-Lease fell short of the ideal was in the matter of its duration. The British Government had paid $6 billion in cash on orders for military supplies placed before the Lend-Lease Act went into effect. From the British point of view, 'equality of sacrifice' required that Lend-Lease be granted retrospectively to cover these expenditures. This, of course, was politically impossible for the United States Government. But continuation of Lend-Lease after the cessation of hostilities might be something else again. As part of the common war effort British reserves had been depleted and British exports drastically reduced. Could not Lend-Lease be used to bring them back to peace-time levels? Or—to make another point—could not the

[1] Minutes of a luncheon meeting between Morgenthau, White, Halifax, and Waley (17 Nov. 1943), recorded by White, 26 Nov. 1943, *White Papers*. After the British representatives left, White and Morgenthau discussed the possibility of getting bases or access to raw materials from Britain in return for permitting an increase in reserves. Ibid.

[2] Communication from Prime Minister to President Roosevelt (9 Mar. 1944), printed in Churchill, *Closing the Ring* (London, 1952), App. C, p. 612. The Prime Minister also took pains to emphasize that the level of British reserves should be considered in relation to the total volume of sterling indebtedness. Publication of the level of British reserves (which Lend-Lease Administrator Leo Crowley had promised to Congress) would be misleading unless accompanied by publication of the size of the sterling balances; but publication of the latter 'would certainly have most injurious effects upon our sterling position'. Ibid. Thus the British and American leaders were caught in a vicious circle. At the same time, the Americans argued that they should not be expected to acquiesce in a higher level of British reserves simply because Britain indulged in over-generous treatment of its sterling creditors.

[3] A third respect in which day-to-day administration of Lend-Lease fell short of 'equality of sacrifice' was in the matter of the categories of goods eligible for shipment. In an ideal system of war supply, it should have made little difference whether aid to Britain included machine guns or prefabricated houses, provided that resources were being optimally employed and the items were going where they were most needed. But in practice the American Administration was hesitant about including certain civilian type goods in Lend-Lease shipments.

expenses of demobilization and enemy occupation be considered as costs of the war itself?

There were a small number of American commentators who took the position that 'rehabilitation is part of the cost of the war, and the principle of equality of sacrifice applies'.[1] But they were in the minority. Although the language of the original Lend-Lease Act might have supported a broader interpretation,[2] Congress sought increasingly in the late war years to limit Lend-Lease to the actual period of military hostilities. Part of the pressure to achieve this result came from American business interests who feared both British export competition and the continuation of government trading in the post-war period.[3] Part resulted from the desire of most Congressmen to make a sharp distinction between war-time aid and post-war reconstruction assistance—and to give Congress greater control of the latter. One example of the Congressional attitude was the amendment to the Lend-Lease Act passed in 1944 which, in the words of Senator Arthur Vandenberg, the leading Republican foreign policy spokesman, aimed 'to confine lend-lease absolutely to the military operation of the war'. In expressing his support for this amendment Senator Tom Connally, the leading Democratic spokesman, declared: 'As one who originally voted for the Lend-Lease Act, I do not think that we ever intended Lend-Lease to serve any purpose except to aid in the military operations carrying on the war.'[4]

That part of the Lend-Lease Act which caused Congress particular anxiety was Section 3(c), under which the President was authorized to exercise his powers even after the end of Lend-Lease 'to the extent necessary to carry out a contract or agreement' made with a foreign government before termination of the programme. In April 1945 the Congress passed a new amendment providing:

> That nothing in section 3(c) shall be construed to authorize the President to enter into or carry out any contract or agreement with a foreign government for post-war relief, post-war rehabilitation or post-war reconstruction; excepting that a contract or agreement entered into in accordance with this act in which the United States undertakes to furnish to a foreign government defense articles, services, or information for use in the prosecution of the present war and which provides for the disposition . . . of any such

---

[1] Staley, op. cit., p. 379. See also 'Postwar Lend-Lease?', *The Christian Science Monitor* (4 Nov. 1944).

[2] Based on a liberal construction of the phrase 'defense of the United States'.

[3] See, for example, 'U.S. Chamber Asks Lend-Lease Limit', *The New York Times* (20 Nov. 1944) and National Association of Manufacturers *Newsletter* (Aug. 1944).

[4] 90 *Cong. Rec.* 4097 (8 May 1944).

defense articles, services, or information after they are no longer necessary for use by such government in promoting the defense of the United States shall not be deemed to be for post-war relief, post-war rehabilitation, or post-war reconstruction.[1]

In unanimously adopting this amendment the House Committee on Foreign Affairs explained that the provision would 'facilitate the separate consideration by the Congress of appropriate measures' to deal with the reconstruction problem.[2] Leo Crowley, the Lend-Lease Administrator, acknowledged that under the amendment he had the responsibility 'to be sure that every contract that is made now for procurement for our allies be screened very, very carefully . . . unless we can certify that supplies can be delivered, in our judgment, in time to be of some help during the actual military operation, we should not enter into any contract to furnish them'.[3] In his view— and that of his deputy, Oscar Cox—the amendment meant that the Lend-Lease administration was now obliged to provide Britain and other allies only with supplies likely to be needed in the conduct of the war and was also obliged to require cash payment for all goods in the 'pipeline'[4] which were eventually delivered and for all unexpended goods of post-war value which had been delivered before the end of hostilities.[5]

Unfortunately, British opinion showed little awareness of these clear statements of American policy. The enthusiastic years of post-war planning had encouraged a tendency to deprecate orthodox means of international finance—a tendency to look forward to a world in which 'lenders will lend and borrowers will not repay'.[6] One scholar pictured the United States facing a glut of surplus production after the war and forecast 'a tremendous development on the lines of Lend-Lease'.[7] Keynes himself inclined to the view that the United States, in its own interest, might wish to continue Lend-Lease for a time after the war. Even the Chancellor of the Exchequer remarked: 'When we turn to the problems of the post-war world we find in the principle of mutual aid the indispensable condition of an improved system of economic and monetary intercourse between

[1] P.L. 31, 79th Congress, 1st sess. 59 Stat. 52 (1945).
[2] 91 *Cong. Rec.* 2156–7 (13 Mar. 1945).
[3] U.S. Congress, Senate, Committee on Foreign Relations, *Extension of the Lend-Lease Act*, Hearings on H.R. 2103, 79th Cong., 1st sess. (Mar.–Apr. 1945), p. 33.
[4] I.e., ordered but not delivered by the end of the war.
[5] Id., p. 35.　　[6] 'Painless Prosperity?', *The Economist*, cxliii (1942), p. 132.
[7] D. Caradoe Jones, Reader in Social Statistics at Liverpool University, reported in 'Post-War Extension of Lend-Lease?', *The Financial News* (23 July 1943).

nations.'[1] The post-war use of Lend-Lease implied in these statements might have been justified on the grounds of 'equality of sacrifice'—at least during a short period of post-war transition; but the prospects for such a programme were not encouraged by contemporary developments in American opinion. In this as in other respects Lend-Lease, no less than the financial accounting of the sterling area, formed an unsound basis for post-war policies of multilateral trade.

PLANNING FOR THE TRANSITION PERIOD

Among the most far-reaching consequences of the Second World War were the changes it brought to the economic positions of Britain and the United States. The contrast was almost complete. The United States achieved a tremendous expansion of its industrial plant. Its national output approximately doubled in real terms and was far more evenly distributed than before the war. The war resulted, it is true, in an over-rapid depletion of domestic mineral resources. But in general the United States faced the peace-time future in better economic health than ever before. If any problem clouded the horizon it was that of fully employing the greatly expanded productive resources.

In the United Kingdom, the situation was not so fortunate. About one-quarter (£7,300 million) of Britain's pre-war national wealth (£30,000 million) had been lost in the war.[2] The main factors were physical destruction (£1,500 million); shipping losses (£700 million); internal disinvestment (£900 million); and external disinvestment (£4,200 million). The serious deterioration in the external position resulted mainly from the liquidation of external investments (£1,118 million); the increase in external liabilities (2,879 million); and the loss of gold and dollar reserves (£152 million). To make matters worse, exports by the end of 1944 had dropped to one-third their pre-war volume.

The decline in exports was particularly alarming in the light of the losses in shipping and investment earnings. To compensate for these losses, exports would have to be increased some 50 per cent. above the pre-war level simply to enable the purchase of the pre-war level of British imports. But this figure was probably too modest: in view of

[1] Sir Kingsley Wood, quoted in 'Mutual Aid for Peace Trade', *The Manchester Guardian* (10 Sept. 1942). See also 'Lend-Lease for Peace', id. (9 July 1942).
[2] These and the following figures are taken from *Statistical Material Presented During the Washington Negotiations*, Cmd. 6706 of 1945. The dates used to compare the pre-war and post-war positions are September 1939 and June 1945.

population increases, the demand for higher living standards, the
need to service new indebtedness, and new requirements for other
(e.g. military) foreign expenditure, the necessary increase in British
exports was probably nearer 75 per cent.[1] It would take at least three
years before such an increase could be achieved; during this time,
Britain would face a deficit in its balance of payments of an estimated £1,250 million ($5 billion). Some form of transitional assistance
was obviously required to avert a fall in British living standards to
a point even below their war-time levels and to facilitate British
participation in the ambitious projects for multilateral trade.

The main elements in the deterioration of Britain's economic position did not become apparent only with the end of the Second World
War. To some extent they were foreseen at the very outset of the
conflict. At an early date qualified opinion in both countries, in the
words of a distinguished American economist, regarded 'the structural change in the English international financial position . . . as
a major world problem upon the solution of which the course of
international relations will fundamentally depend'.[2] It was also per-
ceived that the economic problems facing Britain would be shared by
other countries in Western Europe. How was it, therefore, that the
British and American Governments never matched their long-term
planning with effective planning for reconstruction itself?

The answer to this question requires a brief review of the successive
devices by which the two governments sought to deal with the period
of transition from war to peace. Both the Keynes and White plans in
their original form contemplated that substantial resources would be
devoted to the needs of reconstruction.[3] But, as we have seen, the
financial institutions which emerged at Bretton Woods were not
equipped to be effective institutions of transitional finance. A similar
neglect of the transition problem could be seen in the evolution of
the United Nations Relief and Rehabilitation Administration.[4] At
its inception, U.N.R.R.A. seemed likely to play a major role in
reconstruction. But its functions were progressively confined when,
due to the insistence of the American Congress, rehabilitation was

---

[1] Even this estimate did not allow for price increases and for adverse changes in the
terms of trade.

[2] Alvin Hansen, 'Changes in the Economic Structure Arising Out of the War',
Public Policy, vol. iii (1942), p. 261.

[3] For the role Keynes and White expected their plans to play in the transition period
see Chapter V, *supra*.

[4] This, of course, did not affect Britain directly because Britain was not a recipient
but a contributor to the U.N.R.R.A. programme.

defined as co-terminous with relief. Thus between planning for the long and the short-run there began to appear an increasingly ominous gap.

As the European war drew to a close, concern with this gap could no longer be avoided. The focus for discussion of the transitional problem became the Lend-Lease negotiations on the amount of aid the United States would supply to Britain during 'Stage II'—the period between the German surrender and the final defeat of Japan. At the Second Quebec Conference Roosevelt and Churchill reached informal agreement on this subject. The British Government took the position that American munitions aid should continue during the war against Japan, reduced in proportion to the reduction of the British war effort, while non-munitions aid should be maintained at a point nearer the existing level. According to the British view, Lend-Lease supplies should be sent even if they made possible the release of British manpower for civilian production and an increase in commercial exports. To these propositions Roosevelt expressed general assent. In place of the British formulae, however, he preferred to use absolute figures—$3½ billion in munitions assistance and $3 billion in other aid.[1] A joint Anglo-American committee assigned to work out the details of this understanding reached agreement later on the extent of Lend-Lease aid during 'Stage II' and also on a greater degree of freedom for British export trade.[2] Churchill was full of optimism when he announced the successful completion of the committee's work to the House of Commons: 'Never, I think, has there been a more thorough understanding of the facts of the economic position, and the problems of Great Britain and the United States of America on both sides than we have now been able to reach.'[3]

Was this optimism premature? There were several dangers in attempting to employ Lend-Lease as a vehicle for British reconstruction. The President soon encountered serious opposition from leading members of the Administration. The Secretary of State, as might be imagined, was infuriated at Roosevelt's conduct at Quebec because the tentative promise of aid to Britain 'had attached to it no conditions whatever. There were numerous questions pending between us and Great Britain on which we should seek settlement or action, and the credits would be needed as part of our bargaining position with her.'[4] Henry L. Stimson, the Secretary of War, objected

---

[1] For details of the Quebec discussions on 'Stage II' assistance see Hancock and Gowing, pp. 527–8; Hull, *Memoirs*, vol. ii, p. 1614.
[2] Brown and Opie, pp. 68–69.
[3] 406 H.C. Deb. 69 (30 Nov. 1944).   [4] Hull, *Memoirs*, vol. ii, p. 1618.

on somewhat different grounds. He thought the United States should make a generous contribution to the solution of Britain's transitional difficulties, but he felt the President had no authority to use the Lend-Lease Act for this purpose. The reservations expressed by Stimson, who was noted for his integrity and his liberal outlook, are worth quoting:

I was a witness for the presentations made to Congress and . . . I knew perfectly well that Congress had made the Lend-Lease appropriations on the representations that it was in aid of an actual war effort to help an ally who was actually fighting for us and not for the purpose of rehabilitating a nation which was not fighting or appropriations which were not, in other words, an aid to our own war effort. I therefore thought that if we were going to make use of Lend-Lease appropriations in the post-war period when there was no longer any connection between them and the actual fighting of the recipient, we ought to consult Congress. I did not at all object to the purpose but I thought it would be very dangerous to go ahead under the original authority which was aimed at another objective.[1]

Other obstacles to the Quebec understanding began to emerge. The American Joint Chiefs of Staff held unanimously that Lend-Lease deliveries should be made only in the case of materials which would actually be used in the war.[2] Moreover, the President had no authority under the Lend-Lease Act to make binding commitments about the prospective amount of Lend-Lease aid: appropriations had, as always, to be made by Congress. Thus the British members of the joint committee were bound to be disappointed in their attempt to get American initials on a formal document.[3] As Crowley and Cox later assured a Congressional committee, the British were specifically informed that the promises of Lend-Lease aid were subject to the changing circumstances of the Japanese war, the availability of the necessary supplies, and the appropriation of funds by the Congress.[4]

[1] Excerpts of Stimson's remarks at a Cabinet meeting of 13 Oct. 1944, as recounted in his diary of the same day. Henry L. Stimson and McGeorge Bundy, *On Active Service in Peace and War* (New York, 1947), p. 593. At the time Stimson would have preferred 'a great act of statesmanship on the part of the President' instead of an attempt to use Lend-Lease for this purpose, but acknowledged that this would require 'a great effort of education'. Diary of 22 Nov. 1944, ibid.

[2] William D. Leahy, *I Was There* (New York, 1950), p. 273.

[3] For an account of British disappointment on this score, see Harrod, *Life of Keynes*, p. 591.

[4] These assurances were stimulated in part by the anxiety expressed by Senator Vandenberg, who said he had heard rumours that the United States had made Lend-Lease commitments at Quebec that were not only excessive but unrelated to the prosecution of the war. U.S. Congress, Senate, Committee on Foreign Relations, *Extension of the Lend-Lease Act*, Hearings on H.R. 2103, 79th Cong., 1st sess. (Mar.–Apr. 1945), p. 20. See id., p. 14, for the joint statement issued 30 Nov. 1944 by Secretary

In fact, the President himself is reported to have approved the reservation that the projected programme of Lend-Lease deliveries 'does not constitute any commitment . . . all schedules, both munitions and non-munitions, are subject to the changing demands of strategy as well as to supply considerations and the usual considerations of procurement and allocation'.[1]

There was one further danger in relying upon Lend-Lease as an instrument for British reconstruction. Even if the Administration permitted 'Stage II' assistance to take such a form and reach such a volume as to cover substantial British post-war needs, assistance of this kind could last no longer than the duration of the Japanese war. In Roosevelt's own words, the Quebec talks concerned only 'the scope and scale of mutual Lend-Lease aid between the United States and the British Empire *after the defeat of Germany and during the war with Japan*'.[2] In view of the clear declarations of Congress on this subject, the President could have little hope of extending Lend-Lease once the period of hostilities was over. At Quebec and afterwards the British and American Governments proceeded on the assumption that the Japanese war would last for eighteen months after the war in Europe. But what if the Japanese war should suddenly end?

Neither Bretton Woods, U.N.R.R.A., nor Lend-Lease could be relied on to meet Britain's needs for transitional assistance. The only remaining alternative was some special measure of post-war aid. But on this subject neither British nor American opinion had been prepared to think realistically. Many British officials either refused to consider the need for such aid at all or did their thinking in terms which were politically impractical. In the winter of 1943-4, for example, Sir David Waley told the Americans that he doubted 'whether his government would wish to accept assistance designed to put Britain on its feet during the post-war period. . . . Britain would not want the solution as a free gift from the American

---

of State Stettinius, Morgenthau, and Crowley on the nature of the agreement reached at Quebec.

[1] Leahy, p. 279. The Admiral, who was a close adviser of Roosevelt, adds: 'The President was doubtful about his authority to spend any Lend-Lease money after the war was over. Other people differed with him and said he did have such authority. This question was argued back and forth. . . . Roosevelt did issue an order to the Joint Chiefs of Staff that they were not to use Lend-Lease except to further the progress of the war. He told me that he was trying to adhere to the intent of Congress.' Id., p. 280.

[2] Italics supplied. Sherwood, *The White House Papers of Harry L. Hopkins*, vol. ii (London, 1949), p. 811.

Government'.[1] Later, in the spring of 1945, when Judge Samuel
Rosenman arrived in London on a special investigation of recon-
struction needs, Keynes told him: 'The only possible solution for
Britain's problems today would be another brain-wave by your
President Roosevelt—like Lend-Lease.'[2]

Until the very last moment, the British Government denied all
reports that it was planning to seek special measures of reconstruction aid.[3] Little was done to prepare the public for such a step by
frank discussion of British needs. Newspaper opinion was even
openly hostile to any suggestion that Britain might apply for an
American credit. To some commentators there was something
usurious about the very idea. The *Daily Herald* warned its readers
that 'American financiers have been trying with no success to force
Britain to accept a huge American loan' so that they could get
'hundreds of millions of dollars interest which would be a first
charge on British taxes'.[4] And a Reuter correspondent reported as
late as July 1945 that 'Britain would almost certainly refuse such a
loan, however big it might be or however low the interest rate'—in
fact, British officials and businessmen were 'rather mystified as to
why Americans trouble to discuss the matter'.[5]

American opinion was hardly better prepared to consider special
measures of transitional assistance. For a time the American people
had responded with enthusiasm to appeals for generous measures in
the building of a better world. Their natural idealism and good will
had, more than anything else, ensured approval of the Bretton Woods
institutions. Had these reserves been drawn on to support a timely
programme of world reconstruction, the history of the post-war
period might have read differently. Instead they were largely exhausted in the campaign for two institutions of long-term policy. To
make matters worse, the Administration had found it necessary to
present Bretton Woods as an alternative to special measures of aid
to Britain.[6] Final passage of the Bank and Fund was only secured in

---

[1] This is White's paraphrase of Waley's remarks. White's minutes of the luncheon
meeting of 17 Nov. 1943, cited p. 175, n. 1, *supra*.

[2] Rosenman, *Working with Roosevelt* (New York, 1952), p. 257.

[3] 'Such rumours are quite unfounded', Anderson declared. 'Briton Says Nation
Will Not Beg Case', *The New York Times* (5 July 1945).

[4] 'U.S. Loan Plot Failed' (12 Dec. 1944). The British Treasury was also reported to
be unsympathetic to the idea of an American loan. 'British Found Cold to Dollar
Loan From U.S.', *The New York Herald-Tribune* (10 Dec. 1944).

[5] A grant-in-aid, however, 'would, of course, be accepted'. Sydney Campbell,
Reuter financial editor, 'Says British Wish Grant, Not Loan', *The New York Times*
(4 July 1945).   [6] See Chapter VII, *supra*.

the summer of 1945, and in August the State Department was still attributing reports of a British loan to those who had urged the United States to aid Britain 'rather than subscribe to the International Monetary Fund and International Bank for Reconstruction and Development'.[1]

It was hardly surprising in these circumstances that the American people should be almost entirely ignorant of Britain's precarious economic position. As Penrose recalls,

the political education of congressmen, of large sections of the public and even of official Washington . . . had been wholly neglected . . . the British for some time refrained from circulating in the United States adequate information about or explanation of their position . . . the administration and the wiser men in Congress would have been well advised to have given a full public explanation of the coming economic difficulties of the U.K., showing particularly the extent to which these difficulties arose out of Britain's early stand against the common enemy. But the opportunity to do this was lost.[2]

Anglo-American economic collaboration rested now on a shaky basis. One mischance might shatter the edifice and destroy the multi-lateral projects which the two Governments had so painstakingly devised.

THE END OF LEND-LEASE

The next chapter in Anglo-American economic relations opened with a turbulent rush of dramatic events. President Roosevelt died suddenly and was succeeded on the very threshold of victory by Harry S. Truman. Churchill was replaced by Clement Attlee as Britain's Prime Minister after a totally unexpected electoral victory by the British Labour Party. Atomic bombs were dropped on Hiroshima and Nagasaki. Japan announced its readiness to surrender. The Second World War was over. In the wake of these events the White House issued a terse press release:

The President has directed the Foreign Economic Administrator to take steps immediately to discontinue all Lend-Lease operations and to notify foreign governments receiving Lend-Lease of this action.

The President directs that all outstanding contracts for Lend-Lease are cancelled, except where Allied governments are willing to agree to take

[1] The Department stated flatly that 'the British Government has not approached the Department concerning a loan. *Nor have we any present plans for requesting legislation to authorize such a credit*'. Italics supplied. 'British Loan Plan is Denied by Grew', *The New York Times* (6 Aug. 1945).

[2] Op. cit., pp. 182–3. The futile attempts of Penrose and Ambassador Winant to alert the Administration to this danger are recounted by Penrose in chs. x–xiii.

them over or where it is in the interest of the United States to complete them.[1]

This announcement fell upon Britain like a bombshell from an unexpected quarter. Whitehall had not expected Lend-Lease to be cut off by such precipitate action, without prior notice or consultation. The Parliamentary outcry was immediate. Churchill, now Leader of the Opposition, described the step as 'rough and harsh' and refused to believe it was 'the last word of the United States'. The new Prime Minister, for his part, made it clear that a more liberal interpretation of the Lend-Lease Act had been expected. He declared frankly that the abrupt American decision had put Britain 'in a very serious financial position'.[2]

In the United States little sympathy was shown for these expressions of discomfiture. With only isolated exceptions, the cutting off of Lend-Lease was thoroughly approved. The response of even the most liberal Congressmen testified to the gulf that had grown up between British and American opinion.[3] 'I can't understand their attitude', Senator Robert Wagner exclaimed. Chairman Sol Bloom of the House Foreign Affairs Committee called the British reaction 'unreasonable, especially in view of the fact that the Act made it perfectly clear what was going to happen'. Representative William Colmer added: 'We all naturally assumed that Lend-Lease would cease on V-Day.' The response was even less sympathetic in traditionally anti-British quarters. One unidentified Administration figure told the press that the British were putting on a 'cry-baby act'. The *New York Daily News* compared the British reaction to 'being mad at your rich uncle, who has been giving you hand-outs, because he died'.[4]

Although it was the formal announcement of 21 August that touched off the controversy, the abrupt American action might have been forecast a good deal earlier. At the Potsdam Conference the British and American Chiefs of Staff had debated the Lend-Lease question.[5] The British representatives, citing the Washington agreement on assistance during 'Stage II', asked for a steady flow of American supplies to assist in the job of enemy occupation and in the formidable task of economic reconstruction. The American Chiefs of

---

[1] *The New York Times* (22 Aug. 1945).   [2] 410 H.C. Deb. 955–8 (29 Aug. 1945).
[3] The following expressions of Congressional and Administration sentiment are quoted in 'Capital Resents British Stand on Lend-Lease', *The New York Herald-Tribune* (26 Aug. 1945).
[4] Quoted in the *Daily Mail* (29 Aug. 1945).   [5] Leahy, pp. 376–7.

Staff told the British that there was no authority for the shipment of further Lend-Lease material except that which could be used in the war against Japan. On 5 July Truman issued an order providing that 'issue to Allied Governments of Lend-Lease munitions of war and military and naval equipment will be limited to that which is to be used in the war against Japan, and it will not be issued for any other purpose'.[1] This directive, in the words of the British historians, 'contradicted the principles and plans that had been mutually agreed at Washington'.[2] When Truman arrived in Potsdam, Churchill and the British Chiefs of Staff pressed him to reconsider. Recalling his recent role in the Congress, Truman declared: 'I told the Senate that the Act was a weapon of war only.'[3] At about the same time Crowley repeated Administration assurances that Lend-Lease would be used only to further the conduct of actual military hostilities.[4]

Thus the way in which Lend-Lease was cut off was to some extent predetermined. At the Cabinet meeting where the decision was made, Crowley had only to cite the repeated promises made by the Administration. Lend-Lease was only to aid in the actual prosecution of the war: therefore it had to be cut off immediately. Goods were only to be supplied for use in the war effort: therefore the recipients would have to pay for goods in the 'pipeline'. With an inexperienced President, and one with close associations in the halls of Congress, these arguments proved decisive. Had Roosevelt been alive, or some of Truman's more liberal advisers not been out of Washington,[5] the outcome might have been different. But at most they could have accomplished only a tapering of Lend-Lease until alternative means were found for transitional financing.[6] Such a tapering might have saved Britain the several hundred million dollars of indebtedness

[1] Id., p. 377.

[2] Hancock and Gowing, p. 533.

[3] Leahy, p. 414. Truman admitted, however, that the occupation might be considered as part of the war. Ibid.

[4] U.S. Congress, Senate, *Export-Import Bank Act of 1945*, Hearings on H.R. 3771, 79th Cong., 1st sess. (17 and 18 July 1945), p. 5. Crowley's remarks were reported in *The New York Times* (18 July 1945).

[5] By an unfortunate coincidence both Acheson and Clayton were away—the former in Canada and the latter in London. For the way in which Clayton 'vented the vials of his wrath' on the transatlantic telephone, see Harrod, *Life of Keynes*, p. 596.

[6] Truman himself subsequently authorized the continuation of Lend-Lease shipments to China, on the grounds of that country's grave economic and political difficulties. Perhaps a similar exception might have been made for the United Kingdom, to facilitate the problem of redeploying troops and to help finance the cost of enemy occupation. But in view of the long-standing views of Congress on Lend-Lease it is doubtful whether any Administration could have dispatched a significant volume of assistance to Britain in the tapering process.

incurred for receipt of 'pipeline' supplies after the close of hostilities. But it would not have provided a basic solution. The fundamental errors had already been made.

CONCLUSION

The Second World War inspired an unparalleled degree of economic collaboration between the Western allies. Some aspects of war finance, however, violated the principle of 'equality of sacrifice' and the pooling of resources in the common effort. The main offenders were the system of financial accounting employed between the sterling area countries and certain policies followed in the operation of Lend-Lease. Failure to correct these shortcomings added to the transitional difficulties which threatened to impair the ambitious projects for the achievement of multilateral trade. Unfortunately, neither the British nor the American Governments devised adequate measures to deal with the transitional problem. This gap in the post-war planning became dramatically evident with the abrupt termination of Lend-Lease. Anglo-American negotiations to deal with this problem had now to begin in an unfortunate atmosphere of haste, confusion, and misunderstanding.

CHAPTER X

NEGOTIATING THE LOAN

In the early autumn of 1945 the British and American Governments began a fateful series of negotiations to adapt their war-time alliance to the new requirements of the transition period. The circumstances were not favourable. The sudden end of Lend-Lease had brought an unwelcome atmosphere of haste and a dangerous legacy of mis-understanding. To make matters worse, the two peoples now faced the peace-time future with striking differences in temper and outlook.

Let us try, for a moment, to recapture the mood of that eventful period. It is clear that the thoughts of both peoples had turned in-ward upon domestic concerns. But what different thoughts they were! The people of Britain had known six years of agony and sacri-fice. They had been fortified in their struggle by the promise of a better life in the wake of victory. It was clear, now that victory had come, that this promise could not be realized without new assistance from the United States. Very well, it seemed to them, Britain could made a good case for such assistance. Had they not given dispro-portionately in the common cause? Could they not claim American aid as a matter of right?

On the other side of the Atlantic thoughts ran rather differently. The American people had provided their allies with huge sums to aid in winning the war; they had given additional sums to aid in winning the peace. In their view it was high time to end controls, reduce taxes, and return to 'normalcy'. New products and industrial techniques promised to bring unprecedented comforts to the average American. Vast consumer demands waited to be filled. Surely the rest of the world, with the assistance the United States had already given, would now be able to look after itself.

THE BRITISH APPROACH

This was the environment in which the British Government was forced to appeal for a new measure of American aid. Hints of such an appeal had been slowly accumulating. There had been Churchill's observation: 'We have given in the common cause, and may claim assistance to recover our normal economy from those we have helped to victory.'[1] There had been Anderson's warning that 'we shall have to incur further indebtedness'.[2] There had also been his more detailed statement:

> We emerge from the struggle with a gravely distorted economy, with an enormous burden of external debt and a balance of payments problem such as we have never before had to face. The system of international economic collaboration to be established now must profoundly affect our ability to play any useful part in the affairs of the post-war world and may even involve our very standards of life. We must determine our course of policy not in relation to this particular plan or that but upon a review of our situation as a whole. We must not assume that the cure for all our troubles was found at Bretton Woods. The time is at hand when we must decide and we shall do so heartened immensely by our knowledge of the part which America is clearly determined to play.[3]

What kind of assistance was British opinion prepared to accept? The public was naturally impressed with the disproportionate sacrifices the nation had made in the course of the war. 'We require', said *The Manchester Guardian*, 'an adequate acknowledgement . . . of the price we have paid.'[4] Many appeared to believe that the principle of 'equality of sacrifice' would justify a new appeal for American help and that such help might take the form of a grant-in-aid.

Now, in the face of all the danger signals, even Keynes became enamoured of this idea. His liberal conviction that ideas could conquer vested interests, his tendency to assume that logic and justice must eventually triumph, his faith in the power of his own advocacy —all these encouraged his hopes. He did not perceive that profound changes had taken place in American opinion. Robert Brand and Frank Lee of the British Treasury's delegation in Washington tried to warn him, but they were dismissed as 'black pessimists'. Even Clayton made little impression when he declared flatly that new American aid would have to be in the form of an interest-bearing loan.[5] Keynes still reassured himself by recalling the many times past when American generosity had come at the eleventh hour to lighten the burden of British difficulties.

Thus Keynes held out the hope that the American Government would agree to make $6 billion available as a grant-in-aid, or at the very least, as an interest-free loan. This estimate had unfortunate consequences. In the first place, it generated an entirely unrealistic

---

[1] *The Times* (16 Mar. 1945).   [2] 410 H.C. Deb. 711 (24 Apr. 1945).
[3] *The Times* (5 July 1945).   [4] (9 Sept. 1945).
[5] Clayton made this statement to Keynes during his August visit to London.

climate of opinion in Whitehall. 'He had persuaded them so successfully that the thing could be done that, when it was not done, they
tended to think that it must be owing to his faulty negotiations.'[1] In
the second place, his easy assumption of the case for such a generous
measure of American aid did not sit well in the United States. Keynes
asked one influential American: 'Can't you have another brain-wave
like Lend-Lease to get us out of our difficulties?' He was told in no
uncertain terms: 'No, sir, we're not having any more brain-waves.'

In September 1945 a British delegation headed by Keynes arrived
in the United States seeking a settlement of Britain's Lend-Lease
account and some new measure of American aid. The situation
required the most skilful exercise of the diplomatic art. The British
Ambassador in Washington, Lord Halifax, told the American people:
'We are not coming to you hat in hand as suppliants. We do not
want to ask anything of you which you are not satisfied is in the ultimate interest of your own country.'[2] Keynes struck the same attitude.
In an opening press conference he painted a picture of British self-
reliance and sought to dispel the notion that his country felt aggrieved
by the termination of war-time aid: 'The British Government had no
reason to suppose that Lend-Lease would continue for a significant
length of time after the end of the war or would be available for any
expenditure except that which arose out of the war in its concluding
phases. . . . We have received far too much liberality and consideration in the famous Lend-Lease Act to make any complaint about the
clean cut.'

About the precise terms of the aid Britain was now seeking Keynes
said very little. He only cautioned:

No doubt an easy course would be for you to offer, and for us to put our
names to a substantial loan on more or less commercial terms, without
either party to the transaction troubling to pay too much attention to the
question of the likelihood of our being able to fulfill the obligations which
we are undertaking. . . . We are not in the mood, and we believe and hope
that you are not in the mood, to repeat the experiences of last time's war
debt. We would far rather do what we can to get on as best as we can on any
other lines which are open to us.

If Keynes was vague about the terms of the aid, however, he was

---

[1] Harrod, *Life of Keynes*, p. 597.
[2] *The New York Times* (13 Sept. 1945). The British press greeted this approach with
enthusiasm. See, for example, 'We Don't Come to Beg', the *Daily Express* (13 Sept.
1945); 'Halifax Says Britain Asks No Favours', the *Daily Mail* (13 Sept. 1945);
'Britain "Not A Suppliant" To America', the *Daily Herald* (13 Sept. 1945).

not vague or ambiguous about its purpose. He rested his case for assistance squarely on the mutual interest in a multilateral régime. Without financial help, he declared, Britain would have to retain its war-time controls and develop bilateral trade techniques. With financial aid, on the other hand, the British Government would find it possible 'to work out with you . . . some means of returning at the earliest possible date to normal trade practices without discrimination and to increased freedom and liberality in commercial and tariff policies; in the belief that the resulting general expansion of world trade will result in the final outcome in you and other countries as well as ourselves being much better off on balance than under the first plan'.[1]

This affirmative, businesslike approach made a good impression on American opinion. There was, indeed, no other one available. During the opening days of the official negotiations Keynes brought up the question of 'equality of sacrifice'. He quickly found that the Administration was far more interested in future policies than in past performances. Comparisons about the British and American war efforts served only to stir resentment.[2] The American Government, as Clayton had already indicated, was eager to press ahead with the plans for the reconstruction of multilateral trade. It could not contemplate further financial assistance to Britain unless it received firm promises that Britain would ratify the Bretton Woods institutions and participate in the establishment of an International Trade Organization.

Unfortunately, the British people had little understanding of these facts. They had been told almost nothing about the Anglo-American plans on commercial policy. They had withheld approval of Bretton Woods. They had heard increasing criticism of the multilateral approach. Now they had fought an election mainly on issues of domestic policy and had elected a party which avoided discussion of multilateral trade. Yet here was Keynes making multilateralism the

---

[1] Press conference of 12 Sept. 1945, reported in the *Commercial and Financial Chronicle* (20 Sept. 1945).

[2] The American public did not react favourably to reports that the British were claiming to have made a greater relative contribution to the defeat of the Axis. See, for example, John Crider, 'British Base Plea for Aid on Justice Over War's Costs—They Quote Statistics to Show They Contributed Far More Relatively Than We Did', *The New York Times* (21 Sept. 1945). Naturally a very different response was aroused on the other side of the Atlantic. See the enthusiastic report that Keynes was basing his case 'on the hard statistical contention that Britain's was the greater contribution towards victory'. 'All America Now Knows Facts of Britain's Effort', the *News Chronicle* (22 Sept. 1945).

keystone of his appeal for American aid. Did he do this with the support of his countrymen? If not, the negotiations now beginning were founded on sand; they could only bring new difficulties to the Anglo-American alliance.

TABLE 1

American opinion on the relative importance of foreign and domestic problems

Date										Percentage naming foreign problems as most vital
Nov. 1935	.	.	.	.	.	.	.	.	.	11
Dec. 1936	.	.	.	.	.	.	.	.	.	26
Dec. 1937	.	.	.	.	.	.	.	.	.	23
Jan. 1939	.	.	.	.	.	.	.	.	.	14
Apr. 1939	.	.	.	.	.	.	.	.	.	35
Dec. 1939	.	.	.	.	.	.	.	.	.	47
Aug. 1940	.	.	.	.	.	.	.	.	.	48
Nov. 1941	.	.	.	.	,	.	.	.	.	81
. . .*										
Oct. 1945	.	.	.	.	.	.	.	.	.	7
Feb. 1946	.	.	.	.	.	.	.	.	.	23
June 1946	.	.	.	.	.	.	.	.	.	11
Sept. 1946	.	.	.	.	.	.	.	.	.	23
Dec. 1946	.	.	.	.	.	.	.	.	.	22
Mar. 1947	.	.	.	.	.	.	.	.	.	54
July 1947	.	.	.	.	.	.	.	.	.	47
Sept. 1947	.	.	.	.	.	.	.	.	.	28
Dec. 1947	.	.	.	.	.	.	.	.	.	30
Feb. 1948	.	.	.	.	.	.	.	.	.	33
Apr. 1948	.	.	.	.	.	.	.	.	.	73
June 1948	,	.	.	.	.	.	.	.	.	50
Oct. 1949	.	.	.	.	:	.	.	.	.	34

* Polls taken during the war-time period were omitted because they differed significantly in wording from the pre-war and post-war questions.

Source: Gabriel A. Almond, *The American People and Foreign Policy* (New York, 1950), p. 73. The figures are adapted from polls taken by the American Institute of Public Opinion.

THE AMERICAN RECEPTION

Let us turn now to the other side of the Washington negotiations. The Chairman of the American delegation was Fred Vinson, the new Secretary of the Treasury. Vinson was in charge of that part of the negotiations concerned with the British request for financial aid. The Vice-Chairman of the American delegation was Will Clayton, Assistant Secretary of State for Economic Affairs. Clayton was in charge of that part of the negotiations concerned with the 'Proposals' on commercial policy. These two men may be regarded as symbols of the major influences working to shape American policy.

Fred Vinson was a conscientious, conservative, border-state Democrat who succeeded Morgenthau shortly after Truman became President. The contrast he made with his predecessor told much about the changes that had been taking place in the Democratic Administration. Morgenthau had understood little of politics. He had been a willing supporter of New Deal experiments in the domestic and international field. As a result, he had been an anathema to both Congress and the business community. Vinson, on the other hand, was a more orthodox figure. This homespun alumnus of the House of Representatives was in close touch with the 'grass roots' of America. He was one of a group of Conservative Democrats whose influence in the Administration had been increasing in the late war years. Like other members of that group he had little aptitude or desire for bold innovation. His main objective remained what it had been during his career in elective politics—to discover the popular will and translate that will into government policy.

In the autumn of 1945 the nature of the popular will was unmistakable. There was a noticeable lack of concern with international affairs.[1] The problems of domestic reconversion were uppermost in the public mind. Influential voices, citing the threat of inflation and the unprecedented size of the national debt, counselled against any additional foreign spending. 'Europe should not ignore the fact', ex-President Herbert Hoover declared, 'that we are far more impoverished by this war than by the last one.'[2] Similar warnings were given by another 'elder statesman', Bernard Baruch, who declared himself against aiding Britain or any other country until a national balance-sheet had been drawn up to determine 'whatever we have left over' after taking care of domestic needs.[3] In Baruch's view the United States was preparing to shoulder financial obligations far beyond its capacity to bear. He also argued, as the Administration itself had done during the Bretton Woods debate, that there was

[1] Table 1 provides one measure of the prevailing mood.
[2] *The New York Times* (18 Sept. 1945).
[3] Bert Andrews, 'Baruch Asks Inventory of Nation's Resources', *The New York Herald-Tribune* (4 Nov. 1945).

nothing unique about Britain's predicament. 'If we let England have billions', he warned, 'we will have to let Russia, China, France, Norway, Denmark, Belgium, Holland, Italy and the Balkans have some too.'[1]

Here was one aspect of the public mood of which Vinson was disposed to take account. Another was the anxiety caused by the election of a Labour Government. Baruch warned Congress lest it aid foreign countries 'to nationalize their industries against us'.[2] Others cited Harold Laski, and, ironically, Keynes himself, as irresponsible exponents of Socialist experimentation. Aid to Britain, they argued, would either be wasted or employed to further policies incompatible with American principles of private enterprise. Although most Americans conceded that the domestic implications of Socialism were Britain's own affair, many questioned whether a Socialist Britain could carry out the international objectives of American aid. As the *Wall Street Journal* put it: 'The question of a loan to Britain does not hinge on the political philosophy of her cabinet. It hinges on the question of what policy that government is likely to adopt in its commercial relations with the rest of the world.'[3]

In these circumstances it was not surprising that there was strong public opposition to the idea of a British loan.[4] This fact would have given pause to any Administration, but it had a particular impact in the autumn of 1945. Congress was becoming more and more rebellious. The power and prestige of the Executive was exceedingly low. Even Truman's suggestion for a writing-off of war-time Lend-Lease aroused a storm of opposition.[5] The new President, still unsure of himself, was not yet prepared, as Roosevelt had been, to challenge the legislature with a show of powerful leadership. The result was a stalemate, causing, for a time, the virtual end of effective government. Keynes was hardly exaggerating when he later told the House of Lords that 'during the whole time I was in Washington there was not a single Administration measure of the first impor-

[1] The *Daily Mail* (15 Sept. 1945).

[2] Andrews, op. cit., *supra*. The influence of Baruch's message was considerable. In Walter Lippmann's opinion it 'could hardly have been more subtly contrived to wreck the negotiations and prevent a reconciliation of the British and American views'. 'Mr. Baruch Writes a Letter', *The New York Herald-Tribune* (6 Nov. 1945).

[3] (13 Aug. 1945).

[4] 60 per cent. of those interviewed in a Gallup poll opposed a loan to Britain; 27 per cent. were in favour; 13 per cent. expressed no opinion. The *Chicago Daily News* (10 Oct. 1945).

[5] 'Truman Stirs Bi-party Row on War Debts', *The New York Herald-Tribune* (1 Sept. 1945).

tance that Congress did not either reject, remodel, or put on one side'.[1]

All these developments profoundly influenced Vinson's ideas about the size and the terms of American assistance. Of course, the Secretary of the Treasury was not only interested in domestic politics. He was also interested in finding a solution that would cover Britain's legitimate needs. Unfortunately, he was badly advised in this respect. Some of the blame for this must be placed on Harry White, who still had some of the power he had acquired under Secretary Morgenthau. We have already noted how, during the Bretton Woods debate, White steadfastly belittled the need for a British loan. In that arduous campaign an estrangement had developed between White and two of his most able colleagues, Edward Bernstein and Ansel Luxford. Bernstein and Luxford were more sympathetic than White to British needs. Now, when a technical committee was formed by White to advise on Britain's financial position, the two of them were deliberately excluded. This committee produced extremely modest estimates of Britain's needs for American assistance. Seriously alarmed, Bernstein and Luxford took the unusual step of sending Vinson a memorandum on their own initiative. They warned that the committee's estimates were far too low, that the Anglo-American arrangements would break down, and that the Administration would be forced to come to Congress again for additional aid. Unfortunately, the memorandum came too late to influence the course of the negotiations. By this time the size and terms of the American loan had been finally determined.

So much for the influence on American policy transmitted through the person of Fred Vinson. There was also a second element at work. This was represented by the imposing figure of Will Clayton. Clayton was certainly one of the most striking and original personalities to have served the United States Government in recent years. Born in modest circumstances in Jackson, Mississippi, he came honestly by his reputation as a self-made man. From a $15 a week job as a court stenographer he had risen to become head of the world's largest firm of cotton brokers. His career was eloquent testimony to the tremendous potentialities of unfettered private enterprise. No wonder that at an early date he developed a passionate abhorrence of government interference in economic life.

In foreign economic policy Clayton was an even more uncom-

[1] 138 H.L. Deb. 785 (18 Dec. 1945).

promising exponent of free enterprise principles than Cordell Hull himself. For a time he had regarded the Reciprocal Trade Agreements Act as too cautious an approach to tariff reduction. New Deal policies of agricultural restriction had driven him into the Liberty League, an extreme right-wing political organization. As the war approached, however, he had returned to the Democratic fold to support Hull in his campaign for multilateral trade. His plans for the post-war world were based on the conviction that 'the international economic policies of nations have more to do with creating conditions which lead to war than any other single factor'.[1] He even went so far as to declare: 'If the principles of equality of access on reasonable terms to the trade and raw materials of the world were universally practiced, the appetite for expansion of sovereignty, so productive of international friction, would largely disappear.'[2]

Clayton's attitude in the Washington negotiations was an expression of this philosophy, combined with courage, magnanimity, and goodwill. He had always taken a sympathetic view of the British predicament. He was not a person to shrink from unpopular policies out of fear of domestic political difficulties. At the same time, he was by no means soft or forgetful of American interests. America's primary interest in aiding Britain, so it seemed to him, was the reconstruction of a multilateral régime. If such aid were granted he would insist that it be accompanied by specific commitments to ensure that the aid had its intended effect.

It was no secret that Clayton was displeased at the wide latitude for currency restrictions left by the monetary compromise of Bretton Woods. He was also impatient at the slow progress in the drafting of a code on commercial policy. In his mind the British request for transitional aid offered a unique opportunity to speed things up. The United States could use its vast economic power to promote trade policies in the general interest. It could solve Britain's transitional problem and thus remove what Clayton considered the last legitimate basis for British opposition to a multilateral régime. In this way an acceleration of the Bretton Woods time-table and an Anglo-American understanding on commercial policy became the necessary accompaniments of financial aid to the United Kingdom.

Clayton's own concern that multilateral commitments be linked

---

[1] Letter to David M. Figart, 15 Nov. 1943, *Clayton Papers*.
[2] 'The Implications of International Economic Relations to World Peace', *Dept. of State Bull.*, xiv (1946), p. 678.

to the transitional aid was largely altruistic. But it was reinforced by strong pressure from members of the American business community who had a direct economic interest in the elimination of British trade controls. Clayton's correspondence was filled with complaints from foreign traders about the operation of Imperial Preference, the sterling area dollar pool, and new bilateral payments agreements which Britain had concluded with Sweden and Argentina. These letters warned that support for Bretton Woods, the Reciprocal Trade Agreements programme, and other measures of the Administration's foreign economic policy would be withdrawn unless some tangible benefits for American business were immediately received. One correspondent told Clayton that he opposed the idea of aiding Britain but added that 'if you succeed in doing away with the Empire preference and opening up the Empire to United States commerce, it may well be that we can afford to pay a couple of billion dollars for the privilege'.[1]

The same point was now advanced in public by prominent individuals and business organizations concerned with foreign trade. The National Association of Manufacturers warned that no assistance to Britain could be approved by Congress unless 'the commitments the British make toward relaxing and eliminating discriminatory trade practices are definite, tangible, and practical from the standpoint of American industry'.[2] Similar demands for the elimination of British commercial and financial restrictions were voiced by the U.S. Chamber of Commerce and the National Foreign Trade Council.[3] Banker Winthrop Aldrich urged: 'The British Commonwealth should agree to do away with exchange controls on current account and give up the so-called sterling area . . . relinquish the system of imperial preference and . . . eliminate quantitative trade controls.'[4]

The linking of multilateral policies to transitional aid was urged not only by the business community but also by dominant opinion in the American Congress. On this subject the supporters and opponents of Bretton Woods could finally join ranks. The Administration's foreign economic policy had been based on the argument that prosperity and peace required the abandonment of the practices of

---

[1] Letter to Clayton from General R. E. Wood, Chairman of the Board of Sears Roebuck & Co., 26 Nov. 1945, *Clayton Papers*.

[2] 'British Warned U.S. Will Act if Trade Barriers Continue', *Journal of Commerce* (29 Oct. 1945).

[3] 'Foreign Credit Group Seeks U.S. Aid in Sterling Bloc Areas', *The New York Herald-Tribune* (6 Sept. 1945); 'British Aid Backed with Reservation', *The New York Times* (20 Oct. 1945).   [4] *The New York Times* (5 Oct. 1945).

'economic warfare'. Those who supported that policy could hardly vote assistance to a country which refused to abandon such practices. On the other hand, the Bretton Woods programme had been attacked on the ground that its cost was not justified by sufficient assurances of reform in the economic policies of other countries. These critics could hardly be faced again unless the Administration could get more tangible and immediate economic concessions.

Some indication of the attitude of Congress was provided by a report on post-war reconstruction issued by a special committee of the House of Representatives.[1] This report argued that 'the advantages afforded by United States loans and other settlements are our best bargaining asset in securing political and economic concessions in the interest of world stability'.[2] It urged the Administration to obey 'the statutory intent of the Lend-Lease Act and of the agreements concluded under it' by exacting commitments on multilateral policies 'before any writing off of Lend-Lease'.[3] It also proposed that American reconstruction aid should be provided only to those countries willing to abandon state trading practices and prepared to give 'a guaranty of non-discriminatory treatment for all business of United States citizens'.[4] Finally, it included the specific recommendation that 'a prerequisite to the granting of large-scale loans to England should be the removal of discriminatory treatment, of quotas, exchange controls, and tariff preferences, with an agreed schedule based on the volume of trade, and flexible time schedules for their removal'.[5]

Such were the pressures operating on American policy through the figure of Clayton. How they combined with those to which Vinson was subject may be seen from an editorial in *The New York Herald-Tribune* which appeared shortly before the opening of the Washington negotiations. This editorial warned that the ability of the United States to grant assistance was not unlimited and cautioned against the 'sentimental argument' that aid was due to an impoverished ally. Then it urged that specific conditions be attached to any help given to the United Kingdom:

Enlightened self-interest suggests that we give her what help we can afford on terms that will accomplish two objectives—assist her to self-reliance and prevent her from using the fresh economic strength she gains from our aid

---

[1] U.S. Congress, House, Special Committee on Post-War Economic Policy and Planning, *Economic Reconstruction in Europe*, H. Rept. No. 1205, 79th Cong., 1st sess. 12 Nov. 1945).   [2] Id., p. 13.
[3] Ibid.   [4] Id., p. 44.   [5] Id., p. 29.

against us. We should recognize that Great Britain, with her sterling area and empire preference and acts of discrimination against foreigners has established an economic isolationism more pronounced than this country's with its tariff system. . . . We must bargain with her realistically.[1]

Animated by this 'realistic' attitude, Vinson, Clayton, and the other American negotiators prepared the American reception to the British approach.

NEGOTIATING THE LOAN

On 13 September, after several preliminary meetings between subordinates, Keynes and Halifax led the British delegation through the portals of the Federal Reserve Building for the first formal session of the Washington negotiations. From our previous discussion we can see that major obstacles to agreement lay not only in the genuine differences between the delegations themselves but in the broad gulf that now separated public opinion in their respective countries. One observer went so far as to suggest that the main difficulty facing the negotiators was not 'what would be the right and wise thing to do. . . . What they are trying to decide, and they all of them are seriously troubled about it, is how far Congress and Parliament, the American public and the British, will permit them to solve the problem.'[2]

As if the situation were not difficult enough, yet another problem appeared when the Washington meetings got under way. There was a serious clash in the personalities of the two most important negotiators. Keynes and Vinson could not seem to get along. White had admired Keynes; Morgenthau had been fascinated by him; Clayton and Acheson had become his close friends. But between the grave, cautious border-state politician and the urbane product of Cambridge University there was no *rapport* at all. White and Keynes, it is true, had also differed widely in temperament and social background. But at least they had shared something of the same approach to economic analysis. With Vinson, this unifying factor was not present. Vinson's chief criterion for judging Keynes's economic arguments was what would be accepted by his constituents at home. 'Mebbe so, Lawd

---

[1] 'Time for a Bargain' (13 Sept. 1945). For another expression of this view see 'Banker's Role', *The Christian Science Monitor* (13 Oct. 1945). For one of the few suggestions that assistance to Britain should be based on moral rather than business considerations, see 'The British Problem', *The New York Times* (12 Sept. 1945).

[2] Walter Lippmann, 'Today and Tomorrow', *The New York Herald-Tribune* (4 Oct. 1945).

($ million)

PRE-WAR

1936-8 (average)

Imports	3,500	Exports	1,950
		Net Invisibles	1,350
		Deficit	200
			3,500

HYPOTHETICAL POST-WAR

Year immediately after the transition

Imports	6,500	Exports	5,750
Overseas expenditure	250	Net Invisibles	1,000
	6,750		6,750

Imports, exports and freights are at an assumed price-level double pre-war.

Above assumes nothing for repayment of war debts.

ESTIMATE FOR 1946

Imports	5,200	Exports	2,600 ✓
Overseas war expenditure	1,200 ✓	Net Invisibles	680 ✓
	6,400	Deficit	3,120
			6,400

(Assumed prices approximately double pre-war)

HYPOTHETICAL BALANCE SHEET
during transitional period

Deficit

	$ Million	
1946	3,000	2.3 ✓
1947	1,250	.8 ✓
1948	500	.2 ✓
1949)	250	0 ✓
1950)		
	5,000	3.3

Keynes 5
4.3

Other liabilities	(a)	Settlement of lend-lease etc.
	(b)	Release of sterling to the Sterling Area 1946-50
Available Assets	(c)	Aid from Canada
	(d)	Aid from rest of Sterling Area during 1946
	(e)	Use of reserve etc.

(b) and (d) are each put provisionally at about 1,000 and therefore cancel out over the period as a whole.

4,500

4 4
4 Billion

38
3 Billion

Clayton's copy of estimates used during the loan negotiations.

Keynes, mebbe so', Vinson would say after hearing some particularly brilliant contribution, 'but down where I come from folks don't look at things that way.'

If Vinson showed little interest in the refinements of economic analysis he showed even less appreciation of the shafts of wit which Keynes now broke about his brows. In vain did members of the British delegation warn Keynes that he was dealing with a different type of man than Morgenthau or Acheson. 'Please try to remember', one associate pleaded, 'that you are dealing with Kentucky.' 'Well', said Keynes defiantly, 'Kentucky will have to like it.' Indeed, the more he was warned, the more unmercifully he ragged his adversary. One exchange was particularly memorable. Vinson, to illustrate some point, had grown rather rhetorical. He demanded to know whether Britain's capacity to service a loan would not be enhanced 'if suddenly, tomorrow, you found currency in a cave'. 'Why, of course', Keynes exclaimed. '"Any currency found in caves"—we'll have that in the agreement!' There was a roar of laughter at this *riposte*. Vinson turned black with rage. He did not quickly forget the incident.

The detailed terms of the Washington settlement will be analysed in the next chapter. Here we shall only outline the general course of the negotiations. There were five fundamental issues, all of them somewhat interdependent. The first, of course, was the nature of the American assistance. For almost an entire month this question dominated the negotiations. Keynes was under instructions to negotiate for a grant-in-aid. No one could have made a more powerful case for this solution. But the American delegation stood firm. Vinson and Clayton were in complete agreement that a grant would not be approved by the American people. When it became apparent that nothing could move them a serious schism developed within the British camp. Some members of the British Cabinet wanted to break off the negotiations. Anxious telegrams were sent from London. In effect, they said: 'You were originally sent to negotiate a grant-in-aid. What is this you are drifting into?' Keynes was infuriated by these messages. Now, rather belatedly, he described the true state of American opinion. It was only after some agonizing exchanges that he finally received permission to remain and negotiate within the framework of American demands.

Once it became apparent that a grant-in-aid could not be achieved, Keynes devoted all his energies to securing an interest-free loan. On this subject the two delegations were not so very far apart. Both sides recalled the experience of the previous war debts. They agreed that it would be unwise to burden Britain once again with annual interest charges unrelated to changes in Britain's external position. But interest remained a major issue for domestic political reasons. The American delegation insisted that no loan could be approved by the Congress unless it bore an interest charge at least equal to the cost of borrowing by the American Treasury. The British replied that an interest charge would never be understood in the United Kingdom. In the end, something of a compromise was reached. It was agreed that the loan would carry a modest interest charge of 2 per cent., but that the charge would be waived in bad times when Britain earned an inadequate amount of foreign exchange.

Bound up closely with the question of the nature of the American assistance was the question of its size. The British said they would need aid in the amount of $6 billion. The Americans unanimously regarded this figure as too high, but found it difficult to agree on a counter-proposal. The American technical committee estimated the British balance of payments deficit for 1946–8 at $3·3 billion; it did not consider that this estimate would be affected significantly by the presence of multilateral obligations such as the convertibility of sterling. One estimate of the U.S. Treasury put the British deficit as low as $2·3 billion. These estimates, of course, were of the overall deficit of the United Kingdom alone. There was no thought of a separate dollar balance of payments problem. Nor was any allowance made for a possible drain on the central reserves due to deficits in the overseas sterling area.

Like the decision on the matter of interest, the decision on the size of the financial aid was finally determined more by political than by economic factors. There was never any detailed consideration at a high level in the American Government of just how much assistance Britain required. The question was how much assistance could safely be asked of Congress. The politically cautious Vinson proposed $3·5 billion, Clayton and the State Department $4 billion. The disagreement was eventually settled by Truman himself, who 'split the difference' at $3·75 billion.

In retrospect, these figures may be thought to reflect undue caution. If Congress could be asked for $3·75 billion, why not for $4 or even $5 billion? Within such a margin Congress was unlikely to be difficult, once it had been persuaded of the necessity for the loan itself. It probably made little practical difference, however, even if the Administration was unduly conservative on this matter. The final figure of $3·75 billion was no very great disappointment to the British delegation. Indeed, once a loan with interest had been decided upon, the British lost a lot of their enthusiasm for a larger sum with its heavier burden of annual payments. And in the last analysis Keynes and his associates believed that the amount offered them would be adequate to satisfy British needs.

The remaining issues of the Washington talks concerned the commercial and financial policies of the United Kingdom. As we have seen, Clayton was anxious to press ahead with the Anglo-American commercial policy talks and to link them formally with the financial negotiations. The British delegates were reluctant to do this, both because Whitehall had not entirely made up its mind on some of the commercial policy issues and because they foresaw domestic political difficulties in tying such matters as Imperial Preference to the granting of American aid. Fear on this latter score was soon justified. Reports widely circulated in both countries created the impression that the United States was using the loan as a way of forcing British acceptance of an American trade programme. *The New York Times*, for example, spoke as if the plan for a trade charter were solely an American idea and declared that the British were being asked to 'wipe out their empire (tariff) preference system as a quid for the financial aid'.[1] *The Manchester Guardian* called the proposal for the elimination of preferences a 'new development' as a result of which 'the whole aspect of the negotiations has been changed'.[2] Other British papers carried the same story in alarming banner headlines.[3] In fact, of course, the negotiations on commercial policy had been amicable and had only followed the general lines of the Washington discussions of 1943.[4] The misunderstanding created on this subject might have serious future consequences. It was an expensive price

[1] John Crider (26 Oct. 1945). See also Reston, 'Britain's Cabinet Approves U.S. View on World Trade', id. (7 Nov. 1945). Preferences were not the only measure of trade policy reported as a 'condition' of the loan. See, for example, Reston, 'World Trade Body to Fight Cartels if We Advance Loan, British Agree', id. (9 Nov. 1945).
[2] 'U.S. Asks for Abandonment of Empire Preference' (5 Oct. 1945). See also the *Financial News* of the same date.
[3] ' " Abandon Empire Preference "—Americans Present New Demand ', the *Daily Express* (5 Oct. 1945); 'Empire Preference Must Go, Says U.S.', the *Daily Herald* (5 Oct. 1945); 'U.S. Insists: End Empire Preference', the *Daily Mail* (5 Oct. 1945).
[4] The actual course of the 1945 negotiations on commercial policy and their true relation to the financial negotiations was described in Chapter VIII, *supra*.

for the Administration to pay for the privilege of claiming British endorsement of the 'Proposals' as an additional benefit from aid to the United Kingdom.

Another issue relating to Britain's external economic policy was the convertibility of sterling. Here the difference between the two delegations was on timing rather than on ultimate objective. Keynes had come round to the view that the convertibility of sterling was something fully in the interest of Britain as well as the world at large.[1] But now the American negotiators proposed a rigid commitment forbidding Britain to impose any restrictions on the use of sterling for current transactions after 31 December 1946. Keynes strongly resisted the idea of a fixed deadline—especially one that was only a year away. He did not believe that the anticipated rate of British recovery justified the assumption of such a burden. He was particularly concerned about the adverse effect on Britain's balance of payments of a unilateral commitment to convert foreign holdings of sterling without an equivalent commitment from foreign countries to convert holdings of their currencies. In place of the American proposal he suggested a general pledge to lift financial restrictions at the earliest possible moment. But the American negotiators would not accept this alternative. They were convinced that a fixed timetable was necessary to insure British compliance with multilateral principles and to persuade Congress that a tangible benefit had been received. It was all Keynes could do to get the time-table extended a few months—to one year after the effective date of the agreement.[2] He also managed to insert a saving clause permitting postponement of convertibility in 'exceptional cases' where countries were abusing their convertibility privileges.

The final issue of the Washington negotiations concerned the accumulated sterling balances. American feelings on this subject were understandably strong. In the course of the Washington negotiations the American delegation had agreed to a complete wiping out of Britain's obligations for Lend-Lease materials used during the course of the war. It had also agreed to a generous settlement for Lend-Lease goods of post-war value then in the possession of the United King-

[1] See, for example, Keynes's letter to Philip Cortney (26 June 1945), in which he agreed that 'in order of urgency the main objective to be attained is the free convertibility of the pound sterling'. The letter is reprinted in Cortney, *The Economic Munich* (New York, 1949).
[2] The effective date of the agreement was expected to be some time in Mar. or Apr. 1946, depending on the speed of Congressional action.

dom. The United States Government was prepared to support such a liberal settlement as a means of removing obstacles to the reconstruction of a multilateral trading system. But it expected other countries to do the same. It wanted to ensure that its transitional assistance to Britain would prove really effective and would not be diverted to other ends.

For these reasons the American negotiators pressed for a drastic scaling down of the sterling balances. Indeed, this was one of the assumptions on which the plan for American assistance was based. 'Of course', Clayton assured one of his business associates, 'the bulk of the $14 billion frozen sterling credits is to be written off.'[1] Some members of the Administration wanted to join Britain in negotiations with its sterling creditors. They suggested that the United States should bear part of the cost of the sterling releases offered these creditors in return for a substantial measure of scaling-down. But the British Government opposed all proposals for American participation in a settlement of the balances. Moreover, Keynes was instructed to avoid any specific commitment on the form that this settlement might take. Drafts of an article on the balances to be included in the Financial Agreement were returned by London with wholesale expurgations. This eventually taxed the limits of Keynes's patience. After the return of one such draft he cabled: 'We are negotiating in Washington repeat Washington. Fig leaves that pass muster with old ladies in Threadneedle Street wither in a harsher climate.'[2]

The provision on the balances finally agreed upon at Washington sought to accommodate American desires without giving the specific terms of the final settlement. It noted simply that some balances would be written off, some funded, and some immediately released. Nevertheless, although no specific proportions were published in the Financial Agreement, the British and American negotiators did exchange informal estimates of what the final outcome was to be. One of the British negotiators suggested that about one-third of the balances might be cancelled and 90 per cent. of the remainder funded over a long period. The American negotiators based their financial proposals on the assumption that total releases of sterling balances during 1946–50 would total only £250 million ($1 billion) and would be exactly balanced by net contributions from

[1] Letter to S. M. McAshan, Jr., of Anderson Clayton & Co. (18 Sept. 1945), *Clayton Papers*.
[2] The source for this story is Paul Bareau, 'Future Prospects', in Institute of Bankers, *The Sterling Area* (London, 1949).

the overseas sterling area to the central reserve.[1] It is reported that Keynes himself expressed agreement with at least part of this assumption.[2]

In these various ways the five major issues of the Washington negotiations were finally resolved. But the settlement required nearly three months of intensive, and sometimes bitter, negotiation. The last few weeks were a nightmare for all concerned. The deadline for the conclusion of the talks was ominously near. December 31 was the last date by which Britain could ratify the Bretton Woods agreements and become an original member of the Bank and Fund. Several weeks had to be allowed for Parliamentary debate on these agreements and on the terms of the Washington settlement. In the first week of December time ran out on the two delegations.

There was an atmosphere of suspense and drama about these last few days. With each new concession the United Kingdom had become increasingly restive. The prospect of an interest-bearing loan combined with rigid multilateral commitments finally proved too much for some members of the Cabinet. For one decisive moment, the British Government wavered. It considered recalling Keynes to London for further consultations. But Keynes's health would not permit him to return by air, and the delay of a sea voyage might have meant the end of the financial negotiations. The Cabinet decided instead to send Sir Edward Bridges, a leading Treasury official, in an attempt to secure better terms.

This last desperate expedient proved of no avail. Upon his arrival in Washington Bridges found an American delegation firmly united against further concessions. Either Britain would agree to the existing terms, or the negotiations would end in failure. Faced with this alternative, the Cabinet made the inevitable decision. On 6 December 1945 the Financial Agreement was finally signed.

CONCLUSION

The signing of the Anglo-American Financial Agreement was the occasion for profound relief. It meant, according to Halifax, that 'the cooperation of our two governments has not ended with the end

---

[1] See the last two lines of the mimeographed sheet used by Clayton during the Washington talks and reproduced on p. 200. The document was found among the *Clayton Papers*.

[2] Keynes 'gave the figure of £200 million as the maximum amount of ready cash that Britain should provide in all towards paying off these balances prior to 1951'. Harrod, *Life of Keynes*, p. 608.

PLATE 3

Secretary of State James F. Byrnes signs the Anglo-American Financial Agreement as Keynes (*left*), Halifax, and Vinson (*right*) look on

of the war, and that we mean to go forward side by side along the road to peace'.[1] Behind these hopeful words, however, was considerable ground for misgiving. The negotiations had occurred in a highly tense and critical atmosphere. Their outcome had been determined less by the economic realities than by the pervasive influence of public opinion. The American negotiators, in particular, had been forced to strike a number of compromises between their better judgement and the domestic political mood. Might such compromises have been avoided if the Administration had tried to lead American opinion to a better understanding of the British case? Which was the greater danger—that such an understanding could not have been achieved, or that the negotiators would frame a pseudo-solution which could only lead to new difficulties? As one observer declared: 'Only a genuine settlement is worth proposing and certainly it would be better to plunk for the real thing, even if at first there were strong opposition, than to tinker with some sort of counterfeit which will land us and the rest of the world into another post-war catastrophe.'[2]

Whether the Washington settlement was counterfeit or real will be the next question to command our attention.

[1] *The New York Times* (7 Dec. 1945).
[2] Lippmann, Today and Tomorrow', *The New York Herald-Tribune* (4 Oct. 1945).

CHAPTER XI

THE LOAN AGREEMENT AS AN INSTRUMENT OF MULTILATERALISM

SHORTLY after its signing on 6 December 1945 President Truman predicted that the Anglo-American Financial Agreement would 'set the course of American and British economic relations for many years to come'.[1] This forecast was to be vindicated in ways that its author could hardly foresee. The settlement reached at Washington soon had repercussions which profoundly affected the development of Anglo-American policy toward multilateral trade. It is time to examine the terms of that settlement in some detail. Was it well designed to further the multilateral goal?

THE LEND-LEASE SETTLEMENT

Before turning to the Financial Agreement itself we must first review the terms of the Lend-Lease settlement which was concluded at the same time.[2] In view of the frequent equivocation about repayment of Lend-Lease, the generosity of this settlement certainly surpassed expectation. The war-time Lend-Lease account, in which the United States stood as a net creditor of the United Kingdom to the extent of over $20 billion, was completely wiped out. Some $6 billion in surplus property and Lend-Lease located in Britain at the end of the war was transferred for $532 million—a sum probably well below even its post-war value. For Lend-Lease in the 'pipeline' the American Government asked full payment to the extent of $118 million. This total of $650 million Britain was asked to repay on the same credit terms as the $3·75 billion loan—terms more favourable than those offered to the other recipients of Lend-Lease aid.[3]

From the point of view of the American Government this was a settlement of unprecedented generosity. It was also an act of political

---

[1] Message of the President in forwarding the Agreement to Congress, 92 *Cong. Rec.* 603 (30 Jan. 1946).

[2] 'Settlement for Lend-Lease and Reciprocal Aid, Surplus War Property, and Claims', *Financial Agreement Between the Governments of the United States and the United Kingdom*, Cmd. 6708 of 1945, pp. 6–8.

[3] The Lend-Lease obligations of other allies were covered by Export-Import Bank credits carrying interest charges of 2⅜ per cent. These credits, unlike the one granted to Britain, carried no provision for waiver of interest.

courage, for it was far more generous than the settlement which Congress and the public apparently desired.[1] On the other hand, in the light of 'equality of sacrifice', the writing-off of Lend-Lease consumed in the war was the very least that Britain was entitled to expect. It could even be argued that the requirement of payment for surplus property and 'pipeline' goods was a violation of the principle in the post-war transition.[2] But this was a rather perfectionist point of view: against the forgiveness of $20 billion the failure to forgive $650 million was a relatively minor omission. In general the Lend-Lease settlement, by removing the threat of a large burden of dollar indebtedness, was well designed to implement the multilateral goal.

The settlement, however, had another and more dubious aspect. Following the formula outlined in Article Seven, the writing-off of war-time Lend-Lease was linked with British adherence to multilateral principles. The settlement of Lend-Lease was made 'complete and final'—a matter of no little importance to the United Kingdom. But in making this settlement the two Governments took special note not only of the 'benefits already received by them in the defeat of their common enemies' but also

of the general obligations assumed by them in Article VII of the mutual-aid agreement of February 23, 1942, and the understandings agreed upon this day with regard to commercial policy. Pursuant to this settlement, both Governments will continue to discuss arrangements for agreed action for the attainment of the economic objectives referred to in Article VII of the mutual-aid agreement. The Governments expect in these discussions to reach specific conclusions at an early date. . . . In the light of all the foregoing, both Governments agree that no further benefits will be sought as consideration for lend-lease and reciprocal aid.[3]

Thus the American Administration carried out its plan to exact a British pledge of co-operation in multilateral projects as a 'consideration' for a generous settlement of the Lend-Lease account. There is no doubt that this was in accord with the express desire of Congress.[4] One wonders, however, whether it proved a very useful expedient. When it finally looked into the matter Congress did not, after all,

[1] See the public opinion poll and the recommendations of the Congressional committees cited pp. 172–3 *supra*, as well as the charges subsequently made by the Senate War Investigating Committee that the payments asked by the U.S. in the Lend-Lease settlement with Britain were entirely inadequate. The *Financial Times* (23 Mar. 1946).
[2] For the development of this view, see Sir Hubert Henderson, 'The Anglo-American Financial Agreement', *O.I.S.B.*, viii (Jan. 1946), p. 3.   [3] Cmd. 6708, p. 6.
[4] See the recommendations of the House committee, p. 198, *supra*.

find the British pledge a very convincing 'consideration'.[1] And the linking of the commercial policy 'Proposals' with the Lend-Lease (and Loan) agreements was seriously to prejudice their reception in the United Kingdom.

THE ANGLO-AMERICAN FINANCIAL AGREEMENT

The line of credit—its purpose, amount, and terms

The purposes recited in any agreement provide useful clues to the intention of the parties and an indispensable guide to subsequent interpretation. The line of credit made available by the Anglo-American Financial Agreement was designed 'to facilitate purchases by the United Kingdom of goods and services in the United States, to assist the United Kingdom to meet transitional postwar deficits in its current balance of payments, to help the United Kingdom to maintain adequate reserves of gold and dollars, and to assist the Government of the United Kingdom to assume the obligations of multilateral trade, as defined in this and other agreements'.[2]

The juxtaposition of these various objectives raises an interesting question. What was the principal purpose of the loan—to implement British reconstruction in the various ways specifically mentioned or to facilitate the execution of multilateral 'obligations'? Probably the British and American draftsmen saw no inconsistency here. They could argue, with justice, that progress toward British recovery would be progress toward a multilateral régime. But the reverse proposition was not quite so obvious. The carrying out of multilateral obligations would promote British recovery only if the obligations were reasonable and within the nation's capacity to support. If the obligations were too burdensome or too precipitate they might play havoc with Britain's reserves, balance of payments, and ability to purchase goods in the United States. In such an event a difficult dilemma would confront those in charge of the Financial Agreement.

The possibility of conflict in the purposes of the American aid depended to a large extent on the amount of that aid itself. If the resources made available were infinitely great, all the stated purposes

[1] The Senate War Investigating Committee charged that the asserted 'benefits' involved in the 'consideration' were 'nebulous and require the United Kingdom to do no more than it ought to be willing to do anyway'. *The Times* (23 Mar. 1946).

[2] 'Financial Agreement Between the Governments of the United States and the United Kingdom', Article 3, Cmd. 6708. The complete text of the Financial Agreement is reproduced in an Appendix to the present volume.

could easily be realized. In fact, of course, the resources were definitely limited—a line of credit of $3·75 billion, to be drawn on at such times and in such amounts as was required. Together with the loan subsequently made available by Canada this put $5 billion at the disposal of Britain for use in the transition period.[1] This figure coincided exactly with the estimated transitional deficit put forward by the British during the Washington negotiations.[2] But the British estimate took no account of several unfavourable possibilities—that Britain's terms of trade might take an adverse turn and that large government expenditures might be required throughout the transition period. It took no account of the fact that the carrying out of multilateral obligations might increase the need for financial aid. Finally, it made no allowance for the possibility that as banker for the sterling area Britain might have to support not only its own deficit but the deficits of other sterling countries as well. For all these reasons there was considerable doubt that the assistance was large enough to accomplish its stated objectives.

The aid extended to Britain was in the form of a loan carrying an interest charge of 2 per cent. per annum. Interest and principal were to be repaid in fifty annual instalments, beginning on 31 December 1951. We have already noted that the assistance might have taken the form of a grant-in-aid, had the principle of 'equality of sacrifice' been literally applied. Once this alternative was rejected, the question of interest became important. Here the terms of the Financial Agreement sought to reduce as far as possible the burden upon the British balance of payments. Taking into account the five-year period of grace in repayment of interest, the effective rate of interest was only 1·6 per cent. The annual instalments of interest and principal would be $140 million—by no means a dangerous burden for Britain to assume in years of reasonably prosperous world trade. To ease the burden in a period of economic stringency the Financial Agreement included a provision, without precedent in previous American loan agreements, that interest payments might be waived. The United Kingdom would not be required to pay interest when it considered a waiver 'necessary in view of the present and prospective conditions of international exchange and the level of its gold and foreign exchange reserves' and when its average income from home-produced exports and net invisible transactions in the five preceding years was

---

[1] For the sake of convenience we are lumping together U.S. and Canadian dollars.
[2] *Statistical Material Presented During the Washington Negotiations*, p. 6.

insufficient to pay for a typical pre-war volume of imports.[1] These two conditions were designed to make possible a waiver of interest when Britain was no longer able to maintain its pre-war standard of living consistently with long-term solvency in its financial position.

For a number of reasons, however, the waiver clause was not so helpful as initially appeared. In the first place, the increase in population and the demand for better living standards made the pre-war volume of imports an obsolete basis for measurement.[2] Second, the formula made no allowance for the fact that a portion of Britain's foreign exchange income would be required to service her new burden of external indebtedness. Third, the reference to Britain's average earnings in a five-year period made the waiver unavailable in the face of violent short-run fluctuations in international trade. Finally, and more important than these technical points, the waiver was an unsound device from a political standpoint. However favourably the two Governments might regard use of the waiver, the public reaction was liable to be unfortunate. No prudent British Government would risk losing the goodwill of the American people for the sake of a comparatively trifling saving in external payments.

The transitional assistance subsequently extended by the United States to its other war-time allies (via the Export-Import Bank) contained the requirement that the aid be spent directly for American goods.[3] No such condition was attached to the British loan. This requirement could hardly have been included, since the dollars were partly required to implement the obligation to make sterling convertible. A number of minor restrictions were included, however, which related the line of credit to the other financial obligations of the United Kingdom.

[1] Article 5 (b). The typical volume of imports was fixed at £866 million, the 1936–8 average, this figure to be adjusted to take account of price changes. In calculating Britain's foreign exchange income releases of sterling balances in any year in excess of £43,750,000 were to be counted as capital transactions and not calculated as reductions of net income from invisibles. Thus Britain would not be permitted to take advantage of the waiver simply because it chose to show excessive generosity to its sterling creditors.

[2] In partial reply to this it might be argued that demands for better living standards should not have deserved consideration as long as Britain was living on foreign credit. However true this might be in theory, no British government would find it possible to resist such demands. Moreover, the redistribution of the pre-war national income in favour of the less privileged classes by itself would cause an increase in imports, since these classes would spend a greater proportion of their incomes on the primary products obtained from abroad.

[3] Not a provision of very great significance in the immediate post-war period, when most of the desired goods were only obtainable in the United States.

To begin with, Britain agreed to discharge its other obligations from sources other than the American loan.[1] This provision was designed to prevent use of the loan for payment of the sterling creditors. In fact it provided no such assurance, since there was no way of telling whether sterling obligations were being paid off by loan drawings or by the proceeds of current dollar earnings.

A second restriction was equally dubious. This forbade Britain to borrow from British Commonwealth Governments on credit terms more favourable to the lender than those in the Anglo-American Financial Agreement.[2] Here was an obvious attempt on the part of the American Government to avoid seeming more generous than countries bound to Britain by formal political ties. Whether this had some influence on domestic American opinion it is hard to say; certainly it had doubtful economic justification. It might possibly deprive Britain of valuable assistance from countries less powerful economically than the United States.

The third of the restrictions involved the greatest complications of all. It provided that the waiver of interest could not be invoked unless Britain received a waiver of interest payments on long-term loans arranged with Commonwealth countries and unless releases of sterling balances were 'reduced proportionately'.[3] This was also designed to avoid the appearance of unequalled American generosity and to prevent Britain from favouring its other creditors. In practice it had the unfortunate result of placing yet another qualification on the usefulness of the waiver clause.[4]

The multilateral obligations

One of the purposes of the Financial Agreement was to 'assist the Government of United Kingdom to assume the obligations of multilateral trade, as defined in this and other agreements'. The multilateral obligations included in the Financial Agreement concerned four major subjects—the current transactions of the sterling area countries, the current transactions of the United States, the current

---

[1] Article 6 (i).
[2] Article 6 (ii). The provision applied only to the years 1945–51.
[3] Article 6 (iii).
[4] This provision was apparently based on the assumption that the balances would be largely funded and releases kept under British control. On any other assumption it constituted a very serious impairment of the waiver's usefulness. The provision probably prevented Britain from invoking the waiver in 1952.

transactions of third countries, and treatment of the accumulated sterling balances.

The provision concerning the current transactions of the sterling area countries was drafted in the following terms:

> The Government of the United Kingdom will complete arrangements as early as practicable and in any case not later than one year after the effective date of this Agreement[1] . . . under which . . . the sterling receipts from current transactions of all sterling area countries . . . will be freely available for current transactions in any currency area without discrimination; with the result that any discrimination arising from the so-called sterling area dollar pool will be entirely removed and that each member of the sterling area will have its current sterling and dollar receipts at its free disposition for current transactions anywhere.[2]

One wonders whether this provision ever meant the same thing to the British and American Governments. In explaining the Financial Agreement to Congress and the public, the leading American negotiators held out this provision as the most significant of all the multilateral commitments.[3] As they explained it, the dollar pool had involved serious discrimination against American exports because the sterling area countries had been required to deposit their dollar earnings in London and had been forced to obtain British permission whenever they wanted to spend those earnings on American goods. The Financial Agreement, they promised, would work a major change in the operation of the sterling area by doing away with British control over the dollar earnings of the sterling countries.

The British interpretation of this provision was rather different. The representatives of the United Kingdom had always insisted that the operation of the dollar pool did not in fact prevent each member of the sterling area from having 'its current sterling and dollar receipts at its free disposition for current transactions anywhere'. In their view the dollar pool was a strictly voluntary war-time arrangement by which the sterling area members agreed to exercise self-restraint in dollar spending so as to conserve for urgent uses a pool of common reserves. After the economic difficulties of the war were over, there was hardly any likelihood that the sterling area

---

[1] The effective date of the Agreement was defined elsewhere as 'the date on which the Government of the United States notifies the Government of the United Kingdom that the Congress of the United States has made available the funds necessary to extend to the Government of the United Kingdom the line of credit in accordance with the provisions of this Agreement'. Article 1. In practice the effective date of the Agreement turned out to be 15 July 1946.

[2] Article 7.   [3] See Chapter XII, *infra*.

members would want to continue the voluntary arrangement. In British eyes, therefore, this provision of the Financial Agreement involved no significant change in British policy.

Which of these two views was correct? In the case of such an informal and flexible institution as the sterling area it is difficult to give a definite answer. The truth lay somewhere between the two extremes. It was certainly misleading to maintain that the dollar pool was an instrument of formal control by which the United Kingdom dictated the external policy of the sterling area countries. But it was also misleading to suggest that this provision in the Loan Agreement meant nothing at all and that the dollar pool might never prove inconsistent with multilateral principles. The point can be made by contrasting two possibilities. Suppose each member of the sterling area held its own dollar reserves. Each would naturally be concerned with improving its *net* dollar position: it would try not only to reduce imports but to export as much as possible to dollar markets. Suppose, on the other hand, that the dollar pool was maintained, and that the members of the sterling area agreed to restrict themselves to certain amounts of *gross* dollar spending. In this case the sterling countries would be induced to import less from the dollar area without being induced to export more. Operation of the pool would not merely redistribute the available supply of dollar earnings; it would actually reduce that supply below the level it could otherwise be expected to attain. In short, it might divert trade away from the United States and encourage an artificially high level of trade between the sterling area countries.

Unfortunately, the language of the Financial Agreement was not clearly directed to this legitimate point. It encouraged the misconception that Britain actually dictated the external policies of the sterling area countries. The traditional suspicion with which many Americans regarded the sterling area would be consequently increased. Such suspicion might, in the transition period, be extremely ill-advised. It would certainly be unwise to insist on decentralization of the sterling area and relaxation of its war-time discipline at a time when the sterling countries were desperately short of foreign exchange.

So much for the first of the multilateral obligations in the Financial Agreement. The second concerned British policy toward the current transactions of the United States. The United Kingdom promised that beginning with the effective date of the agreement it would not restrict payments for the purchase of American goods permitted to be imported into the United Kingdom and would not restrict the use of sterling balances owned by United States residents provided such balances arose out of current transactions.[1] By themselves these provisions effected no change in British policy: at the time of the Financial Agreement Britain was controlling its imports from the United States by means of restrictions on goods rather than by means of restrictions on payments.[2] The provisions were supplemented, however, by another commitment—that after 31 December 1946 Britain would not discriminate against the United States in its quantitative trade controls.[3] This commitment was rather more significant. Its purpose was to ensure that Britain did not use quantitative restrictions on the importation of goods to evade its obligations on the financial side. Certain exceptions were nevertheless permitted. Britain was allowed to discriminate for the purpose of using inconvertible currencies accumulated prior to 31 December 1946.[4] It was also permitted to discriminate when the discriminatory restrictions were merely alternatives to the financial restrictions permitted under the 'scarce currency' provisions of the Articles of Agreement of the International Monetary Fund.[5]

Despite these exceptions, the commitment to non-discrimination was too tightly drafted. The deadline of 31 December 1946 was only a year away. What would be the outcome if transitional difficulties persisted and currencies remained inconvertible? Britain would have a large deficit in its trade with the United States; its normal surpluses in trade with other countries would yield only inconvertible currencies which could not be employed to purchase dollar goods. Under the terms of the non-discrimination clause Britain would have to cut down purchases not only from the United States, whose currency it did not possess, but from other countries, whose currencies it did. The obvious injustice of this measure would have serious economic and political repercussions. In such a situation there would be little prospect of invoking the exception permitting discrimination in accord with the 'scarce currency' clause of the Fund Articles. Given the various safeguards against Fund lending for reconstruction purposes, the Fund was unlikely to be short of dollars during the transition period. Thus the

---

[1] Article 8 (i).   [2] I.e., by import licensing rather than by exchange control.
[3] Article 9.   [4] Article 9 (a).
[5] Article 9 (c). A third exception permitted Britain to employ 'measures not involving a substantial departure from the general rule of non-discrimination' to assist 'a country whose economy has been disrupted by the war'. Article 9 (b).

non-discrimination provision, however logical it may have appeared, might not prove flexible enough in the face of unforeseen transitional difficulties.

Probably the most important of the multilateral obligations in the Financial Agreement was the obligation to make sterling generally convertible for current transactions within one year after the effective date of the Agreement.[1] Since other provisions already assured 'convertibility' of sterling earned by residents both of the overseas sterling countries and the United States, this provision entailed a new obligation only in favour of third countries—the most important of them in Western Europe and South America. The legal form of the obligation was a promise by both the United States and the United Kingdom not to restrict payments and transfers for current transactions; specifically, not to take advantage of the transition period provisions of the Articles of Agreement of the International Monetary Fund.

To this undertaking there were two major exceptions similar to those included in the non-discrimination provision: the obligation did not apply with respect to sterling accumulated before the obligation became effective and did not prohibit restrictions employed in accordance with the 'scarce currency' provisions of the International Monetary Fund.[2] Like the non-discrimination provision, the obligation to make sterling generally convertible was stated to be 'in anticipation of more comprehensive arrangements by multilateral agreement' and was to expire on 31 December 1951.[3] The 'more comprehensive arrangements' presumably referred to the end of the Fund's transition period and to the coming into effect of an international trade charter. No attempt was made to define the situation that would occur in the event that these 'more comprehensive arrangements' never came into force.

The convertibility obligation, it must be emphasized, applied only to the use of sterling for current transactions. The drafters of this provision, like the drafters of the International Monetary Fund Agreement, assumed that it was possible to control capital movements while simultaneously permitting freedom in current transactions. But they were aware that in some situations convertibility might be abused and employed as a device for illegal capital transfer. Consequently they provided a kind of escape clause. Convertibility was to take effect one year after the effective date of the Agreement

---

[1] Article 8 (ii).   [2] Article 8 (ii) (a) and (b).   [3] Article 8 (iii).

unless in 'exceptional cases' after consultation the parties agreed otherwise.[1] This would make it possible to suspend convertibility with respect to those countries which were not taking adequate measures to confine convertibility to current transactions.

In the light of historical hindsight it is easy to be over-critical of the convertibility provision. It would be unfair to say that all the difficulties of the provision could have been appreciated at the time, or that it was doomed from the very outset. On the other hand, even in the light of the information then available, the deadline of eighteen months should have been regarded as dangerously short. The danger would not have been so great if other countries had been under a similar obligation to make their currencies convertible, or if the size of the financial assistance had been substantially larger. As it was, however, Britain was provided with assistance just sufficient to cover its own deficit; no margin was provided for the drain on British resources that might result from the convertibility obligation.

The fact is that the negotiators did not fully understand the economics of convertibility. They did not appreciate the difficulty in which Britain might find itself in the event that it went on accumulating inconvertible currencies while other countries, deliberately restricting imports from the United Kingdom, presented large sterling surpluses for conversion. Given this hazard of making one currency convertible in a generally inconvertible world, and given also the general uncertainties of the transition period, the use of a rigid time-table was certainly injudicious. It would have been much wiser if the date for implementation of convertibility could have been left to a joint Anglo-American board or even to the authorities of the International Monetary Fund.

The last of the multilateral obligations in the Financial Agreement concerned the accumulated sterling balances. This was drafted in terms much less precise than the obligations already discussed—necessarily so, since Britain was powerless to make commitments concerning the reduction of debts owed to third parties. The Financial Agreement stated simply that the Government of the United Kingdom 'intends to make agreements with the countries concerned, varying according to the circumstances of each case, for an early

---

[1] The escape clause in Article 8 (ii) permitted a *postponement* of convertibility to a 'later date'; the escape in 8 (ii) (b) permitted a *suspension* of convertibility at any time during the life of the Fund's transitional period. An escape clause permitting *postponement* also qualified the obligations to end the dollar pool and to convert releases of the sterling balances.

settlement covering the sterling balances accumulated by sterling area and other countries prior to such settlement. . .'.[1] This wording made it clear that sterling balances of non-sterling area countries were involved as well as sterling balances of sterling area countries, and that the anticipated settlements would embrace balances accumulated after the war (but prior to the settlements) as well as those accumulated during the war itself. Although the exact nature of the settlements was not spelled out—the agreements were to vary 'according to the circumstances of each case'—it was stipulated that the balances would be divided into three categories:

(a) balances to be released at once and convertible into any currency for current transactions, (b) balances to be similarly released by instalments over a period of years beginning in 1951, and (c) balances to be adjusted as a contribution to the settlement of war and post-war indebtedness and in recognition of the benefits which the countries concerned might be expected to gain from such a settlement.[2]

The Government of the United Kingdom agreed that it would 'make every endeavour to secure the early completion of these arrangements'.[3] It also agreed that 'any sterling balances released or otherwise available for current payments will, not later than one year after the effective date of this Agreement unless in special cases a later date is agreed upon after consultation, be freely available for current transactions in any currency area without discrimination'.[4]

These provisions represented a compromise between two different views on the sterling balances question. The American negotiators wanted a drastic scaling down of the sterling debts. They argued that Britain's other war-time creditors should show generosity equivalent to the generosity shown by the United States. They expressed anxiety lest the balances be used by Britain to gain markets at the expense of American export trade. Most important, they pointed out that the balances constituted a threat to Britain's external equilibrium and hence an obstacle to British participation in a multilateral régime.

These were all sensible arguments. But the solution proposed by some of the Americans was not so sensible. In certain quarters there was a tendency to treat the sterling balances as if they were no different than the Lend-Lease account and to suggest that they could be cancelled by Anglo-American fiat. This approach ignored a number of economic and political obstacles. For one thing, elementary justice might require a very different measure of scaling down for some of

---

[1] Article 10 (i).   [2] Ibid.   [3] Ibid.   [4] Article 10 (ii).

Britain's poorer sterling creditors than for an economically powerful country like the United States. For another thing, a large part of the sterling balances were privately held and could be handled only with considerable difficulty. Finally, many of the sterling creditors were independent countries who would demand to be consulted on the terms of settlement; they could not be expected to acquiesce in a bilateral agreement to which they were not parties. For all these reasons any attempt to achieve a final solution to the problem of the balances through the instrument of the Financial Agreement was bound to end in failure.

But if the position taken by some of the American negotiators was impractical, what judgement should be passed on the British approach? From the very earliest discussions on the International Monetary Fund the British representatives had resisted suggestions that the balances be made a subject of international concern. They gave the impression that offers of outside assistance would not be welcome and determined to seek a solution by themselves. This attitude betrayed a vast over-confidence in Britain's economic position and a serious underestimate of the danger which the sterling balances posed for the execution of Britain's multilateral obligations.

In truth, no adequate solution of the sterling balances problem could be found on a bilateral basis. Multilateral objectives could only be served in this case by multilateral negotiations—by an acknowledgement that the problem of war-time indebtedness concerned all the United Nations and demanded a collective solution. This was the approach originally hoped for by Churchill himself. If a United Nations conference had been called to deal with the problem the United States could have bargained forgiveness of the Lend-Lease account against a scaling down of the sterling obligations. The onus of responsibility for the settlement would have been shared. With the weight of the United States and other countries behind it, Britain would have enjoyed prospects for a satisfactory settlement that it never could have enjoyed alone.

Unfortunately, there was no disposition to try this approach in the autumn of 1945. The sudden end of war-time collaboration had left Britain in a desperate position; no one wanted to risk the delay that such a conference would have entailed. Moreover, neither the British nor the American Government was sufficiently sensitive to the needs of the under-developed countries who were among the largest sterling creditors. India and Egypt, to take two obvious examples, would not agree to a drastic scaling down of their sterling balances unless they were assured that capital would be made available from another source. No other source, of course, was then available or in immediate prospect. Private capital movements would require time to recover their normal volume; even when they had recovered they would not reach the kinds of projects for which financing was most urgently required. The International Bank had a conservative constitution and only limited resources; it would not even begin operations for many months. What the major sterling creditors required was a large volume of new funds made available either as grants-in-aid or as loans on extremely easy credit terms. The main contributor of these funds would have to be the United States. But there was no prospect at all that the United States was prepared to accept responsibilities of this kind.

Thus neither Britain nor the United States was ready to face up to a thorough-going solution to the problem of the sterling balances. Instead the two Governments improvised an illusory settlement—one which appeared to accommodate both their interests but which in the end could satisfy neither. The British were far too optimistic about the arrangements that would be made with the sterling creditors. They left the Americans with the impression that the balances would be almost entirely scaled down or funded. There was simply no adequate basis for the assumption that such an outcome would be achieved. The leaders of the British Government, pursuing the line of least political resistance, were contemplating no bold surgical operation. They would simply send delegations to each individual creditor, asking for generous treatment. Just what would they have to bargain with in such negotiations? Each creditor would hold out for the best possible terms, watching jealously lest another should receive more favourable treatment. The resulting settlements could hardly promote the purposes for which the United States had determined to extend the line of credit.

Provision for consultation and escape

The Anglo-American Financial Agreement included a number of multilateral obligations with specific time limits. Convertibility of sterling earned by American residents was to take place upon the effective date of the Agreement. Non-discrimination in the use of quantitative restrictions was to take place by 31 December 1946. Convertibility of sterling earned by residents of the sterling area and other countries was to take place within one year of the effective date of the Agreement.

The use of these specific target dates was particularly inappropriate in the uncertain economic conditions of the early transition period. The cause of multilateralism would have been better served by a more flexible arrangement enabling the parties to make periodic appraisals of the economic circumstances. Convertibility of sterling was not something which could be decreed with assurance eighteen months in advance. Nor could it be carried out successfully without close consultation between Britain and the United States and a certain amount of co-ordination of their domestic and external policies. The Financial Agreement made no provision for this consultation and co-ordination. Such an omission would hardly have been justified in a private financial contract. How much less was it justified in an instrument of collaboration between two great countries.

The Financial Agreement contained only two provisions permitting possible modification of its multilateral undertakings. The first was the general provision that either of the parties might 'approach the other for a reconsideration of any of the provisions of this Agreement, if in its opinion the prevailing conditions of international exchange justify such reconsideration, with a view to agreeing upon modifications for presentation to their respective legislatures'.[1] This provision was of limited value. Legislative discussion might be long; it might be acrimonious; it was a cumbersome and inefficient way of making adjustments. What was needed was a more informal mechanism for adapting the Agreement to changing circumstances.

The only evidence of such a mechanism in the Agreement was the phrase providing that the time limits for the three major 'convertibility' obligations were to apply unless in 'exceptional cases' after consultation the parties agreed otherwise. This provision did at least avoid the necessity for legislative approval. But its value as a mechanism of adjustment was also doubtful. The use of the phrase 'exceptional cases' as opposed to 'exceptional circumstances' was designed to ensure that the clause could only be invoked in the cases of particular countries which permitted abuse of the convertibility privilege. The provision was not intended to cover the case of a general international payments crisis necessitating postponement of the

[1] Article 12.

convertibility obligations.[1] One could always hope, of course, that the two Governments might some day agree upon the broader interpretation. But the failure to provide consultative machinery reduced the likelihood that any such adjustment would be made in time.

CONCLUSION

The outcome of the Washington negotiations was hardly more reassuring than the circumstances in which they began. It was true that the Lend-Lease settlement, while falling short of complete conformity with 'equality of sacrifice', did represent a generous and courageous contribution to the multilateral goal. But the Anglo-American Financial Agreement, concluded in the name of multilateralism, represented a less fortunate instrument for the achievement of this objective. The line of credit was liberal in its size and terms—but not liberal enough to inspire complete confidence that the multilateral undertakings could be successfully carried out. The undertakings themselves were too tightly drawn and tied to unduly short and rigid time limits. The Agreement made inadequate provision for adjustment and for consultation between the parties. These were only the most obvious difficulties; to make matters worse, the debate on the Agreement now beginning in the two countries was further to prejudice the prospect of a successful outcome.

---

[1] During the Congressional hearings on the Financial Agreement, Administration witnesses took pains to emphasize that the 'exceptional cases' clause was intended to cover situations arising with individual countries and was not intended to permit the United Kingdon to maintain restrictions generally on a world-wide basis in conditions which might be described as exceptional:

'MISS SUMNER: Any time Britain wants to come over and consult with its friends in the Treasury or the State Department, those things can be waived. Congress has voted the $3·750 million and the bureaucrats can change the Agreement.

'MR. CLAYTON: It is well understood, Miss Sumner, that this has reference to some exceptional, and it says exceptional, cases. . . . I assure you that it does not materially affect the agreement on the part of Britain to make all sterling convertible within one year after the Agreement.'

U.S. Congress, House, Committee on Banking and Currency, *Anglo-American Financial Agreement*, Hearings on H. J. Res. 311, 79th Cong., 2nd sess. (May–June 1946), p. 659. See the subsequent interpretation to the same effect by Dalton, 443 H.C. Deb. 401–2 (24 Oct. 1947).

CHAPTER XII

PASSING THE LOAN

THE signing of the Financial Agreement on 6 December 1945 was by no means the end of this important episode in Anglo-American economic relations. It was still necessary to secure approval of the Agreement on both sides of the Atlantic. The consequences of rejection by Parliament or Congress would be extremely grave. The United Kingdom would have to do without $3·75 billion in transitional assistance from the United States and perhaps also the $1·25 billion which Canada had agreed to grant on similar terms. Far from receiving additional credits to wind up its Lend-Lease account, Britain might be asked to make payment immediately, either in cash or in some other form, both for Lend-Lease of post-war value and for articles consumed in the course of the war. Deprived of transitional aid from the United States and Canada and faced with this additional burden of repayment, Britain would face a drastic cut in its living standards and a serious setback in its reconstruction plans.

There were still other things at stake. Rejection of the Financial Agreement might shatter the whole structure of economic co-operation on which the two countries had lavished such time and effort. Without the loan, Britain would not join the Bretton Woods institutions.[1] Without Britain, the Fund and Bank could not begin operations.[2] For the same reasons, there would be little prospect for the early establishment of an International Trade Organization. Thus rejection of the Financial Agreement would not only upset existing plans for the revival of multilateral trade; it would blight the outlook for multilateralism for an indefinite future. It was clear that grave matters hung in the balance.

[1] The British leaders made it clear on several occasions that the American loan was for Britain a prerequisite to Bretton Woods. See Dalton's statement on this point during the loan debate. 417 H.C. Deb. 431 (12 Dec. 1945).
[2] By 31 Dec. 1945 neither Australia nor New Zealand had ratified the Bretton Woods agreements and India had only ratified provisionally. Had Britain failed to join the Bank and Fund it is unlikely that these three countries would have done so. Their absence, coupled with that of Britain and the Soviet Union (which also failed to ratify), would have prevented ratification by countries with 65 per cent. of Fund and Bank quotas as required by the Articles of Agreement.

But rejection of the Financial Agreement was not the only source of danger. Even approval might be achieved in such circumstances as to prejudice the possibility of success. The cause of Anglo-American co-operation would not be served if the Agreement were passed in an atmosphere of misunderstanding, with contradictory expectations about the way in which it was to be carried out. Unfortunately, there was a real possibility that this might happen. The gulf between British and American opinion had grown so wide that only a courageous effort of education on the part of the two Governments could put things right. 'How difficult it is for nations to understand one another', Keynes was moved to exclaim, 'even when they have the advantage of a common language. How differently things appear in Washington than in London, and how easy it is to misunderstand one another's difficulties and the real purpose which lies behind each one's way of solving them. . . . Everyone talks about international co-operation, but how little of pride, of temper or of habit anyone is willing to contribute to it when it comes down to brass tacks.'[1]

The great debate now unfolding on the Anglo-American Financial Agreement was to provide a telling illustration of the truth of this statement.

THE BRITISH DEBATE

The British debate was short and intense. A few days after the signing of the Financial Agreement the Government presented Parliament with an omnibus resolution expressing approval of the Financial Agreement, the Lend-Lease settlement, Bretton Woods, and the commercial policy 'Proposals'.[2] Since the deadline for British ratification of the Bretton Woods agreements was 31 December 1945 there was no time for delay. Only three weeks remained for Parliamentary and public discussion.

Thanks to constitutional and political complications, the outcome was by no means assured. True enough, the Labour Government was supporting the multilateral projects. It had a large majority in the House of Commons. By the exercise of party discipline it could assure affirmative votes from all but a handful of recalcitrant members. But the House of Lords was in the hands of the Conservatives, and this chamber still retained some of its old power to de-

---

[1] 138 H.L. Deb. 777–8 (18 Dec. 1945).
[2] 417 H.C. Deb. 422 (12 Dec. 1945). Parliament was not actually asked to 'approve' the 'Proposals' but only to 'welcome the initiative' of the United States Government in presenting them.

Q

lay.[1] Although the Conservative leaders had supported the multilateral plans as members of the war-time Government, they were reluctant to share responsibility for the Washington settlement as members of the Opposition. To make matters worse, the Labour Ministers found themselves in the anomalous position of supporting a programme that seemed inconsistent with their plans for greater government ownership and control. Only the Liberals, reduced to a small minority, were free to provide unqualified support. Thus the Washington settlement, even if not rejected, would meet with precious little enthusiasm on either side of the House.

The attack on the Agreement

If any doubt remained about the precarious state of Anglo-American economic collaboration it was dispelled by the hostile comments that marked the opening of the British debate. Feeling ran high in many quarters. Robert Boothby told the House of Commons that the Agreement was 'an economic Munich' and warned the Labour Government that it had no mandate to 'sell the British Empire for a pack of cigarettes'.[2] From the Government backbenches the left-wing Richard Stokes was moved to exclaim that the majority of Americans were 'extremely ignorant . . . in the adolescent state . . . and . . . do not understand the international trade problem'.[3] His sentiments were echoed by Jenny Lee, the energetic wife of Aneurin Bevan, who declared: 'There is no wisdom in this loan, and there is no kindness in it. There is nothing in the terms of this loan which give us any reason to suppose that an administration which could offer a niggardly, barbaric and antediluvian settlement such as this loan, can solve the unemployment problem in their own country much less help the world.'[4]

Strong language was not employed by extremists only. Said Viscount Simon: 'I do not suppose there ever has been a very important international agreement put before Parliament for acceptance in which it was found that the conditions aroused in this country such deep anxiety and widespread mistrust.'[5] Oliver Lyttleton, another

---

[1] Under the Parliament Act of 1911 the House of Lords could, by withholding its approval, delay legislation for two years, except in the case of a 'money bill', which became an Act even without the Lords' consent if they failed to pass it after one month. It was not clear whether the motion moved by the Chancellor could be considered a 'money bill'. But in any case, rejection or amendment in the Lords would have meant the expiration of the 31 December deadline.

[2] 417 H.C. Deb. 468–9 (12 Dec. 1945).   [3] Id., cols. 708–9 (13 Dec. 1945).

[4] Id., col. 669 (13 Dec. 1945).   [5] 138 H.L. Deb. 688 (17 Dec. 1945).

Conservative, expressed the opinion that the terms of the Financial Agreement were 'so onerous . . . as nearly to defeat the objects which both borrower and lender have in transacting the loan'.[1] In a widely quoted letter to *The Times* Sir Hubert Henderson concluded: 'The financial agreement with the United States is for a loan upon conditions which are calculated to ensure default.'[2] The severity of the criticism and the widely differing sources from which it came prompted *The Economist* to observe: 'In the complex of agreements that have been bound together—the Loan Agreement, Bretton Woods, and the commercial proposals—there is something to displease everybody.'[3]

One of the most obvious irritants lay in the terms of the credit itself. Public opinion might not always follow the complex arguments about convertibility, Bretton Woods, and commercial policy, but the fact that the United States had chosen to charge interest to its war-time ally was palpable enough to be generally understood.[4] Parliament and the press expressed this mood. Churchill declared he was 'astonished' that the United States had decided to charge interest 'in the special circumstances in which we find ourselves'.[5] Keynes added: 'I shall never so long as I live cease to regret that this is not an interest-free loan . . . what a difference it would have made to our feelings and to our response!'[6] Anderson went so far as to suggest that the assistance should not have been a loan at all but should have taken the form of 'an adjusted payment, in conformity with the principles of equal sacrifice and the clean slate; principles for which, until recently, there was powerful backing on both sides of the Atlantic'.[7] In these circumstances it was perhaps inevitable that little attention should have been given to the complete writing off of war-time Lend-Lease, an omission that encouraged inaccurate charges that Britain was being treated less generously than after the First World War[8] or even 'like a defeated nation, in the way Ger-

---

[1] 417 H.C. Deb. 574 (12 Dec. 1945).   [2] (12 Dec. 1945).

[3] 'Second Thoughts', cxlix (1945), pp. 849–50.

[4] According to a Gallup poll taken shortly after the Parliamentary debate the most widespread ground of public opposition to the loan was the nature of the credit terms; the financial and commercial policy undertakings did not appear among the major reasons for complaint. The *News Chronicle* (14 Feb. 1946).

[5] 417 H.C. Deb. 713 (13 Dec. 1945).

138 H.L. Deb. 784–5 (18 Dec. 1945).

[7] 417 H.C. Deb. 446 (12 Dec. 1945). This theme was echoed widely in the press. See, for example, *The Manchester Guardian* (4 Dec. 1945): 'It was wrong and short-sighted to make this contribution a loan at all, and we are certain that before ten years have gone our American friends will blame us bitterly for having allowed them to commit this same mistake twice in a generation.'

[8] Boothby declared: 'Lord Baldwin has been much criticised for the 1923 debt

many was treated under the Dawes and Young loans'.[1] One of the most bitter comments on the credit terms appeared in *The Economist*: 'It is aggravating to find that our reward for losing a quarter of our national wealth in the common cause is to pay tribute for half a century to those who have been enriched by the war.'[2]

It was not the terms of the credit, however, but the conditions which it appeared to carry, that caused the deepest and most enduring resentment. On this subject, the approach of the British and American Governments now appeared in fundamental contrast. In the view of the American Government there was a distinction between asking for the surrender of bases or raw materials, on the one hand, and for agreement on principles of financial and commercial policy, on the other. The Administration had steadfastly resisted Congressional pressure to seek the former; but it felt it had the right and duty to seek the latter. As the National Advisory Council explained: 'No sovereign nation will in return for a loan grant concessions which impair its sovereignty, endanger its security, or arouse the opposition of its people and, of course, the United States has no disposition to seek such concessions.' Nevertheless, it was 'appropriate' both that assistance should be linked to the adoption of multilateral policies and that 'the attitude of the United States toward making a loan should be conditioned upon the attitude of the borrowing countries' toward such matters.[3] In the words of Clair Wilcox, the new Director of the State Department's Office of International Trade Policy, the multilateral obligations attached to the loan could provide no cause for complaint because 'these matters are . . . commitments that Britain is enabled to make by virtue of the loan. . . . Our negotiators did not seek concessions that would have been extraneous to the loan, *concessions that would have challenged British sovereignty and affronted British pride*.'[4]

This analysis reflected an imperfect understanding of British opinion. As we have already seen, Bretton Woods and the commercial policy programme had aroused strong resistance in the United Kingdom. On the Right Wing of political opinion, these projects were

settlement; but the terms he obtained then were princely by comparison with these terms.' 417 H.C. Deb. 457 (12 Dec. 1945).

[1] H. Norman Smith, 417 H.C. Deb. 469–70 (12 Dec. 1945).

[2] 'Second Thoughts', cxlix (1945), p. 850.

[3] *Report to the President on the Activities of the National Advisory Council*, House Doc. No. 497, 79th Cong., 2nd sess. (4 Mar. 1946), p. 7.

[4] Italics supplied. 'What Do We Get?', speech to the Pennsylvania State Chamber of Commerce (7 May 1946).

regarded as a threat to domestic industry and to Imperial economic arrangements; on the Left, as a menace to full employment and the welfare state. Although opposition to multilateralism was strongest on the extreme fringes of the two political parties, doubts and reservations had begun to cloud even moderate opinion. By the end of the war the future of British policy was still in doubt. In these circumstances it was extremely unfortunate for the British Government to have to wrap the multilateral programmes in a single package, link them to an unpopular loan, and press for a quick decision. To those who had been sceptical of multilateralism, the whole procedure reeked of blackmail. Lord Woolton, the Conservative leader, spoke of 'dollar dictation'. He exclaimed: 'I do not like this tacking on a loan to Bretton Woods. It is not a respectable way to treat a great country.'[1] *The Economist*, which had been reserving judgement on Bretton Woods, was moved to observe: 'Nothing could be less democratic and more devious than the way in which the whole subject has been withheld from authoritative discussion until it is now rushed through under pressure of a threat.'[2] And G. D. H. Cole now charged that the American Government was using 'our own economic difficulties arising out of the war as an opportunity to prevent our Government from applying its socialist principles in international trade'.[3]

Even those willing to take a more charitable view of American behaviour were alienated by the circumstances in which Britain had been asked to subscribe to multilateral principles. A significant comment was made by Lord Lindsay of Birker:

I think that one of the difficulties about the relations between these two great countries which we both inherited from our spiritual ancestors, the Puritans . . . is the habit of looking down with ineffable superiority on other people. When we do that to each other it is really more than we can bear

[1] 138 H.L. Deb. 715 (17 Dec. 1945).
[2] 'Second Thoughts', cxlix (1945), p. 850.
[3] 'Loan May Kill State Trading in U.K.', *Reynolds News* (21 July 1946). Substitute the word 'Imperial' for 'socialist' and the same argument could be found in L. S. Amery, *The Washington Loan Agreements* (London, 1946). Amery said: 'The British Empire is the oyster which this loan is to prise open. Each part of it, deprived of the mutual support of Empire Preference, is to be swallowed separately, to become a field for American industrial exploitation, a tributary of American finance, and, in the end, an American dependency.' Id., p. xi. The opponents of multilateralism put particular emphasis on the charge that Bretton Woods and the commercial policy 'Proposals' were 'conditions attached to the loan'. Empire Industries Association, *Statement of the Executive Committee* (10 Dec. 1945). Government spokesmen were not very firm in rebutting this charge. See the ambiguous answer of Cripps, 418 H.C. Deb. 487–8 (12 Dec. 1945), and the misgivings accordingly expressed by *The Times* (23 Jan. 1946).

and when the Americans do it to us it riles us very much indeed. The kind of impressions you have got of these negotiations, of the Americans looking down at us as people who did all kinds of wicked tricks and using their powers to make us very good children, was very hard to bear, considering the facts.[1]

So great was the general irritation at the linking of multilateral conditions with financial aid that Britain's own stake in multilateralism was in grave danger of being obscured. This result was natural enough. The Americans had demanded certain things in return for their financial aid. These things might well be in the interest of the United States. It was hard to believe they were in the interest of Britain as well. Thus much more emphasis was placed on the short-term disadvantages of the multilateral undertakings than on the long-term advantages of multilateral trade.

The undertakings which aroused the most violent reaction were those embodied in the Financial Agreement itself. There was, first of all, the convertibility provision. Convertibility, the Government had once affirmed, was very much in Britain's interest. But now, in order to have American aid, Britain was forced to achieve it in accord with a short and inflexible time-table. Hugh Dalton, Chancellor of the Exchequer, had to confess that the obligation had been accepted only 'with very great reluctance' and only because 'we felt we must meet them on this point sooner than break the whole negotiation'.[2] Churchill made the remarkable observation that the provision was 'so doubtful and perilous that the best hope is that in practice it will defeat itself, and that it is in fact too bad to be true'.[3] And Anderson argued that however desirable convertibility might be, it should not have been imposed on Britain by a contractual arrangement with another country:

Convertibility, in my view, is a thoroughly good thing; it was always a goal to be aimed at, to strive for; but left to ourselves we would have proposed to approach convertibility by degrees, to approach it tentatively, and not until we had found in practice that we could undertake the obligation of convertibility and continue under that obligation, should we accept the *de jure* liability which this Agreement puts upon us.[4]

[1] 138 H.L. Deb. 839 (18 Dec. 1945). See also the comment of the *Financial Times*: 'All this talk about "assisting the Government of the United Kingdom to assume the obligations of multilateral trade" is sheer poppycock. Our trade has always been multilateral. . . . Man for man, we export more than twice as much as the United States of America and import five times as much.' 'American Trade With the British Empire' (12 June 1945).   [2] 417 H.C. Deb. 439 (12 Dec. 1945).
[3] Id., col. 714 (13 Dec. 1945).   [4] Id., col. 451 (12 Dec. 1945).

The commitment to abolish the sterling area dollar pool was another undertaking in the Financial Agreement that aroused serious distrust of the multilateral programme. Left to its own devices Britain would have had little interest in maintaining the dollar pool. Indeed, it would have had little prospect of doing so. The members of the sterling area would not want to continue for very long the war-time system of informal restraint. If they were to continue to bank in London they would want to recover the uninhibited right to use their balances which they enjoyed before the war. As Keynes put it:

I wonder how much we are giving away there. . . . We cannot force these sterling area countries to buy only from us, especially when we are physically unable to supply a large part of what they require. It seems to me a crazy idea that we can go on living after 1947 by borrowing on completely vague terms from India and the Crown Colonies. They will be wanting us to repay them. . . . Two-thirds of what we owe to the sterling area is owed to India, Palestine, Egypt and Eire. Is it really wise to base our policy on the loyalty and goodwill of those countries to lend us money and leave out of our arrangements Canada and the United States?[1]

All this was true enough. But now Britain had accepted a specific commitment to make the foreign exchange earnings of the sterling area countries freely available for current transactions anywhere. The critics of multilateralism could charge that vital interests had been sacrificed. Boothby could allege that the obligation meant 'the abolition of the sterling area'.[2] Others asserted that it would deprive Britain of her overseas markets and would result in the abandonment of the sterling countries to the economic orbit of the United States. For months criticisms of the Financial Agreement talked of 'the folly of destroying the sterling area'.[3] The Government did little to discourage such misconceptions. As late as the autumn of 1946 Dalton was asked whether Britain 'would dissolve the sterling area in accordance with the terms of the American loan agreement'. He replied: 'You may ask me when, but not if. That undertaking will be kept.'[4]

---

[1] 138 H.L. Deb. 788–9 (18 Dec. 1945).

[2] The phrase appeared in a motion moved by Boothby and Squadron-Leader Hollis to postpone debate on the loan and other agreements. For the full text of the motion, see *The New York Times* (8 Dec. 1945).

[3] See, for example, 'American Trade With the British Empire', the *Financial Times* (12 June 1946). See also the statement of the City Editor of *The Manchester Guardian*: 'By next summer we must break up the sterling area . . .' (15 July 1946).

[4] *The Times* (28 Sept. 1946).

The defence of the Agreement

The attack on the Agreement was strong and passionate; the Government's defence was weak and almost apologetic. The general strategy was to stress the evil effects of rejection rather than the beneficial effects of approval. Primary emphasis was placed on Britain's need for the loan. Without the American dollars, the Government declared, Britain would not be able to obtain the foodstuffs, raw materials, and manufactures necessary for the maintenance of tolerable living standards and the urgent job of reconstruction. Dalton put the matter poignantly:

> Let us look at the alternative—an alternative not selected according to the fancy of an ingenious Hon. Member, but dictated by the inevitable and ineluctable facts. Our stock of gold and dollars is running low. Every Monday, in the Treasury, they place before me a statement showing how much gold and dollars we still have. The curve goes so-and-so; but it tends downwards. Without new dollar resources, we could not much longer afford to purchase any supplies which have to be paid for in dollars. The dollars would not be there . . . we should have to undergo greater hardships and privations than even during the war; and all those hopes of better times, to follow in the wake of victory, would be dissipated in despair and disillusion.[1]

The second argument on which the Government relied was that rejection of the Agreement would have adverse repercussions on Anglo-American relations. This argument had to be handled with care. Many members of Parliament, like some members of Congress, saw their country as an intermediary in controversies with the Soviet Union. They would be alarmed by the suggestion that the loan was the prelude to an Anglo-American alliance. The point had to be made in a more general way:

> Finally, and perhaps most serious of all, the rejection of these Agreements would mean the dissipation of all hopes of Anglo-American co-operation in this dangerous new world into which we have moved. We and the Americans, if peace is to be assured, must learn to live and work together. The rejection of these Agreements would not only be an economic and financial disaster for this country of ours, but it would be not less a disaster for the whole future of international co-operation.[2]

These were the two main elements in the Government's case. But what of that expressly stated purpose of the Financial Agreement—

[1] 417 H.C. Deb. 441 (12 Dec. 1945).
[2] Dalton, 417 H.C. Deb. 443 (12 Dec. 1945).

'to assist the United Kingdom to assume the obligations of multi-lateral trade'? On this subject the voice of the Government was evasive and uncertain. We have already noted how it stressed the exceptions and escapes in presenting Bretton Woods and the 'Proposals'. In these cases such tactics might not occasion immediate difficulty—after all, they were long-term instruments, broadly drafted to accommodate divergent views. But the danger was rather more imminent in the case of the Financial Agreement itself. Here the period of grace was only eighteen months: implementation of its multilateral undertakings could only be assured if British opinion was determined to employ the measures necessary to carry them out.

Unfortunately, these requirements were rather overlooked in the course of debate. The Government was reluctant to complicate an already dangerous situation by taking a firm stand on the importance to Britain of multilateral trade. It was easier to argue that the multilateral commitments had been an inevitable concession to the United States—or simply to minimize their importance altogether. It was easier also to assign to the United States the main responsibility for making the Agreement work. A considerable amount of time was devoted to stressing America's responsibility to maintain full employment, reduce tariffs, and lend more freely to the rest of the world. Keynes himself stated that if a fundamental disequilibrium appeared in world trade, the Americans 'would consider it their duty to find a way out'.[1] Foreign Secretary Ernest Bevin declared: 'It has been said that, inevitably, this will lead to another repudiation. That is in the hands of the United States, and nobody else.'[2] Newspaper comment took a similar line. Said *The Times*: 'The responsibility for the success of the policy to which this country is jointly committed rests primarily on the United States.'[3] *The Economist* added: 'The Anglo-American loan agreement is the key-stone of an arch of policy that rests wholly on the twin pillars of stability in American foreign and domestic economies.'[4]

That the United States shared a heavy load of responsibility for the success of the Financial Agreement no one could seriously deny. There was a danger, however, in the disproportionate emphasis given

---

[1] 138 H.L. Deb. 792 (18 Dec. 1945). Keynes added confidently that 'all the most responsible people in the State Department and in the Treasury, have entirely departed from the high tariff, export subsidy conception of things, and will do their utmost with, they believe, the support of public opinion in the opposite direction'. Ibid.

[2] 417 H.C. Deb. 734 (13 Dec. 1945).

[3] 'Fruits of the Loan' (16 July 1946). See also the *Scotsman* (15 July 1946).

[4] 'Warning From the West', cli (1946), p. 1.

to this fact. Hardly anything was said of certain essential requirements in British policy. The Government made no mention of the need for Britain to undertake domestic fiscal and monetary policies consistent with its external obligations. On the contrary, it devoted considerable efforts to showing that full employment and domestic planning would not be impeded by the multilateral arrangements. Nor did it explain the critical importance of the problem of the sterling balances. No one explained that the American negotiators considered the funding and scaling down of a large majority of the balances a major prerequisite to the successful implementation of the terms of the Financial Agreement. Indeed, when Government spokesmen mentioned the balances they deliberately avoided words that might suggest such a drastic solution. Dalton said simply that some of the balances would be freed, some funded, and the rest 'adjusted, *perhaps*, *in some cases*, adjusted downwards, as a contribution by the sterling area countries to a reasonable settlement of this war debt problem'.[1] This was hardly the spirit in which the problem had been approached during the negotiations themselves.

Thus the case for the Financial Agreement and the other multilateral projects received a weak and incomplete presentation. There was really only one man who was able to recapture the vision of a healthy, free-flowing, and open system of trade based on the close economic collaboration of Britain and the United States. This was Keynes himself. In his famous defence of the Agreement before the House of Lords he dealt a hard blow to the opponents of multilateralism. With merciless sarcasm he dismissed their programme as an attempt 'to build up a separate economic bloc which excludes Canada and consists of countries to which we already owe more than we can pay, on the basis of their agreeing to lend us money they have not got and buy only from us and one another goods we are unable to supply'.[2] In a ringing peroration he recalled the economic and political interests of Britain in a multilateral régime:

These policies seem to me to be in the prime interest of our country, little though we may like some parts of them. They are calculated to help us regain a full measure of prosperity and prestige in the world's commerce. They aim, above all, at the restoration of multilateral trade which is a system upon which British commerce essentially depends. . . . The separate economic blocs and all the friction and loss of friendship they must bring with them are expedients to which one may be driven in a hostile world,

[1] Italics supplied. 417 H.C. Deb. 430 (12 Dec. 1945).
[2] 138 H.L. Deb. 790 (18 Dec. 1945).

where trade has ceased over wide areas to be co-operative and peaceful and where are forgotten the healthy rules of mutual advantage and equal treatment. But it is surely crazy to prefer that. Above all, this determination to make trade truly international and to avoid the establishment of economic blocs which limit and restrict commercial intercourse outside them, is plainly an essential condition of the world's best hope, an Anglo-American understanding, which brings us and others together in international institutions which may be in the long run the first step towards something more comprehensive. Some of us, in the tasks of war and more lately in those of peace, have learnt by experience that our two countries can work together. Yet it would be only too easy for us to walk apart. I beg those who look askance at these plans to ponder deeply and responsibly where it is they think they want to go.[1]

This speech provided a badly needed lift to the supporters of the Agreement. A few days earlier, the motion approving the Financial Agreement, Bretton Woods, the Lend-Lease settlement, and the 'Proposals' had been roughly handled in the House of Commons. The final vote, 343–100, with 169 abstaining, gave an entirely inadequate picture of the divided character of Parliamentary sentiment. Churchill and a majority of the Conservative party abstained from voting, and many Conservatives, defying their leaders, voted against the agreements. The Government was also faced with a revolt in its own ranks. Quite a few of the Labour members who voted for approval (e.g. Crossman, Bevan, Zilliacus) did so only under pressure of the 'three-line whips'.[2] In the House of Lords, threats of a Conservative uprising had persisted until the eleventh hour. They collapsed after the unconvincing performance of Beaverbrook and the masterly statement of Keynes.[3] With the end of the political debate, the fever of controversy subsided. At last one could try to put in perspective the strident and immoderate comment. Keynes wrote to an American friend: 'We are, I think, justified in being critical, but we are not so ungrateful or unreasonable as you might suppose through reading the newspapers.'[4]

In the last analysis, the nation seemed to be reconciled to the Financial Agreement. When it came to a decision, the majority of the press and the public were on the side of approval.[5] Acceptance,

---

[1] 138 H.L. Deb. 793–4 (18 Dec. 1945).

[2] I.e., the most stringent possible exercise of party discipline.

[3] The salutary effect of Keynes's speech on public opinion was remarkable. For one ndication of its effect compare the editorial comment in *The Manchester Guardian* before and after its presentation.   [4] *Letter to Professor Viner, January 4, 1946.*

[5] Except for the Beaverbrook papers, virtually the entire press supported ratification. So, apparently, did most of the interested public, according to a Gallup poll

however, came not from choice, but from necessity. The debate had injured the cause of Anglo-American understanding; perhaps, too, it had also jeopardized the prospects of those very multilateral objectives which the Financial Agreement was designed to achieve.

THE AMERICAN DEBATE

The British debate had hardly subsided when the American debate began. On 20 January President Truman forwarded the Financial Agreement to Congress with an appeal for speedy approval. Like the Fund and Bank, the British loan was presented for approval by majority vote of both Houses of Congress. Another lengthy debate on American foreign economic policy was now at hand.

TABLE 2

American Attitudes toward the British Loan, June–August 1946

(Asked in June): There's talk now about the United States lending a large amount of money to England. How do you feel about that?

(Asked in August): You probably know that Congress recently voted to lend a large amount of money to England. How do you feel about that?

	June %	August %
Approve	10	18
Approve with qualifications or uncertainty	28	19
Undecided, don't know	13	12
Disapprove with qualifications or uncertainty	8	8
Disapprove	40	42
Opinions not ascertained	1	1
	100	100

Source: Leonard S. Cottrell and Sylvia Eberhardt, *American Opinion on World Affairs* (Princeton, 1948), p. 130.

The Agreement in danger

It had been clear at the outset of the Washington negotiations that American opinion was ill-prepared for a new measure of financial aid to the United Kingdom. Misgivings expressed then about the political prospects were now confirmed. Opinion polls continued to report

published in the *News Chronicle* (14 Feb. 1946). Out of all those questioned 72 per cent. said they had been following the debate on the Financial Agreement; 50 per cent. approved acceptance; 17 per cent. opposed; 5 per cent. were undecided. In response to the question: 'Do you believe that by keeping up austerity Britain could reconstruct her industry and trade without borrowing from America?' 32 per cent. said 'yes'; 47 per cent. 'no'; 21 per cent. 'don't know'.

that a majority of the public opposed the loan.[1] Letters to Congressmen also contained a preponderance of adverse comments, increasing the anxiety of legislators that in an election year a vote for the loan might be political suicide. One can get an idea of the pressure put on the Congress from an entry in the diary of Arthur Vandenberg, the Republican Senator who had recently abandoned isolationist views:

> The British loan is a tough conundrum for me and for my Republican colleagues. . . . I have a feeling we ought to 'go along' with this loan for the sake of some nebulous affinity which the English-speaking world must maintain in mutual self-defense. But I also confess my feeling that about 90 per cent. of my constituency will be unimpressed by this ideology . . . and will soon become very vocal against this whole postwar fiscal prospectus. I freely confess my own perplexity. . . . The whole thing has been badly handled. It can easily become a major tragedy.[2]

These fears were shared by other close observers of the Washington scene. One veteran journalist reported that the Congressional hearings were beginning 'in an atmosphere of defeatism and pessimism' and added that 'very real doubt exists whether Congress will approve the loan proposals'.[3] In London Sir Stafford Cripps admitted grimly, 'it looks as if Congress may possibly turn it down'.[4]

The situation was a grave one. A majority of newspapers and business organizations were for the loan, but it was proving difficult to arouse support in Congress and the public at large. The main problem was one of general indifference. Domestic problems loomed very large: in addition to high taxes the public was plagued by the rising cost of living and a serious wave of strikes. In these circumstances those who sought aid for foreign nations had to bear a very heavy burden of proof. Why—it was typically asked—should Britain have a loan at a lower rate of interest than that charged to returning servicemen on housing loans? Why should more assistance be given to Britain when so much remained to be done at home?

In certain circles the loan was not simply regarded with indifference but with active, bitter hostility. This attitude was summed up in the words of the Congressman who thought the loan would 'promote too damned much Socialism at home and too much damned Imperialism abroad'.[5] Here, indeed, were the two major bogeys.

---

[1] See, for example, the poll results presented in Table 2.
[2] Personal memorandum of 19 Dec. 1945, Arthur H. Vandenberg, Jr. (ed.), *The Private Papers of Senator Vandenberg* (Boston, 1952), p. 231.
[3] Marquis Childs in the *Washington Post* (16 Feb. 1946).
[4] *The Times* (28 Feb. 1946).
[5] Representative Emmanuel Celler, quoted in the *Daily Mail* (7 Dec. 1945).

Fear of Socialism did much to alienate members of the business community who might otherwise have supported the loan. Clayton was besieged with anxious queries from prominent financial and commercial leaders who were alarmed by certain policies of the new British Government—particularly the decisions to nationalize steel and not to open the Liverpool Cotton Exchange.[1] The subject of Imperialism could also be counted on to complicate matters. Irish voters recalled traditional grievances; Jews injected the increasingly explosive issue of Palestine; other ethnic groups joined in opposition. The venerable standards of the American Revolution were raised again. One Congressman announced that he would not vote one dollar for Britain 'as long as they have got the crown jewels in London'.[2] And an irate Senator insisted: 'The British Loan is not to provide relief for starving people. It is to provide relief for a decadent empire. My slogan is: "Billions for the relief of starving children but not one cent of American taxpayers' money for the relief of Empires".'[3]

Opposition to the British loan stemmed from very diverse sources, but the serious arguments employed by the opponents fell into two categories. Both, it must be admitted, derived considerable support from the Administration's hitherto universal approach to political and economic affairs. On the political side, American leaders had put great emphasis on the danger of special alliances and accords within the general family of nations—alliances which might derogate from the authority of the United Nations Organization, lead to the formation of political 'blocs', and thus enhance the danger of war. How far the majority of Americans had accepted this philosophy could be seen in the reaction that greeted Churchill's proposal at Fulton, Missouri, for an Anglo-American alliance to resist Soviet expansion. Overnight the great war leader had become the subject of the most violent criticism. *The Economist* correctly observed: 'The notion of close Anglo-American co-operation as the necessary backbone for UNO, which in Britain is a wholly sensible and reasonable idea, still looks to the American mind very much like the juxtaposition of two contrary ideas.'[4]

In such a climate of opinion the critics of the loan could make a case of great persuasiveness. Was not the loan the first step toward

[1] The letters and telegrams from Bernard Baruch had a particular acerbity. *Clayton Papers.*

[2] Representative Dewey Short, quoted in the *Daily Mail* (7 Dec. 1945).

[3] Senator Edwin Johnson in a nation-wide broadcast reported in *The New York Times* (17 Feb. 1946).   [4] 'The Two and The One', cI (1946), p. 361.

the very alliance that Churchill proposed? Administration leaders such as Henry Wallace strove hard to rebut this idea.[1] But anxiety still persisted. One Congressman feared that approval of the loan would mean 'adding fuel to the war between the United States and Russia'.[2] Several members of the House Banking and Currency Committee warned: 'This loan will give impetus to Anglo-American imperialistic elements. Later the American people will be told this loan was advance guarantee of American money, guns and boys for all future British Empire needs and desires.'[3] Even more moderate figures such as Senator Vandenberg expressed concern, noting that 'if we grant a loan to England and then deny one to Russia (if she asks for it as she undoubtedly will) we have thereby made further co-operation among the Big Three impossible (which, incidentally, would be the end of UNO). . . . If we are going ultimately to deny a Russian loan, perhaps it would be better not to open up . . . at all.'[4] And the *Wall Street Journal* summed up:

This country's reaction to Mr. Churchill's Missouri speech must be convincing proof that the United States wants no alliance or anything that resembles an alliance with any other nation—at least none outside the American continent. The instinctive reaction was one of strong opposition to any such arrangement when it is presented to the American people for what it is. It seems time to raise the question of whether we may not be getting ready to act without exactly realizing what we are doing.[5]

The second line of attack on the loan was encouraged by the hitherto universal approach of the Administration in the economic

[1] Wallace said that the loan to Britain was no prelude to an Anglo-American alliance and that he would not be supporting it if it were. U.S. Congress, Senate, Committee on Banking and Currency, *Anglo-American Financial Agreement*, Hearings on S.J. Res. 138, 79th Cong., 2nd sess. (Apr.–May 1946), p. 303.
[2] Jesse Sumner, quoted in *The Times* (15 July 1946). Another member of Congress employed a homely illustration to sum up his concern: 'Here is British Imperialism, in friction today with Russia. We walk over to Britain and say "Here, we are on your team. Here is a new shotgun". Well, if there were two neighbors and they were having trouble over the lot line and we walked up and gave one of them a shotgun and later on there was some shooting we would not have helped to quiet things even though we hoped we were quieting them down.' Representative Howard Buffett, U.S. Congress, House, Committee on Banking and Currency, *Anglo-American Financial Agreement*, Hearings on H.J. Res. 311, 79th Cong., 2nd sess. (May–June 1946), p. 373.
[3] Minority Report of the Committee, quoted in *The New York Times* (18 June 1946).
[4] Personal memorandum of 19 Dec. 1945, *Vandenberg Papers*, p. 231.
[5] 'Loans and Alliances' (19 Mar. 1946). It is interesting to note that Keynes himself, viewing the American debate from afar, thought 'the one criticism that . . . would really contain some truth would be the charge that by making this loan to England, America was in effect underwriting British policy in other parts of the world'. Paraphrase of his remarks in Memorandum of Conversation with Lord Keynes at the British Treasury, 24 Jan. 1946, by William H. Taylor, U.S. Treasury Representative, *White Papers*.

field. As we have already noted, the Bretton Woods debate had distracted attention from the grave character of Britain's transitional difficulties and the unique importance of British and Commonwealth policy in the organization of multilateral trade. Ignorance of Britain's economic difficulties had grown to appalling proportions. It was widely asked why Britain of all countries deserved a special measure of assistance. Some Congressmen wanted to know why Britain couldn't solve its own problems by borrowing money from the British public instead of the United States. Senator Taft, whose understanding of economic problems was far above average, declared that Britain's transitional needs could be met by a loan of $1·25 billion.[1] Some opponents of the loan, encouraged perhaps by exaggerated descriptions of the sterling 'bloc' and Imperial Preference, claimed that in reality Britain had at its disposal the vast economic resources of the Commonwealth. The United Kingdom, one Congressman alleged, 'has about $8,000,000,000 in dollar assets lying around in other countries, several billions in dollars in cash now. She has about $15,000,000,000 in gold mines, about $8,000,000,000 assets in diamond mines. She is far from being strapped.'[2]

America's economic interests in solving Britain's transitional problem might have been more apparent had the Administration not made such ambitious promises for the universal approach to reconstructing world trade. Multilateralism, after all, was supposed to have been America's reward for a liberal settlement of Lend-Lease and a handsome contribution to the Bretton Woods institutions. Why, then, the critics asked, was still more aid required to achieve the same result? One opponent of the Loan reminded the Administration that Britain

made a commitment in Article 7, and they got 20 billions of aid in connection with that, net. Is it not reasonable for us to expect some accounting made of that promise before we get into a series of new deals? ... It seems to me that to turn around and make the same deal over again in a little different fashion without some reason to believe that there has been a reformation in the meantime might call for another disillusionment, and the American people, the electorate in this country, are getting pretty well fed up on disillusionment.[3]

In reply to this line of argument, some Administration spokesmen contended that 'it was always understood' that additional aid to

[1] 92 *Cong. Rec.* 4113 (24 Apr. 1946).
[2] Representative William Barry, House Hearings, p. 417.
[3] Representative Howard Buffett, id., p. 423.

Britain would have to be provided to facilitate her participation in a multilateral régime.[1] This suggestion was heatedly rejected by one indignant Congressman:

I certainly do not think that was stated at the time of the hearings of Bretton Woods, when they were taking place up here before this committee; in fact, then the proponents of Bretton Woods were opposing a key currency approach and the key currency approach people were opposing Bretton Woods. The general argument advanced by most of them was to take Bretton Woods, and then you do not have to bother with all these other details, and instead of having the onus of financial arrangements between the United States and some other country which will cause hard feelings if they do not happen to materialize as planned . . . you will have the International Bank handling it and the blame or credit will be distributed generally among the nations of the world.[2]

Senator Taft also offered his recollections:

A year ago, when we had the Bretton Woods agreements up for consideration, and it was proposed that the way to meet the whole problem was to make the British a loan, rather than through Bretton Woods, Mr. White, of the Treasury, came before the committee in executive session and said that the British are all right, they do not need a loan, or, if so, it can be worked through the Export-Import Bank. He was afraid it would interfere with the Bretton Woods agreements. He said the British expect most of the $14,000,000,000 [sterling balances] will be forgiven. He said the British have a great deal of money here, and he gave us the figures. . . .[3]

Certainly it was rather late to stress the multilateral benefits which might result from special assistance to the United Kingdom. As Taft objected, the new assistance was 'sought for the exact purpose that Bretton Woods was sought'.[4] It would be no easier to win the sceptics over after some of the remarks made about the Financial Agreement during the debate in the United Kingdom. As one supporter of the loan complained, the critics were now saying 'that Britain does not want the loan, Bretton Woods, or a trade agreement, and has plainly told us that she cannot fulfill its terms'.[5] The British debate had also undermined the confidence of tentative supporters of the loan like Senator Vandenberg: 'Our prospective debtors are already beginning to "shylock us" before the papers are signed. We are notified in advance that we are going to get no good will out of

---

[1] William McChesney Martin, Jr., President of the Export-Import Bank, in House Hearings, p. 454.   [2] Congressman John Kunkel, id., at pp. 454–5.
[3] 92 *Cong. Rec.* 4111 (24 Apr. 1946).   [4] Id., p. 4114 (24 Apr. 1946).
[5] *The New Republic* (16 Jan. 1946).

this largesse. If we are not going to get good will what are we going to get?'[1]

To Vandenberg's question the critics of the loan were already suggesting a number of answers. The multilateral commitments, they charged, were a 'laughable' benefit for American aid.[2] They demanded more direct concessions—rights in raw materials, owner-ship of airfields, even the wholesale transfer of British territory. Without a campaign for the loan of great persuasiveness there was a genuine danger that these conditions might now be attached by the American Congress.

The campaign for multilateralism

The powerful opposition aroused by the British loan placed the Administration in a difficult position. It was not willing to present the loan as a generous measure on behalf of a war-time ally; it was equally unwilling to present it as an investment against Soviet im-perialism. The battle for the Agreement would have to be fought on the same basis as the battle for Bretton Woods and the Reciprocal Trade Agreements Act. In short, the Agreement would have to be presented as a harbinger of multilateral trade and, consequently, of world prosperity and world peace.

Thus the familiar arguments for multilateralism were presented once again—sometimes in extreme form. First came the political argument. According to Secretary of State James Byrnes: 'If we fail to make this loan, Britain will be forced to do business by barter with a bloc of nations. These nations will be forced to do business with Britain in preference to other nations, which means dividing the world into economic blocs, thereby endangering the peace of the world.'[3] Next came the economic argument. Testifying on behalf of the Administration, Eric Johnston stated that rejection of the loan would mean 'inevitable depression' for the United States,[4] while Wallace said such a step would 'reduce our exports below the prewar level with far-reaching consequences for our economy as a whole'.[5]

---

[1] Personal memorandum of 19 Dec. 1946, *Vandenberg Papers*, p. 231.

[2] *Barron's Weekly* (11 Mar. 1946).

[3] Quoted in the *Daily Telegraph* (7 Dec. 1945). See also 'Wallace Warns of Atomic Risk if Congress Bars British Loan', *The Christian Science Monitor* (12 Mar. 1945).

[4] Johnston also said the loan would create 5 million jobs for Americans. *The New York Times* (20 Mar. 1946).

[5] House Hearings, p. 404. The Administration put great emphasis on this argument. Vinson told the Senate Banking and Currency Committee, for example: 'The financial agreement will open up the markets of England and many other countries to our exporters. This means more exports for our farmers and manufacturers, more jobs for

Summing up both the political and economic dangers, Vinson warned: 'Two rival blocs would mean economic warfare . . . world trade would be destroyed. . . . We would find our trade decreased, and our people unemployed. England would find her standard of living deteriorated and her people impoverished. . . . The consequences to world prosperity and to world peace would be disastrous.'[1]

In such exaggerated form these arguments were fraught with complications for future policy. There might well be, as we have seen, a link between multilateralism and world peace. But in the circumstances of 1945 it could hardly be maintained that British restrictions represented warlike acts, threatening to produce military conflict between a 'sterling bloc' and a 'dollar bloc'. There might also be a link between America's prosperity and America's export trade. But the amount of the loan was too small in relation to the gross national product to provide a significant stimulus to American employment; in any case, the major danger in the early transition period was not depression but inflation, which the loan to Britain could only aggravate. Moreover, the dogmatic assertions about the incompatibility of British restrictions with peace and prosperity might prove embarrassing at a future date if Britain found it impossible to remove these restrictions and America had to assent to their retention in the interest of the two countries.

But there was a more immediate difficulty with these arguments. As the critics had been quick to point out, they had already been employed to secure passage of the Bretton Woods agreements. Why could not Britain's needs be met by a loan from the International Bank? The Administration's answer was that the Bank was 'not intended to deal with special needs of this sort. The Bank's resources must be used for long-term reconstruction and development purposes. The proposed loan to England was a long-term emergency

our workers, more profits for business, and higher income for all our people.' Quoted in U.S. Congress, Senate, Committee on Banking and Currency, *Implementation of the Financial Agreement Between the United States and the United Kingdom*, S. Rept. 1144, 79th Cong., 2nd sess. (Washington, 1946), p. 12. Such promises seem to have impressed the special interest groups who supported the loan. See, for example, the statement of Edward A. O'Neal, President of the American Farm Bureau Federation: 'Unless credit is advanced to the United Kingdom, Britain's only alternative is the placing of certain limitations upon trade with the non-sterling area. American agriculture cannot afford to have these restrictions on trade. . . .' Id., p. 14.

[1] U.S. Congress, Senate, Committee on Banking and Currency, *Anglo-American Financial Agreement*, Hearings on S.J. Res. 138, 79th Cong., 2nd sess. (Apr.–May 1946), p. 14.

credit unsuited to the operations and purposes of the Bank.'[1] This was not a very helpful answer for those who had been led to believe that the Bank would carry the major burden of international lending in the transition period. To many Congressmen it suggested that the United States was preparing to make a large number of special loans outside the Bretton Woods institutions. If the Financial Agreement was to be passed, the Administration would have to quiet misgivings on this score.

This was the very thing it now proceeded to do. 'This credit is not a precedent for anything', Byrnes explained. 'It is unique because the position of Britain in world trade, her need for working capital, and the effect upon world trade of her acquiring that working capital, all are unique.'[2] In other words, Britain was a key country whose recovery was essential to the reconstruction of multilateral trade. How much this sounded like the 'key currency' approach! The official rationale might have been written by Professor Williams himself:

> The proposed loan to Britain . . . is a special case. . . . No other country has the same crucial position in world trade as England. Because of the wide use of the pound sterling in world trade, the large proportion of the world's trade which is carried on by the countries of the British Empire and the extreme dependence of England upon imports, the financial and commercial practices of Britain are of utmost importance in determining what kind of world economy we shall have.[3]

This belated emphasis on Britain as a key country in the reconstruction of multilateralism made an effective argument for the British loan. But it had to be accompanied by assurances on two important points. The first was that the measure of assistance now proposed would be sufficient to achieve its designated purpose. Some Congressmen already considered that they had been misled about the adequacy of Bretton Woods. They wanted now to be clear about the adequacy of the loan:

MR. SMITH. You would not want to say that in a year from now you will not be before this committee to ask for another foreign loan.

---

[1] U.S. Treasury, *Questions and Answers on the Anglo-American Financial Agreement* (Washington, 1946), p. 10.

[2] Address to the Foreign Policy Association, 11 Feb. 1946, *Dept. State Bull.*, xiv (1946), p. 269.

[3] U.S. National Advisory Council on International Monetary and Financial Policy, *The Foreign Loan Policy of the United States*, House Doc. No. 489 (21 Feb. 1946), p. 3. Almost identical language may be found in U.S. Treasury, *Questions and Answers*, p. 15.

MISS SUMNER. To Britain?

MR. SMITH. To Britain, yes.

MR. CLAYTON. Yes, I say to you definitely that I will not be here a year from now asking for another loan to Britain.

MR. SMITH. Two years from now.

MR. CLAYTON. Yes, two years from now.

MR. SMITH. How long do you think it will be before you come before us?

MR. CLAYTON. I do not think I will ever come again for that purpose.

MR. SMITH. But you are not sure?

MR. CLAYTON. Well, Mr. Smith, there are few things of which I can be absolutely sure in this life, but I feel very positive that I will not.[1]

Thus this measure of assistance to Britain was going to be the last. But there was still the second difficulty. What would the loan do for multilateralism that had not been done already by the Bank and Fund? Here again the Administration expressed itself in unequivocal terms. When Truman submitted the Financial Agreement to Congress he stated that 'its most important purpose from our point of view is to cause the removal of emergency controls exercised by the United Kingdom over its international transactions far more speedily than is required by the Bretton Woods Agreements'.[2] This was the heart of the Administration's case. The United States was investing $3·75 billion in order to speed up the Bretton Woods time-table from five or more years to only one. This was what Vinson had in mind when he insisted that the Financial Agreement embodied not 'just a loan' but 'a contract with rights and obligations for both parties',[3] and what prompted Clayton to describe the Agreement as 'the greatest single factor thus far in the postwar foreign economic policy of the United States'.[4] In the Administration's eyes the loan would remove the last remaining obstacle to Britain's whole-hearted participation in a multilateral régime. 'If the agreement is ratified', Clayton summed up, 'we will have multilateral trade.'[5] Given the loan, Vinson promised, Britain would '*immediately* accept the principles of fair and non-discriminatory currency and trade practices'.[6] It was on the basis of these assurances that Congress considered the British loan.[7]

---

[1] House Hearings, p. 261.   [2] 92 *Cong. Rec.* 603 (30 Jan. 1946).
[3] *The New York Times* (6 Mar. 1946).
[4] 'The British Loan and American Foreign Trade', *Dun's Review* (11 May 1946), p. 74.   [5] House Hearings, p. 220.
[6] Italics supplied. Foreword to U.S. Treasury, *Questions and Answers*, p. 2.
[7] The assurances were explicitly incorporated in the Majority Report of the Senate Banking and Currency Committee, p. 6.

In specifying the changes which the loan would bring to British trade policies, the Administration made some ambitious claims. Naturally, it emphasized that the signing of the Financial Agreement had been accompanied by British approval of the main lines of the 'Proposals'. Unfortunately, on some occasions it also gave the impression that the loan had purchased British agreement to American views on commercial policy and that the last remaining obstacles to the successful creation of an International Trade Organization had finally been removed. In citing the benefits America would receive from the loan Vinson declared: 'Britain has agreed that she will support the *American* proposal for an international trade organization to reduce trade barriers and eliminate trade discriminations. . . . England's support for *our* proposal *assures* the success of the United Nations trade conference to be held this year.'[1] Following this line Byrnes promised that if the loan were approved the United States could look forward 'with considerable confidence' to 'the elimination of preference'.[2] And Clair Wilcox told a group of business leaders that thanks to the Socialist Government's endorsement of the 'Proposals', 'we have Britain's pledge that her foreign economic policy will henceforth be devoted to restoring an international order that is favorable to the preservation and expansion of private enterprise'.[3]

The tendency of the Administration to claim too much for the Financial Agreement was illustrated with particular clarity in the case of the provision calling for abolition of the sterling area dollar pool. The Administration encouraged the public to believe that Britain had been forcibly controlling the trade of the sterling area countries, that this control had been outlawed by the Financial Agreement, and that the loan would consequently bring great rewards to American export trade. Clayton told a press conference the day the Financial Agreement was signed: 'With the aid of this credit Britain is enabled to abolish the sterling area dollar pool within one year from the effective date of the agreement, so that whatever sterling is earned in Britain by any part of the world will no longer be treated as a frozen balance to be paid only with British or sterling area goods, but will become a balance which can be used for buying in any country in the world. That is the first very obvious and concrete benefit that the United States will derive.'[4]

---

[1] Italics supplied. Senate Hearings, pp. 23–24.
[2] Address to the Foreign Policy Association, *Dept. State Bull.*, xiv (1946), p. 270.
[3] Speech to the Pennsylvania State Chamber of Commerce (8 May 1946).
[4] *The New York Herald-Tribune* (7 Dec. 1945).

PLATE 4

Clayton (*top and bottom left*) and Vinson (*middle left and upper right*) present their case for multilateralism in Congressional hearings on the Anglo-American Financial Agreement.

Such a statement, of course, bore very little relation to the true state of affairs. Sterling earned by the sterling area countries was not 'frozen'; the dollar pool, as we have already noted, was a voluntary arrangement by which the sterling countries sought to conserve their limited dollar resources for most essential needs. Yet Clayton continued to talk this way in his testimony before Congress. He told the House Banking and Currency Committee that the dollar earnings of overseas members of the sterling area were 'not available to them in buying United States goods for the simple reason that under the sterling dollar pool arrangement they must deposit these dollars in London in the pool and *no longer have any control over them*'.[1]

Statements of this kind did not help to enlighten American opinion. One of the country's leading financial journals now reported that if the Financial Agreement were passed American business firms would be able to sell to sterling area countries 'without waiting for the transaction to be approved in London'.[2] On the floor of the House the Democratic Majority Leader declared: 'One of the primary purposes of the financial agreement is to break up the tight British sterling area bloc. . . . Once these provisions go into effect, Britain will no longer control the trade of the countries which make up the sterling area. These countries will once more be free to buy wherever they please.'[3] Another Congressman, asked why he was supporting the loan, replied: 'This loan was negotiated by our old friend, Fred Vinson. He never sold the United States down the river. You can be sure that he drove as good a bargain as could be had. If we're going to help our foreign trade we're going to have to break that [sterling] bloc. And that's what Fred Vinson did.'[4]

It was left, however, for a prominent labour union to present the most ingenious interpretation of all:

As we understand this agreement it will mean that:

(1) The dollar receipts of Empire countries will no longer be administered from London. Each Empire country will retain its own dollar receipts and administer them itself.

(2) The sales of Empire countries to Great Britain will no longer be paid for in inconvertible pounds, which can only be spent for Empire goods. . . .

These are great concessions. They greatly loosen the commercial bonds of Empire. And in political and economic terms these changes greatly advance

[1] Italics supplied. House Hearings, p. 640.
[2] *The Wall Street Journal* (15 Mar. 1946).
[3] Representative John McCormack, 92 *Cong. Rec.* 8823 (12 July 1946).
[4] Representative Frederick Smith, reported in *The New York Times* (9 July 1946).

the cause of self-determination of peoples and democratic self-government all over the world.[1]

Was such misunderstanding of the Financial Agreement the necessary price of its approval? It might be awkward at some future date for the Administration to explain that despite the Financial Agreement the sterling area countries were continuing to bank their foreign exchange earnings in London. It might be awkward, too, to explain the maintenance by these countries of consultation and self-discipline if the sterling area was confronted with a financial crisis. Whatever their temporary effect, the Administration's arguments were sowing dragon's teeth for an eventual harvest.

The new factor in American policy

But the Administration's campaign was not destined to be success-ful even in the short run. The bold claims about multilateralism evoked little enthusiasm from the general public. Most private citizens who supported the loan did so for humanitarian or political reasons unconnected with the issue of multilateral trade.[2] Most important of all, a clear majority of the Congress was not convinced that the asserted financial and commercial benefits justified the expenditure of $3·75 billion. As a result, Congress did not approve the loan by March or April as the negotiators had planned. The Senate debate dragged inconclusively into May when, as a measure of desperation, Alben Barkley, the President *pro tem*, refused to permit consideration of any other legislation until his colleagues had acted on the loan. As late as July, when the measure went to the House of Representatives, it was considered 'in definite danger'[3] and 'very much touch and go'.[4]

But there was a new factor working for approval of the Financial Agreement. In the ten months between the time Keynes arrived in Washington and the close of the American debate, relations with the

[1] Statement by John Edelman for the Textile Workers Union in support of the loan, House Hearings, p. 522.

[2] The authority for this statement is a series of confidential surveys made available to Clayton during Jan.–July 1946. According to one of these surveys only 35 per cent. of those who said they had heard of the Agreement had any idea that the United States would get benefits other than interest and even among this 35 per cent. a large number mentioned wholly imaginary benefits such as ownership in British bases and various political concessions. *Clayton Papers.*

[3] Danger to British Loan Seen as 75 in House Attack It', *The New York Times* (4 July 1946).

[4] Stewart Alsop, 'British Loan Seen in Jeopardy; Congress Opposition Grows', *The New York Herald-Tribune* (1 July 1946).

Soviet Union were steadily deteriorating. In December there was the impasse of the Foreign Ministers in New York; then, in early spring, the Soviet threat to Iran and Gromyko's boycott of the United Nations. Now the State Department had to face another difficult meeting with the Russians in Paris. In these circumstances some Congressmen who had been unimpressed by the commercial benefits of the loan were getting ready for a second look. But the Administration hung back from making an explicit admission of the real state of relations with Russia. Accordingly, it was reluctant to present the loan as an investment in the political and economic strength of the non-Soviet world.

As prospects for the loan darkened, some commentators became critical of this reluctance. One journalist observed: 'The Administration may be overstressing the trade aspects of the British credit. . . . The main purpose of the proposed credit is not to benefit the U.S. financially, or, in the narrow sense, commercially. It is political and strategic to help Britain to recover her strength.'[1] Another complained:

Despite repeated urgings from both House and Senate Administration leadership, the State Department has insisted on discussing the loan in purely economic terms. Perhaps this is right; the loan was certainly negotiated without political second thoughts. Yet, in view of the appalling world situation, the choice between a strong and friendly Britain and a weak and resentful Britain condemned to a future of endless austerity by a vote of Congress does not seem a difficult choice to make.[2]

It mattered little, however, whether this new argument was officially employed. After the Iranian episode the importance of the Soviet factor could no longer be ignored. By March events at Lake Success were beginning to show the limitations of the United Nations in the face of the intransigence of a great power. Commenting on the American debate, *The Manchester Guardian* now observed that support for the loan had risen 'beyond all expectations' and added somewhat uneasily that 'the loan has now taken on quite a new and possibly false function as an investment against Russian imperialism'.[3] A notable symptom of the new mood was the intervention made by

---

[1] Ernest K. Lindley, the *Washington Post* (17 Feb. 1946).

[2] Stewart Alsop, op. cit.

[3] (16 Mar. 1946). The British press showed a marked lack of enthusiasm at the emergence of this new factor. *The Economist* observed: 'If the loan goes through, the balance will have been tilted in its favour by the belief that it represents an investment in security against Russian expansionism. This may well be the first fruit of Fulton. It is an unpalatable coating for the pill.' 'The Loan Hearings', cl (1946), p. 455.

Joseph P. Kennedy, a former Ambassador to Britain not noted for his friendship to that country. Kennedy attracted wide attention by proposing a grant-in-aid to Britain on the grounds that 'the British people and their way of life form the last barrier in Europe against Communism; and we must help them hold that line'.[1] Perhaps the most powerful appeal of all was made by Senator Vandenberg. In April, before departing for the Paris meeting of the Foreign Ministers, Vandenberg announced on the floor of the Senate that he had finally decided to support the loan. He warned his colleagues: 'If we do not lead some other great and powerful nation will capitalize our failure and we shall pay the price of our default.'[2] This was the turning-point in the Senate debate. On 10 May, after disposing of nine crippling amendments, the Senate finally approved the Agreement.

In the House of Representatives, where the Administration anticipated even greater difficulty, the Soviet factor also exerted a decisive influence. Here approval of the loan would require support from a number of wavering Republicans. The prospects for their co-operation were greatly enhanced by the forceful testimony in committee of witnesses such as Charles S. Dewey, a Republican banker who had vigorously opposed Bretton Woods. Dewey stated quite frankly that the economic arguments for and against the loan were now entirely overshadowed 'due to the fact that certain conditions exist in the world today which we did not foresee when the war terminated. . . . This loan, to me, will be the means, and probably the last chance we have, of bringing back to our side very willing nations who might, due to force of circumstances and difficulties, slip under the general influence of the Russian ideology of government.'[3] The impression made by warnings of this kind became apparent at a dinner held by Clayton to muster support from a group of Republican Congressmen who had not yet taken fixed positions on the loan. After the meeting was over one of the Congressmen wrote to Clayton: 'I find that the economic arguments in favor of the loan are on the whole much less convincing to this group than the feeling that the loan may serve us in good stead in holding up a hand of a nation whom we may need badly as a friend because of impending Russian troubles.'[4] Clayton wrote back: 'I am sure you are right in your analysis of the reaction of our friends the other evening on this British loan'.[5]

[1] 'Kennedy Backs Aid to Britain As Gift', *The New York Times* (4 Mar. 1946).
[2] 92 *Cong. Rec.* 4080 (22 Apr. 1946).   [3] House Hearings, p. 357.
[4] Letter from Representative Christian Herter to Clayton, 8 May 1946, *Clayton Papers*.   [5] Letter of 10 May 1946, id.

In the final stages of the House floor debate the Financial Agreement needed all the help this new argument could supply. To begin with, the situation in Palestine deteriorated. Bevin made the tactless remark that the American people supported a home for the Jews in that country 'because they did not want too many of them in New York'.[1] Congressmen from New York and other Eastern states were instantly swamped with protests and some who had been considered 'safe' on the loan actually changed their positions.[2] To make matters worse, an unrepentant isolationist now won a resounding victory in a Nebraska election for a vacant Senate seat. Political experts interpreted this as a warning of 'grass-roots' dislike of the loan which would 'send a good many trembling Congressmen into the ranks of the opposition'.[3] At the eleventh hour it looked as if the loan was lost.

But these adverse factors assumed their proper proportions in the final stages of the House debate. Majority leader McCormack set the tone in his opening speech. The Soviets, he declared, 'are challenging our civilization directly and other civilizations indirectly'. He warned his colleagues lest 'we leave those countries who look toward Washington with a friendly eye no alternative but to be subjected to the sphere of influence of Moscow'.[4] At this one wavering Congressman rose to announce his support of the loan, asserting that McCormack's argument 'hits the nail squarely on the head'.[5] Minority leader Jesse Wolcott, who had expressed doubts about the loan as a commercial proposition, now stated that the new political aspect 'transcends dollars and cents'. He concluded: 'In our actions today we determine for years to come whether there shall be a coalition between the British sphere and the American sphere or whether there shall be a coalition between the British sphere and the Soviet sphere.'[6] Perhaps the most influential voice of all was that of Speaker Sam Rayburn. He intoned gravely:

I do not want Western Europe, England, and all the rest pushed toward an ideology that I despise. I fear if we do not co-operate with our great natural ally that is what will happen. . . . If we are not allied with the great British democracy, I fear somebody will be and God pity us when we have no ally across the Atlantic Ocean and God pity them too.[7]

[1] *The New York Times* (13 June 1946).
[2] The situation was saved to some extent by statements of responsible Jewish leaders that the loan issue should be decided on its merits.
[3] Joseph and Stewart Alsop in the *Washington Post* (14 June 1946).
[4] 92 *Cong. Rec.* 8824 (12 July 1946).
[5] Id., p. 8825.   [6] Id., p. 8913.   [7] Id., p. 8915.

Shortly after these statements the Financial Agreement was passed. The American debate was finally over.[1]

How decisive had been the Soviet factor? In a comment on the debate, *The New York Times* declared: 'Ever since majority leader McCormack spoke strongly yesterday on the urgency of Anglo-American solidarity in the face of the opposing ideology, speaker after speaker asserted that it was the political importance of Anglo-American solidarity rather than any technical aspects of the Agreement which compelled them to vote for the resolution.'[2] But there is a more precise way of gauging the impact of the new argument. The Financial Agreement had been approved by votes of 46–34 in the Senate and 219–155 in the House. Although these appeared to be comfortable majorities, the true balance of forces was revealed by the voting on critical amendments. In the Senate McFarland had proposed an amendment providing for the outright transfer to the United States of British bases in the Western hemisphere. Had this amendment been passed it would have required renegotiation of the entire Agreement—with little prospect of Parliamentary approval. It was defeated by a vote of 45–40. A change in only three votes could have unravelled the whole complicated structure of Anglo-American economic collaboration. The roster of those who opposed this amendment[3] contained some unexpected names—Ferguson, Hickenlooper, Wiley—Republican Senators with isolationist views. It would be comforting to think that these men had been newly converted to the importance of multilateral trade. But their voting record on other parts of the Administration's foreign economic programme indicated otherwise. It was more likely (though not, of course, susceptible to proof) that the dominant consideration had been the Soviet factor.[4]

In the last analysis the Administration's traditional arguments had

[1] It may be interesting to note that in the final stages of the House debate Cordell Hull emerged from retirement to announce his support for the loan. He issued a characteristic broadside against economic blocs and discriminatory practices which might promote 'economic war instead of economic peace'. *The New York Times* (12 July 1946). Congressmen were now distinctly uninterested in these traditional arguments.
[2] *The New York Times* (14 July 1946). To the same effect is the report in the *Daily Telegraph* (15 July 1946).   [3] 92 *Cong. Rec.* 4599–4600 (8 May 1946).
[4] The argument made with reference to these three Senators above can be applied to Congressional Republicans generally. Because of the defection of some Southern Democrats and Democrats from Jewish and Irish constituencies, the Administration needed considerable support from the Republicans in order to pass the loan. It got what it needed: Republican voting for and against the loan was 17–18 in the Senate and 61–122 in the House. This was far more favourable than the Republican performance on previous foreign economic measures put forward by the Administration.

not saved the loan. It had been the new realization that economic assistance to Britain was an important investment in the political and economic stability of a gravely threatened Western world.

CONCLUSION

On 15 July 1946 President Truman signed the legislation authorizing the British loan. A grievous setback for multilateralism had been successfully avoided. But the long and acrimonious debate had left some ugly scars. A turbulent scene took place in the House of Commons. 'The House', said Dalton, 'will, I am sure, share the satisfaction of His Majesty's Government that the United States Congress has approved the Loan Agreement.' A chorus of 'No's' came from the irreconcilables; one member was on his feet demanding to know 'in what period the Chancellor expects to go into a huddle for the elimination of Imperial Preferences, and the sell-out of the Empire?'[1] *The Manchester Guardian* declared: 'The British public, it is only honest to say, has watched the progress of the loan through Congress with something like horror. Most people must often have felt they would like to withdraw the whole thing rather than be under obligation to a legislative body containing so many ignorant and ill-natured members.'[2] Many were now prepared to agree with *The Economist* which warned that the American Congress could no longer 'be relied upon to pursue with any consistency the policy of moderation and liberality without which the whole structure of the loan, of Bretton Woods and of non-discriminatory trade is built on sand'.[3]

Indeed, there had been an unfortunate inevitability in the sequence of events. The inadequacies of the war-time financial accounting, the omissions in planning for the transition period, the dissolution of collaboration at the end of the war, the gulf in Anglo-American attitudes during negotiation of the loan—each had been the legacy of its predecessor and all had combined to produce not merely a bitter debate on the loan agreement but a debate which encouraged drastically different expectations for the future. British opinion had accepted the multilateral undertakings as the unfortunate accompaniments of a badly needed loan. Now it assigned to the United States the primary responsibility for their fulfilment. American opinion had been told that the loan would bring far-reaching and immediate

---

[1] Beverley Baxter, 425 H.C. Deb. 882 (15 July 1946).
[2] (15 July 1946).   [3] 'The Loan in Congress', cl (1946), p. 743.

changes in British trade policies. Now it awaited their execution. At
the same time, final American acceptance of the loan had been
secured out of concern with the Soviet factor. In these confused
circumstances, was there any hope that the terms of the Financial
Agreement would be carried out? Without future collaboration of
unprecedented skill, the stage was set for disaster.

PART IV

MULTILATERALISM IN PRACTICE

CHAPTER XIII

SAVANNAH: TWO CONCEPTIONS OF FINANCIAL COLLABORATION

EVEN as the Financial Agreement was making its tortuous way through the American Congress, attention was turning back again from the transitional to the long-term problems. The inaugural meeting of the International Monetary Fund and the International Bank for Reconstruction and Development was scheduled to take place at Savannah, Georgia, in March 1946. This meeting would test the degree of genuine consensus that had been reached on international financial policy during the Anglo-American negotiations of 1943–44. Keynes assured a friend that Savannah would be 'just a pleasant party'.[1] But his preliminary conversations with American officials indicated that some controversial issues were still unresolved. During one of these discussions Keynes expressed anxiety lest a 'decision as to the size of the staff of the Fund should precede *determination of its functions*'.[2] Perhaps, beneath his external optimism, Keynes harboured forebodings of the difficulties to come.

THE ISSUES AT SAVANNAH

At first sight the principal items on the agenda at Savannah seemed innocent enough—the choice of a permanent site for the Fund and Bank and the determination of the functions and salaries of their Executive Directors. But there was a deeper issue behind all of these matters. Were the Fund and Bank purely financial institutions whose direction could be entrusted to a group of international civil servants? Or did their operations have such economic and political implications as to require close control by the member governments? The Articles of Agreement signed at Bretton Woods made no clear choice for either alternative. It remained for Savannah to decide between them.

---

[1] Harrod, p. 625.
[2] Italics supplied. Paraphrase of Keynes's remarks in William L. Tomlinson, Memorandum of Conversation with Lord Keynes on Scheduling the First Meeting of the Board of Governors Under the Bretton Woods Agreements, 19 Jan. 1946, *White Papers*.

S

The first major item on the agenda was the site of the two institutions. At Bretton Woods the British had reserved their position on the decision to locate the Fund and Bank in the United States. Now, finding it impossible to reverse that decision, they sought at least to place the headquarters in New York rather than in Washington. Keynes was anxious that the institutions should be kept clear of 'the politics of Congress and the nationalistic whispering gallery of the Embassies, and Legations'.[1] He was supported by a number of other delegates who were equally reluctant to locate the new institutions in the capital of their wealthiest and most powerful member. They argued that 'the Fund as an international institution should not be associated too closely with the capital of any nation . . . the staff and officials should be in an atmosphere conducive to allegiance to the Fund'.[2] But the American delegation,with Vinson at its head,was committed in advance in favour of Washington. As Keynes later reported:

. . . Mr. Vinson told me that the American delegation had decided that both institutions should be placed in Washington and that this was a final decision the merits of which they were not prepared to discuss. The U.S. Administration, he said, was entitled to decide for themselves what location within the U.S. was to be preferred. . . . Unfortunately Mr. Vinson, before warning us or seeking our views, had thought fit to take his proposition direct to the President and to obtain his authority to make this an absolute instruction to the American Delegation from which they were not to be free to depart in any circumstances.[3]

Since the United States was the host country for the two institutions as well as their most important member, the outcome of this controversy was virtually assured. The Committee on Site voted for Washington and justified its decision in the following terms:

The Fund, as an intergovernmental institution, should be free of any possible influence from economic, financial or commercial private interests. In recent years there has been a shift from New York to Washington of international financial policy making. The judgment of the government of the country in which the Fund is to be located should be given substantial weight. Washington, D.C. affords a better opportunity for the members to communicate with the representatives of their respective governments. In Washington the officers of the Fund would have ready access to data and material relating to the economies of many countries.[4]

[1] Memorandum on Savannah, 27 Mar. 1946, Harrod, p. 630.
[2] Report of the Committee on Site, *Selected Documents—Board of Governors Inaugural Meeting*, International Monetary Fund (Washington, 1946), p. 29.
[3] Memorandum on Savannah, *supra.*
[4] Report of the Committee on Site, *Selected Documents*, p. 29.

This decision was an important victory for the idea of close national control of the Bretton Woods institutions. It was to have a profound effect on their future development.

The second dispute that arose at Savannah concerned the official duties of the Executive Directors of the two institutions. The Articles of Agreement of the International Monetary Fund provided that the ordinary business of the Fund should be handled by a Managing Director and a staff of international civil servants. They also provided for Executive Directors selected by the member Governments who would make more important policy decisions. The Articles specified that the Executive Directors 'shall function in continuous session at the principal office of the Fund and shall meet as often as the business of the Fund shall require'.[1] These Directors were likely to behave as representatives of their respective Governments. Thus the extent of their activity at the Fund's headquarters had an obvious bearing on the extent to which the Fund would be subjected to national control.

The specific question that now divided the British and American delegates was 'whether Executive Directors and Alternates must devote full time to the business of the Fund or whether Executive Directors and Alternates might be engaged part-time in some other occupation and receive remuneration therefrom'.[2] The British Government wanted to minimize the influence of national governments in the Fund's daily operations; it hoped the Directors and Alternates might hold other posts, such as responsible positions in their respective Treasuries. The American Government wanted to be sure of a powerful voice in the day-to-day operations of the Fund; it wanted the Directors and Alternates to devote full time to the business of the Fund. The matter was finally resolved by providing: 'It shall be the duty of an Executive Director and his Alternate to devote all the time and attention to the business of the Fund that its interests require, and, between them, to be continuously available at the principal office of the Fund.'[3]

This language represented no clear victory for the viewpoint of either side. Indeed, it may be said to have begged the question entirely. Certainly there would be very different interpretations of the

[1] Article XII, Section 3 (*g*). The same terms were used in Article V, Section 3 (*e*) of the Articles of Agreement of the International Bank.

[2] Report of the Committee on Functions and Remunerations, *Selected Documents*, p. 31.

[3] By-laws of the International Monetary Fund, id., p. 12.

requirement that the Executive Directors be 'continuously available'. And in view of the contrasting conceptions of the nature of the International Monetary Fund there would be substantial differences about the time and attention that 'its interests require'.

The third and final issue dividing the British and Americans was the remuneration to be given the Executive Directors. In conformity with its desire for full-time Directors the American delegation proposed salaries of $25,000 (net of taxes) and finally won approval for the figure of $17,500.[1] Acceptance of these high salaries was a decisive victory for the American conception. For Keynes, whose disappointment had been accumulating with the other reversals, it proved to be the last straw. He characterized the figures as 'scandalous'.[2] They would lead, he argued, to 'justified public criticism' of 'such high emoluments for so large a body of officials'.[3] In the end it was the one decision made at Savannah on which he refused to place his Government's approval:

These decisions, however mistaken in our opinion, have nevertheless been made. The difficulty of the resulting dilemma which faces us is obvious. A more unpleasant duty than that which falls to me today I have seldom experienced. I do not wish to deprive any man, especially old and respected friends, of their due and proper reward, but in our view so large a body of persons cannot properly be remunerated on the very high level proposed, which equals or exceeds the highest remuneration available in most countries for public service. My country feels, therefore, that they cannot share in any way for the responsibility of this decision.[4]

Back in England Keynes's words attracted wide attention. The setback on the issue of salaries was represented as a serious contradiction of British expectations: 'It had been hoped', *The Manchester Guardian* complained, 'that the "Bretton Woods" scheme would be managed by truly independent experts, judging economic needs on their merits and giving impartial advice to all. It would be difficult enough to make such a spirit grow in the political setting of Washington, but the arrangements now made seem to have made this even less likely.'[5]

---

[1] It was agreed, however, that the salaries would be scaled down proportionately in accordance with the amount of time which the Executive Directors did not devote to Fund business.

[2] *The New York Herald-Tribune* (16 Mar. 1946).

[3] *The New York Times* (17 Mar. 1946).

[4] The *Financial Times* (18 Mar. 1946).

[5] *The Manchester Guardian* (20 Apr. 1946).

TWO CONCEPTIONS OF FINANCIAL COLLABORATION

We must now turn from the specific disputes that arose at Savannah to a more detailed examination of the different conceptions from which they sprang. The underlying issue had both economic and political aspects. On the economic side, there was the original difficulty that had been encountered in the very earliest Anglo-American negotiations. Was the institution for monetary co-operation to be 'active' or 'passive'? The Joint Statement of 1944 had decided that the Fund should be 'passive' in the sense that it could not buy and sell foreign currencies on its own initiative, but would have to await requests for assistance by the member countries. But had it also decided that the Fund would exercise no discretion in dealing with such requests? The American answer was firmly in the negative. The American Treasury regarded the Fund as an instrument for the achievement of free and non-discriminatory currency practices; it was unwilling to accept an interpretation that would remove an important sanction for the achievement of this goal. Moreover, Congress had been assured that Fund members did not have automatic drawing rights, but were subject to continuous supervision under the Articles of Agreement.[1]

White had occasion to state the American view with considerable firmness. During discussion of the salaries of the Executive Directors he said:

The controversy stems from the issue as to what is the major role which the Fund and the Bank, and particularly the Fund, shall play. It has been our belief from the beginning that the Fund constitutes a very powerful instrument for the coordination of monetary policies, for the prevention of economic warfare, and for an attempt to foster sound monetary policies throughout the world. As part of the necessary machinery to implement those objectives, it was regarded by the United States and others as essential that there be large resources available to the Fund. But I should like to call your attention to the fact that those large resources were regarded as one of the instruments to make possible the broader purposes of the Fund, purposes which are set forth in Article I of the Articles of Agreement. The resources were but a part of the organization and function of the Fund. . . .[2]

White went on to state that the questions now dividing the delegates at Savannah stemmed 'from something that goes very far back, from something that ran right through the discussions with

[1] See p. 135, supra.
[2] Meeting of the Board of Governors of the International Monetary Fund, 16 Mar. 1946, Fund Doc. 27, p. 10, World Fund and Bank Inaugural Meeting.

regard to the proposals that were before us from the beginning, from the very first conversation that we had with our British friends several years ago'.[1] The British, he recalled, had proposed the creation of an International Clearing Union, which would provide members with an automatic source of credit. Even when the Clearing Union was abandoned, the British had sought to make the operations of the International Monetary Fund as automatic as possible, leaving little discretion to the Fund to pass upon the exchange practices of its members. The British had held that point of view sincerely and had made a good case for it—'but it is a point of view that we did not agree with and it is a point of view that the majority of members at Bretton Woods did not agree with, as indicated from the kind of document that emerged'.[2] The Articles of Agreement, White concluded, embodied the American conception of the Fund as an active monitor of exchange practices. This conception could not be circumvented by tampering with the Fund's organization:

> We feel that any attempt to weaken that aspect of the Fund's operations is a threat to the Fund. We do not believe that the Fund, no matter how wisely managed by a managing director, could begin to achieve the objectives that we hope. And we do not believe, further, that it is wholly to be expected that once an issue has been decided it should be again raised in various directions and by indirection. We submit that the thesis that salaries should be lower than necessary to attract competent men is not only a blow at the prestige of the group, not only a threat to the competence of the group, but may become, I hope undesignedly, an instrument to divert the purposes and divert the general policy of the Fund so that it will come closer akin to the hearts of those who foresee in the Fund little else than a source of credit. . . .[3]

These were strong words. Keynes replied rather coldly that the British 'were and remain in accord with the functions of the Fund as set forth in the Bretton Woods final act, which took, in our judgment, a sufficient account of our views about the limitations within which it was advisable that the Fund should work'.[4] There was little doubt about what those views were. The British Government believed that Fund members could dismantle their economic defences only if given unencumbered access to Fund resources. Drawing rights could not be made dependent on Fund approval of a member's economic policies without violating this principle. The Fund had been accepted by

---

[1] Ibid.   [2] Id., p. 11.   [3] Id., p. 12.   [4] Id., p. 13.

Parliament only after great emphasis on its value as a source of liquidity and only after the most detailed assurances that it would not interfere in the domestic affairs of its members. If the American view expressed at Savannah were pressed to its logical conclusion it might undermine the fundamental assumptions on which British approval had been based. 'Had it not been on the explicit undertaking by the Americans to drop their initial idea of the schoolmistress that the British had agreed to the non-Unitas version of the Fund? Now the Americans were slipping back to their old bad ways of thought. It is not surprising that Keynes was maddened.'[1]

The American views on access to Fund resources, however, represented no 'slipping back' to 'old bad ways of thought'. To gain approval for the Fund the Administration had found it necessary to allay Congressional fears that the institution might become a sieve for the outpouring of American dollars. The Bretton Woods Agreements Act subjected the United States Executive Directors to close control by the American Government. The Act also required the Directors to seek an interpretation that the Fund could only employ its resources for 'current monetary stabilization operations to afford temporary assistance to members in connection with seasonal, cyclical, and emergency fluctuations in the balance of payments' and not 'to provide facilities for relief or reconstruction on the part of any member'. These provisions reflected the desire of Congress to protect the Fund's resources from dissipation in the transition period. Unfortunately, in the case of countries suffering from large transitional dollar deficits, it was impossible to ensure that Fund assistance would be used only for stabilization purposes. The only way to safeguard the Fund's resources was to suspend the drawing rights of countries which could not convince the Executive Directors that they had surmounted their principal transitional difficulties.[2]

Such an outcome was rather different from what British opinion had been led to expect. During the British debate there had been indications that a number of British leaders regarded the Fund as a source of support in the transition period. Keynes himself had been troubled by the implications of the Bretton Woods Agreements Act. Although he considered some of its provisions 'unexceptionable' he had mentioned 'certain aspects of them we do not altogether like'.[3]

[1] Harrod, pp. 634–5.
[2] Authority for such action could be found in Article XX, Section 4 (*i*).
[3] *Letter to E. M. Bernstein, May 29, 1945.*

One of these had been the proposed interpretation about use of the Fund's resources:

> If the . . . amendment is to be regarded as no more than high-lighting what is already written in Article XIV (1), clearly there is no harm in that. If, however, the amendment were taken literally as limiting the rights of a country in using the Fund, it would, I should have thought, be impracticable. It is impossible to earmark money, and when a country, which in fact is in the course of reconstruction or getting straight after the war, uses the Fund, it is impossible to say in any particular case exactly to what purpose that particular dollar is devoted.[1]

According to this line of reasoning the impossibility of 'earmarking' money made it futile to try to protect the Fund's resources by inspecting the merits of each request for financial aid. Thus there could be no restrictions at all. This was the very opposite conclusion from that reached by Keynes's counterparts in the United States.[2]

What can be said in retrospect of the contrasting positions of the two Governments? Given the position of equilibrium that was expected to prevail in the long-run, much might be said for Keynes's view that the resources of the Fund should be automatically available to Fund members. But given the state of general disequilibrium that existed in the transition period, it is difficult to see how his position could have been accepted. During the transition the natural equilibrating forces would not be at work; it could not be assumed that funds requested for stabilization purposes would normally be repaid within a short time period. The fact that money could not be 'earmarked' suggested the futility of checking each particular request for aid; but it did not remove the need for close supervision by national representatives. It would still be necessary to determine which nations had made sufficient strides in recovery to become eligible for automatic drawings. The United States, whose currency was almost universally demanded for reconstruction purposes, could not be expected to leave this determination to a group of international civil servants. In the transition period monetary stabilization could not be achieved 'automatically' according to a set of rules—this was the time members would insist on the closest control over the Fund's operations.

---

[1] Ibid.

[2] Presumably Keynes was still willing to restrict drawings in the exceptional circumstances contemplated in Article V, Section 5, where a member was 'using the resources of the Fund in a manner contrary to the purposes of the Fund'. But this placed the burden of justifying restriction of drawing rights on the Fund, whereas the American interpretation placed the burden on individual members to justify their right to draw.

The appropriate instruments of that control were the Executive Directors. However acceptable the British position might have been for long-term policy, it was not well suited to the immediate problems facing the delegates at the Savannah Conference.[1]

But the Anglo-American differences at Savannah must not be discussed solely in economic terms; they had their political aspects as well. Morthenthau and White had aimed to transfer the control of international finance from Wall Street to Washington. They expected the Bretton Woods institutions to accomplish this transfer. Financial policy, in their view, would now be freed from the intrigues of vested interests. It would be made by 'financial institutions run by financial people' so that the financial needs of a country would 'be taken care of wholly independent of the political connection'.[2] The Bank and Fund were to develop into supra-national institutions concerned only with their members' economic needs.

What Morgenthau and White failed to see was that the transfer of decision-making from New York to Washington might not have this effect at all, but might actually increase the nationalistic and political components of international financial policy. The insistence of Congress that the American Executive Directors be subjected to close control by the American Government was an inkling of things to come. When Vinson succeeded Morgenthau as Secretary of the Treasury the weakness of the White–Morgenthau view became finally apparent. The new Secretary had to make policy in an imperfectly organized world; the United Nations was yet untried and tensions were developing with the Soviet Union. Decisions made at the headquarters of the Fund and Bank might have important political consequences affecting the national security of the United States. Vinson was quick to appreciate this fact. Shortly after Savannah he wrote: 'The business of the Fund and Bank involves matters of high economic policy. They should not become just two more financial

---

[1] There was an argument against the British position even on long-term grounds. By 1946 it was clear that many of the members of the International Monetary Fund would engage in complete or partial state-trading, or at least in large-scale planning in the domestic economic sphere. It could no longer be assumed that balance of payments disequilibria were temporary and self-correcting phenomena; surpluses and deficits in the balance of payments would be the result, to a large extent, of conscious governmental decisions. In the absence of natural equilibrating forces, protection of the Fund's resources and the enforcement of monetary discipline would have to be achieved by a good deal of conscious planning and control by the Executive Directors. See Raymond F. Mikesell, 'The Role of the International Monetary Agreements in a World of Planned Economies', *Jour. of Pol. Ec.*, lv (1947), p. 47.

[2] See also Morgenthau's statement quoted p. 11, *supra*.

institutions.'[1] According to one financial writer the Administration had come to the conclusion that 'there is no separating the political and economic angles of a loan'—therefore operations of the Bank and Fund would be 'as political as a troop movement'.[2] In its evolution to world leadership the United States was becoming increasingly aware of the political implications of its economic strength.

This was not the trend in American policy for which Keynes had hoped. In the provisions of the Bretton Woods Agreements Act he had already found cause for misgiving:

> The proposal to make the American Director subject to an advisory council is . . . a purely domestic matter, to which we cannot object. Some of us, however, had been hoping that the officials of the two bodies would, in the course of time, come to regard themselves as primarily international officials, taking a world, objective outlook, and only where clearly necessary grinding their own national axes. So one would have wished to minimise, rather than maximise, their national representative character and their position as delegates from outside authorities.[3]

The Savannah Conference brought the full realization of these early forebodings. Keynes expressed his disapproval with the following simile:

> I hope that Mr. Kelchner has not made any mistake and that there is no malicious fairy, no Carabosse, which he has overlooked to ask to the party. For if so the curses which that bad fairy will pronounce will, I feel sure, run as follows:—'You two brats will grow up politicians; your every thought and act shall have an *arrière-pensée*; everything you determine shall not be for its own sake or on its merits but because of something else.'
>
> If this should happen, then the best that could befall—and that is how it might turn out—would be for the children to fall into an eternal slumber, never to waken or be heard of again in the courts and markets of mankind.[4]

Here was a poignant appeal for the restoration of the idealistic spirit in which the two institutions were originally conceived. But was there any real hope in the circumstances of 1946 that this original spirit could prevail? The prospects might have been different had the

---

[1] Fred M. Vinson, 'After the Savannah Conference', *Foreign Affairs*, xxiv (1946), p. 622.

[2] Sylvia Porter, 'U.S. to Exploit World Bank', the *New York Post* (9 May 1946).

[3] *Letter to Bernstein, supra.*

[4] Harrod, p. 632. Vinson was greatly displeased by this speech. One observer recalls that he grumbled: 'I don't mind being called malicious, but I *do* mind being called a fairy!'

United Nations been made into a genuine instrument of world government. In reality, however, it was only a loose association of states retaining a large measure of national sovereignty. As long as nations were unwilling to surrender their sovereignty in the political field, was it realistic to expect them to do so in the economic? The granting and withholding of short and long-term credits would have important political repercussions, and the largest prospective creditor, the United States, could not be expected to forego the political advantages of its economic strength. Thus political as well as economic factors brought eventual victory to the American conception of financial collaboration.

CONCLUSION

The Savannah Conference revealed a serious division between the United States and Britain on the character of the financial institutions they had constructed in the war. The British, led by Keynes, inclined toward the view that the Fund and Bank should be purely financial institutions, directed mainly by a staff of international civil servants. The Americans, led by Vinson, sought to subject the institutions to close control by national governments. The political and economic circumstances of the transition period made it virtually inevitable that the American viewpoint should finally prevail.

Although the American conception of financial collaboration was justified by the circumstances, it was not presented at Savannah in the most fortunate way. The American delegation made no secret of the fact that it considered itself to hold the balance of economic and political power. This alienated British opinion and produced reactions far out of proportion to the particular differences dividing the two countries. One British newspaper complained that

the conference appears to have been a most unhappy experiment in post-war monetary co-operation. The American Treasury, which in these matters seems at present to take the lead over the State Department, massed its voting powers and ran the conference in a rigidly domineering manner. Every proposal put forward by the American delegation was pressed through with steam-roller tactics, and the delegation seems to have made no secret of its belief that the United States, which pays the piper, has a right to call the tune. In fact, the worst fears of those who had always warned us that this was what the United States meant by international economic co-operation were borne out at Savannah.[1]

[1] *The Manchester Guardian* (23 Mar. 1946). See also the *Financial Times* (25 Mar. 1946).

Above all, Keynes was shaken by the results. In contrast to his confident manner a few months before, he now had little heart to defend American policy. 'Thus before his eyes, the warning of his critics seemed to be coming true . . . at Savannah, it seemed as if all his fine protestations on behalf of American goodwill and co-operativeness were belied. . . . His castles were falling around him.'[1] It was a bitter blow for the man who had become such an ardent exponent of Anglo-American collaboration. When death claimed him a few weeks later, the cause of multilateralism sustained a grievous loss. In view of the increasing gulf between British and American opinion, it was a loss which that cause could ill afford.

[1] Harrod, p. 635.

CHAPTER XIV

LONDON: TWO CONCEPTIONS OF COMMERCIAL COLLABORATION

THE Bretton Woods institutions were now officially launched on their respective careers. But there was still no equivalent organization for collaboration on the commercial side. During 1946 measures were taken to remedy this omission. In February the Economic and Social Council of the United Nations appointed a Preparatory Committee of nineteen countries to draft a convention for the consideration of an International Conference on Trade and Employment.[1] The Committee was to have on its agenda the main lines of action laid down in the 'Proposals for Consideration by an International Conference on Trade and Employment' drafted by the British and American negotiators in the autumn of 1945. In anticipation of the first meeting of the Preparatory Committee, the United States published a 'Suggested Charter for an International Trade Organization of the United Nations'.[2] The 'Suggested Charter' was put forward simply as a basis for discussion and was designed to 'clarify possible obscurities and remove any misunderstandings to which the condensed language of the "Proposals" may have given rise'.[3] Finally, at Church House, London, in October 1946, the Preparatory Committee gathered to begin work on the Charter for the International Trade Organization.

Although the commercial policy negotiations had now been generalized to include other countries, the future of the I.T.O. still lay very much in the hands of Britain and the United States. Without agreement between these two countries, progress on the Charter would be impossible. With Anglo-American agreement, the prospects were good for a successful outcome. In their opening statements at London both countries expressed their continued allegiance to multi-

[1] The countries appointed as members of the Preparatory Committee were Australia, Belgium, Brazil, Canada, Chile, China, Cuba, Czechoslovakia, France, India, Lebanon, Luxembourg, Netherlands, New Zealand, Norway, South Africa, the U.S.S.R., the United States, and the United Kingdom. The U.S.S.R. decided not to attend the meetings of the Preparatory Committee.
[2] The text of the 'Suggested Charter' may be found in United Nations, Economic and Social Council, *Report of the First Session of the Preparatory Committee of the United Nations Conference on Trade and Employment* (London, 1946), E/PC/T/33, pp. 52–67.
[3] Clayton, Foreword to the 'Suggested Charter'.

lateralism in the field of commercial policy. Sir Stafford Cripps, welcoming the delegates on behalf of the United Kingdom, stressed the importance of finding

> some method acceptable to all the main nations which will insure a degree of order in the international economic sphere and so will remove that fear that will otherwise prevent us from embarking upon an expansionist policy for world trade. Just as in the political sphere we seek some corporate security for the world; so in the economic sphere we need to regulate the use of economic armaments.[1]

This approach was enthusiastically endorsed by Clair Wilcox, the head of the American delegation, who went so far as to call the drafting of the Charter the most urgent task confronting the United Nations in the international economic field. 'Of the many tasks of reconstruction that now remain', he said, 'ours is by all odds the most important.'[2] In confident terms Wilcox expressed the State Department's faith in the universal validity of multilateral principles:

> Every nation stands to gain from the widest possible movement of goods and services. . . . That international trade should be abundant, that it should be multilateral, that it should be non-discriminatory, that stabilization policies and trade policies should be consistent—these are propositions on which all nations, whatever their forms of economic organization, can agree.[3]

Of the wide range of issues discussed at London, only three need concern us here. These were the ones that formed the heart of the earlier Anglo-American commercial policy discussions. One of them—the tariff-preference issue—caused no particular difficulty. The compromise struck in the 'Proposals' was retained. The Draft Charter that emerged at London embodied the unconditional most-favoured-nation clause, excepting from the clause all existing margins of preference.[4] It provided that members should enter upon request 'into reciprocal and mutually advantageous negotiations . . . directed to the substantial reduction of tariffs and the elimination of import tariff preferences'.[5] The real test of Anglo-American agreement on this obligation would come with the opening of the specific tariff and preference bargaining set for Geneva in the spring of 1947. At London it was the other two issues that were of central importance—

---

[1] Preparatory Committee, First Session, Plenary Meetings, *Verbatim Records*, E/PC/T/PV/1 (15 Oct. 1946), p. 8.
[2] *Verbatim Records*, E/PC/T/PV/2 (16 Oct. 1946), p. 3.   [3] Ibid.
[4] I.e., all the preferences existing *after* the tariff-preference bargaining to occur in 1947.   [5] Article 24 (1).

the relation between multilateral trade and employment, and the elimination of quantitative restrictions.

THE EMPLOYMENT ISSUE

The relation between trade and employment policy probably evoked more discussion than any other issue at the London Conference. How were these policies to be related—either in framing the objectives of the Charter or in defining its specific obligations? According to Wilcox, the first principle to be embodied in the Charter was 'that existing barriers to international trade should be substantially reduced, so that the volume of such trade may be large'.[1] According to Cripps, the prime object was to 'achieve an agreement as to the manner in which the nations can co-operate for the promotion of the highest level of employment and the maintenance of demand and can bring some degree of regulation into world trade and commerce'.[2] The differences in emphasis reflected in these statements provided a warning of the difficulties that were now to come.

The American position on the relation between multilateral trade and employment was much the same as it had been in the earlier negotiations. The United States recognized no less than Britain that high levels of employment and effective demand were desirable objectives and that the failure to achieve them would hinder the expansion of world trade. But in drafting specific obligations for members of an International Trade Organization the Americans found a difference between 'asking a man to obligate himself to remain prosperous and asking him to agree to a rule against deliberate attacks on the prosperity of his neighbors'.[3] In the American view, the reduction of trade barriers was something a Government could effectively promise to accomplish; the maintenance of full employment was not. Accordingly a commitment on employment could not be 'as absolute as in the case of other matters which lie entirely within the volition and control of nations'.[4]

There was a second point to be considered. Legitimate differences might exist between nations on how to define the employment objective and on the relative weight to be put on this objective as com-

[1] *Verbatim Records*, E/PC/T/PV/2 (16 Oct. 1946), p. 4.
[2] Id., E/PC/T/PV/1 (15 Oct. 1946), p. 4.
[3] Harry C. Hawkins, 'Problems Raised by the International Trade Organization', in Seymour Harris, *A Foreign Economic Policy for the United States* (Cambridge, 1948), p. 276.   [4] Ibid.

pared with the objective of expanding real income. By its rejection of the Full Employment Act of 1945 the American Congress had indicated that it did not want to bind itself in advance to 'Keynesian' methods of maintaining full employment. The Employment Act passed instead in 1946 spoke of 'high and productive' employment and left the Executive free to employ a variety of less clearly specified methods. Was it not unfair to conclude from these developments that the United States was indifferent to the employment problem? As Wilcox put it, there seemed to be some 'impertinence' in the assumption that the United States was 'both ignorant of the problem of stability and indifferent to it'.[1]

These views on the employment issue were reflected in the American 'Suggested Charter'. This document followed closely the language agreed to in the 'Proposals'. In particular, the 'Suggested Charter' retained the 'undertaking' that each nation should 'take action designed to achieve and maintain full employment within its own jurisdiction through measures appropriate to its political and economic institutions'.[2] It also retained the provision that no nation should seek to maintain employment through measures likely to create unemployment in other countries.[3] Finally, it embodied the suggestion that, under the aegis of the Economic and Social Council, members should exchange information on employment problems, consult regularly on employment, and hold special conferences in the case of a threat of widespread unemployment.[4] At the same time, the 'Suggested Charter' made no attempt to elaborate on the provisions of the 'Proposals'. And it indicated that the employment provisions were to be included in one of the chapters of the trade charter rather than in a separate convention on employment policy.[5]

In contrast to their American counterparts, the British delegates came to the London Conference with the intention of achieving a substantial expansion of the employment obligations. In so doing they appear to have been under considerable pressure from domestic opinion. The literature on home and foreign economic policy was now fairly saturated with the subject of full employment.[6] It was

---

[1] *A Charter for World Trade* (New York, 1949), pp. 33–34.

[2] 'Suggested Charter', Article 4. The mention of 'full employment' probably went beyond what the Congress would have liked, but the situation was safeguarded by the phrase 'through measures appropriate', &c.   [3] Article 5.   [4] Article 6.

[5] The 'Proposals' did not specify a separate convention on employment policy, but their format rather hinted at this result, since it put 'Proposals Concerning Employment' on a parity with 'Proposals Concerning an International Trade Organization'.

[6] One of the most influential books was that by Sir William Beveridge, *Full Employment in a Free Society* (London, 1945), which adopted an ambitious definition of the

widely predicted that a serious American depression would develop within the coming year. This prospect was the most frequently cited ground for misgiving about British participation in the I.T.O.[1] A typical statement was that of Hugh Gaitskell, a prominent member of the Labour Party's right wing: 'If you can maintain full employment in America, then the prospects for freedom from trade restrictions are bright.'[2]

Here again was the familiar assumption made in the Clearing Union that the failure to maintain full employment would be the only—or at least the major—threat to equilibrium in the balance of payments. There appeared to be little recognition that the over-zealous pursuit of full employment might provide an equally important source of difficulty. Indeed, some British leaders appeared to believe that domestic expansion would be positively helpful—even if pushed beyond the full employment goal. Herbert Morrison went so far as to declare: 'Our full employment policy means that for a long time to come we will have a *shortage of labour*. That is one of the biggest contributions we can make to sound and prosperous world trade. And, therefore, to world peace.'[3]

The British Government, of course, was by no means unique in its concentration on the problem of full employment. Other countries at London, notably Australia and New Zealand, went much farther in emphasizing the importance of domestic expansion. Their views were made known to the British Government at the customary meeting of Commonwealth representatives held prior to the London Conference. The proposal now advanced by the British Government was much milder than the plans proposed by these countries.

The British Government put before the London Conference some draft passages for inclusion in a Convention on International Employment and Trade Policy.[4] It proposed that the employment obligations 'might either take the form of a separate Convention (signed at the same time and by the same countries as the articles of the Trade Organization) or form part of a general Convention which would

objective (employment of 97 per cent. or more of those willing and able to work) and proposed to achieve it by the widespread use of central planning and direct controls.
[1] See, for example, the comments in *The Times* and the *Financial Times* (27 Nov. 1946).   [2] *The New York Times* (24 Oct. 1946).
[3] Italics supplied. *The Times* (5 Nov. 1946).
[4] 'Draft Passages on Employment for Inclusion in a Convention on International Employment and Trade Policy', Annex A of 'Memorandum by the United Kingdom Delegation on International Employment Policy', in First Session of the Preparatory Committee, Committee I (Employment and Economic Activity), *Working Papers*, E/PC/T/C.I/W.3.

also establish the International Trade Organization and contain the specific articles of agreement of that Organization'.[1] The passages stated in unambiguous terms that full employment was 'the main condition for the maintenance of satisfactory levels of living' and that its maintenance on 'a reasonably assured basis' was 'essential . . . to the expansion of international trade'.[2] Nothing was said of the contribution of freer trade to employment. As the British commentary explained:

The fundamental advantage of more liberal international trading conditions is not so much that it will give a greater volume of employment all round, but that it will raise output per head all round by allowing each country to concentrate more on the production of those goods and services which it is relatively most fitted to produce. . . . We must not get into the position in which it is assumed that, if trading conditions can be liberalised, employment will thereby automatically be maintained. The maintenance of employment, on which all our hopes for a permanent liberalisation of trading conditions must ultimately rest, requires separate and positive action.[3]

The draft provisions put forward by the British delegation made full employment policies not simply the concern of the Economic and Social Council but also of the I.T.O. itself and of the various specialized agencies of the United Nations. Beyond this they did three main things. First, they laid down specific international obligations with respect to national economic policy. Second, they related these obligations and the commercial policy obligations in such a way that countries pursuing full employment at home might have safeguards against the spread of deflationary pressure from abroad. Third, they called for positive measures of international collaboration for the maintenance of full employment.

With respect to the first subject, the draft passages contemplated two distinct obligations. To begin with, countries were obliged to take measures to achieve and maintain full employment and to avoid falling into a slump which might prejudice the achievement of full employment in other countries. The specific obligations proposed on this score did not appear to differ materially from those which appeared in the 'Proposals'. But the British commentary which accompanied the draft passages placed great emphasis on one conception that had not been expressly embodied in the 'Proposals'. It stated that the

[1] British Memorandum, p. 1. In the end the British decided to drop the idea of a separate Convention.
[2] Annex A, id., p. 2.　　　　　　　　[3] Explanatory Note, Annex B, id., p. 9.

maintenance of full employment was 'a duty which each government owes not merely to its own nationals, but to the world as a whole. Accordingly, it must be a basic element in any international employment policy to secure from governments—particularly the governments of the main trading nations—an unambiguous recognition of their international responsibility in this regard'.[1] Moreover, the commentary read as if an obligation to adopt effective employment policies was virtually the same thing as the successful achievement of full employment: 'The adoption of effective domestic measures for the maintenance of full employment is the essential basis. If all important countries adopted effective policies of this kind, no international depression need ever develop.'[2]

The American negotiators regarded these statements with a certain amount of scepticism. They were not so certain that the only barrier to the maintenance of full employment was unwillingness to adopt the necessary policies. They considered that the simple undertaking embodied in the 'Proposals' and the 'Suggested Charter' was sufficient. They were not convinced of the need for an explicit statement that the maintenance of full employment was an obligation owed by a government not only to its own citizens but to other governments as well. This notion, they argued, was implicit in the employment undertaking anyway—to spell it out in formal terms would only antagonize certain segments of American opinion. But these objections were not pressed too hard. In the end the Draft Charter included the explicit statement that the avoidance of unemployment was a matter 'not of domestic concern alone, but . . . a necessary condition for the expansion of international trade'.[3] A lengthy exposition of this view was included in the Report of the Conference.[4]

Rather more difficulty was caused by the second of the obligations proposed by the British with respect to national economic policy. Each Government was obliged to 'take action through measures appropriate to its political and economic institutions to correct a fundamental disequilibrium in its balance of payments which persistently creates balance of payments difficulties for other countries and so prejudices them in the maintenance of full employment'.[5] The

---

[1] Annex B, id., p. 4.   [2] Annex B, id., p. 5.   [3] Article 3 (1).
[4] *Report of the First Session of the Preparatory Committee of the United Nations Conference on Trade and Employment*, part II, chapter I (Achievement and Maintenance of High and Steadily Rising Levels of Effective Demand, Employment and Economic Activity), E/PC/T/33, pp. 4–6.   [5] British Memorandum, Annex A, p. 2.

British commentary declared that this was a necessary supplement to the obligation to maintain full employment. It argued that

a deflationary pressure may . . . be caused by a country which is not actually experiencing serious unemployment. For example, a country may be persistently buying from abroad or investing abroad appreciably less than it is selling abroad. Indeed, the excess of its sales of exports may be the means whereby it is maintaining its own employment. This is, however, likely to exercise a deflationary pressure on other countries and to intensify their problem of maintaining their own employment. . . . What particular measures should be adopted (e.g. the stimulation of imports or the removal of special encouragements to exports, an appreciation of the country's exchange rate, an upward revision of its internal price and cost structure, an increase in foreign investment, etc.) should, of course, be left to the country concerned to determine.[1]

This statement was unaccompanied by any reference to the policies of deficit countries: it appeared to place responsibility for curing a balance of payments disequilibrium on the surplus countries alone. It recalled the formulation of the problem contained in the Clearing Union—a formulation that had been unacceptable to the United States. Here was the question of creditor-debtor responsibility all over again. On this subject there had been no noticeable reduction in the gap between British and American opinion. Wilcox considered the British proposal 'clearly inadmissible. It applied exclusively to the United States. It carried the possible implication that instability in other countries was attributable solely to the United States. And it imposed an obligation on the United States alone.'[2]

Once again, however, the American delegation was forced to accept a compromise. An article appeared in the London Charter expressing the agreement of members 'that, in case of a fundamental disequilibrium in their balance of payments involving other countries in persistent balance of payments difficulties, which handicap them in maintaining employment, they will make their full contribution to action designed to correct the maladjustment'.[3] Moreover, the Report of the Conference embodied the emphasis on creditor responsibility contained in the British memorandum.[4]

---

[1] Annex B, id., pp. 4–5.   [2] *A Charter for World Trade*, p. 137.
[3] London Charter, Article 7.
[4] 'It was not suggested that countries, which are experiencing difficulties through unfavourable balance of payments, may not themselves be partly responsible for the maladjustments. . . . But insofar as the pressure on their balance of payments is due to the failure of countries with excessively favourable balances of payments to spend their external purchasing power on imports or to utilize it for productive investment abroad,

Thus the British delegation achieved a certain measure of success in gaining recognition for the first of its three major proposals on employment policy. Its second proposal was designed to relate the obligations on national economic policy to the obligations on commercial policy. In the words of Professor Meade, who sat for Britain on the First Committee, 'there must be in the international settlement which we are now devising sufficient escape clauses, let-outs, special arrangements, call them what you will, which will enable those countries which are adopting internal measures for full employment to protect themselves against a world depression if such a world depression should show itself'.[1] To meet this need the British memorandum tentatively suggested the following passage for inclusion in the employment Convention:

The Governments on whose behalf this agreement is signed request the United Nations, acting through the machinery of the Economic and Social Council, to accept the obligation of giving an opinion, if the International Trade Organization so requests, and after consultation with the other specialised agencies concerned, (a) whether inability of a country or group of countries to carry out the policies contemplated in this Agreement is making it difficult for another country or group of countries to maintain a high level of employment, and (b) if so, whether the terms of the international agreement to which the country or countries so affected are parties, provide adequate opportunity for remedial action without a temporary release from obligations under the International Trade Organization.[2]

Here the United Kingdom seemed to be suggesting the inclusion of an employment 'escape clause' which would release the I.T.O. members from their multilateral obligations in the event of an American slump. The idea of such a clause was vigorously championed by the Australian delegation. The British Government was obviously taking account of the Australian view, yet seemed not entirely to have made up its mind. Although Meade declared that the clause 'required careful consideration', he also said it was 'not at all certain' that its

the main responsibility for the necessary re-adjustment should not fall on the countries which are under pressure.' Part II, chapter I, section E. 2, London Report, p. 5. Mention was also made of appropriate measures which the creditor might take to correct the disequilibrium—'the stimulation of imports or the removal of special encouragements to exports, an appreciation of the country's exchange rate, an upward revision of its internal price and cost structure, an increase in foreign investment, etc.' These were the specific measures suggested in the British memorandum and were similar to the main lines of action envisaged for the creditor countries in the Clearing Union.

[1] First Session of the Preparatory Committee, Committee I (Employment and Economic Activity), *Verbatim Records*, E/PC/T/C.I/PV/2, p. 40.

[2] British Memorandum, Annex A, p. 3.

inclusion would be necessary.[1] And the British commentary explained that the clause would be rendered superfluous if sufficient safeguards were embodied in various other parts of the I.T.O. Charter.[2]

This in fact was the course that was finally adopted. The idea of an employment 'escape clause' was set aside. Its main objectives were achieved by expanding the freedom of countries to employ quantitative restrictions on balance of payments grounds.[3] Moreover, the nullification and impairment provisions of the Charter were drafted to embrace obligations on national economic policy as well as commercial policy obligations.[4] Thus the failure of a member to maintain full employment or to cure a balance of payments surplus which handicapped other members in maintaining full employment might release the other members from their specific obligations with respect to trade restrictions. Finally, the I.T.O. was instructed to have regard in the exercise of its functions to 'the need of Members to take action within the provisions of the Charter to safeguard their economies against deflationary pressure in the event of a serious or abrupt decline in the effective demand of other countries'.[5] This provided explicit recognition of the fact that members might be released from their multilateral obligations in the event of an American slump.

The third major British proposal concerned international action for the maintenance of full employment. The 'Proposals' and the 'Suggested Charter' had provided for the study and the exchange of information on employment problems, regular consultation on such problems, and the holding of special conferences in the event of widespread unemployment. The British proposal went beyond these provisions. It envisaged an undertaking by members to participate in arrangements 'for the co-ordination of the action of the various specialised agencies in the field of employment policy'.[6] The British were extremely cautious in suggesting this line of action, since 'at the present stages of international economic organization, the direct action necessary to maintain the total world demand for goods and services at a high and stable level must, in the main, be the sum of individual national efforts'.[7] Nevertheless, they maintained that the contribution of the specialized agencies in the employment field

[1] E/PC/T/C.I/PV/2, pp. 43 and 64.
[2] British Memorandum, Annex B, paras. 10–11, p. 6.
[3] See *infra*, pp. 280–4.
[4] London Draft, Article 35.   [5] London Draft, Article 8.
[6] Annex A, section (4) (ii), p. 3.   [7] Annex B, para. 12, p. 6.

might be 'really appreciable'.[1] Consequently, they suggested that the Economic and Social Council, together with the specialized agencies, should consider what action might be taken along the following lines: the promotion of stability in the incomes of primary producers; co-operation to synchronize credit conditions and influence terms of borrowing; contra-cyclical timing of international public works; and the promotion of a flow of capital in time of depression to countries whose balance of payments needed support in order to enable them to maintain domestic employment.[2]

Of these four lines of action only the second offered any hope of immediate advance. The first contemplated the device of the buffer stock, a subject which had already been unsuccessfully explored with the United States. The third could only be pursued by an agency with much greater resources for public investment than the International Bank, and there was little prospect for the creation of such an agency. The fourth line of action involved the same kind of obligation on creditor countries which had caused such strong American resistance to the Clearing Union, for it envisaged measures 'to finance the trade deficits of the "full employment" countries by increasing the export of capital from the countries in which the depression was developing'.[3]

The London Conference avoided exploration of these controversial suggestions by drafting a resolution for later adoption by the conference which would adopt the I.T.O. Charter. This resolution requested the Economic and Social Council to undertake studies along the four main lines suggested by the British memorandum.[4] At the same time, an article was inserted in the London Charter providing that national action to maintain full employment should 'so far as possible, be supplemented by international action sponsored by the Economic and Social Council of the United Nations and carried out in collaboration with the appropriate inter-governmental organizations'.[5] The British suggestions for international action to maintain full employment were thus removed from the jurisdiction of the I.T.O. and assigned to organs of the United Nations, with little prospect for immediate action.[6] It was apparent that British misgivings on the I.T.O. resulting from concern with full employment would have to

---

[1] Annex B, para. 12, p. 6.
[2] Annex A, section (5), p. 3, and Annex B, part III, pp. 6–8.
[3] Annex B, part III, para. 24, p. 8.   [4] London Report, p. 6.   [5] Article 3 (2).
[6] In February 1947 the Economic and Employment Commission of the United Nations, a permanent body dealing with these matters under the supervision of the

be satisfied by the general obligations inserted on this subject and by various negative safeguards providing 'let-outs' from multilateral obligations.

THE ISSUE OF QUANTITATIVE RESTRICTIONS

The second fundamental Anglo-American issue which arose at the London Conference concerned the elimination of quantitative restrictions. In the 'Proposals' of 1945 the two Governments had agreed in principle that quantitative restrictions should be eliminated. The most important exception related to restrictions imposed to safeguard the balance of payments. Restrictions imposed on these grounds were to be governed during the post-war transition period by principles which would 'promote the maximum development of multilateral trade' and which 'in no event would be more restrictive of such trade' than the principles applicable to the use of financial restrictions under the transitional provisions of the Articles of Agreement of the International Monetary Fund.[1] Determination of the length of the transition period was to occur by a procedure analogous to that provided in the transitional provisions of the Fund Articles. Both during and after the transition period the use of quantitative restrictions was to be governed by fixed criteria. After the transition period these restrictions were to be non-discriminatory, except in cases where 'their application would have the effect of preventing a member from utilising inconvertible currencies for buying needed imports'.[2]

At the London Conference the American Government set out to achieve more specific limitations on the use of quantitative restrictions than those contained in the 'Proposals'. Its 'Suggested Charter' fixed the end of the transition period at 31 December 1949. Up to this date members of the I.T.O. would be entitled to employ quantitative restrictions for balance of payments purposes provided only that they consulted with other members affected by such restrictions. At the end of that period these restrictions were to be removed.[3] From then on restrictions would be permitted only to 'arrest a long continuing

Economic and Social Council, assigned the four suggestions for international action to its Sub-Commission on Employment and Economic Stability. The Sub-Commission did not meet until November 1947.

[1] 'Proposals Concerning an International Trade Organization', chapter III, section C, 2, b.

[2] Chapter III, section C, 7. There were certain other minor exceptions that need not concern us here, such as the exception permitting discrimination pursuant to action taken under the 'scarce currency' clause of the Fund Articles.

[3] Article 20, 2.

or large deficit in the Member's balance of payments' or 'in the case of a Member with very low monetary reserves, to forestall a large deficit in the Member's balance of payments'.[1] Members employing such restrictions would be obliged to consult with the I.T.O., which would have the power to request their removal, and, in the event that they were not removed, to authorize aggrieved members to retaliate against the offender.[2] Discrimination in the use of quantitative restrictions would be permitted only to facilitate the use of inconvertible currencies accumulated before 31 December 1948.[3] Thus the 'Suggested Charter' sought to confine the use of balance of payments quantitative restrictions to a relatively brief transition period; and to ensure that such restrictions would be employed thereafter only in the event of severe balance of payments difficulties and only in conformity with the principle of non-discrimination.

The position of the United Kingdom toward the use of quantitative restrictions on balance of payments grounds was now somewhat ambivalent. On the one hand, the British Government wanted defences during the transition period and in a time of an American slump; on the other, it wanted to remove restrictions imposed upon its exports by other countries. As one of the British delegates declared: 'We are a country which, as a result of the war, is faced with acute balance of payments difficulties over time, but nevertheless the solution of our balance of payments problem depends upon the expansion of our exports, and therefore, upon the very moderate use of Q.R.[4] under these provisions by other countries.'[5]

On balance, however, the British delegates found the provisions of the American 'Suggested Charter' far too restrictive. They wanted to dispense with the idea of a short transitional period. They rejected the idea of consultation with affected members before 31 December 1949 and with the I.T.O. after it. They wanted consultation with the I.T.O. only where new restrictions were imposed or existing restrictions intensified. In general, the British delegates took the view that each country should be free to determine, in the light of the principles of the I.T.O., whether or not to impose quantitative restrictions for balance of payments purposes. 'Clearly the international organizations cannot be empowered to force members to adopt one sort of remedial measure rather than another . . . that particular power was

---

[1] Article 20, 3(a).   [2] Article 20, 3(c).   [3] Article 22, 2.
[4] Quantitative restrictions.
[5] Clark, Committee II, Sub-Committee on Quantitative Restrictions and Exchange Control, *Verbatim Records*, E/PC/T/C.II/QR/PV/3, p. 15.

pretty explicitly taken away from the Fund in the Fund Agreement, and we do not see how it could possibly be given to I.T.O.'[1]

The London Charter embodied a number of specific concessions to the British desire for greater freedom in the use of quantitative restrictions. It contained no such short transition period as had been envisaged in the 'Suggested Charter'. Its criteria governing the use of balance of payments quantitative restrictions applied only to new or intensified restrictions—not to already existing ones. Moreover, these criteria permitted the use of restrictions 'to stop or forestall the imminent threat of a serious decline in the level of monetary reserves' or 'in the case of a Member with very low monetary reserves to achieve a reasonable rate of increase in its reserves'.[2] This wording provided much more assurance than the 'Suggested Charter' that defensive measures could be taken against an American slump, since restrictions could be imposed in advance of a deficit in the balance of payments. On the other hand, the codification of such a large measure of freedom for the use of quantitative restrictions raised the possibility that the 'exception' might eventually devour the rule.

Beyond the question of the freedom to be permitted for quantitative restrictions generally was the specific question of the appropriate scope for discrimination. Here again the British position was ambivalent. Once sterling became a convertible currency, a situation required by the Loan Agreement within but a few months, British exports might become the subject of discrimination by dollar-hungry countries just as much as the exports of the United States. Moreover, Britain was already tied to non-discrimination in the use of quantitative restrictions by the terms of the Loan Agreement. For these reasons, it might be wise to tie other countries to non-discrimination as tightly as Britain was tied. On the other hand, in the long run all currencies were supposed to become convertible and the provisions of the Loan Agreement would be superseded by the 'more comprehensive arrangements' of the I.T.O. It might be prudent, therefore, to include some provisions for a limited amount of discrimination—provisions Britain could rely on should its transitional difficulties persist.

Britain's nicely balanced interest in discrimination received expression in the final provisions of the London Charter. Like most of the other members of the Preparatory Committee, Britain was unwilling to accept the stringent requirement of the 'Suggested Charter' that discrimination be permitted only for the use of inconvertible currencies

---

[1] Clark, id., p. 16.   [2] Article 26, 2(a) (i) and (ii).

accumulated in the war and early post-war years. The United States eventually had to bow to the general conviction that discrimination might be required for a longer period. The London Report put forward the case of a country having a favourable balance of payments with a country having an inconvertible currency. If the exports of the first country could not be transferred readily to countries with convertible currencies this country might find it more desirable to increase its imports from the country with the inconvertible currency —even on a discriminatory basis—than to accumulate inconvertible balances.[1] To cover such a possibility the London draft omitted the time limit on balance of payments quantitative restrictions laid down in the 'Suggested Charter' and authorized members to discriminate in the use of these restrictions—provided that the discrimination enabled them to obtain additional imports over the level they could obtain in the absence of discrimination and provided the discrimination had equivalent effect to exchange restrictions permitted to those members under the Fund Articles.[2] Discriminatory restrictions permitted under this exception were to be reviewed before 31 December 1951 'with a view to the earliest possible elimination of discriminations . . . which restrict the expansion of world trade'.[3] In this way the Preparatory Committee, while granting substantial scope for discrimination, at least retained the principle that discrimination should not be permanent.

Thus the London Charter embodied substantial exceptions allowing scope for the use of quantitative restrictions generally and for discrimination in their application. These exceptions represented major departures from the full rigour of multilateral principles. Nevertheless, the exceptions stopped far short of giving countries complete freedom in the use of quantitative restrictions. Moreover, their insertion was somewhat ameliorated by the presence of provisions giving the I.T.O. fairly extensive powers of review and supervision.

Less defensible were the provisions inserted at the behest of Britain and certain other countries concerning the relation between their domestic policies and their commercial policy obligations. Some of the language now incorporated in the London Charter, far from suggesting that quantitative restrictions were generally to be avoided, seemed actually to encourage members to employ them:

Members may need to use import restrictions as a means of safeguarding

[1] Part II, chapter III, section c, 3.
[2] Article 28 (1) (d) (iii) and (iv).   [3] Article 28 (3).

their external financial position and as a step towards the restoration of equilibrium on a sound and lasting basis, particularly in view of increased demand for the imports needed to carry out their domestic employment, reconstruction, development or social policies.[1]

As if this general statement were not enough, the Charter contained the specific provision that the I.T.O., in reviewing the use of restrictions by particular countries,

shall not recommend the withdrawal or general relaxation of restrictions on the ground that the existing or prospective balance of payments difficulties of the Member in question could be avoided by a change in that Member's domestic employment, reconstruction, development or social policies.[2]

This clause went far beyond its counterpart in the Articles of Agreement of the International Monetary Fund. As we noted earlier,[3] the exemption for domestic policy in the Fund Articles applied only to decisions upon requests for exchange depreciation; it did not apply to decisions on the use of exchange restrictions. Nor did it foreclose the possibility of criticizing a country's domestic policy. But the clause in the London Charter made it possible for countries to maintain restrictions indefinitely by continually postponing internal correctives. It appeared to place internal policies above criticism and to subordinate international to domestic economic objectives. It was an unfortunate addition to the ambitious project for commercial collaboration.

CONCLUSION

The First Session of the Preparatory Committee to draft a Charter for an International Trade Organization had offered a further occasion to explore the critical issues of commercial policy still outstanding between Britain and the United States. The occasion had not been used in the most fortunate possible way. Each Government had pressed specific commitments to which the other was not entirely prepared to adhere. On the one hand, the United Kingdom took the initiative on the issue of the relation of employment to trade policy. Despite the misgivings of the American delegation it succeeded in inserting provisions designed to place upon the United States an international responsibility for maintaining full employment and for correcting

---

[1] Article 26 (1).

[2] Article 26 (3)(e). The far-reaching implications of this provision were somewhat tempered by the subsequent statement that in carrying out their domestic policies members would 'pay due regard to the need to restore sound and lasting equilibrium in their balance of payments'. Ibid.   [3] See pp. 115–16, *supra*.

disequilibria in its balance of payments. On the other hand, the United States took the initiative on the issue of quantitative restrictions. It advanced detailed rules confining the use of these restrictions to a number of carefully defined circumstances. The price of getting agreement on these rules was the insertion of a large number of exceptions, including an exemption for domestic policy broader than any that had been inserted in the other newly-fashioned agencies of international economic collaboration.

Was it possible, in the light of these facts, to regard the London Charter as a genuine advance over the 'Proposals' of 1945? The United States and Britain had tried with understandable zeal to gain recognition for commercial policy principles that seemed in their respective national interests. But if the principles were not mutually acceptable they would eventually be diluted to the point of meaninglessness or frustrated by the insertion of crippling exceptions. This was in fact what had happened at London to certain provisions on employment and quantitative restrictions pressed unreasonably by the British and American Governments. There was little prospect that these provisions would cause any change at all in national policies. In each country, as a matter of fact, the provisions sponsored by the other were already being explained away. The main emphasis was given to the purely negative safeguards inserted to protect existing domestic policies. In Britain, for example, *The Manchester Guardian* declared:

> Doubts about the wisdom of the original proposals were caused mainly by fears about unemployment and about our balance of payments. They might make it impossible to erect safeguards against the spread of an American slump. And the rules might be too rigid to allow us to correct the violent distortions in our external financial position caused by the war. The proposals now agreed to go far to allay both of these fears.[1]

The American Administration, defending the Charter in a Senate committee, was appeasing the critics along similar lines:

THE CHAIRMAN [Senator Millikin]. . . . Now, what would this International Organization have the right to say to us? What could it demand of us in the way of performance of the obligation that we have here . . . to take action 'designed to achieve and maintain full and productive employment', and so forth?

MR. WILCOX. The Organization would not have the right to say anything to us or to demand any particular action of us . . .

[1] (27 Nov. 1946).

. . . .

THE CHAIRMAN. Then we have full and complete control over what we shall do?

MR. WILCOX. Yes, sir.

. . . .

THE CHAIRMAN. Well, then, what is the purpose of the direction? If each member retains within itself full discretion over the subject, why talk about it in the Charter? Will not each member continue to do so just as it has in the past?

MR. WILCOX. Well, I think you are probably right.[1]

It did not look as if the provisions on employment and quantitative restrictions that had divided Britain and the United States would effect very great changes in actual policies. Little, therefore, had been gained by their insertion. Had anything been lost? The answer would soon be clear. However little influence such provisions might have on actual policies, they would serve as convenient targets for the critics of multilateralism now gaining strength in the two countries. Additional conferences to draft the Charter still lay ahead. More detailed provisions were being prepared. Without unusual restraint on the part of Britain, the United States, and the other participating Governments, the I.T.O. might eventually collapse of its own weight.

[1] U.S. Congress, Senate, Committee on Finance, *International Trade Organization*, Hearings on Trade Agreements System and Proposed International Trade Organization Charter, 80th Cong., 1st sess. (Mar.–Apr. 1947), vol. i, pp. 98–99.

CHAPTER XV

THE END OF BRETTON WOODS

THE meetings at Savannah and London occasioned numerous disagreements between the United States and Britain on the best means of implementing a multilateral régime. But the two Governments were still at one in proclaiming multilateralism as a desirable objective and in anticipating its early achievement after the solution of transitional difficulties. They expected the multilateral system to take shape quickly on the three major supports founded originally by Anglo-American collaboration—Bretton Woods, the Anglo-American Financial Agreement, and the I.T.O. Unfortunately, they did not reckon with the events that lay ahead in 1947. In that decisive year a grave political and economic crisis beset the Western world; the three supports of multilateralism began to crumble; and the prospects for the speedy restoration of multilateralism were blighted for the indefinite future.

The first of the three supports to show the effects of the crisis was the one constructed at Bretton Woods. The architects of the Fund and Bank expected these institutions to play a significant part during the transition period in leading the world back to free and non-discriminatory currency practices. They assumed that the Fund and Bank would satisfy the needs of the United Nations for financial assistance, with the help of the special measures of relief and reconstruction already devised. They assumed that one by one the members of the Fund would abandon their transitional restrictions and embrace the full code of multilateralism laid down in the Articles of Agreement. Finally, they assumed that the Bretton Woods institutions would operate in a united and peaceful world in which the economic needs of all nations would be satisfied without regard to political considerations. The crisis of 1947 was quickly to destroy all these assumptions. Thus, although it did not destroy the institutions themselves, it may justifiably be said to have marked 'the end of Bretton Woods'.

THE LAST ILLUSIONS

In late September 1946 the delegates of some forty countries gathered in Washington for the first annual meeting of the Board of

Governors of the International Monetary Fund and the International Bank for Reconstruction and Development. They showed no lack of faith in the war-time assumptions. The leaders of the American and British delegations in particular continued to be absorbed by the same issues of long-term policy that had occupied their Governments during the war. Neither appeared to foresee the new and more urgent problems that would soon demand their attention.

American opinion was still preoccupied with the danger of excessive currency fluctuations, exchange restrictions and other forms of 'economic warfare'. A typical comment appeared in *The New York Times*:

The American people have made it clear that they are behind . . . the Bretton Woods agreements because they do not want another world war and because they realize the importance of the economic and social causes of world wars. Between 1918 and 1939 the world staggered through a state of economic chaos, with various alterations in exchange rates and one discrimination piled on top of another in many kinds of trade barriers. For example, when an American businessman sold goods abroad on a ninety-day account for a certain amount of sterling, francs or other currency, he seldom knew what these would be worth in American dollars at the end of ninety days. If Bretton Woods and Savannah restore confidence in the value of what a trader gets for what he sells foreign trade should flourish again . . . and should constitute a most important factor in reaching . . . successful reconversion in the fullest sense of the word.[1]

This was the kind of thinking that still dominated official policy. The primary concern of the United States Treasury was to avoid the recurrence of the currency disorders that followed the previous armistice and to prevent war-time exchange restrictions from hardening into a permanent pattern. John Snyder, the new Secretary of the Treasury, expressed this view forcefully at the Bank and Fund meetings. He called for immediate action by the Fund to restore a régime of free and stable currencies:

Active leadership on the part of the Fund . . . is essential if world trade is to be restored to a high level and if economic warfare among nations is to be avoided. . . . A function of the Fund which I want to emphasize is that of promoting common standards of fair practice in monetary and financial relations among nations. . . . Our success can be measured by our development of acceptable standards to which all countries are willing to adhere. . . . We cannot afford to permit economic warfare to weaken the bonds which hold the United Nations together.[2]

[1] Russell Porter, 'Reconversion Record' (17 Mar. 1946).
[2] International Monetary Fund, *First Annual Meeting of the Board of Governors,*

In general, Snyder left no doubt that the American Government expected the Bretton Woods institutions to play a major role in the transition period as well as in the long run:

> If I may be permitted to express the keynote of this second meeting of the Board of Governors, it is this: *Let us lose no time in speedily activating the Fund and Bank as effective instruments in a world sorely in need of their services.*
> The Fund and Bank were designed to meet both the immediate postwar and the longer term monetary and financial needs of the world.[1]

Just what did Snyder mean by 'activating' the International Monetary Fund? He certainly did not mean that the Fund should become an active provider of financial aid. In accordance with the Congressional mandate, the American Executive Director had obtained an interpretation that Fund resources were to be used only for short-term stabilization purposes and not for rehabilitation and reconstruction.[2] Moreover, the First Annual Report of the Executive Directors announced the intention of the Directors to 'exercise the power to limit or postpone exchange operations with countries whose economies are so out of balance that their use of the Fund's resources would be contrary to the purposes of the Fund Agreement or prejudicial to the Fund or the members'.[3] At the outset, therefore, the Fund adopted the American view that the difficulties of the transition period required a careful husbanding of its limited resources.

Clearly, what Snyder wanted to 'activate' was not the Fund's lending authority, but only its authority to police exchange practices. But could the Fund be put into operation in this lop-sided way? The power to offer or withhold credit was one of its primary sanctions against improper monetary policies. If the Fund was to withhold its resources altogether, what lever could it employ to hasten its members to acceptance of their multilateral obligations? 'Activating' the Fund in such a manner might inspire hopes that could not be fulfilled and turn the institution into a nagging but impotent harbinger of the multilateral régime.

Report of the Executive Directors and Summary Proceedings, September 27 to October 3, 1946 (Washington, 1946), pp. 35–36.

[1] Italics in original. Id., p. 33. [2] Id., p. 106.

[3] The resources of the Fund would thus be 'limited to use in accordance with its purposes to give temporary assistance in financing balance of payments deficits'. Id., p. 24. At the same time the Report acknowledged that the Fund might have to take risks in the transition period not justified in normal circumstances. Ibid.

U

The British approach to the Fund and Bank meeting was no less hampered by a preoccupation with war-time conceptions. Dalton, now Chancellor of the Exchequer and British Governor of the Bank and Fund, told a reporter that the one phrase uppermost in his mind during these meetings was 'full employment'.[1] Acting on behalf of his Government he sought an interpretation of the Fund Articles that 'steps which are necessary to protect a member from unemployment of a chronic or persistent character arising from pressure on its balance of payments, are among the measures necessary to correct a fundamental disequilibrium'. This interpretation was designed to permit a devaluation of sterling in the event that external forces threatened to cause a fall in British employment without actually causing a deficit in the British balance of payments. It was inspired by the old fear, so persistently expressed during the Bretton Woods debate, that membership in the Fund would be an obstacle to the achievement of full employment. There was no doubt that this fear was still widespread. The British press devoted considerable attention to the proposed interpretation and expressed some anxiety that it might be rejected.[2] In fact the interpretation aroused little controversy and was speedily adopted at the annual meeting.

The British preoccupation with full employment proved just as inappropriate as the American preoccupation with the dangers of 'economic warfare'. There was little real danger that the Fund would refuse legitimate requests for depreciation and would force deflation on helpless members. Quite the opposite: when the Fund finally began operations in March 1947 it accepted without protest the existing par values certified by most countries. It was far more likely that the Fund would become the unwilling repository of over-valued exchange rates than an obstacle to legitimate depreciations. In truth, the real danger threatening Fund members in the transition period was not depression, but inflation; not undue dependence on economic fluctuations abroad, but inadequate responsiveness to the invigorating influence of the world market. In the closing months of 1946 this fact was not yet seen. Nearly everyone was preoccupied with the inter-war experience and the potentially restrictive influence of the

---

[1] *The Times* (28 Sept. 1946).

[2] See, for example, the *Financial Times* (29 Mar. 1946). Much was also made of the interpretation by conservative American opinion, which expressed the fear that it would throw a 'monkey wrench' into the Fund machinery and leave the United States defenceless against a series of competitive depreciations of the pound sterling. See 'A Crippled Monetary Fund', the *Wall Street Journal* (5 Oct. 1946).

gold standard. Even Managing Director Camille Gutt, hardly a rabid inflationist, was emphasizing that the Fund 'replaces the old but today ineffective gold-standard rule that a country must adjust its national economy to external pressure . . .'.[1] How a country could ever achieve equilibrium unless it did 'adjust its national economy to external pressure' was never satisfactorily explained.

Thus did the war-time attitudes dominate official thinking toward the Fund and Bank in the autumn of 1946. One of the results was a dangerous complacency about the ability of the two institutions to meet the needs of the transition period. Nowhere was this complacency more notable than in the United States. The prevailing over-confidence was reflected in the message Truman sent to Congress in March 1946 transmitting the report of the National Advisory Council on American lending policy:

> It is expected that the International Bank will begin lending operations in the latter half of 1946 and that during the calendar year 1947 the International Bank will assume the primary responsibility for meeting the world's international capital requirements that cannot be met by private investors on their own account and risk.[2]

To justify this conclusion the Council stated that the most urgent needs for assistance in the eighteen months ending in June 1947 could be met by existing relief and reconstruction programmes and by an additional $3½ billion in Export-Import Bank lending.[3] Secretary Snyder revealed that these optimistic estimates were still influencing American policy when at the September meetings of the Board of Governors he repeated the prediction that the International Bank would assume the 'primary responsibility' for reconstruction financing.[4] As late as December 1946 experts of the Federal Reserve Board estimated that the world's unsatisfied needs for dollars in 1947 would amount only to $3½ billion—needs which could be financed without difficulty out of foreign gold and dollar holdings, the British credit, and Export-Import Bank loans. The remainder of

---

[1] 'The International Monetary Fund and Its Functions', *Proc. Am. Ac. Pol. & Soc. Sci.*, xxii (1947), p. 157.

[2] *Statement of the Foreign Loan Policy of the United States Government*, House Doc. No. 489, 79th Cong., 2nd sess. (Washington, 1946), p. 3.

[3] Id. The Council proposed that the lending power of the Export-Import Bank, already increased in 1945 from $0·7 to $3·5 billion, should be increased again to $4·75 billion. Congress displayed such opposition, however, that the suggestion was abandoned. In the summer of 1946 the Export-Import Bank announced its intention to leave the field of reconstruction and return to short-term operations of the pre-war type. [4] *Summary Proceedings*, p. 34.

these needs, they declared, could be satisfied 'without excessive strain by the new international institutions, even if hopes for a resumption of private foreign investment in this country are not realized'.[1]

One reason for American complacency lay in the ambitious claims that had been made for the Bretton Woods institutions and the deceptively large resources they appeared to have at their disposal. Throughout 1946 the Administration spoke of the Fund and Bank in greatly exaggerated terms. The United Nations General Assembly was told that no new measures of reconstruction aid were necessary because the Bretton Woods institutions would make available 'some fifteen billion dollars for assisting countries in acquiring the foreign exchange necessary for the reconstruction and development of their economic life and for the stabilization of their currencies'.[2] Clayton, in an attempt to justify the termination of U.N.R.R.A., went even further. He declared not only that 'fifteen billion dollars' had been made available by the Bank and Fund but that measures had been taken 'for the provision of a total of nearly 30 billion dollars of foreign exchange to countries which need it'.[3] Clayton concluded that although these resources were not equally distributed to all countries 'the buying power which these funds will generate will circulate around the world and will be a very great contribution to economic recovery everywhere'.[4]

The misleading nature of these statements should have been readily apparent. The Bretton Woods institutions did not have $15 billion ready for use in the reconstruction period. The Bank had immediately available for lending from its own resources only the 2 per cent. of its capital subscribed in gold and the additional 18 per cent. of paid-in subscriptions, of which only the American ($635 million) had been put at its disposal. Even taking account of the unpaid portion of the American subscription, the Bank's potential lending power was still only $3·2 billion. Moreover, it was becoming apparent by the time of the first annual meeting of the Board of Governors that the Bank would not be ready to begin lending operations 'in the latter half of 1946',[5] as originally planned. As for the Fund, it was not designed for reconstruction at all and its management had determined to conserve its resources in the transition period.

---

[1] 'International Transactions of the United States in the First Postwar Years', *Fed. Res. Bull.*, xxxii (1946), pp. 133–4.
[2] U.S. Delegation to the U.N., Press Release No. 78 (14 Nov. 1946).
[3] 'Clayton Replies to Gravy Train', letter of Clayton in the *Washington Post* (18 Aug. 1946).   [4] Ibid.   [5] Truman's message, p. 291, *supra*.

How then could it be claimed that the Bretton Woods institutions, combined with existing measures of emergency aid, would meet the world's reconstruction needs? The fact was that the optimistic American estimates were founded on wishful thinking. The Administration leaders had promised Congress that the British loan would be the final measure of American assistance. To admit their mistake and make yet another request for aid to foreign countries was a course that was fraught with difficulty. It was much simpler to believe that the need for such aid did not exist. In this state of self-deception the American Government continued to temporize until the spring of 1947. Then came the rude awakening.

BRETTON WOODS IN CRISIS

The founders of the Bretton Woods institutions had assumed that after a short period of post-war adjustment the world would move quickly toward political as well as economic equilibrium. On both counts this assumption was finally shattered in the spring of 1947.

The contrast between the expectation and the reality was particularly dramatic in the political field. Instead of moving toward 'one world' the United Nations found themselves divided into two hostile camps, each dominated by a colossus of unprecedented power. On the one side was the United States, which demobilized its military establishment and abandoned close war-time collaboration with its Western Allies. On the other was the Soviet Union, which maintained its armed forces at an ominous size and expanded its control over a growing number of satellite countries. The resulting disequilibrium was now too serious to ignore. The defeat of Germany, followed by the deliberate dismantling of its industrial plant, left a political vacuum on the continent of Europe which dynamic and aggressive Soviet power seemed only too likely to fill. The Western nations, divided from one another by history and tradition, gravely weakened by two world wars, stood helpless before the overwhelming might of their Eastern neighbour. The Governments of France and Italy were gravely challenged from within by local Communist parties; Greece and Turkey seemed in equally grave danger of aggression from without. It was clear that the Allied victory had not brought the hoped-for universal society governed by the rule of law, but a divided world drifting toward civil strife, revolution, and possibly even full-scale war.

The expected trend toward equilibrium was no more evident in economic affairs. In 1946 the United States ran an export surplus of $8·2 billion. In 1947 this surplus, instead of diminishing, rose further to $11·3 billion.[1] The main area of disequilibrium, as in the political field, could be found in Europe. The consolidated deficit of the European countries in their trade with the rest of the world reached $5·8 billion in 1946 and $7·5 billion in 1947.[2]

How could such huge surpluses and deficits be explained? In part, of course, they could be explained by deficiencies in European production—by the inadequate output of critical commodities such as coal and steel and by the lagging agricultural effort. But this was only part of the story. On the whole the production record of the European nations (excluding Germany) exceeded expectation; it was, to take one standard of measurement, notably better than after the First World War.[3]

The main difficulty now lay elsewhere. There was, to begin with, the deterioration in the so-called 'invisible' items of Europe's balance of payments. In 1938 the European countries had offset a $2·1 billion deficit in their merchandise trade with a surplus of the same amount from invisible transactions. By 1947 the pre-war income from invisibles had turned into a deficit of $0·6 billion—an adverse change of $2·7 billion. This reflected various costs of the Second World War and its aftermath: the liquidation of overseas investments, the accumulation of external indebtedness, the loss of shipping, and the continued burden of foreign military and political expenditures.

Even more drastic than the adverse change in invisibles was the deterioration in the merchandise account. Between 1938 and 1947 the merchandise deficit of the European countries increased by $4·8 billion. Some $3·6 billion of the increase was due to the rise in world prices above pre-war levels.[4] The rest was due to the fact that in 1947 European imports were 114 per cent. and European exports only 81 per cent. of their 1938 volume.

---

[1] *Report on the Activities of the National Advisory Council from October 1, 1947 to March 31, 1948*, House Doc. 737, 80th Cong., 2nd sess. (Washington, 1948).

[2] These figures and the statistics used in the following analysis are drawn from three reports of the Economic Commission for Europe: *A Survey of the Economic Situation and Prospects of Europe* (Geneva, 1948); *Economic Survey of Europe in 1948* (Geneva, 1949); and *Economic Survey of Europe Since the War* (Geneva, 1953).

[3] 95 per cent. of the 1938 level in 1946–7 as compared with 83 per cent. of the 1913 level in 1920.

[4] The value of the pre-war merchandise deficit was increased simply by virtue of the general increase in commodity prices; there was no appreciable change in Europe's terms of trade.

The whole of the change in import and export volumes could not be explained by inadequate production. Much of it resulted from far-reaching alterations that had taken place in the pre-war structure of international trade. The political crisis had disrupted trade between Eastern and Western Europe, making the West much more dependent than formerly on non-European sources of foodstuffs and raw materials. Even trade between the Western European countries was inhibited by the loss of pre-war commercial contacts and the spread of restrictions and bilateral practices. Finally, the war had shifted the source of many American imports from Europe to the Western hemisphere. It was largely for these reasons that Europe was importing fully seven times the value of what it was exporting to the United States and that the anticipated progress toward equilibrium was replaced by the now famous symptom of economic imbalance—the 'dollar shortage'.

The Bretton Woods institutions were not designed to operate effectively in this condition of growing political and economic disequilibrium. The political difficulties of the transition period quickly dispelled the notion that the operations of the two institutions could be wholly 'independent of the political connection'.[1] The Soviet Union, to begin with, did not even ratify the Bretton Woods agreements. This increased the relative voting power of the Commonwealth and the United States and enhanced the possibility that the Fund and Bank would be instruments of Anglo-American—and especially American—policy. Moreover, as relations with the Soviet bloc deteriorated, the political significance of Fund and Bank operations naturally increased. Several of the Soviet satellites were members of the institutions. The United States was understandably reluctant to permit the granting of financial assistance to members of an increasingly hostile bloc of nations.

Indeed, the growing hostility between East and West was forcing the American Government to seek ever greater control over the disposition of the resources it was making available to other nations. At the time of the Bretton Woods conference the United States had been strongly in favour of providing economic aid through international institutions. After several years of practical experience with U.N.R.R.A. this was no longer true. The American Government had watched with increasing discomfort as millions of dollars of its relief supplies were delivered to Soviet satellites. The discomfort became

[1] See p. 11, *supra*.

particularly acute in the case of Yugoslavia, a country with whom relations had seriously deteriorated after the shooting down of American aircraft. One of the major factors in the American decision to seek an end to U.N.R.R.A. was the desire to avoid a repetition of the Yugoslav experience. As Acheson explained, the American people and the American Congress had decided that the United States should no longer grant large sums 'under conditions which would leave little or no effective control by the grantor of these funds'.[1]

In the case of the Bretton Woods institutions, of course, American resources had already been put under international control. But it was not too late to ensure that the resources of the Fund and Bank were employed in conformity with American political interests. The powerful voice which the United States had in the operation of these institutions soon began to make itself felt. The political question came up most directly in the case of the Bank. Although the Articles of the Bank required it to be non-political in its lending policy, the Bank made it clear almost from the very beginning of its operations that it would take account of political factors in considering requests for assistance from members of the Soviet bloc:

Though the Bank is precluded from making or denying loans to achieve political objectives, there is an obvious and necessary interrelation and inter-action between political events and conditions in any country. The soundness of a loan depends fundamentally on the financial and economic prospects of the borrower. In so far as those prospects may be affected by the conditions of political instability or uncertainty in the borrowing country, those political conditions must be taken into consideration.[2]

In accordance with this interpretation the Bank in the autumn of 1947 refused to extend a loan to Poland on the ground that Poland's refusal to attend the Paris Conference on European Recovery raised doubts about its independence from Russia and its standing as a good credit risk.[3]

The economic as well as the political disequilibrium had a profound influence upon the operations of the Bretton Woods institutions. As its members suffered from increasingly severe dollar deficits, the Fund took greater measures to protect its resources. In an important interpretation of their powers in June of 1947 the Executive Directors declared that they could look behind the representations made by applicants for assistance and could determine whether in

---

[1] (8 Dec. 1946). *Dept. of State Bull.*, xv (1946), p. 1007.
[2] *Second Annual Report of the Executive Directors* (Washington, 1947), p. 17.
[3] *The New York Times* (5 Nov. 1947).

fact the applicants needed loans for the purposes stipulated in the Fund Articles.[1] To put it bluntly, the Fund was not going to grant assistance to members unless it was assured that the aid would be used for short-term stabilization purposes and not for purposes of reconstruction. Since few members could give such assurances in the first half of 1947 the Fund engaged in virtually no exchange operations.

To justify their conservative policy the Executive Directors recalled that the Fund was 'intended as part of the permanent machinery of international monetary relations rather than as an emergency device to meet the special needs of the postwar years'.[2] It added that 'the Fund's objectives can only be fully realized in a world in which the war-damaged and war-devastated countries have restored their productive efficiency to the point where they can achieve balance in their international payments with a level of trade conducive to their own and the general well-being'.[3] This position was firmly approved in a subsequent report of the U.S. National Advisory Council:

It was clearly the intent of the agreement not to bar countries from using the Fund's resources during the postwar reconstruction period, but these resources were to be used only for the purposes of the Fund and not contrary to its articles. . . . Therefore the Fund, while aiding the war-torn countries by the sale of dollars to them, was required to exercise careful judgment, and its sales of currency have been made only after careful study of the economic and financial conditions of the members applying. There was a very real danger that, if the Fund's resources were used in large part by countries in the process of reconstruction . . . the long-range purposes of the Fund would be lost sight of and its resources would be quickly exhausted before the date at which the Fund could become fully effective in maintaining exchange stability and preventing discriminatory exchange practices.[4]

Not until conditions of equilibrium were restored, therefore, could the Fund assume a significant role as a provider of financial aid.

The Fund's conservative lending policy in the face of the economic crisis of 1947 aggravated the mistrust of the institution that had been accumulating in Britain since the conclusion of the Savannah Conference. During the debate on Bretton Woods British opinion had been led to regard the Fund as an automatic source of credit and hence as a useful support in time of financial need. Now, instead, the

[1] *Second Annual Report of the Executive Directors*, p. 3.   [2] Id., p. 2.   [3] Ibid.
[4] *First Special Report of the National Advisory Council on the Operation and Policies of the International Monetary Fund and International Bank for Reconstruction and Development*, House Doc. No. 656, 80th Cong., 2nd sess. (18 May 1948).

Fund was withholding its resources. Moreover, it was asking payment of Britain's substantial contribution in gold and dollars. Thus
it had turned out to be a net drain on British resources. Some critics,
angered by this fact, urged the Government to draw out the dollar
equivalent of its contribution.[1] And *The Economist* spoke for many
when it declared: 'To see the International Monetary Fund—the
chosen instrument for "promoting exchange stability"—playing an
almost entirely passive role in the international payments crisis that
is now engulfing the world is hardly conducive to creating the necessary goodwill and confidence which the new institution will need if
it is to satisfy the great purposes for which it was founded—and for
which, after all, such heavy hard currency expenditures have been
incurred.'[2]

Instead of providing help in the crisis, the Fund's role became increasingly remote. It could do little more than acquiesce in the
spread of exchange restrictions. Every one of its members except the
United States and some minor Latin American countries was availing
itself of the transitional provisions. In these circumstances, exchange
restrictions could no longer be regarded as temporary and exceptional
accompaniments of the transition; they were symptoms of a deeper,
world-wide disequilibrium—a disequilibrium with which the Fund
was powerless to cope. In mid-1949 the Executive Directors finally
wrote a poignant epitaph to war-time hopes. They had to confess,
after four years of peace, that 'dependence on bilateral trade and inconvertible currencies is far greater than before the war'.[3]

The Bank was no better suited to play its appointed role in the
deteriorating economic environment. At Bretton Woods there had
been hopes for an early resumption of private foreign investment. It
had been assumed that the Bank could engage in large guarantee
operations on behalf of foreign governments who wished to have
access to private capital. But the political and economic situation in
1947 was so uncertain that there was little hope for revival of the
foreign bond market. At the same time, the Bank had only limited
resources available for direct lending. Therefore it had to make a
direct approach to private investors with its own securities. Since the
United States was the major source of private capital, the Bank
had to gain the confidence of Wall Street. The last traces of the
policy identified with Morgenthau and White had to be expunged.

---

[1] The *Financial Times* (17 Sept. 1946).   [2] cliii (1947), p. 294.
[3] *Fourth Report of the Executive Directors* (Washington, 1949), p. 3.

Accordingly, in February 1947, major changes occurred in the personnel of the Bank. John J. McCloy, a Wall Street lawyer, replaced Eugene Meyer as President; two Wall Street financiers, Eugene Black and Robert L. Garner, became Vice-President and United States Executive Director. These changes were additional indications that the Bank would confine itself to specific projects justifiable on a commercial basis. It was now more obvious than ever that the Bank could not be the 'primary' source of reconstruction aid. As the Bank itself was ready to admit: 'Because the requirements are greater than anticipated, because the scope of activity and loanable resources of the Bank are limited, it is manifest that the Bank can provide only part of the answer to the problems which confront the world today.'[1]

THE EMERGENCE OF A NEW APPROACH

The Bretton Woods institutions could not work effectively in the crisis that beset the Western world in the spring of 1947. Bold new measures were needed to deal with the growing political and economic disequilibrium. Such measures could only be initiated by the one country with the political and economic power to carry them out: the United States. But would America act—and soon enough to avert disaster? The survival of freedom in Western Europe was now at stake. As one observer put it: 'There is something in the present situation that is very reminiscent of 1940, when also it was very clear that Europe could only be saved by America, but nobody could see how America could be persuaded, in time, to undertake the rescue operation.'[2]

That the United States was persuaded to act in time is now a matter of history. Many men deserve the credit for this fact, including, at the highest level, George C. Marshall, the new Secretary of State, and Dean Acheson, his Under-Secretary. An important role was also played by Will Clayton. As we have seen, Clayton was among the most outspoken in insisting that a multilateral system could be restored with the existing measures of economic aid. The turning-point in his thinking occurred when he visited Europe in the early weeks of 1947. Clayton found that the severe winter just coming to an end had played havoc with European production and transport. In one country after another he was met with appeals for additional American aid. In several cases he saw that without such aid the exist-

---

[1] *Second Annual Report of the Executive Directors* (Washington, 1947), p. 3.
[2] 'Dollars for Europe', *The Economist*, clii (1947), p. 834.

ing governments might capitulate to local Communist movements. He realized, in short, that he would have to revise his earlier assumptions about the post-war political and economic environment.

Upon his return to the United States Clayton put his impressions on paper in the form of a memorandum:[1]

The reins of leadership [he wrote] are slipping from Britain's hands. They will be picked up either by the United States or by Russia. If by Russia, then the balance of world power will turn against America and war will be likely within a generation. If by the United States, there is a good chance that war can be averted.

Communist movements are threatening established governments in every part of the globe. These movements, directed by Moscow, feed on economic and political weakness. The countries under Communist pressure require economic assistance on a large scale if they are to maintain their territorial integrity and political independence.

At one time it had been expected that the International Bank could satisfy the needs for such assistance. But it is now clear that the Bank cannot do this job.

The United States is faced with a world-wide challenge to human freedom. The only way to meet this challenge is by a vast new programme of assistance given directly by the United States itself.

Thus tended the thoughts of Clayton—and other Administration figures—in the opening weeks of 1947. The occasion for translating these thoughts into action was not long in coming. At the end of February the United States learned that Britain was being forced to reduce its overseas commitments and was planning to withdraw its forces from Greece. Truman and Marshall summoned Congressional leaders to the White House to inform them of the gravity of the situation. They outlined the political and strategic implications of the British withdrawal and the need for the United States to assume the burden which the British were no longer able to bear. A few days later the British Government informed the United States officially that it would withdraw its forces from Greece by the end of March. The President acted swiftly. On 12 March he appeared before both Houses of Congress and requested the immediate appropriation of $400 million for economic and military assistance to Greece and Turkey. The President said:

I believe that it must be the policy of the United States to support free peoples who are resisting attempted subjugation by armed minorities or by outside pressures.

[1] What follows is a rough summary of the contents of this memorandum, the text of which has not yet been made public.

I believe we must assist free peoples to work out their own destinies in their own way.

I believe that our help should be primarily through economic and financial aid which is essential to economic stability and orderly political processes.[1]

This was the Truman Doctrine, the first step in the new approach to world affairs which the crisis of 1947 had forced upon the American Government. The second step followed quickly. By the end of March it was clear that economic recovery in Europe could not be assured by stopgap aid to individual countries. Item after item had been added to the programme for post-war assistance, yet many countries were still dependent on American aid. A unified, long-term programme of recovery would have to replace the piecemeal approach. But to spur the American Government to action there was needed still more dramatic evidence of the relation between European recovery and the security of the United States.

That evidence was supplied at the Moscow Conference in April 1947. There, due to Russian intransigence, the Foreign Ministers of the war-time allies made no progress at all in drafting a treaty of peace. The attitude of the Soviet Government, Marshall found, stemmed in no small part from its confident assumption that Western Europe, weakened by economic difficulties, would soon be in Communist hands. He returned from Moscow convinced that no progress could be made in negotiations with the Russians until the health of Europe had been restored.

After this event the Administration became more outspoken in alerting the American public to the growing emergency. On 8 May 1947 in Cleveland, Mississippi, Acheson made a bold statement of the situation. First he outlined America's stake in the economic recovery of other nations:

It is generally agreed that until the various countries of the world get on their feet and become self-supporting there can be no political or economic stability in the world and no lasting peace or prosperity for any of us. Without outside aid, the process of recovery in many countries would take so long as to give rise to hopelessness and despair. In these conditions freedom and democracy and the independence of nations could not long survive. . . .[2]

[1] For the text of this message and other documents relating to the Greek-Turkish aid programme see 'Aid to Greece and Turkey', *Dept. of State Bull.* (Supp., 4 May 1947).

[2] *Dept. of State Bull.*, xvi (1947), p. 992.

Then he warned frankly of the need for new sacrifices:

The facts of international life . . . mean that the United States is going to have to undertake further emergency financing of foreign purchases if foreign countries are to continue to buy in 1948 and 1949 the commodities which they need to sustain life and at the same time rebuild their economies. Requests for further United States aid may reach us through the International Bank, or through the Export-Import Bank, *or they may be of a type which existing national and international institutions are not equipped to handle and therefore may be made directly through diplomatic channels. But we know that further financing, beyond existing authorizations, is going to be needed.*[1]

Finally, on 5 June, Marshall made his famous speech at the Harvard commencement exercises. He explained that although planning for the transition period had correctly estimated the extent of visible destruction in Europe, it had not grasped the full implications of the dislocation of the entire fabric of the European economy. European recovery was going to require much more time and effort than had yet been anticipated.

The truth of the matter is that Europe's requirements for the next three years for foreign food and other essential products—principally from America—are so much greater than her present ability to pay that she must have substantial additional help, or face economic, social and political deterioration of a very grave character. . . . The United States should do whatever it is able to do to assist in the return of normal economic health in the world, without which there can be no political stability and no assured peace. Our policy is not directed against any country or doctrine but against hunger, poverty, desperation and chaos. Its purpose should be the revival of a working economy in the world so as to permit the emergence of political and social conditions in which free institutions can exist. Such assistance, I am convinced, must not be on a piecemeal basis as various crises develop. Any assistance that this Government may render in the future should provide a cure rather than a mere palliative.[2]

Marshall added that before the United States could proceed further in its efforts to assist in recovery, 'there must be some agreement among the countries of Europe as to the requirements of the situation and the part those countries will take in order to give proper effect to whatever action might be undertaken by this Government'. Although he made no specific promise of assistance, he declared that the United States would help in the drafting of a programme of European recovery and would lend 'its support of such a program so far as it may be practicable for us to do so'. A week later he added

[1] Italics supplied. Id., p. 993.   [2] *The New York Times* (6 June 1947).

that Europe's reconstruction needs might require outside assistance of some $5 or $6 billion a year for several years.[1]

At the eleventh hour, with a swiftness seldom displayed by democratic governments, the United States had finally adjusted its wartime conceptions to the urgent requirements of the transition period. The new measures devised to deal with the post-war disequilibrium soon overshadowed the financial institutions designed in the war. The normal objectives of the International Monetary Fund were gradually subordinated to the immediate requirements of European recovery. In the year beginning 1 July 1947 the Fund abandoned its conservative lending policy and extended $610 million in aid to member countries.[2] Many of these loans could hardly be considered for short-term stabilization purposes, but they did serve to fill the gap until the new measures of European aid were passed by the American Congress. Then, when the European Recovery Programme was finally launched, the Fund announced that its resources would no longer be made available to recipients of Marshall Aid except in 'exceptional or unforeseen cases'.[3] It added: 'The Fund and members participating in ERP should have as their objective to maintain the resources of the Fund at a safe and reasonable level during the ERP period in order that at the end of the period such members will have unencumbered access to the resources of the Fund.'[4] As a result of this decision the Fund engaged in virtually no exchange operations during the early years of the Marshall Plan.

The operations of the International Bank also yielded priority to the new programme of reconstruction aid. During the period when the Marshall Plan was being discussed the Bank's Directors 'took the position that, until the form and content of the European Recovery Program . . . had taken shape, the Bank could not make large loans to Europe'.[5] On the other hand, it was 'the intention of the Bank to supplement ERP . . . primarily by financing projects which involve permanent additions to production capacity'.[6] In practice, of course,

---

[1] Id. (13 June 1947).
[2] Of this amount Britain drew $300 million, virtually the whole amount of its drawing rights for one year. This represented a sharp reversal in British policy. According to Harry White, the United Kingdom had declared at the Savannah Conference that it 'did not intend to utilize its quota with the Fund because it expected to be able to make the necessary adjustments without doing so'. Rough draft of a speech introducing an amendment to the fund agreement, 19 May 1948, *White Papers*.
[3] *Third Annual Report of the Executive Directors* (Washington, 1948), p. 74.
[4] Ibid.
[5] *Third Annual Report of the Executive Directors*, p. 8.   [6] Id., p. 13.

the Western European countries preferred Marshall Aid to assistance from the Bank, since the former came as grants or loans on easier credit terms than the Bank could make available. Therefore, as the Marshall Plan gained momentum, the Bank moved out of the reconstruction field. It turned instead, somewhat modestly at first, to the job of helping underdeveloped countries in their programmes of economic development.

Thus were the operations of the Fund and Bank subordinated to the requirements of the Marshall Plan. The objectives of these institutions were overshadowed in a similar way. The immediate goal of the Marshall Plan was the economic recovery of Western Europe. One of the major obstacles to this goal was the network of restrictions existing among the European countries. The economic 'integration' of Western Europe quickly became a dominant theme of the new programme. The emphasis in American policy changed from the pursuit of multilateralism on a universal scale to pursuit of multilateralism within a specific region. There was, of course, no necessary inconsistency here. The regional programme, once successful, might lead to a new attempt to reconstruct multilateralism on a world-wide basis. Nevertheless, it was somewhat paradoxical to find the United States supporting institutions like the Organization for European Economic Co-operation and, eventually, the European Payments Union, which reduced trade and payments restrictions on an intra-European basis and authorized substantial 'discrimination' against dollar goods. This was another respect in which the spirit of Bretton Woods had suffered a major eclipse.

CONCLUSION

The crisis of 1947 made it apparent that the conditions of political and economic equilibrium which had been anticipated at Bretton Woods would be markedly absent in the post-war period. The American Government set out to restore equilibrium with the Truman Doctrine and the Marshall Plan. These two policies stemmed from the recognition that multilateralism could not be achieved simply by a few transitional measures alone but would require a long-term attack on the underlying causes of the world-wide disequilibrium. In this new attempt to restore political and economic equilibrium the permanent institutions devised in the war could play only a minor role. With the beginning of the European Recovery Programme the Fund practically ceased exchange operations and the

Bank left the field of reconstruction lending. The emphasis shifted from the pursuit of world-wide multilateralism through the Bretton Woods institutions to the more limited objective of the recovery and 'integration' of Western Europe. In the spring of 1948, shortly before his resignation from the Fund, White was forced to admit: 'A candid appraisal of the contributions which both institutions have so far made toward the stated objectives would force us to the conclusion that achievement has been much less than anticipated.'[1] It was a difficult admission for White to make. The Bretton Woods institutions had disappointed the hopes of their principal author.

[1] Rough draft of speech introducing an amendment to the Fund Agreement, 19 May 1948, *White Papers*.

CHAPTER XVI

THE END OF THE LOAN

THE second instrument of multilateralism to feel the impact of the 1947 crisis was the Anglo-American Financial Agreement. The growing political and economic disequilibrium had undermined its foundations no less than those of Bretton Woods. Unfortunately, the American and British Governments were slow to recognize this fact. The United States responded to the general European crisis with the Truman Doctrine and the Marshall Plan; but it took no similar initiative to adapt the Loan Agreement to the particular difficulties of the United Kingdom. Britain, in turn, seemed unable either to make the Agreement work or to achieve its orderly modification. Instead, the two Governments drifted along, clinging to a rigid and obsolete instrument of their own making. By the time they were moved to action the loan had been exhausted; its main objectives had been overthrown; and a major setback had been dealt to the attempted revival of multilateral trade.

THE APPROACH OF THE CRISIS

Anglo-American opinion on the Financial Agreement displayed the same kind of premature optimism that it had displayed with respect to Bretton Woods. To some extent this optimism appeared to be justified by the events of 1946. In that year Britain's economic position improved beyond expectation. It had been estimated at the time of the loan negotiations that British exports would recover their pre-war level by the second half of 1946.[1] In fact, British exports passed that level in May and were running at 111 per cent. of the pre-war level in the fourth quarter of the year. Imports in the same quarter were kept down to 72·2 per cent. of their pre-war level.[2] For the year as a whole Britain's overall balance of payments deficit was only £344 million ($1,376 million), less than half the deficit of £750 million ($3,000 million) that had been estimated at the Washington talks.[3]

[1] Cmd. 6707 of 1945, p. 5.
[2] *Economic Survey for 1947*, Cmd. 7046 of 1947.   [3] See Table 3.

TABLE 3

United Kingdom Current Account Balance of Payments, 1938 and 1946–7

millions of £ sterling

Items	1938	1946	1947
Visible trade	−302	−176	−425
Invisible items			
Interest, profits, and dividends (net) . .	+175	+71	+80
Shipping (net)	+20	+29	+33
Government payments (net) . . .	−16	−363	−230
Other items	+53	+95	−3
Balance in respect of invisible items . .	+232	−168	−120
Total current balance	−70	−344	−545

Source: Bank for International Settlements, *The Sterling Area* (Basle, 1953), p. 38.

Encouraged by these omens, Dalton announced that the export drive had 'succeeded beyond expectation and beyond estimate'.[1] He painted a rosy picture of the economic future: 'I have been able, as Chancellor, to meet all the demands on the public purse literally with a song in my heart. If we keep going together as we have since V-J Day, the shortages and frustrations which still afflict us will disappear like the snows of winter, and give place to the full promise of springtime.'[2] Press comments were hardly less buoyant. One British newspaper boasted that 'Britain's own position has been wonderfully transformed since a year ago' and declared that the country could now confront the United States 'as an equal partner in reconstruction'. 'We have shown convincingly', it concluded, 'that we can stand on our own feet economically again.'[3] At about the same time an American newspaper reported: 'It's no longer a question of "export or starve" in Great Britain, as the British export drive is succeeding far beyond the most optimistic hopes of her government and trade authorities.'[4]

In actual fact, the position was not nearly as good as first appeared. The low import volumes and the relatively small deficit in the balance of payments were partly a reflection of Britain's inability to obtain

[1] 430 H.C. Deb. 1425 (26 Nov. 1946).   [2] *The Times* (21 Oct. 1946).
[3] The *Daily Herald* (27 Sept. 1946).
[4] 'British Drive for Exports Succeeds Beyond Hopes', *The New York Herald-Tribune* (4 Aug. 1946).

supplies urgently needed in its reconstruction effort. Moreover, although the overall deficit was less than half of what had been anticipated, Britain's drawings on the American loan continued at about the expected rate.[1] Press reports in both countries put most of the blame for this fact on the rapid rise in American prices. But a more basic factor was the structural problem that Britain shared with Europe generally—the need for large imports of essential Western Hemisphere foodstuffs and raw materials beyond the capacity to export to that area. Britain was taking 42 per cent. of its imports from the New World and sending there only 14 per cent. of its exports in return.[2] This development posed a grave problem in view of the world-wide nature of the 'dollar shortage'. For Britain could no longer get dollars from surpluses with third countries to offset its bilateral deficits with the United States, Canada, and other countries of the dollar area. Thus Britain's dollar deficit might well exceed its overall deficit—a danger that had not been anticipated in fixing the size of the American Loan. The 'double balance of payments problem' was first called to public attention by Sir Stafford Cripps, President of the Board of Trade, in November 1946. Cripps warned: 'We must try to get nearer to balance not only of our total trade but hard currency trade as well and unless we succeed in doing that in the next year or two we shall find ourselves in the position of having to take some drastic action to carry on.'[3]

These forebodings were realized with a devastating swiftness. Instead of improving, Britain's overall balance of payments deteriorated markedly in 1947, showing a deficit of £545 million ($2,180 million) for that year as compared with £344 million ($1,376 million) in 1946. Britain's dollar deficit fully confirmed the fears expressed by Cripps; it rose above the overall deficit to a figure of $2,646 million. The combined dollar deficit of Britain and the rest of the sterling area reached $1,900 million in the first half of 1947 and $2,231 million in the second half—$4,131 million for the year as a whole! Drawings on the American loan quickly reflected these developments. They reached $500 million in the first quarter of the year and $950 million in the second. It was becoming clear that the credit would be exhausted much sooner than expected—certainly by the beginning of 1948.

[1] $600 million in 1946. Unless otherwise indicated, statistics on loan drawings and on the dollar drain are taken from *United Kingdom Balance of Payments 1946 to 1950*, Cmd. 8065 of 1950.
[2] Cmd. 7046 of 1947, p. 19.   [3] *The Times* (29 Nov. 1946).

What was the reason for the drastic deterioration in Britain's external position? The claims on British resources from within and without obviously exceeded the country's economic capacity. One major source of weakness lay in the invisible accounts. As we pointed out earlier, Britain's earnings from foreign investments, shipping, and entrepôt trade were greatly reduced by the war. Yet despite its impoverishment Britain was still trying to bear its accustomed responsibilities as a great world power. Due to the unsettled political situation in Europe and Asia its overseas expenditures were continuing at much higher levels than had been expected at the end of the Second World War. The British Government had to maintain sizeable military forces abroad; it had to pay a considerable part of the cost of maintaining occupied Germany. The military payments alone accounted for the whole of Britain's deficit in 1946. Unfortunately, international tensions were now increasing and there was little prospect of a German peace treaty. It was clear that Britain could no longer support such overwhelming burdens.[1]

TABLE 4

United Kingdom Government Payments and Receipts
1946–7

millions of £ sterling

Items	1946	1947
Payments:		
Military	374	209
Administrative, diplomatic, &c..	20	25
Relief and rehabilitation* . .	123	118
Colonial grants . . .	10	7
Total	527	359
Receipts:		
War disposal, settlements, &c. (net)	164	129
Total payments (net) . . .	363	230

* Including net amount allocated to Germany.

Source: Bank for International Settlements, *The Sterling Area* (Basle, 1953), p. 39.

The main element in Britain's worsening balance of payments, however, was not the external payments on Government account.

[1] Details on the burden of external Government expenditures are presented in Table 4.

It was the deterioration in the balance of visible trade. The full measure of this deterioration was becoming apparent in the early summer of 1947. The volume of British exports had stopped rising; in the second quarter of 1947 it dropped down below the level reached in the third quarter of 1946. The export target of 140 per cent. of pre-war volume set for the end of 1947 had to be postponed in June to mid-1948. Meanwhile, British imports, which had been projected at $5,800 million for the year as a whole, were running at an annual rate of $6,600 million in May and June. The deterioration was particularly severe in trade with the Western Hemisphere. With this region alone there was a deficit in visible items of $1,300 million for the first half of the year.[1]

The unexpectedly large deficit in visible trade was partly due to the general rise in prices which increased in money terms the gap between British imports and British exports. It was partly due also to a deterioration of some 10 per cent. in the terms of trade. Neither of these eventualities had been accounted for in the Washington negotiations. Added to these difficulties were some equally unanticipated short-term factors—the bad harvest in the autumn of 1946 and the severe winter of 1946-7. This winter—the worst in recent history— put an intolerable strain on Britain's resources of fuel and transport. It was a piece of bad luck that dealt a fatal blow to the existing timetable for industrial recovery. To a considerable extent, therefore, the grave deterioration in the visible trade balance was due to causes beyond the control of the British Government.

But the state of Britain's visible trade could not be blamed entirely on fortuitous events. In large measure it reflected Britain's failure to adapt with sufficient energy to its new and less favourable longterm position. It was clear from the outset that the terms of the Financial Agreement could only be fulfilled by a heroic effort of self-denial on the part of the British people. Their Government would have to restrain inflation, proceed cautiously with expenditures on investment and social services, and take drastic measures to increase the output of such critical commodities as coal. This was a formidable and austere programme to offer to any democratic electorate. It was not an easy programme to offer the British people after the ambitious promises that had been made them in the course of the war. And, unfortunately, it was not the programme undertaken in

---

[1] The above data on the British position in the first half of 1947 are taken from 'The British Crisis', *Fed. Res. Bull.*, xxxiii (Sept. 1947), p. 1071.

the early post-war years by Britain's Labour Government. The British leadership in 1946–7 sponsored an inflationary monetary and budget policy, a large volume of capital investment, and substantial expenditures on food subsidies and social services. These led to an excessive demand for imports and left inadequate resources free to produce the required recovery in British exports.

The domestic economic policy of the British Government had another unfortunate aspect. The emphasis on full employment, easy money, and social services created an unreal atmosphere that insulated the average British citizen from the deteriorating external position. As *The Economist* put it: 'The community is faced with the necessity for the most bitter economy of its resources; but fewer of its individuals have a personal economic problem to face than ever before. . . . Of course they do not react to a national emergency that is something they read about in the papers and do not experience in their own lives.'[1] The Chancellor of the Exchequer himself seemed not entirely aware of the relation between his domestic economic policies and the worsening state of external trade. With apparent surprise he noted that 'the contrast is most remarkable between the great difficulty of the overseas position . . . and the relative ease of the purely domestic financial position, in which things are very much better and easier than we would have had any reason to expect two years ago'.[2]

Thus the necessary domestic adjustments were postponed. On 8 July, when the adverse trend of the first six months must have been fully apparent, the Government announced only token measures to meet the crisis. These measures were so modest that even after taking them into account the overall deficit for the year ending June 1948 was officially estimated at £450 million ($1,800 million)—one-third larger than the deficit for 1946! But as Herbert Morrison explained: 'The first duty of this Government to our own people, and also to the world, is to keep Britain in full production, in full employment, in good health and in good heart. . . . The Government are quite clear, having given deep and prolonged thought to this matter, that they should not impose cuts of a scale which would require a drastic adjustment of our standard of living until it is perfectly clear and certain that this is the only course open to us.'[3]

---

[1] 'The Lash of Adversity', cliii (1947), p. 226.
[2] 440 H.C. Deb. 741–2 (18 July 1947).
[3] 439 H.C. Deb. 2065 (8 July 1947).

If it was not 'perfectly clear and certain' to the Government that a 'drastic adjustment' was now required it could hardly be apparent to the public at large. On 15 July the multilateral obligations of the Financial Agreement would take full effect. Yet few public comments showed awareness of the implications of this fact. The complacent attitude was encouraged by Dalton's confident assurance on 8 July that 'in large measure 15th July has already been discounted and the additional burden of assuming these new obligations under the Anglo-American Loan Agreement will be noticeably less than many people suppose'.[1] The 15 July deadline passed with few warnings of impending disaster. *The Banker* even boasted that Britain had 'handsomely' lived up to its obligations 'apparently to the surprise of American financial opinion' and concluded: 'The fateful day so anxiously awaited has come and gone, and brought with it no consequential disaster, nor is any in sight.'[2]

The succeeding days brought a rude awakening. In the week beginning 20 July the dollar drain reached $106 million. The next week it was $126 million; the week after that $127 million; in the week ending August 16 it was $183 million. In order to keep reserves steady at $2·5 billion, the Government had to make increasingly heavy drafts on the American Loan. By 16 August only $850 million remained. The loan at this rate would scarcely last another month.

Events now moved swiftly. On 18 August a British delegation headed by Sir Wilfrid Eady flew to Washington. It was the beginning of the end for Britain's brief encounter with the full obligations of multilateral trade.

THE AGREEMENT AND THE CRISIS

Some eighteen months after the signing of the Anglo-American Financial Agreement the British and American Governments were once more reviewing their economic relations in the American capital. But the circumstances were strikingly different. Then the negotiators had been confidently planning for Britain's speedy reconstruction and its early participation in a multilateral régime. Now they were meeting to avert the imminent exhaustion of Britain's reserves and to extricate Britain from multilateral commitments it could no longer maintain.

We may use this occasion as a focus for analysis. There are two basic questions: What effect did the Financial Agreement have on

[1] 439 H.C. Deb. 2150 (8 July 1947).   [2] lxxxiii (1947), p. 59.

the crisis? What effect did the crisis have on the Financial Agreement? In the following pages we shall try to answer these questions with respect to each of the multilateral obligations.

Convertibility

The most urgent item on the agenda of the emergency meeting in Washington was convertibility of the pound sterling. Eady announced at the outset that this obligation of the Financial Agreement could no longer be supported by the United Kingdom. Two days after his arrival, on 20 August 1947, the British Government suspended convertibility.

What influence did convertibility have on the crisis? Let us begin by asking what convertibility actually meant. As we noted earlier, the essence of the convertibility obligation was that the sterling earnings of countries outside the sterling and dollar areas should be freely available for current transactions by 15 July 1947. In preparation for this deadline the British Government had negotiated a series of bilateral agreements with these countries, beginning with the Anglo-Argentine Agreement of September 1946. The agreements created special Transferable Accounts which could be debited for current transfers to any country in the world.

Although we shall not go into the technical details of the Transferable Account System, one important observation must be made. The British Government considered it impractical to scrutinize in London each individual transaction that involved a non-resident. Therefore it left to the monetary authorities of each foreign government the responsibility for supervising the Transferable Accounts and insuring that withdrawals were made for current transactions only. On the competence and good faith of these authorities rested the only assurance that convertibility privileges would not be abused. Whether or not this precarious method was the only one available to implement convertibility need not concern us now. The point is that its implications had never been made clear to the United States when the original convertibility commitment was drawn up. Nor were the interested American agencies consulted on the development of the Transferable Accounts in advance of 15 July. They were simply notified that this system had been chosen to carry out the convertibility obligation. Anxiously, but without the power to influence events, they had to watch that system develop from afar.

By the late spring of 1947 agreements opening Transferable

Accounts had been concluded with a large number of Britain's major trading partners. Since the agreements took effect immediately upon ratification, convertibility was operative over a wide area well in advance of 15 July. Shortly before that date the British Government invoked the clause of the Financial Agreement permitting postponement of convertibility in the 'exceptional cases' of fourteen countries with whom agreements had not yet been concluded or whose monetary authorities could not be relied on to restrict convertibility to current transactions.[1] Nevertheless, sterling was in fact convertible on 15 July for the world's major trading countries.

In assessing the burden of this obligation on Britain's economic position three facts deserve special emphasis. First, the obligation related only to payments for current transactions. Second, this was a right which Britain's trading partners would have demanded in any case, even apart from the obligation under the Loan Agreement. Countries such as Argentina and Belgium, two of Britain's main suppliers who customarily ran a surplus with Britain in current trade, would not have been willing to accumulate large amounts of sterling which could not be used in meeting their own dollar deficits with the United States. Finally, convertibility had been put into effect gradually over a period of nine months. For all these reasons, one would not have expected the drain on British reserves due to the convertibility obligation to have been either sudden or severe.

This reasoning found widespread British support in the weeks before the suspension of convertibility. Dalton told the House of Commons that

the question of convertibility is not principally a question of what is written in the Anglo-American Agreement, but what is written in the realities of life in these countries. All these countries . . . are running very short of dollars and are increasingly demanding from us sterling convertibility at once into dollars, quite apart from any obligations of the American agreement. If we did not agree to give them convertible sterling, they would invoice the bills in dollars straight away. That should be clearly understood.[2]

The burden of convertibility was also minimized in much informed press comment. *The Manchester Guardian*, for example, acknowledged that there might be 'some extra drain' when the convertibility provision became fully effective but added that 'the number of dollars we

[1] Correspondence of July 14–15, 1947 Relating to the Postponement in Certain Cases of the Obligations Under Sections 7, 8 (II) and 10 of the Anglo-American Financial Agreement, Appendix B of *Report of the Activities of the National Advisory Council on International Monetary and Financial Problems, April 1, 1947 to September 30, 1947* (Washington, 1947), p. 21.   [2] 441 H.C. Deb. 1667 (7 Aug. 1947).

PLATE 5

Above: U.S. and British financial experts meet to deal with the British crisis in August 1947. *Below*: Sir Wilfrid Eady (*right*) confers with John Snyder

have to surrender in this way is unlikely to be very large'.[1] Similarly, *The Economist* spoke of 'the uncertain and probably small additional cost of . . . convertibility'[2] and urged that the convertibility arrangements completed on 15 July should not be regarded 'as part of the price reluctantly paid for financial assistance from the United States. They are rather in the logical line of development of sterling exchange control and in keeping with the great tradition of sterling as a world currency.'[3]

This appeared to be the logic of economics; but what appeared to be the logic of statistics proved more persuasive. In 1946, when the convertibility requirement had hardly begun to take effect, the monthly dollar drain was $75 million. In the first half of 1947, as convertibility was extended over a wider area, the monthly drain was $315 million. In July, when the deadline was passed, the monthly drain was $498 million, and in August, for the twenty days convertibility was in force, the monthly rate was $650 million.[4] In announcing the suspension of convertibility Dalton cited 'the world-wide and ever-increasing shortage of dollars which now prevails' and the insupportability of an arrangement 'under which the heavy burden of the desperate dollar shortage of so many other countries was simply shifted to our shoulders, by reason of the fact that sterling, alone of all the other currencies of the European belligerents, was freely convertible'.[5]

Dalton's statement was the signal for a dramatic reversal of opinion towards the convertibility commitment. The obligation, which a few weeks earlier had been regarded as 'in the logical line of development' of British policy[6] was now viewed as an onerous burden that had been forced on Britain by the United States. In a subsequent debate on the nation's economic situation Dalton referred to the clause as one which even in 1945 he had foreseen as 'dangerous and objectionable'.[7] In an attempt to reconcile this with his statements of early summer, he explained:

We always had a fear—but it would not have been wise constantly to give utterance to it—that it might prove in the end to be unworkable in the

[1] (3 June 1947).   [2] 'Sterling After July 15', clii (1947), p. 1032.
[3] 'After July 15', cliii (1947), p. 117.
[4] The figures are taken from Economic Co-operation Administration Special Mission to the United Kingdom, *The Sterling Area: An American Analysis* (London, 1951), p. 98.
[5] Radio broadcast of 20 Aug., reported in *The Times* (21 Aug. 1947).
[6] Note 3, *supra*.
[7] 443 H.C. Deb. 399 (24 Oct. 1947). This was rather an over-statement. Although Dalton did criticize the convertibility clause during the debate on the Financial Agree-

economic conditions of the world; but having undertaken the obligation we were clearly bound in honour to go all out to observe it, and furthermore, having once undertaken it, it would have been great folly to have given any appearance of hanging back from it.[1]

The British press was quick to join in assigning to the convertibility commitment a large measure of blame for the dollar crisis. *The Economist* declared that the events of 20 August had been of the 'greatest importance' because the obligation of convertibility, one of the 'crippling conditions' of the Loan Agreement, had 'vanished'; it rejoiced that the Government was free at last to devise policy 'in the way best calculated to serve Britain's needs and interests'.[2] The City Editor of *The Manchester Guardian* charged that convertibility had 'deprived Britain of its most powerful bargaining weapon' and complained that it had been 'madness to impose it on us . . .'.[3] Innumerable speeches and articles told the British public that convertibility was an evil provision that had dealt a grievous blow to British recovery.[4]

What support can be found for this view? The fact that the dollar drain increased with the negotiation of the Transferable Account agreements and subsided with the suspension of convertibility does not prove that convertibility was a major cause of the crisis. As we have seen, the approach of the 15 July deadline was accompanied by a steady deterioration in Britain's balance of visible trade. It may be argued, of course, that the deterioration in the visible trade balance was due in part to convertibility, since some countries enjoying the convertibility privilege may have deliberately restricted their imports from Britain as a means of gaining additional sterling for conversion. But this can hardly be the whole, or even a major part, of the answer. The basic cause of the deterioration in Britain's visible trade balance lay in the domestic economic situation described earlier. Moreover, the dramatic increase in the dollar drain during the months of July and August indicated that convertibility was not being restricted to

ment (see p. 230, *supra*) he also said of the American desire for the clause: 'I think their argument has cogency. The transitional period is going to be easier and our difficulties are going to be much less severe because we shall have the dollar credit available for what would otherwise be the most difficult years of trade.' 417 H.C. Deb. 439 (12 Dec. 1945).   [1] 443 H.C. Deb. 400 (24 Oct. 1947).
[2] 'A Curse on the Tinker', cliii (1947), p. 345.   [3] (4 Sept. 1947).
[4] For a notable exception, see 'Convertibility in Retrospect', *The Times* (7 Oct. 1947): 'It is not easy to prove that the original acceptance of convertibility by July 15 of this year was necessarily a mistake. . . . It is important to recognize now that the failure was due more than anything else to the deterioration of the United Kingdom's own balance of payments, that convertibility did not in fact affect the duration of the dollar credit to any major extent. . . .'

current account. Large capital transfers were taking place—something that was neither authorized by the convertibility provision nor envisaged by its authors.

Admittedly, the available evidence on this latter point is only circumstantial; for precise conclusions one would require a detailed account of the transactions which occurred during this period. Nevertheless, some approximation to the real state of affairs can probably be made. It has been estimated that the drain of dollars to Transferable Account countries rose from $60 million in the first six months of 1947 to $300 million in the period 1 July–20 August.[1]

TABLE 5

Spending the American Loan, 15 July 1946 to 20 August 1947

	$ million			
	Net direct U.K. expenditure in West. Hem.	Net overseas sterling area expenditure in West. Hem.	Transferable £–$ conversion	Total
1946: 15 July–31 Dec.	850	−150	50	750
1947: 1 Jan.–30 June	1,300	270	60	1,630
1 July–20 Aug.	420	250	300	970
Total	2,570	370	410	3,350

Source: 'Inquest on the Dollars', *The Banker* (Oct. 1947), p. 15.

Conversions during 1 July–20 August by Argentina and Belgium alone amounted to $93·2 million and $137·2 million, respectively, compared with $74·8 million and $73·2 million in the entire first half of the year.[2] This suggests that a number of Transferable Account countries did not abide by either the spirit or the letter of their agreements. Residents of these countries noted Britain's greatly adverse balance in visible trade and its increased rate of drawings on the American loan. They put these facts together with the fact that the date for the implementation of convertibility had been determined, not by the British Government in its own good time, but by a fixed obligation drafted eighteen months earlier. Accordingly they had little confidence in Britain's ability to maintain convertibility. They pressed for

[1] See Table 5.
[2] Estimates given by Dalton, 443 H.C. Deb. 219 (5 Nov. 1947).

dollars as quickly as possible whenever they were entitled to payment on current account. They also engaged in capital transfers under the guise of current transactions—transfers facilitated by the sizeable sterling balances which, despite the provisions of the Financial Agreement, still remained available for immediate spending.[1] In short, Britain's creditors passed an unfavourable judgement on Britain's economic prospects and employed every available means of exploiting their convertibility privileges before it was too late.

Strictly speaking, therefore, the obligation to make sterling convertible for current transactions was not itself a major cause of the economic crisis which beset Britain in the summer of 1947. The drain on British reserves resulted mainly from the failure to carry out convertibility in the limited sense required by the Anglo-American Financial Agreement and from the failure to carry out certain other provisions of that Agreement. The negotiations at Washington in 1945 assumed that convertibility would be confined to current transactions and that the bulk of the old sterling balances would be segregated and brought under control. The violation of the latter assumption—and perhaps also the former—was evident well in advance of 15 July. This fact coupled with the increasing rate of the dollar drain should have provided a clear warning that the convertibility experiment could not succeed. Why, then, was the deadline for convertibility not postponed?

Herein lies one of the most fascinating minor mysteries of our recent past. It is a mystery which to this day admits of no simple or certain solution. An adequate answer must draw attention to at least two factors. The first is the short-sightedness of certain British and American leaders. The second is the defective international instrument they inherited from the negotiations of 1945.

On one side of the Atlantic, to begin with, was the traditional British pride. The authors of British financial policy were justly proud of their country's financial eminence and its reputation for carrying out its solemn obligations. Britain, they seemed to say, had made a bargain with the United States; it would honour it, even in adversity, to the last iota of its wealth and strength. This reasoning had about it a glorious Old World flavour. Here, several months after the crisis, is Lord Catto, Governor of the Bank of England, still justifying the decision to go ahead with convertibility:

The obligation to attain convertibility on or before the 15th July, 1947, was clear and unequivocal. My Lord Mayor, there are too many people

---

[1] The subject of the sterling balances is discussed in the following sub-section.

about in the world today who think that matters of this kind can be dealt with, not as honour requires, but as expediency dictates! And that kind of reasoning is partly the cause of the world's troubles, for it breeds that lack of trust between nations which is such a feature of world politics at the present time.[1]

But pride was not the only factor at work in British policy. There was also the familiar error of complacency. Dalton's principal advisers in the Treasury and Bank of England told him in advance of 15 July that convertibility could be successfully carried out. The statistical information at their disposal did not show the full amount by which the dollar drain was exceeding Britain's deficit on current account. They thought the increase in the dollar drain was due only to temporary factors such as the winter fuel crisis. They could not believe that, given the choice, a vast number of Britain's customers would choose to hold dollars instead of sterling or that they would help themselves greedily in flagrant violation of their 'gentlemen's agreements'. As Lord Catto explained:

Many and careful arrangements were made before 15th July. Confidence was returning; sterling balances were being more and more freely held in London as in the days before the war, and there was a possibility that convertibility of sterling on current account might be feasible; at any rate, we were obliged to try. And it might have succeeded had it not been that confidence became undermined by the balance of payments crisis in this country and, indeed, all over the world. Suddenly, everybody wanted dollars, and convertibility, even for current transactions, became too great a strain and had to be suspended.[2]

It would appear, therefore, that the British Government had by no means determined to secure a postponement of the convertibility obligation. The American Government saw even less reason for delay. The responsibility for the execution of the Financial Agreement rested upon the United States Treasury. John Snyder, the new Secretary of the Treasury, was even more conservative in outlook than Vinson had been. His attitude toward the Financial Agreement was less that of a statesman interpreting an instrument of high international policy than that of a St. Louis banker claiming his rights under a mortgage agreement or contract of sale. In the months before 15 July he was unrelenting in his insistence that the British live up to the very letter of the Financial Agreement.

A sample of Snyder's approach was afforded by his reaction to a

[1] Speech at the Lord Mayor's Dinner, Mansion House, reported in the *Financial Times* (10 Oct. 1947). [2] Ibid.

provision in the Anglo-Argentine payments agreement. Argentina, according to this provision, was to use its accumulated sterling balances to offset any future deficit in its trade with the sterling area. Snyder pointed out that the provision violated the requirement of the Financial Agreement that releases of sterling balances should be available for spending in any currency area. He warned the British Government that the 'difficulties' they might encounter in carrying out the Financial Agreement could not 'be regarded as justifying commitments which contravene' its express terms. 'I think you can realize', he added significantly, 'the importance we attach to the fulfilment of the obligations undertaken . . . by your Government.'[1] On the eve of the 15 July deadline the Treasury was equally firm in rejecting some of the British requests for postponement of convertibility with respect to specific countries.[2] And in April 1947 the inter-departmental group organized under Treasury leadership to study the operation of the Financial Agreement concluded that the United States should turn down any British request for a general postponement of the convertibility obligation.[3]

Both sides, therefore, were guilty of inertia. But it would be wrong to suggest that there was no awareness at all of the impending disaster. Although some British leaders were unduly optimistic, there were others who saw serious risks in undertaking convertibility in the face of such a heavy adverse balance of trade and such a large amount of uncovered liabilities. Had there been an honourable way out, they might have won the day for postponement. Similarly, there were American leaders who viewed the situation with considerable alarm. Some Treasury officials expressed increasing anxiety at what appeared

[1] Letter from Snyder dated 27 Jan. 1947 included in exchange of notes between the United States and the United Kingdom, printed 433 H.C. Deb. 22 (10 Feb. 1947). In all fairness to Snyder it should be pointed out that he was only attempting to carry out his responsibility as the principal American officer charged with the administration of the Financial Agreement. His vigilance was undoubtedly approved by a considerable section of the American Congress. Following publication of these notes one member of the House of Representatives called attention to 'the amazing revelation that Great Britain is not adhering to the letter of this agreement' and declared that Britain's behaviour was 'disappointing the people of this country who sympathised with the supposed objectives of this loan'. He urged his colleagues to make sure that in the future the American people were not taxed in order that loans could be made 'to nations that violate the principles of sacred agreements'. Representative Dorn, 93 *Cong. Rec.* 798 (5 Feb. 1947).

[2] It rejected requests for postponement, for example, with respect to Switzerland and China.

[3] This conclusion was qualified, however, by the observation that a final decision on such a request could only be made in the light of the circumstances in which the request was made.

to be the unduly large amount of capital transfers.[1] State Department leaders such as Marshall and Clayton were gravely concerned with the political and economic implications of the dollar drain. Probably they would have fought for postponement of convertibility had the British made a request supported by sufficient evidence. In the last analysis, the straw that tipped the balance against postponement may not have been the inertia of certain British and American leaders but the inadequate nature of the Agreement itself.

The main causes of this inadequacy have already been described. First, there was no provision for continuing consultation. As a consequence, the American leaders were not kept adequately informed of the facts of the British crisis—facts necessary to support any American initiative in favour of postponement.[2] Second, there was no provision under which postponement without legislative approval could be authorized. The British leaders were afraid to ask for modifications in the Agreement that would require an appeal to Congress. The only possibility left was the phrase about postponement of convertibility in 'exceptional cases'. But the British recalled how the Americans had fought against this provision; they knew the narrow interpretation it had been given in the United States. Thus the British leaders did not think there could be a general postponement of convertibility by informal consultation between the two Governments. In Dalton's words, 'no general postponement could have happened without a long debate in Congress'.[3] In this way the two Governments were finally trapped in verbal meshes of their own making. Neither was able to take the initiative. 'As in some silly Victorian novel, each side waited for the other to speak first.'[4]

The limitations of the Financial Agreement became particularly apparent after Eady's arrival in Washington. As we have seen, Eady announced at the outset that the British Government had decided to suspend convertibility. Having informed the American Government of this unilateral decision, he proceeded to express the hope that some way would be found to reconcile it with the terms of the Financial Agreement. Since the need for suspension was urgent, there was no opportunity to submit amendments of the Agreement to

---

[1] They simply assumed, however, that the British were aware of the problem and would find a solution.

[2] How deficient American information was can be seen by the fact that as late as 2 June 1947 the inter-departmental group concerned with the Financial Agreement thought Britain's current account deficit for 1947 would be about the same as its deficit for 1946.   [3] 443 H.C. Deb. 402 (24 Oct. 1947).

[4] Joseph and Stewart Alsop, *The New York Herald-Tribune* (25 Aug. 1947).

Parliament and Congress. He therefore suggested that the British
action should be justified under the provision calling for suspension
of convertibility in 'exceptional cases'.[1]

But the American representatives at the Washington discussions
could not agree to this direct method of relieving Britain's difficulties.
According to the American Treasury, the clause in question permitted
suspension of convertibility only in individual (and exceptional) cases
where there was a danger that the convertibility privilege would be
abused. The assurances given to Congress would be violated if the
British were permitted under this provision to make a general and
indefinite suspension of convertibility. The American representatives
stated, therefore, that they could not acquiesce in a general suspension of convertibility except on one condition—that the United Kingdom designated the suspension as purely temporary and promised
to resume convertibility in a comparatively short time as soon as
measures had been taken to prevent abuse of convertibility privileges. This the British representatives were now unwilling to do. They
no longer considered that the dollar drain was due to improper
capital transfers alone—even convertibility on current account was
henceforth insupportable. Nor did they think it would prove possible
in the near future to ensure a system of current account convertibility
against abuse. For these reasons they rejected the condition for a
general suspension of convertibility put forward by the United States.

The difficulty was now revealed in its sharpest form. To put it
bluntly, the British wanted to suspend convertibility in circumstances
for which the Agreement had made no provision. There was no alternative, in the American view, but publicly to accept the fact that
Britain had defaulted on its solemn obligation. Snyder therefore
proposed an exchange of notes in which the British Government
would announce its unilateral action while the American Government would simply take note of this action and suspend the balance
of the credit. To British eyes, this seemed a rather harsh proposal.
What effect would such a public default have on world opinion—
particularly on opinion in the United States? There was also the
danger that an unsympathetic note from the American Government
suspending the balance of the credit might further undermine confidence in Britain's position and increase the rate of the dollar drain.

---

[1] As we noted in Chapter XI, Section 8 (ii) provided for *postponement* of convertibility until a later date; Section 8 (ii) (b) provided for *suspension* of convertibility
without reference to a later date. Since convertibility had already been undertaken,
only 8 (ii) (b) was still available.

At last, after two days of almost continuous negotiation, a compromise was agreed upon. In an exchange of notes released on 20 August,[1] Dalton notified the American Government that convertibility was suspended. But the action was described as 'of an emergency and temporary nature which His Majesty's Government consider to be within the intentions and purposes of the Financial Agreement and which they hope will enable them to take appropriate action to insure that the limited dollar resources of the United Kingdom are available for the purposes contemplated by the Financial Agreement and are not diverted to other ends'. Dalton reaffirmed that the 'full and free convertibility of sterling' was still 'a long-run objective'. He cited the clause of the Financial Agreement providing for suspension of convertibility in 'exceptional cases' after consultation, indicating that Britain might have to make continuing use of that provision and adding that no further drawings would be made on the credit until those consultations had been carried out. Responding on behalf of the United States, Snyder took 'sympathetic note' of the grave drains on Britain's dollar resources—drains which had run 'at a rate greatly in excess of the normal flow of current transactions with consequent peril to the re-creation of the multilateral payments system which is a major objective of the Anglo-American Financial Agreement'. He made special acknowledgement of the British assurance that their action was 'of an emergency and temporary nature, and is deemed by you essential to afford the United Kingdom Government an opportunity for instituting measures to protect the system of convertibility from abuses which endanger its survival'.

This exchange was a reasonably successful attempt to extricate the British and American Governments from the embarrassing position in which they had been placed by the tightly drafted provisions of the Financial Agreement. It allowed them to maintain that the suspension of convertibility was within the terms of the Agreement and was of a temporary and emergency character; it also left open the possibility that a permanent suspension might have to be negotiated. The official position taken by the United States Treasury in response to Congressional inquiries was that the suspension would give the British time to renegotiate the Transferable Account agreements and

---

[1] Correspondence of August 20, 1947, Relating to Modification of the System of Transferable Accounts, Appendix C of U.S. National Advisory Council, *Report on Activities, April 1, 1947 to September 30, 1947*.

ensure that convertibility was restricted to current transactions only. The Treasury also gave assurances that if Britain proved unable to resume convertibility the Financial Agreement, in accordance with its terms, would be renegotiated and submitted in revised form for Congressional approval.

TABLE 6

United Kingdom Gold and Dollar Reserves
Selected dates 1938 through 1947

$ *million*

Date	Current value*	Value in terms of 1938 purchasing power		Changes in reserves (from previous date)
		Value	Per cent. of 1938 reserves	
31 Aug. 1938 . . .	4,190	4,190	100	
31 Dec. 1946 . . .	2,696	1,409	36	−1,494
31 Mar. 1947 . . .	2,380	1,259	30	−316
30 June 1947 . . .	2,410	1,223	29	+30
30 Sept. 1947 . . .	2,383	1,192	28	−27
31 Dec. 1947 . . .	2,079	985	23	−304

* Official and estimated private holdings of gold and dollars, United States and Canadian dollars expressed in terms of United States dollars at current exchange rates.

Source: Table 37, E.C.A. Special Mission to the U.K., *The Sterling Area* (London, 1951), p. 135.

It soon became apparent, of course, that there was no prospect of an immediate resumption of convertibility. The formula adopted in the exchange of notes only postponed the problem of the basic inconsistency between the Loan Agreement and the British action. The problem came to a head again in December 1947. The British financial position was still serious. Marshall Aid was months away. To fill the gap in its balance of payments Britain had to exhaust its drawing rights in the International Monetary Fund and dip further into its rapidly shrinking reserves.[1] In these circumstances the $400 million remaining of the American loan assumed major importance. Unless it was once more made available British reserves would have to be reduced well below the minimum of financial safety. But how, under the original exchange of notes, could such action be allowed?

[1] See Table 6 for Britain's reserve position in the autumn of 1947.

Could the United States permit withdrawal of the $400 million if convertibility were not resumed?

The answer to this question was finally given in the affirmative. The American Treasury had to accept the fact that the convertibility provision had broken down. Snyder confessed to Congressional leaders that there was no immediate prospect that the British would comply with their obligations under the Financial Agreement. Despite this fact he urged that Britain should be permitted to draw upon the remainder of the loan. He argued that in the long run such liberal action would do more to serve the purposes of the Financial Agreement than a narrow interpretation of its terms. The Congressional leaders, now absorbed with Marshall Aid and new problems of Soviet–American relations, were not disposed to raise objections. Consequently, after another exchange of notes in which both Governments again invoked the objectives of the Agreement, the British resumed drawings on the credit. Thus did the letter of an unwise provision give way before the obvious interests of Britain and the United States.

Perhaps a moral can be drawn from this confused sequence of events. The convertibility provision had been tightly drafted to ensure that an important step toward multilateralism would be achieved. In fact, the provision advanced multilateralism not at all; it proved no stronger than the genuine determination of the two Governments to take all the measures necessary to assure success. Indeed, the very specificity and rigidity of the provision—the fixed time limit and the inadequate opportunity for escape—actually set back the cause they were designed to serve. For they encouraged an abortive try at convertibility which brought considerable discredit to the multilateral goal. But before describing the effects of this failure on Anglo-American opinion, we must examine the relation to the crisis of the other major provisions of the Financial Agreement.

The sterling area arrangements

Two other provisions of the Financial Agreement which bore an important relation to the 1947 crisis may be conveniently considered together—the treatment of the accumulated sterling balances and the operation of the sterling area 'dollar pool'. As we noted earlier, the balances were to be divided into three categories—some written off as a contribution to the war effort, some funded, and some made immediately available for spending in any currency area. During the

Washington negotiations the American Government had been led to believe that about one-third of the balances would be written off and the large majority of the remainder funded. The Financial Agreement had been drafted on the understanding that the bulk of the balances would be brought under British control and that the total of releases to sterling area countries in 1946–50 would be limited to some £200–250 million. It had also been understood that these releases would be offset by equivalent contributions from the overseas sterling area and thus would involve no net drain on the central reserves.[1]

There was little in the terms of the Financial Agreement that encouraged the achievement of such a satisfactory settlement. Instead of providing a broad and comprehensive approach to the problem of inter-allied indebtedness, the Agreement simply left it to the United Kingdom to make 'every endeavour' to reach a solution on its own. Once the Financial Agreement was signed, there was probably only one way to achieve a settlement of the balances in accordance with the spirit of the Washington negotiations. That was for the British Government to perform a drastic surgical operation—removing the bulk of these balances from the banking system and replacing them with non-negotiable certificates of indebtedness. In short, the British would have to make a unilateral declaration that the balances could not be considered as ordinary commercial debts. All negotiations about scaling-down, funding, and immediate releasing would then be based on that assumption.[2]

We have already indicated three powerful forces in Britain working against a solution of this kind. The first was the attitude held by the Bank of England and, to some extent, by the Treasury, that the sterling balances must be regarded as solemn financial obligations. The second was the attitude of many officials in the Board of Trade, that the balances would be a convenient device for the expansion of British exports. The third was the attitude of the Foreign Office and the Labour leadership, that a drastic solution of the sterling balances problem might jeopardize progress towards Indian independence within the British Commonwealth. The convergence of these forces in British policy removed all hope for a satisfactory solution. Instead, the problem of the sterling balances was hardly faced at all. A few

---

[1] See pp. 205–6, *infra*.
[2] A strong case on behalf of this approach is made in Harrod, *The Pound Sterling*, Essays in International Finance No. 13 (Princeton, 1952), pp. 10–15.

months after the signing of the Financial Agreement the British Government informed the United States that, for the most part, there would be no blocking or funding of the balances, and perhaps even no segregation of old sterling from sterling earned in current transactions. There would only be informal agreements with the sterling creditors on the rate at which drawings on the balances might be made. Moreover, there would be no permanent settlements providing for scaling-down of the balances, but only temporary settlements for four or five years after which the position with respect to the balances could be reviewed.

The American Government expressed considerable anxiety about these arrangements. It held that they were inconsistent with the spirit of the Washington Agreement, particularly with the objective of achieving a just settlement of inter-allied indebtedness and removing a major obstacle to multilateral trade. But the British Government declared that no other alternative was available. The major sterling creditors were not anxious to negotiate; indeed, they were holding back from negotiations in the hope of getting better terms. Since the British claimed to be making 'every endeavour' to reach a solution, the Americans could not charge them with violating the Agreement. Once again a situation had arisen for which no provision had been made. The United States could only express its misgivings and stand helplessly by.

The resulting outcome was in sharp contrast to what had been anticipated at the time of the Washington negotiations. In August 1947 Dalton revealed that the sterling balances, far from having been scaled down, were at an all-time high of £3,559 million.[1] He added that of these only £1,700 million—less than half—had been formally blocked. The rest were within the control of Britain's creditors, such as the £400 million owed to Australia, New Zealand, and South Africa—countries with whom Britain had 'not thought it necessary to enter into formal arrangements'. About £500 million in unblocked balances was held by countries outside the sterling area, mainly by countries of Western Europe. Finally, some £200 million was left as working capital for use by countries whose balances had been subjected to blocking.

This handling of the sterling balances was clearly inconsistent with the understanding that the bulk of the balances would be brought under control by the 15 July deadline. The only thing to prevent the

[1] 441 H.C. Deb. 1670 (7 Aug. 1947).

conversion of this huge mass of free sterling was the self-restraint of the holders—a weak safeguard in the circumstances of 1947. As the crisis deepened in the spring and summer, several Transferable Account countries drew heavily on their free balances. The sterling area countries did the same. Added to this drain was the drain due to the conversion into dollars of agreed releases from blocked balances. Thus was one of the basic assumptions of the Financial Agreement gradually destroyed.

The failure to solve the sterling balances problem caused a drain on British reserves in two major ways. In the first place, it facilitated abuse of their convertibility privileges by the Transferable Account countries. Residents of these countries got dollars not only with their own sterling balances but also with amounts of old sterling that came into their hands from trade with the sterling area countries. In the second place, the failure to bring the balances under control encouraged a direct run on the central reserves by members of the sterling area. The available statistics cannot pretend to any great precision; but they are reliable enough to suggest the general trend. During the period 15 July–31 December 1946 the overseas sterling area contributed some $150 million to the central reserves from dollar earnings in the Western hemisphere. This was in accord with the pre-war pattern in which the dollar surplus of the overseas sterling area helped offset the dollar deficit of the United Kingdom. But in 1947 this situation abruptly changed. In the first six months of that year the overseas sterling area drew $270 million net from the central reserves for dollar spending in the Western hemisphere. Between 1 July and 20 August it drew no less than $250 million.[1]

What was the explanation for the sudden alteration in the pre-war pattern of settlement? The balance of trade between the overseas sterling area and the United States had become drastically adverse. In pre-war days the exports of these countries to the dollar area had been sufficient to pay for 115 per cent. of their dollar imports; in 1947 they were sufficient to finance only half of those imports.[2] Normally the overseas sterling countries could not have supported such an adverse change in their balance with the dollar area—they would have needed net dollar earnings to offset their deficit with the United Kingdom. Now, however, they had their large accumulated balances to draw upon, in addition to new British capital which was currently

[1] See Table 5, p. 317.
[2] E.C.A. Mission to the U.K., *The Sterling Area*, p. 66.

being supplied. Much of their greatly increased dollar spending was made possible in this way.[1]

The large net dollar drawings by the overseas sterling countries provided an ironic contrast to the Financial Agreement's celebrated stricture against continuation of the dollar pool. Far from being hindered in their dollar spending by the United Kingdom, the overseas sterling countries were placing an intolerable burden on the central reserves by their independent and undisciplined economic policies. But British and American press comment showed little understanding of this fact. British critics of the Financial Agreement railed against the obligation to end the 'dollar pool' as if a tightly disciplined sterling system were suddenly going to end on 15 July. American observers were hardly better informed. When the deadline arrived *The New York Times* referred to Article 7 as the 'main obligation' of the Agreement and announced solemnly that 'today the Empire dollar pool is dissolved'.[2] And *The New York Herald-Tribune* declared that the coming into force of the provision would mean 'a sort of breaking up of one big bottleneck into a lot of little bottlenecks. Instead of a British dollar pool controlling the spending of all dollars coming into the sterling area, the individual countries will now begin setting up their own controls to see that dollars are carefully spent.'[3]

In fact, of course, 15 July brought little change in the operation of the sterling area. The system of voluntary war-time restraint between the sterling countries had already been dissolved—and for reasons other than the 'dollar pool' provision of the Financial Agreement. As we have just noted, the overseas sterling area countries were making large drafts upon the central reserves, adding to the dollar drain which finally forced the suspension of convertibility. The resulting peril to the central reserves finally brought this to an end. In September an emergency meeting was held of Commonwealth representatives who were in London for the annual meetings of the Bretton Woods institutions. The members of the sterling area reviewed their export and import programmes in the light of the dollar crisis and agreed upon certain policies to carry them to June of 1948. Their final communiqué declared:

The discussions have emphasised the importance to the economies of all the countries in the sterling area of the central reserve system which has

---

[1] Although statistical information is inadequate, the above conclusion seems justified because there was no comparable deterioration in the United Kingdom's current balance with these countries. For more detailed estimates of the amount of dollar drain chargeable to the old sterling balances, see Harrod, *And So It Goes On* (London, 1951), pp. 76–77. [2] (16 July 1947). [3] (16 July 1947).

served so well for so many years. Following on the conference the representatives attending it will report to their respective Governments, who will
be able to consider what reductions in hard currency expenditure are
possible and what assistance can be given in other ways to the strengthening
of the sterling area's gold and dollar reserves. Some of the Governments
concerned have already announced modifications in their import programmes which will reduce the claim upon the central reserve for gold and
dollars.[1]

This sounded very much like a revival of the war-time system.
Dalton said it was now 'clear that we must all keep in constant touch
so as to minimise, by common agreement, the drain upon the gold
and dollar resources which are the reserves, not only of the United
Kingdom, but of the Sterling Area as a whole'. He added that it
would 'be necessary to hold further meetings of this kind at frequent
intervals'.[2] Subsequently the various Dominions announced their
intention to live within their current dollar incomes and so avoid
drawing upon their accumulated sterling balances. To most British
commentators this signified 'the reconstitution of the sterling area
dollar pool'.[3] Beaverbrook's *Daily Express* ran the triumphant headline 'Empire Dollar Pool Goes On', and rejoiced in the revival of a
system 'under which the Bank of England controls all the dollar
earnings and payments of the Empire and other countries in the
sterling area'![4]

Thus another obligation of the Financial Agreement was finally
overturned. The wheel had gone full cycle. The 'dollar pool' provision had been designed to avoid discrimination against American
goods by the overseas sterling countries. But the urgent need in the
transition period was to restrain these countries from excessive dollar
spending. The voluntary system of self-restraint that proved essential
amid the stresses of war was proving no less essential amid the uncertainties of peace. For such an eventuality the Financial Agreement made no provision. Instead it encouraged a heated doctrinal
controversy about a system which needed to be judged calmly in
pragmatic terms. It distracted attention from the real danger—the
collapse of sterling area discipline. This failure was encouraged and
aggravated, in turn, by the inadequate handling of the sterling
balances. In the matter of the sterling area arrangements, therefore,
the errors of policy were severe. Once again, as in the case of the

---

[1] *The Times* (7 Oct. 1947).
[2] Speech at the Mansion House, the *Financial Times* (10 Oct. 1947).
[3] The *Observer* (14 Sept. 1947).   [4] (7 Oct. 1947).

convertibility clause, the Financial Agreement made little contribution to their timely correction.

Non-discrimination

Next to convertibility the most important item on the agenda of the emergency meetings of August 1947 was the question of non-discrimination. As we noted earlier, the non-discrimination clause of the Financial Agreement was inserted to ensure that Britain did not evade its obligations in financial policy by inconsistent measures in the commercial field. Under this provision Britain could not restrict the importation of American goods without restricting the importation of the same products from other sources. In other words, the system of import licensing could not make distinctions between different foreign countries; importers of products subject to licensing had to be free to make their purchases solely on the basis of commercial considerations—price, quality, and other terms and conditions of sale. To the American Government this seemed a reasonable requirement, since in normal circumstances it would promote trade along the lines of comparative advantage and increase the real income of all countries.

Unfortunately, however, the summer of 1947 was not a normal time. There was a world-wide shortage of dollars, and Britain was faced with a dollar deficit that exceeded its deficit on overall account. In such a situation rigid adherence to non-discrimination might cause considerable hardship. If Britain were required to import solely on the basis of commercial considerations without regard to its available holdings of foreign exchange it would quickly exhaust its dollar resources and be left with an unusable supply of inconvertible currencies.

The drafters of the Financial Agreement were not unaware of this possibility. They had specifically provided that Britain should be excused from non-discrimination where the scarce currency provision was invoked by the International Monetary Fund. But this exception did not help in the present situation. As we have seen, the Fund had not engaged in active lending operations; hence there was no threat of dollar scarcity *in the Fund* and no use of the scarce currency clause.[1] For other countries, who could avail themselves of the Fund's transi-

---

[1] The Fund was to invoke the scarce currency clause only when 'it becomes evident . . . that the demand for a member's currency seriously threatens the Fund's ability to supply that currency'. Article VII, Section 3 (*a*).

tional provisions, this caused no hardship. But Britain had foresworn resort to these provisions under the terms of the Financial Agreement. In its case, given the terms of the non-discrimination clause, the failure to invoke the scarce currency exception might be very significant indeed.

So far, however, we have discussed the problem from the theoretical standpoint. In practice it was not yet clear that the non-discrimination clause was causing serious difficulty for the United Kingdom. In the first place, the clause was interpreted to permit discrimination in favour of one another by Britain and the colonies.[1] In the second place, it did nothing to prevent Britain from discriminating in favour of its major suppliers in Europe. The Agreement specifically permitted discrimination 'to assist . . . a country whose economy has been disrupted by war'.[2] This was interpreted to include, at the very least, all of the countries which had been occupied by the Axis. Although such discrimination was designed to assist the more unfortunate of Britain's trading partners, it could not be ruled out because it was assisting Britain as well. Finally, the non-discrimination clause did not apply to purchases by the British Government, which now accounted for a major share of Britain's import trade.

There was yet another practical reason why, at the time of Eady's visit to Washington, the non-discrimination clause was working no great hardship. This was the pervasive condition of supply scarcity existing outside the dollar area. Britain could not very well give preference to non-dollar supplies if such supplies were simply not available. As of mid-1947 there were very few items desired by British importers that were denied them by the non-discrimination clause. In the second half of 1947, as more supplies became available in the non-dollar area, this situation might change. But, as Attlee confessed on 6 August, up to that time the non-discrimination clause had been 'hardly operative at all. It is because of low production in

---

[1] The British Government notified the United States in April 1947 that it proposed to authorize such discrimination. The American Government made no objection. Secretary of State Marshall made a public announcement of these facts on 23 July. *Dept. State Bull.*, xvii (1947), p. 228. In view of the fact that American antipathy to discrimination was originally caused by preferential practices in colonial empires this must be regarded as an extremely significant event. The reaction from the American press was generally favourable. See, for example, 'Small Favor, Big Results', *The Christian Science Monitor* (25 July 1947); 'Stretching the British Loan', *The New York Herald-Tribune* (24 July 1947); 'Relief for Britain', *The New York Times* (24 July 1947).

[2] Article 9 (b). Discrimination for this purpose was not to involve 'a substantial departure from the general rule of non-discrimination'.

other countries that we have been driven to buy so largely from the Western hemisphere.'[1]

Unhappily, these facts were not entirely understood by the British public. On its face the non-discrimination clause seemed to say that if Britain did not have the dollars to buy certain essential commodities in the United States it could not buy the same commodities from anyone else. It was of little use to point out the detailed exceptions permitted by the Agreement or to draw attention to the practical limitations of supply scarcity in non-dollar countries. The apparent injustice of the principle itself in the light of Britain's growing economic difficulties was bound to inspire intemperate and often inaccurate criticism. Many commentators, for example, were not aware that the non-discrimination provision did not apply to imports from the colonies. Thus the *Scotsman* complained: 'Already consumers are aware of the effects of the operation of the Article. On account of the dollar stringency . . . we have been obliged to cut down imports of American tobacco, but we cannot increase our purchases from Rhodesia.'[2] In the same vein, a Member of Parliament declared: 'It is quite clear that the whole of our trade is being hampered by Article IX of the American Loan Agreement; not only our trade with our Colonies, but our trade with our Dominions, and also our trade with those countries in South America that are anxious to trade with us.'[3] Even *The Times* seemed to be confused on this score and expressed concern lest the non-discrimination clause upset the Government's plans for a Colonial Development Corporation to stimulate the production of needed foodstuffs and raw materials.[4]

But these were comparatively minor misinterpretations. Many critics misunderstood the meaning of non-discrimination itself. Some charged inaccurately that Britain was obliged to cut down imports from the non-dollar area in the same proportion as it restricted dollar trade.[5] Others had the impression that Britain had to maintain the same quantitative relation between imports from the United States and the Empire as in pre-war years.[6] So serious did these misconceptions become that on at least one occasion American spokes-

---

[1] 441 H.C. Deb. 1494 (6 Aug. 1947). Attlee added, however, that the situation was changing and that with the new import cuts then proposed the clause would begin to be a 'very real factor'.   [2] (16 July 1947).
[3] Major R. H. Turton, 440 H.C. Deb. 823 (18 July 1947).   [4] (17 July 1947).
[5] See, e.g., the letter to *The Times* of L. S. Amery (21 Apr. 1947).
[6] 'What Is Discrimination?', the *Financial Times* (3 July 1947).

men had to assure the British public that the non-discrimination provision did not forbid the buying of goods in non-dollar markets
when prices there were lower![1]

By the summer of 1947 the outcry against the non-discrimination
clause had become too powerful to ignore. A sample of the press
comment may suggest its intensity. In the opinion of the *Financial
Times* revision of the clause was—next to the Marshall Plan—'probably the most important of current Anglo-American questions'.[2]
The Banker described the provision as being of 'crucial and urgent
importance' compared with which convertibility was of 'much less
significance'.[3] The *Scotsman* declared that of all the Loan provisions
'none is more crippling to British freedom of action or is having a
more harmful effect upon the efforts of the British people to improve
their standard of living . . .'.[4] The *Daily Mail* reported protests against
'needless austerity'[5] and exclaimed: 'Plainly the Article—the notor-
ious Article 9—will have to go unless Britain is to starve.'[6] A Parliamentary uproar began, culminating in a motion to obtain release
from the obligation entirely.[7] In mid-July a *New York Times* correspondent reported: 'At this moment, it is Clause 9 of the American
Loan Agreement that is most in the public eye and resentment against
it is universal.'[8]

The widespread public criticism of the non-discrimination clause
put great pressure on the British Government. So also did the
developing economic situation. The provision had not yet caused
serious harm; but it might soon begin to do so. To meet the growing
crisis a drastic new import programme was being devised which
might involve substantial departures from the rule of non-discrimination. As supply prospects in non-dollar countries improved the
British Government did not want to be restricted, however slightly,
by the terms of the Financial Agreement. Therefore, while Eady did not
ask at Washington for complete annulment of the non-discrimination

[1] Snyder had to explain to sceptical British journalists during a visit to London that
'definitely Britain can always buy in the cheapest market under Article 9'. Lewis
Douglas, the American Ambassador to Britain, also scored the 'misconception' that
under the non-discrimination clause Britain had to reduce its purchases in other
countries to the same extent that it reduced purchases in the U.S. Snyder joined in
emphasizing that 'that is not the American interpretation'. *The New York Times*
(16 Sept. 1947). [2] (25 June 1947). [3] lxxxiii (1947), p. 5.
[4] (16 July 1947). [5] (14 June 1947). [6] (26 Aug. 1947).
[7] The motion was made by Boothby and Squadron-Leader Hollis. *The New York
Times* (15 July 1947) observed that the motion would 'be endorsed silently and probably in speeches by a majority of M.P.'s even though they would not vote for it'.
[8] Herbert L. Matthews, 'Economics Strain U.S.-British Ties', *The New York Times*
(20 July 1947).

PLATE 6

Hugh Dalton (*left*) and Snyder during Snyder's visit to London in September 1947

provision, he did ask for an interpretation liberal enough to accommodate the new import programme that would shortly emerge.

Once again, the inflexible nature of the Financial Agreement provided an impediment to easy adjustment. As we have already noted, the International Monetary Fund had made no declaration that the dollar was a scarce currency. In the absence of such a declaration the American representatives at the Washington talks did not see how the existing condition of exchange stringency could provide a basis for modification of the non-discrimination provision. Yet they did agree in applying the clause to 'take into consideration the unusual aspects of the financial position of the United Kingdom'.[1] This meant that as long as Britain was short of dollars the United States would not object if Britain conserved its available supply by buying wherever possible in soft-currency markets—even if this meant buying goods which could be bought more cheaply in the United States.

Thus, in private, the necessary accommodation was finally made. But the inflexible language of the Financial Agreement forced the American leaders to keep up appearances. Snyder reacted violently when it was suggested that the United States had sanctioned a modification of the non-discrimination clause. At one press conference he banged his fist on the table and declared: 'I categorically asked Sir Wilfrid Eady if he was asking for any change in this clause and he replied "No". There has been no kind of deal, or arrangement, or otherwise that could violate either the spirit or the letter of the Loan Agreement.'[2] In London a few weeks later Snyder repeated this denial. 'So far we have found no breach of Article 9', he said. He reminded representatives of the British press that the United States believed in 'flexibility of contract' and declared that the British authorities 'have found they have ample room to act under the terms of the Loan Agreement'.[3] The American Embassy in London amplified these remarks with the following statement:

In his statement to the Press on 15th September last, Mr. John W. Snyder, the United States Secretary of the Treasury, pointed out that when any two Governments work out an agreement it must be kept flexible. This was the spirit of the original loan negotiations, and it is the purpose

[1] U.S. National Advisory Council, *Report on Activities, April 1, 1947 to September 30, 1947*, p. 4.
[2] 'No Agreement on Article 9', *The Manchester Guardian* (28 Aug. 1947). See also 'Mr. Snyder: No Agreement to Alter Loan', *Daily Telegraph* (28 Aug. 1947).
[3] 'Snyder Denies U.S. Is Curbing Britain', *The New York Times* (16 Sept. 1947).

and intention of the officials of the two Governments who are presently dealing with this problem.

The framers of the Anglo-American Financial Agreement specifically recognized the existence of unusual aspects of the United Kingdom position requiring certain deviations from any inflexible rule on non-discrimination.

It is basic to an understanding of Section 9 of the Agreement to appreciate that it was never intended to constitute a strait jacket on British trade.[1]

Britain was now free to discriminate against American goods in favour of all non-dollar suppliers. The President of the Board of Trade forwarded the American Embassy's statement to the House of Commons with the assurance that this would take care of Britain's needs in the existing emergency.[2] The Government now announced that it would 'do all in their power to find new sources of supply. . . '.[3] In drawing up the new import programme it determined to conserve its dollar resources for goods that could only be obtained in the Western Hemisphere. It would obtain other goods in the non-dollar area even if they were more expensive than identical goods in the United States.

Discrimination finally had official sanction. In principle this seemed an important matter. But its practical significance was not so clear. After the new import programme was drawn up an estimate was made of the imports from non-dollar sources that were likely to involve discrimination against the United States. These amounted, in all, to less than 2 per cent. of all imports.[4]

This review of the relation between the non-discrimination provision and the crisis of 1947 leads to the same conclusion reached earlier with reference to convertibility and the sterling area arrangements. In and of itself, the provision was not a major cause of Britain's economic difficulties. At the same time, it was ill-suited to the growing dollar crisis and hindered timely Anglo-American arrangements to alleviate the drain on British reserves. Like its companion provisions, it caused widespread resentment and misunderstanding on both sides of the Atlantic and profoundly affected public attitudes toward multilateral trade. With an elaboration of this last important point we shall conclude our discussion of the Financial Agreement.

---

[1] The *Financial Times* (19 Sept. 1947).
[2] 443 H.C. Deb. 54–55 (Written Answers) (28 Oct. 1947).
[3] 443 H.C. Deb. 5 (21 Oct. 1947).
[4] Aggregate estimates of this kind, of course, may understate the importance of critical individual items. Nevertheless, the figure does suggest the relatively small amount of discrimination that it was actually practicable to undertake.

THE AGREEMENT AND PUBLIC OPINION: THE
CONSEQUENCES OF A FALSE START

It is frequently misleading to draw parallels between the behaviour
of individuals and the behaviour of nations. Yet one term normally
reserved for the study of human neurosis seems unusually well suited
to explain the impact of the British crisis on both sides of the Atlantic.
Britain's brief and ill-starred flirtation with multilateralism was, in
the language of psychiatry, a 'traumatic experience'. The events of
1947 have profoundly influenced British and American policy even
to this very day.

The British reaction

It is a poignant moment in history when a whole people is forced
to face new facts in its national life and reshape its entire attitude
toward the future. Such a moment occurred for Britain in the summer
of 1947. The economic realities were no longer the exclusive concern
of a small group in Whitehall; they were beginning to be understood
by the public at large. The revelation brought some bitter inquiry.
What had happened to the greater security and higher living standards that had been promised in the darkest days of the war? Who
was responsible for this nightmare prospect of endless austerity and
desperate struggle for economic survival?

In the aftermath of disaster a scapegoat was sought in all directions.
Conservative spokesmen blamed the Labour Government. Labour
spokesmen blamed industry, the weather, and adverse conditions
abroad. But on one cause of the crisis nearly all could agree—the
Anglo-American Financial Agreement.

Two main charges were now heard. In the first place, the American
loan had largely been wasted: 'It would not be so bad if we had had
goods and services from it, but it is estimated that a good half or
more of it vanished in a few days when the convertibility clause
came in.'[1] In the second place, the loan and its attendant conditions
had helped bring on the financial crisis. 'There was no need for the
American Loan', declared a correspondent of the *Sunday Express*.
'It brought no wealth to Britain and it sapped the determination of
the country.'[2] 'Britain must accept no more loans from America',

---

[1] Harold Roberts, 443 H.C. Deb. 197 (22 Oct. 1947). Even Churchill declared that
the loan had been 'frittered away' on foodstuffs and luxuries and had provided no
lasting aid to British recovery. *The Times* (5 Aug. 1947).

[2] David Roberts (9 Nov. 1947).

declared the *Evening Standard*. 'The last one was not needed. . . .
This great country is in danger of being beaten down and impoverished by loans.'[1] These extreme expressions found echoes even in more
moderate opinion. The *Scotsman*, for example, declared:

> Without the Loan, we should probably by now have been in a much
> worse state of austerity, *but there is some cause to doubt whether it has
> improved our long-term prospects for recovery*. By the conditions of the loan
> agreement we tied ourselves to an American policy of economic inter-
> nationalism, and surrendered the main weapons we might have used to
> correct our unbalanced situation by direct action.[2]

The widespread feeling of frustration and disappointment produced some bitter criticism of the United States. Particularly violent
comment was heard during Eady's visit to Washington. 'Bourbon-
sipping' John Snyder was pictured as a 'chief inquisitor' who was
using techniques of the 'Star Chamber' against British representatives.[3] Nothing less than outright control of Britain's domestic
economic affairs was said to be the demand of the Americans.[4] One
journal told its readers that Britain had been 'called upon to account
for her management of domestic affairs in the capital of a foreign
power . . . the British people [are] no longer masters in their own
house'.[5] And another declared that 'the British people would prefer
to go hungry and work out their own salvation, rather than live on
American charity with such strings attached to it'.[6]

In the House of Commons Sidney Silverman asked: 'Is there
anybody who denies that the economic troubles of this country are
directly attributable to American financial and economic policy?'[7]
In the fever of controversy, old complaints were revived: Britain
had borne a disproportionate share of the war burden; the Americans had not implemented the principle of 'equal sacrifice'; Lend-
Lease had been cut off in violation of America's solemn obligations.[8]
Troubled by the British mood one American correspondent reported a
crystallizing of opinion among moderates . . . which makes the present
trend here both national in scope and very important in its bearing on

---

[1] (29 Sept. 1947).   [2] Italics supplied. (4 Mar. 1948).
[3] James Brough in the *Daily Mail* (21 Aug. 1947).   [4] Ibid.
[5] The *Evening Standard* (21 Aug. 1947).
[6] The *New Statesman and Nation* (23 Aug. 1947).
[7] 443 H.C. Deb. 939 (29 Oct. 1947).
[8] 'We had a solemn agreement with them that they would see us through, and they
only saw us half-way through.' Alfred Edwards, 443 H.C. Deb. 795 (24 Oct. 1947).
Silverman even suggested that the Americans were not 'within their legal rights' in
terminating Lend-Lease. 443 H.C. Deb. 942 (29 Oct. 1947).

Anglo-American relations. . . . It comes from a long-maturing conviction that post-war United States does not understand the disproportionate war burden carried by this and other European countries and that the paths of Europe and the New World are diverging. So far, this divergence is economic at the base and political only in its overtones. It has not become primarily political or extended into the field of military solidarity. But once the disappointment settles down into a kind of conviction, it is difficult to reverse the trend.[1]

The anti-American reaction described in this report received one of its most striking expressions in the pages of *The Economist*, which placed on the United States the main responsibility for Britain's difficulties and announced that it was finally out of patience with American demands:

The fault for the present crisis—if fault there must be—is far more America's than Britain's. . . . The world-wide dollar crisis, which hurled the convertibility provision into a disaster, is due to the fact that the American balance of payments has got out of control. Nothing could have been done about any of these things by any British action or inaction. Contributory negligence there has been from the British side, but it has been of smaller importance.

. . . .

American opinion should be warned that over here, in Great Britain, one has the feeling of being driven into a corner by a complex of American actions and insistencies which, in combination, are quite intolerable. Not many people in this country believe the Communist thesis that it is the deliberate and conscious aim of American policy to ruin Britain and everything that Britain stands for in the world. But the evidence can certainly be read that way. And if every time that aid is extended, conditions are attached which make it impossible for Britain ever to escape the necessity of going back for still more aid, to be obtained with still more self-abasement and on still more crippling terms, then the result will certainly be what the Communists predict.[2]

Such an outburst of resentment against America was unfortunate. Still, it would probably pass in time. There was, however, another and more lasting consequence of the 1947 crisis. This was the reaction against multilateralism itself—a reaction that died hard, if, indeed, it ever died at all. One theme now ran like a *leitmotif* through nearly all comment, moderate as well as extremist: *we must not make the same*

---

[1] Saville R. Davis, 'British Crisis Strains Links with U.S.', *The Christian Science Monitor* (27 Aug. 1947).

[2] Italics supplied. 'Inconvertible Again', cliii (1947), p. 306.

mistake again. Here, for example, was the *Financial Times*, reacting to a report that the United States had hit upon some new kind of intra-European convertibility scheme: 'Already, we may claim to have sacrificed far more than we can afford in the interests of multi-lateral trading, without having derived any benefit whatever from it. . . . *This is a case for looking before we leap a second time.*'[1] The same point was made by an article in *The Banker*:

> The Americans seem to entertain hopes that the retreat from such forms of multilateralism as had begun to emerge may be ended by the granting of liberal aid to Europe under the Marshall Plan. But European nations are not likely to respond. *Britain's experience with convertibility will surely give rise to a resolute determination to refuse American aid which has economic strings attached.*[2]

There was now nearly universal agreement that, for the time being, multilateralism should be abandoned. When, if ever, could it be restored? The crisis had inspired profound misgivings about multilateralism, even as a long-term objective. The *Scotsman's* formulation was typical: 'To insist on the inclusion of convertibility, non-discrimination and multilateral trading in the loan agreement *might* have been all right in a stable world but not in the chaotic conditions of the immediate post-war period.'[3] And *The Times* declared:

> Clearly the existing state of the world puts the idea of genuine 'multi-lateralism' out of reach just now. It is impracticable now because of the one-sided nature of world production, *and in the next stage, when the world has recovered, it may be impracticable because of the one-sided nature of world trade*, with the United States intent upon selling much more than it buys. . . . *Whether desirable in principle or not*, the possibilities of the so-called 'bilateral' method of obtaining and paying for supplies from overseas must now be energetically examined.[4]

Such statements suggested that multilateralism might play little part in the achievement of equilibrium—even in the long run. Indeed, *The Economist* now argued that multilateralism would have to be set aside 'until the whole fundamental problem of disequilibrium between the Eastern and Western hemispheres has been solved'.[5] This, it was expected, would take a very long time. Cripps was saying, for example: 'By the end of 1948, as far as we can foresee, the

---

[1] Italics supplied. (6 Oct. 1947).
[2] Italics supplied. C. Gordon Tether, 'Bretton Woods and the Crisis', lxxxiv (1947), p. 32.
[3] Italics supplied. (21 Aug. 1947).   [4] Italics supplied. (22 Aug. 1947).
[5] 'Sterling's Future Role', cliii (1947), p. 333.

same elements of disequilibrium will be there as today, though that force, we hope, will not be quite so great. We shall still be faced, *in 1949 and the succeeding years*, with a large dollar deficit. . . .'[1] If this bleak diagnosis was correct, multilateralism would have to be indefinitely postponed.

In the general reaction against multilateralism it was frequently forgotten that many of the provisions of the Loan Agreement were once thought to be in Britain's long-term interest. *The Economist*, for instance, which had noted earlier that convertibility 'should not . . . be regarded as part of the price reluctantly paid for assistance from the United States'[2] now declared that convertibility 'was not a chosen objective nor was it a party objective. It was an inescapable part of the price for a loan which most people were agreed Britain had to have'.[3] The *Yorkshire Post* now recalled that during the loan negotiations the British delegates had sought in vain 'to persuade the American negotiators that in asking for convertibility they were asking for something that would not assist but hamper the development of international trade'.[4] Such comments gave new encouragement to traditional exponents of bilateralism:

Even though Britain is finding herself forced back into bilateralism by factors beyond her control, there can be no doubt that, under the influence of the recent experience, British opinion, too, has moved considerably in favour of it. Many people have realized that, so long as Britain has an adverse trade balance, she cannot afford to return to multilateralism. . . . There are even some people who, learning from the lessons of the past few months, have come to the conclusion that bilateralism is worth having for its own sake.[5]

Thus the traditional critics of multilateralism hailed the crisis as their final vindication. 'In the end', said the *Daily Herald*, 'it is likely to have been worth while proving by hard experience to the world and to American opinion in particular, that the dream of freely convertible currencies and "multilateral" trade is just not practicable in the contemporary world.'[6] *The Economist* provided the most influential statement of this position. It drew two conclusions from the crisis—first, that the American balance of payments could no longer be expected to right itself automatically through tariff cuts or large-scale lending; second, that for countries as dependent as

---

[1] Italics supplied. 443 H.C. Deb. 288 (23 Oct. 1947).   [2] p. 315, *supra.*
[3] 'Sterling's Future Role', cliii (1947), p. 331.   [4] (21 Aug. 1947).
[5] Paul Einzig, 'The Case for Bilateralism', *The Banker*, lxxxiv (1947), p. 27.
[6] (2 Aug. 1947).

Britain on international trade 'non-discrimination and economic stability are incompatible with each other'. 'It is much the most likely
contingency', *The Economist* concluded, 'that the problem of the
American balance of payments will have to be solved in the great
majority of years in the same way in which it is being solved in
1947—by a universal restriction by all other countries of their
purchases from the U.S.'[1]

This, then, was the final irony. The Loan Agreement, designed to
foster multilateralism, had precisely the opposite effect. Not only did it
fail to effect any permanent change in British trade or financial policy;
it shook the faith of many in the desirability of multilateralism and
greatly strengthened the hand of the traditional critics of that objective.

The American reaction

The impact of the British crisis was no less profound on the other
side of the Atlantic. The American people had made what seemed to
them a generous loan—a loan that had been presented as a harbinger
of prosperity and multilateral trade. Until the spring of 1947 they
had little notice that British recovery was not proceeding according
to plan. Now, suddenly, the loan was almost gone, and the British
predicament seemed worse than ever. So much had been promised—
so little had been achieved. Who was responsible for the failure?

The American critics of the multilateral projects, no less than their
British counterparts, now had a chance to reap the harvest. Taft
expressed the growing suspicion that American generosity had once
more been wasted. The loan, he said, 'has nearly all been spent on
food, films, and tobacco, with the result that at the end of a year, so
far as England is concerned, we are where we started'.[2] Other commentators, ignoring such causes of the dollar drain as the abuse of
convertibility, the excessive spending of overseas sterling countries,
and the heavy burden of British external commitments, placed full
responsibility for the crisis on the domestic policies of the Labour
Government. *The New York Times*, for example, said the crisis
reflected a failure of the British productive effort under Socialism[3]—
ignoring the fact that the record of British recovery was without
equal in Western Europe.[4] In some quarters there was a stark failure

[1] 'Articles Seven to Ten', cliii (1947), p. 228.
[2] 'Loan "Mistake" Says Taft', Reuter dispatch in the *Daily Mail* (23 July 1947).
[3] (31 July 1947).
[4] With the single exception of Ireland, which suffered no damage in the war. See
Economic Commission for Europe, *A Survey of the Economic Situation and Prospects
of Europe* (Geneva, 1948), p. 3.

to understand the complex causes of the dollar drain. One *New York Times* financial writer exclaimed: 'Why talk of the vagaries of the weather when withdrawals totalled $700,000,000 in July alone, a rate equivalent to more than twenty-five billions over three years? When we say that Britain is facing a "dollar shortage" what we really mean is that she is facing a penalty for her failure to solve the problem of production.' Having made this statement, the writer then went on to ask: 'Is production—is postwar recovery—perhaps incompatible with socialism?'[1]

A large segment of the American press, naturally anti-Socialist in its sympathies, found in the British crisis an occasion to attack the Labour Government.[2] There was a tendency to oversimplify the problem and to attribute all British difficulties to the nationalization programme or even to a simple unwillingness to work. 'The impression is widespread in this country', declared the *Chicago Daily News*, 'that the resolution to face hard reality and buckle down to work was overlong in coming. . . . The United States is willing to help to every reasonable extent, in self-interest as well as in friendship. But, as it has been phrased, we are not willing to work six days a week to help people who work five.'[3] Supplementing the view that the Socialists had mismanaged the internal situation was the view that they had badly bungled their external finance—a view reinforced by the suddenness with which the crisis had come and the lack of warning given by Whitehall. A British correspondent reported from Washington that 'while there is a widespread and genuine sympathy for Britain's plight and her people's sharpened austerity, there are indications in the press and Government of an irritation that the British Government should have been taken so suddenly unawares and that within a matter of weeks there should be such complete change of opinion in official London concerning Britain's financial future'.[4]

Despite widespread criticism of British policies, however, American opinion was sympathetic to revision of the Financial Agreement. It was even coming round to acceptance of Britain's need for additional aid. Indeed, the British crisis of 1947 provided a final spur to the revolution in American thinking which had begun during the

[1] Edward H. Collins, 'Economics and Finance' (11 Aug. 1947).
[2] Especially the conservative financial press led by such papers as the *Wall Street Journal* and militant anti-British publications such as the *Chicago Tribune* and the *New York Daily News*.
[3] Quoted in a summary of American opinion by the U.S. Information Service (26 Aug. 1947).
[4] Frank Oliver in the *Sunday Times* (10 Aug. 1947).

debate on the Loan Agreement and which had been accelerated by the accumulating symptoms of political and economic imbalance. At the end of the war American opinion had tended to regard Britain as a political and economic rival, providing only somewhat less of a threat to American objectives than the Soviet Union itself. By the summer of 1947 a substantial change had taken place. Events had begun to show that Britain and the United States had similar interests throughout the world; that these interests were gravely threatened by the Soviet Union; and that Britain was America's most important ally in the job of containing Soviet power.

American opinion not only developed a greater awareness of the political importance of a strong and friendly Britain; it also began to make a more realistic estimate of British strength. At the end of the war Americans tended to regard Britain as one of the three great 'super-powers'. The extent to which the war had undermined the foundations of British strength and reduced its capacity to shoulder world-wide commitments was hardly realized. An outstanding example of this failure in American thinking was the fruitless Anglo-American controversy over the allocation of German occupation costs. Secretary of State James F. Byrnes had proposed an even split of Bizonia's external deficit, which had been estimated for 1947 at $400 million for the British zone and $200 million for the American. When Ernest Bevin, the British Foreign Minister, had said that Britain would be unable to shoulder such a burden, Byrnes had announced that the United States would bear an extra amount of the cost only if the United Kingdom agreed to exchange occupation zones. That, Byrnes recorded, gave Bevin a 'good answer' for his anxious Treasury advisers. 'I thought it unwise for Britain to be in the position of a poor relative or a junior partner by contributing less than 50 per cent. They are a proud people. It would be apt to cause irritation. It seemed much better to aid Britain in some other way.'[1]

Britain's sudden withdrawal from Greece and Turkey and the sharp deterioration of its economic position provided powerful antidotes to this sort of thinking. Britain's weakness and the threat this posed to American security was impressed not only on Administration leaders but on the public at large. *The New York Times*, in a notable editorial, summed up the changing mood:

The emergency in Britain has shocked this country. . . . It has suddenly projected before our imagination the picture of a world without British

[1] *Speaking Frankly* (New York, 1947), pp. 196–7.

power, without the balance wheel of British moderation, without the weight of Britain in the democratic scale.

The consequences to us of such a void in the economic and political universe in which we live are as alarming as was the fear of British defeat which impelled us to help Britain long before we were forced into open war. What we fought for was survival—the survival of the freedoms on which our system of government and way of life are based. Without these freedoms, we see even better now than then, America as we understand it could not live. But it is equally important to see that the same danger still exists in the perilous transition to peace. The gravest threat to the democratic system now lies in the discouragement of democratic peoples. If the British people lose courage, for example, lose incentive to go on fighting, lose the sense of invincibility they continue to feel in today's breakdown ... our democracy and the cause of democracy are immeasurably weakened in the world. The United States cannot let this happen.[1]

This new approach to Britain's difficulties produced a different attitude toward the Anglo-American Financial Agreement. 'The need of a Britain as economically strong as possible is a political need of the United States. If the operation of the British Loan Agreement weakens Britain as a world power, that will be to the United States' disadvantage.'[2] Such a formulation of the problem discouraged rigid enforcement of multilateral obligations. If convertibility could not be implemented without draining British reserves, then sympathetic consideration of its suspension was necessary.[3] If the sterling balances could not be scaled down without causing serious disaffection in strategic areas, then these political factors would have to be decisive.[4] If Britain could show that the 'dollar pool' and Imperial Preference contributed to its economic strength, then the United States would have to refrain from asking their elimination:

The nature of the changes [the British] ask in the [loan] agreement are in line with the latest developments in American trade policy ... Special trade arrangements now qualify for American approval when they can be shown to be beneficial to world trade. This throws a more favourable light on the 'sterling area' which Britain has just been forced officially to relin-

---

[1] 'We Stand By Britain' (14 Feb. 1947).

[2] 'Britain's Dollars: Make Them Last', *The Christian Science Monitor* (7 Aug. 1947).

[3] *The New York Times*, for example, suggested (19 July 1947) that Britain might have asked 'that the timetable for return to convertibility be slowed down'. The *Times* concluded: 'It would have had little difficulty in making a case for such a plea.'

[4] British policy toward the Indian and Egyptian balances was now held to touch 'the question of military security in the Middle East and Far East. ... Those who criticize it have not found alternatives to satisfy such men as Foreign Minister Ernest Bevin and Secretary of State George C. Marshall, who have heavy stakes in that part of the world.' Saville R. Davis, *The Christian Science Monitor* (28 Aug. 1947).

quish, and indeed even on the system of special trade preferences which has for years operated among the members of the British Commonwealth.[1]

Thus, when it came to a choice, American opinion subordinated the immediate enforcement of multilateralism to the political and economic interests of the Western World.

CONCLUSION

The Anglo-American Financial Agreement proved a defective instrument for the achievement of multilateral trade. By providing Britain with a considerable amount of dollar aid and by making detailed provision for the resumption of multilateralism it appeared to solve the transitional problem. This was a dangerous illusion: it encouraged the British and American Governments to regard as solved a problem they had only put off to the future. The dollar aid could not achieve its purpose unless Britain put a tight rein on domestic consumption and investment, unless the accumulated sterling balances were brought under control, unless the overseas sterling area maintained its war-time policy of restraint, and unless abuse of the convertibility privileges was avoided. Perhaps no Agreement, no matter how well drafted, could have achieved all these things in the conditions of the post-war world; but an effective instrument of Anglo-American collaboration would at least have alerted the two Governments to the dangers and enabled them to take common measures to forestall disaster. Thus, for example, it would have provided for joint consultation on the technical measures to implement convertibility and on the treatment of the accumulated sterling balances. Such consultation might not have brought a complete solution to these problems; but it would at least have initiated changes in the time-table for resuming multilateral trade. Instead, the Financial Agreement combined rigid deadlines for multilateralism with inadequate consultative machinery to ensure that the deadlines were met. It forced the two Governments to fence at long range over the interpretation of legal commitments, instead of enabling them to work together to solve their common problems. The result was an abortive attempt at multilateralism which sapped the political and economic strength of the free world and a false start which profoundly weakened the cause of multilateralism in Anglo-American opinion.

[1] *The Christian Science Monitor* (4 Aug. 1947).

It must be confessed, however, that the very failure of the Financial Agreement may have had some beneficial results. It dramatized the weakened economic position of Britain and spurred that country and other members of the sterling area to make necessary revisions in their internal and external economic policies. It impressed American opinion with the extent of British weakness and with the vital stake of the United States in the restoration of British power. Would it also stimulate some overdue adjustments in the system of Anglo-American economic collaboration? One anxiously hoped that it would. As *The Christian Science Monitor* put it:

Assessing blame is a profitless business, particularly if it provokes recriminations and hardens self-justification. But reviewing the loan's record of failures can help if it awakens in both countries a willingness to confess mistakes and an awareness that a far better effort must be made to understand the other's needs, feelings, and political difficulties.

Such progress could occur in three stages:

A first step should be more adequate realization of the urgency of Britain's need. A second should be better understanding of the fact that Britain is the key advance sector in the whole anti-Communist line. . . . The third step should be bold measures to help Britain hold the fort—not only by new financial advances but by such public understanding and official teamwork as produced the destroyer and Lend-Lease plans and won the war.[1]

The United States was on its way to negotiating these first two steps. It remained to be seen whether, in conjunction with Britain, it was capable of negotiating the third.

[1] 'For Bolder Aid to Britain', *The Christian Science Monitor* (28 Aug. 1947).

CHAPTER XVII

THE END OF THE I.T.O.

WE have observed the decline of two of the main instruments for the achievement of multilateral trade. It remains now to describe the fate of the third—the still uncompleted project for commercial collaboration aimed, among other things, at 'the reduction of tariffs and other trade barriers' and at 'the elimination of all forms of discriminatory treatment in international commerce'.[1] The extent of Anglo-American agreement on these objectives would be tested in three specific ways. First, there would be the round of tariff and preference bargaining whose results would be embodied in a General Agreement on Tariffs and Trade. Second, there would be the negotiations to complete the drafting of the Charter of the International Trade Organization. Third, there would be the campaign to win approval for the I.T.O. in Britain and the United States. These crucial tests of Anglo-American economic collaboration will form our next and final subject of concern.

TARIFFS AND PREFERENCES: THE DAY OF RECKONING

The terms of the tariff-preference settlement remained one of the great unresolved Anglo-American issues. On the level of general principle, agreement had already been achieved. The London Draft of the I.T.O. Charter had incorporated the basic provisions of the 'Proposals': no new preferences would be created nor existing preferences increased; reductions in the most-favoured-nation rate would automatically reduce the margins of preference; existing international commitments would not stand in the way of agreed reductions in preference. There was also agreement on the oldest and most basic commitment of all—the obligation (as it was now stated) to enter upon request into 'reciprocal and mutually advantageous negotiations . . . directed to the substantial reduction of tariffs . . . and to the elimination of import tariff preferences'.[2] But what would happen when the time came to implement this

---

[1] Article Seven of the Mutual Aid Agreement.

[2] London Draft, Article 24 (1). The same commitment was embodied in the final version of the I.T.O. Charter adopted at Havana, Article 17. *Havana Charter for an International Trade Organization*, Dept. of State Publ. 3206 (Washington, 1948).

commitment in actual negotiations? The answer would be given when the members of the Preparatory Committee arrived in Geneva in the spring of 1947 to negotiate the General Agreement on Tariffs and Trade.

The prelude to Geneva

Will Clayton and his State Department deputies looked forward to Geneva with considerable anticipation. They would bring with them the greatest tariff-reducing powers ever delegated to American representatives. They considered that their authority to reduce American tariffs to 50 per cent. of 1945 levels would make possible, if not the complete elimination of Imperial Preference, then at least the elimination of all the individual preferences which had been major obstacles to American export trade.

This eagerness to achieve the elimination of Imperial Preference was not just an expression of America's traditional hostility to trade discrimination. It was the result of a very contemporary political need. The Republican victory in the Congressional elections of 1946 posed a serious threat to the reciprocal trade agreements programme and the emerging Charter of the I.T.O. Clayton badly needed a major achievement to lay before Congress in the trade field. What he hoped for was nothing less than a front-page headline reading 'Empire Preference System Broken at Geneva'. As one observer put it, Clayton and his advisers would regard the Geneva Conference as a success 'only if the Imperial Preference system is thoroughly wrecked beyond hope of repair'.[1]

Now, as the Geneva Conference was about to begin, the Department of State went on record to this effect. The Republican-controlled Senate Finance Committee was questioning Harry Hawkins on the London Draft of the I.T.O. Senator Millikin, its new chairman and a lifelong opponent of liberal trade, recalled the obligations undertaken by Britain in Article Seven of the Mutual Aid Agreement. Would the Geneva Conference see the fulfilment of those obligations? Would it bring the elimination of Imperial Preference?

MR. HAWKINS. . . . In theory, you have not yet got absolute assurance that anything is going to happen to the British preferences. But in practical fact, something is going to happen, I am quite confident. If it did not happen, then this whole thing is in danger.

[1] Michael Hoffman, 'U.S. Due to Seek Tariff Showdown', *The New York Times* (19 Aug. 1947).

THE CHAIRMAN. I am very glad to have your frank recognition of that, and it follows from that that if it is the judgment of the Congress that nothing is going to happen, then there is no sense in proceeding with this organization.

MR. HAWKINS. The Congress will have a chance to judge that.[1]

A few minutes later the Committee was given more specific assurances:

THE CHAIRMAN. In other words, it follows that if these preferences cannot be eliminated there is no point in the Charter. Is that correct?

MR. HAWKINS. Yes; and the action contemplated on the tariffs. When you say eliminated, it does not necessarily follow that they will all be gone, but the parts that hurt will be gone. . . .

THE CHAIRMAN. But if the real substance of the preferences is not eliminated, there will be no point to the Charter and it will probably not come before the Congress.

MR. HAWKINS. I should think that would be it.[2]

The impression left by Hawkins's testimony was that the State Department considered the elimination of Imperial Preference the *sine qua non* of the I.T.O. This was most unfortunate. In Britain, the uncompromising supporters of Preference—the Conservative backbenchers, the Beaverbrook press, the British Empire League—were in a defiant mood. The Anglo-American Financial Agreement, with its appearance of bargaining commercial concessions for economic aid, had increased the virulence of their protests. One Member of Parliament now declared that there was 'nothing the United States could offer, no concession, that would justify one move towards the elimination . . . of Imperial Preference'.[3]

If the Government tries to eliminate Empire Preference a number of us will conduct such a nation-wide campaign in this country as will light the very beacons on the hills. We will attack them in the market place, in the towns and the cities, we will rouse this whole country against them in such a crusade as will overcome this Government, because we will not have it.[4]

Even more ominous than the increasing vehemence of traditional

---

[1] U.S. Congress, Senate, Committee on Finance, *International Trade Organization*, 80th Cong., 1st sess. (Mar.–Apr. 1947), p. 195.   [2] Id., p. 196.
[3] Beverley Baxter, 425 H.C. Deb. 1639 (19 July 1946).
[4] Id., col. 1639. An idea of the intensity of feeling of the Preference forces can be had by reading the literature put out during this period by the Empire Industries Association and the British Empire League. See also L. S. Amery, *The Washington Loan Agreements* (London, 1946); and Henry Drummond-Wolff, *British Declaration of Independence* (London, 1947).

spokesmen for Imperial Preference was the movement on the part of moderate opinion. Many who had supported the formula embodied in Article Seven and the 'Proposals' were becoming sceptical of its practical application in the Geneva negotiations. By the spring of 1947 it was doubtful that a majority of either political party would support anything approaching the elimination of Preference in the circumstances that now prevailed. The very distinction between tariffs and preferences, so important a part of the war-time agreements, seemed to have been forgotten. The retrogression had gone so far that on the eve of the Geneva negotiations *The Times* could describe as an 'evident and outstanding weakness' of the American approach the 'refusal to treat tariffs and preferences on an equal footing'.[1] It added that 'this has given rise to the *remarkable* formula that the object of these negotiations is the "reduction" of tariffs and the "elimination" of preferences. To this doctrine, in its full literal interpretation, *Britain could not in practice agree for obvious reasons. . . .*'[2]

The hardening of British opinion on Imperial Preference was encouraged by three contemporary developments in American policy. The first was the Republican victory in the Congressional elections. This event was widely interpreted to mean that the United States was no longer prepared to abide by its part of the Article Seven bargain—in short, that there would not be the 'substantial' reduction in American tariffs which was promised in return for the elimination of Preference: 'The ascendancy of Mr. Cordell Hull in American thinking on tariffs is over. The high-tariff party is back. . . . The condition of an American low-tariff policy under which Britain agreed to abjure "discriminatory practices" is unlikely to materialise.'[3] Churchill made a notable speech in the House of Commons in which he contrasted American assertions that Britain was committed to the elimination of Preference with the high-tariff reputation of the Republican Party:

It would be a great surprise to me, at least, if a Republican Congress were to embrace Free Trade so wholeheartedly, completely, and passionately, and to promote such a casting down of tariff walls of all kinds as to call in question, even as a matter of discussion, the comparatively small, modest Preference duties which have been built up in the British Commonwealth of Nations, which have become part of our supreme common life and which are even more important to us as symbols of our indissoluble

---

[1] (10 Apr. 1947).   [2] Italics supplied. Ibid.
[3] 'The Republicans Return', *The Economist*, cli (1946), p. 738.

union than for their commercial advantages, which are, none the less, considerable.[1]

The second development in American policy that helped to harden British opinion on Imperial Preference was President Truman's directive of February 1947 on the administration of the trade-agreements programme.[2] This directive was designed to appease Republican leaders who had doubts about the Reciprocal Trade Agreements Act and the tariff bargaining scheduled to begin at Geneva. But in actual fact it involved no very serious compromise with protectionist opinion. The President rejected the proposal by Senators Vandenberg and Millikin that all future tariff concessions should be limited in advance by a Tariff Commission determination of the 'peril points' beyond which they could not go without injury to a domestic industry.[3] His directive incorporated only their second proposal—that the Administration should insert an 'escape clause' in every trade agreement providing for the withdrawal or modification of concessions which caused or threatened to cause such injury.

How important a change did this directive represent? As we noted earlier, the Administration had already adopted the practice of inserting an escape clause into its trade agreements; in asking additional tariff-reducing powers in 1945 it had promised to continue to do so. Moreover, the escape clause provided in Truman's directive was closely circumscribed. It could be invoked to withdraw or modify a concession only when foreign goods were being imported in increased quantities, when such imports were the result of the tariff concession, and when they caused or threatened to cause 'serious injury' to a domestic industry.[4] Withdrawal or modification of a concession was allowed only to the extent and for such time as was necessary to prevent the injury. In just one respect did the directive suggest a retreat to a less liberal trade policy. It transferred the administration of the escape clause from an inter-departmental executive committee to the Tariff Commission, an organization which was likely to be more receptive to complaints from domestic

[1] 430 H.C. Deb. 21–22 (12 Nov. 1946).

[2] Executive Order 9832 Prescribing Procedures for the Administration of the Reciprocal Trade Agreements Program, February 25, 1947, 12 *Fed. Reg.* 1363.

[3] Joint Statement by Chairman of the Senate Foreign Relations Committee (Vandenberg) and the Chairman of the Senate Finance Committee (Millikin) on Reciprocal Trade Agreements, February 7, 1947, 93 *Cong. Rec.* 957 (10 Feb. 1947).

[4] The importance of these criteria can be seen from the fact that in the period 1947–53 they were satisfied on only six occasions on items accounting for a total of only $3 million in import trade.

producers. But this was an inadequate basis for saying that the directive was a fundamental departure from previous policy.

British opinion, unfortunately, found little consolation in these facts. *The Economist* called the order 'a very sad relapse from recent practice'[1] and the 'worst possible introduction to the Geneva talks next month'.[2] It attached little importance to the limitations governing use of the clause and envisaged a 'clamour which will greet the Tariff Commission on every occasion that domestic trade shows some signs of falling away, on each occasion that an individual business finds that it has fallen below its sales quota'.[3] Robert Boothby, ignoring the careful language of the directive entirely, told the House of Commons that the United States could now 'terminate any concession which, in fact, increases American imports'.[4] For weeks after its publication the directive was the subject of Parliamentary criticism and several Members declared flatly that it made 'nonsense' of the whole programme of commercial collaboration.[5]

The third development in American trade policy that alienated British opinion was the conclusion of the U.S.–Philippine trade agreement of 1946. Before receiving their independence the Philippines had occupied a position within the American customs area, so that Philippine goods entered duty-free into the United States. It was considered that the sudden termination of this status would produce very grave disturbances on the Philippine economy. The U.S.–Philippine agreement was designed to provide a period of transition to full tariff autonomy. It provided that existing American tariff rates would be put gradually into effect on Philippine goods to the extent of 5 per cent. a year over a period of twenty years. This was clearly a preferential tariff arrangement, albeit a temporary one.

The U.S.–Philippine trade agreement was widely cited in Britain along with the U.S.–Cuba preference system as yet another departure by the United States from the letter of its own law. Lennox-Boyd quoted Truman's statement that 'the political independence of the Philippines is totally inadequate without economic stability' and exclaimed 'well, that has been our argument throughout, justifying Imperial Preference in the Colonies and Dominions'.[6] He concluded that the new agreement 'absolutely knocks the bottom out of any

---

[1] clii (1947), p. 330. [2] 'The Vandenberg Tariff', clii (1947), p. 377.
[3] Ibid. [4] 434 H.C. Deb. 1066 (10 Mar. 1947).
[5] Walter Elliot, 435 H.C. Deb. 874 (24 Mar. 1947). A similar viewpoint was expressed by Douglas Dodds-Parker and Sir Peter Bennett, id., cols. 947 and 980.
[6] 425 H.C. Deb. 1630 (19 July 1946).

A a

argument that we are under a moral obligation to abrogate Imperial Preference. . . . I hope, fortified by extracts of that kind, the Financial Secretary will go to the forthcoming trade talks with America determined to keep our Imperial Preference, and to use to them some of the arguments that have been used to justify this agreement with a foreign country.'[1]

The full measure of the difficulty that would confront the United States in seeking the elimination of Imperial Preference was made dramatically apparent in the Parliamentary debate held shortly before the opening of the Geneva Conference.[2] A coalition of Conservatives and left-wing Labourites put the Government squarely on the defensive. These critics announced their opposition to the tariff-preference formula laid down in Article Seven, the 'Proposals', and the draft I.T.O. Charter; they demanded to know whether, in the forthcoming tariff bargaining, the Government was really intending to carry it out. 'If, in the opinion of the Government', Beverley Baxter asked, 'the advantages offered in world trade are great enough, will the Government then consider the absolute elimination of Imperial Preference with all that elimination will mean? Will they go as far as elimination if, in their opinion, they are getting a bargain which is worth it?'[3] Surely, if the tariff-preference formula meant anything at all, there would have to be an affirmative answer to this question. Yet Sir Stafford Cripps, President of the Board of Trade, said simply: 'If the Hon. Member is speaking of the elimination of all preferences, we do not see any prospect of anything of that sort happening.'[4] What, then, was meant by the 'elimination of import tariff preferences'? In British minds the distinction between tariffs and preferences seemed to have been entirely obscured. Harold Wilson, summing up for the Government, now described the forthcoming negotiations as merely 'a continuation of the trade negotiation of 1938 with America . . . a negotiation in which we *reduced* . . . preferences in return for a reduction in United States tariffs'![5] These assurances helped to quiet Parliamentary misgivings. But the day of reckoning was now at hand.

The day of reckoning

In April 1947 the world's major trading nations gathered in Geneva for tariff bargaining on the largest scale ever attempted. To a

[1] Id., cols. 1629–31.   [2] 435 H.C. Deb. 865–999 (24 Mar. 1947).
[3] Id., col. 892.   [4] Ibid.   [5] Italics supplied. Id., cols. 994–5.

considerable extent the success of this bargaining would depend on the tariff-preference settlement worked out between the Commonwealth and the United States. The opening events were not encouraging. The leader of the British delegation, Sir Stafford Cripps, told a press conference that even if the American negotiators offered to reduce all tariffs by 50 per cent.—the full extent of their authority—Britain would still be unwilling to eliminate Imperial Preference.[1] This unsettling announcement had hardly been made when the conference was threatened from another quarter. In mid-June, after several weeks of debate, the American Congress passed a bill providing price supports for the domestic wool industry and an increase in the wool tariff. The Congressional action cast a pall over the Geneva negotiations. Wool was one of the most important American import items on which concessions were desired. Several delegations, including those of the United Kingdom and Australia, threatened to bolt the conference if the wool bill became law.

Clayton had to move rapidly to avert disaster. He flew to Washington and forcibly told the President that passage of the wool bill would wreck the Geneva conference and set back the whole liberal trade programme. In the end, Truman vetoed the bill. He also authorized Clayton to offer a 25 per cent. reduction in the existing duty. Adjournment of the Geneva Conference was thus averted. But the incident raised additional doubts about the capacity of the United States to make good on its commercial policy promises.

These events were only the beginning of the difficulty. When the negotiators began to trade offers on tariffs and preferences it quickly became apparent that there was no meeting of minds on the *quid pro quo* that was to make possible the 'reduction' of tariffs and the 'elimination' of preferences. The disagreement was very largely an Anglo-American affair since the Dominions did not, for the most part, show their former enthusiasm for the Preference system. It was political developments in Britain and the United States that now imposed the gravest obstacle to a satisfactory settlement. This obstacle was made more serious by the lack of very close personal relations between the British and American negotiators. Meade and Hawkins, two of the most important figures in the war-time talks, had come to be most cordial friends. No such *rapport*, unfortunately, now existed between their successors. Here was another major factor working for the breakdown of the tariff-preference formula.

[1] *The Manchester Guardian* (12 Apr. 1947).

The course of the negotiations can be quickly summarized. The American delegates offered tariff reductions of 50 per cent.—the full extent of their authority—on a wide range of import items. In return they were offered mainly bindings of existing preferences and hardly any elimination of preferences at all. The British offers with respect to the preferences which Britain enjoyed in other parts of the Empire were particularly disappointing. Most of the offers were for a reduction of less than one-third in the preference margin. Complete elimination of preference was offered on only two items—salmon and motorcycles—which comprised (according to American calculations) only 0·04 per cent. of Empire imports from the United States! In the opinion of the Americans, the British offers did not represent any appreciable progress toward the elimination of the Preference system.

Now, in the hard light of practical bargaining, the durability of the war-time consensus was put to the test. Clayton cited the words of Article Seven and the 'Proposals'. In his view they meant that if the United States would liquidate the Smoot-Hawley tariff Britain would liquidate Imperial Preference. The United States, he declared, was now offering, not simply to liquidate Smoot-Hawley, but to return to the relatively low tariff rates of 1913. There could be no doubt, therefore, that the elimination of Preference was finally in order.

Sir Stafford Cripps firmly resisted this interpretation. He too cited the terms of the Anglo-American agreements. He reminded Clayton that the concessions had to be 'mutually advantageous'—not just in terms of paper concessions, but in terms of trade likely to flow. Already, he said, Britain was at a disadvantage: while preferences were permanently bound against increase American tariff concessions were bound only for three-year periods and even then could be withdrawn at any time under the escape clause. If all these factors were taken into account, Cripps declared, it would be clear that the offers made by the United Kingdom were entirely consistent with its solemn obligations.

News of this deadlock soon began to darken reports from the Geneva Conference. The American public was told that Britain was backing out of its commitments to eliminate Imperial Preference and that its 'persistent refusal to bargain realistically' was 'threatening to make a farce' out of the attempt to lower trade barriers.[1] The

---

[1] Hoffman, 'British Accused of Stalling in Tariff Parley at Geneva', *The New York Times* (8 Aug. 1947). See also 'Imperial Trade Preferences Balk U.S. Aims', *The New York Herald-Tribune* (31 July 1947).

British public was told that the American tariff offers were never 'substantial enough in terms of the additional trade likely to flow to justify the "elimination" of any large number of preferences . . .'.[1] One British newspaper announced with finality that the tariff-preference settlement envisaged at the time of the Loan Agreement had been 'postponed if not jettisoned *sine die*'.[2]

Everything conspired now to aggravate the tariff-preference impasse. Britain's economic fortunes reached their lowest ebb in these unfortunate summer months. Resentment was increasing against the terms of the American Loan. The public was in no mood to accept new demands for non-discrimination:

> Though greater reductions [in preferences] might have been possible in more normal circumstances, it is considered that, having regard to Britain's balance of payments difficulties, this is about the worst moment for surrendering safeguards of any kind, and particularly those that derive from Imperial Preference. It is also recalled that the United States has twice before imposed conditions that could not be fulfilled—namely, the instance, first, of non-discrimination in the Loan Agreement, and secondly, of convertibility.[3]

The British representatives at Geneva served clear notice of the nation's mood. Harold Wilson declared that Britain's economic difficulties would not permit it, for some time at least, to embrace any more obligations of multilateral trade. Indeed, he warned that

> . . . the methods we may have to use in the intervening months and years may appear to be opposed to the principles of the Draft [I.T.O.] Charter. Many of us will certainly have to assist our position by agreements with particular countries, some of whom are represented here. . . . *In our own case we shall find it necessary and desirable to have even closer economic co-operation with other countries of the Commonwealth.*[4]

The American delegation at Geneva was now in a difficult position. Congress had been given the impression that Britain would eliminate Imperial Preference. The British Government was refusing to do so. What would be the consequences of this refusal? The co-operation of Congress would be needed to facilitate modifications in the Anglo-American Financial Agreement. It would be needed also to pass the programme of Marshall Aid, of which Britain would be a major beneficiary. For these reasons Clayton considered greater Preference

---

[1] *The Times* (3 Oct. 1947). See also *The Economist* (14 June 1947), p. 941.
[2] The *Glasgow Herald* (25 Aug. 1947).   [3] *The Times* (1 Oct. 1947).
[4] Italics supplied. Preparatory Committee of the United Nations Conference on Trade and Employment, First and Second Sessions, Plenary Meetings, *Verbatim Records*, E/PC/T/PV.2/6, p. 31.

concessions an absolute necessity. But if the elimination of Imperial Preference was a political necessity for Clayton, its maintenance was just as great a necessity for the British leaders. A substantial element in both Britain's major parties now desired not simply the maintenance, but even the increase, of Commonwealth economic ties. The Conservative Party's Annual Conference resolved with enthusiasm that 'trade between different parts of the Empire shall not be hampered by any agreement with any foreign power'.[1] And Ernest Bevin, the Labour Government's Foreign Minister, now proposed an Empire Customs Union as a way out of Britain's economic difficulties.[2]

Faced with the impossibility of reaching immediate agreement, the State Department sought a formula which would avoid the need for immediate British action but would give to the American public the appearance of preserving in principle the advantages that had been claimed for Article Seven and the 'Proposals'. Clayton made a 'final offer'—a three year moratorium on the elimination of Preference followed by step-by-step elimination over a period not to exceed ten years. In the latter part of September even this proposal was rejected by the British Cabinet. A carefully composed reply declared that Britain could not promise now to eliminate Preference at some specified future time in complete ignorance of the economic conditions that would then prevail and of the concessions that would be offered in return. The note added, however, that Britain would be ready for further discussions on tariffs and preferences after as short an interval as three years in the light of all the circumstances prevailing at that time.

This posed an ugly dilemma for Clayton and his colleagues. Either they would accept an agreement without much progress toward the elimination of Preference or they would have no agreement at all. After anxious deliberation they decided to choose the former alternative. It was simply not worth breaking up the Geneva Conference over the issue of Imperial Preference. Such a dramatic failure would have a far worse effect on American opinion than the failure to eliminate Imperial Preference. Accordingly, the two Governments set about to put as good a face as possible on their tariff-preference differences. The United States accepted the modest concessions offered by Britain in the preferences Britain enjoyed in the

---

[1] *The Times* (13 Oct. 1947).

[2] Id. (4 Sept. 1947). Since there was not the slightest practical prospect of a customs union between the Commonwealth countries Bevin's proposal amounted to a call for a reinforced system of Imperial Preference.

Dominions.[1] By way of compensation the Dominions agreed to greater reductions in the preferences they enjoyed in the United Kingdom. In this way, at the last moment, the Geneva Conference was finally saved.

On 29 October 1947 Harold Wilson announced the terms of the tariff-preference agreement in the House of Commons. He declared that the Geneva negotiations had not weakened 'in any way' the economic arrangements that had been developed between the nations of the British Commonwealth.[2] A White Paper presented to Parliament a few weeks later repeated this assurance. It reported that the concessions made by Britain and the other members of the Commonwealth did not 'by any means involve an abandonment of the essential structure' of Imperial Preference.[3] But an aroused public opinion was not so easily appeased. It had been widely reported that the United States was threatening to withhold Marshall Aid unless greater Preference concessions were received.[4] *The Economist* declared that Britain's consent to the tariff-preference settlement had been 'only secured by threats'.[5] And the more extreme supporters of Imperial Preference, unimpressed by the modest nature of the Preference concessions, now exclaimed: 'The Big Bad Bargain is sealed! The Big Black Pact is made! . . . The citadel of Imperial Preference is breached.'[6]

The State Department did its best to conceal its disappointment at the final terms of the tariff-preference settlement. It announced that preferences had been 'substantially reduced' on a 'significant part' of American trade and entirely eliminated 'on a considerable list of products which the United States exports'.[7] These claims seemed rather ambitious, in view of the facts. Although reductions of some significance had been achieved in preferences enjoyed by Commonwealth countries in the United Kingdom, the United States had made very little progress in eliminating preferences enjoyed by

[1] These concessions had been increased slightly from the extremely small offers made at the beginning of the negotiations.

[2] 443 H.C. Deb. 879 (29 Oct. 1947).   [3] Cmd. 7258 of 1947, p. vi.

[4] See, for example, 'Cut Tariffs—Or No Aid, Says U.S.', the *News Chronicle* (11 Oct. 1947). For a survey of British opinion on this point, see Saville R. Davis, *The Christian Science Monitor* (26 Sept. 1947).

[5] 'Mr. Clayton Goes', cliii (1947), p. 630.

[6] The *Daily Express* (18 Nov. 1947). See also Empire Industries Association and British Empire League, *The Geneva Trade Agreement*, Monthly Bulletin No. 81 (Nov.–Dec. 1947).

[7] U.S. Department of State, *Analysis of the General Agreement on Tariffs and Trade*, Dept. of State Publ. 2983 (Washington, 1947), p. 1.

Britain in the Commonwealth countries. Preferential margins remained unchanged on items accounting for 70 per cent. of Britain's
pre-war exports to the Commonwealth which were subject to Preference.[1] Preferences were terminated completely on items accounting
for only 5 per cent. of Britain's exports receiving preferential treatment. This was a very small step in the direction of the 'elimination'
of Imperial Preference that had been forecast in the earlier Anglo-
American economic agreements.

TABLE 7

The Elimination of Preferences Granted by Commonwealth Countries
to the United Kingdom

	Total value of preferences guaranteed to United Kingdom in 1938	Percentage reduced by less than 35%	Percentage reduced by 35% or more	Percentage eliminated	Percentage unaffected
	£ million	*Percentage*			
Canada . . .	16	27	11	18	44
Australia . . .	35	17	3	1	79
New Zealand . .	21	11	24	2	63
South Africa . .	15	..	8	3	89
India and Pakistan .	7	21	2	13	64
Total . . .	94	15	10	5	70

Note: Percentages are based on U.K.–Commonwealth trade in 1938.
Source: Cmd. 7258.

Thus, in the last analysis, there was little practical benefit from the
tariff-preference distinction on which the United States had placed
such great importance. The emphasis on the 'elimination' of Preference
served only to antagonize British opinion and to distract attention from
the broader aspects of the Geneva settlement. Taken as a whole, the
gains from this settlement were not insubstantial. The United States
had made concessions—often up to the full limit of 50 per cent.—on
import items worth $1,766·5 million in 1939.[2] In return, the United
States had received concessions on export items worth $1,192 million
in 1939.[3] The concessions made by the United States brought the

[1] See Table 7.
[2] This was 78 per cent. of total U.S. imports in that year. Department of State,
op. cit., p. 133.   [3] Ibid.

American tariff to its lowest level since the comparatively moderate Underwood Tariff of 1913. How much trade would be facilitated by these concessions was not yet clear, in view of the still substantial height of many American duties and the wide use of direct controls by other countries. But a good beginning toward trade liberalization had nevertheless been made.

There was still another ground for satisfaction. The General Agreement on Tariffs and Trade had an importance that went far beyond the specific tariff and preference concessions. It provided a forum for the discussion of trade problems and a mechanism by which the Contracting Parties could modify their tariff concessions in the light of changing economic and political conditions. It also provided a set of commercial policy principles to assure that the tariff concessions were not offset by other instruments of trade restriction. In most cases the G.A.T.T. rules were simply a shortened version of principles already incorporated in the Draft Charter of the I.T.O. They would be superseded once the I.T.O. itself came into existence. Once again, therefore, we must return to the negotiations on this latter project.

THE COMPLETION OF THE CHARTER

The final drafting of the I.T.O. Charter took place at two long and arduous sessions of the Preparatory Committee—the first at Geneva in the spring of 1947, the second at Havana the following winter. These negotiations met their greatest difficulty on two unresolved issues of decisive importance for Anglo-American commercial collaboration. The first, to which we have already had occasion to refer, was the issue of discrimination in the use of quantitative restrictions. The second, which we have not yet mentioned, concerned the special exceptions designed to promote the development of under-developed countries.[1]

Exceptions for discrimination

The London Conference had reached general agreement on the subject of quantitative restrictions to protect the balance of payments. At Geneva and Havana the central issue became discrimination in the use of these restrictions. As we have seen, the gathering economic

---

[1] In addition to sources specifically cited the author has drawn in the following sections upon information provided in William Adams Brown, *The United States and the Restoration of World Trade* (Washington, 1950).

crisis was undermining support for non-discrimination in the United Kingdom. The British Government was resisting American demands for the elimination of Preference and was soon to seek modification of the non-discrimination clause of the Anglo-American Financial Agreement. It also decided to propose alterations in the non-discrimination provisions of the London Draft Charter.

The London Draft permitted an I.T.O. member to discriminate in the use of quantitative restrictions where the discrimination provided the member with additional imports and the quantitative restrictions were equivalent to exchange restrictions permitted to that member under the transitional provisions of the International Monetary Fund. Before 31 December 1951 departures from the rule of non-discrimination were to be reviewed by the I.T.O. 'with a view to the earliest possible elimination of discriminations . . . which restrict the expansion of world trade'.[1] In the months that elapsed between the London and Geneva Conferences the British Government decided that these provisions were badly suited to British needs. Under the Anglo-American Financial Agreement Britain had foresworn resort to the transitional provisions of the Fund Articles. Therefore it would be the one country prevented from discrimination under the generous exception of the London Draft. As sterling became convertible, it might find itself severely discriminated against on all sides without being able to discriminate in return. The British Government was also uneasy about the provision for a review of discrimination after 31 December 1951. There was a growing fear that the transition to multilateralism might require a longer period. As Sir James Helmore, the British delegate at Geneva put it, 'for the countries advancing this Charter to take it upon themselves to say that by 31st December 1951 all discriminations will be wrong, when we have admitted that throughout 1948–49–50 some of them may be right, seems to me to be attaching to ourselves altogether too much importance'.[2]

The American delegates, however, opposed any major change in the London formula. They complained that they were already under attack from domestic critics for having permitted too much freedom to discriminate. It was one thing, the Americans argued, to permit discrimination in a carefully defined transition period; it was another to permit countries to go on accumulating inconvertible currencies

---

[1] London Draft, Article 28 (3).
[2] Second Session of the Preparatory Committee, Commission A, *Verbatim Records* (9 July 1947), PC/T/A/PV. 28, p. 35.

and discriminating into the indefinite future. There was no justification for any further loosening of the London provisions. In the American view, 'the achievement of expansion of trade and the achievement of non-discrimination are the same thing . . . an attempt to secure more international trade by methods of discrimination is an illusory pursuit . . .'.[1]

The majority of the delegates at Geneva now regarded this formulation with extreme scepticism. They regarded the non-discrimination clause of the Anglo-American Financial Agreement as an object-lesson for future policy. The I.T.O. Charter, they argued, should not be made so restrictive. As the French delegate put it, 'I think the experience of the past years has shown that the obligations of the United Kingdom to act according to the provisions of Article 27[2] has somewhat delayed the restoration of Europe'.[3] Despite American objections, the provisions on discrimination were thoroughly revised. Countries were no longer required to discriminate in a manner equivalent to the discrimination permitted under the Fund Articles. They were now permitted to relax quantitative restrictions in a discriminatory manner without regard to the restrictions permitted by the Fund, provided only that in so doing they obtained additional imports above the total they could obtain by adhering to the rule of non-discrimination.[4] Nevertheless, some limitations on discrimination were maintained. In carrying out discrimination under this new provision countries were obliged to act in accordance with a number of carefully enumerated (if rather ambiguous) criteria—for example, they were not to obtain the additional imports 'as part of an arrangement by which the gold or convertible currency which the Member Country receives directly or indirectly from its exports to other Members not party to the arrangements is appreciably reduced below the level it could otherwise have been reasonably expected to attain'.[5] Moreover, discrimination was permitted only 'when substantial and widespread disequilibrium prevails in international trade and payments'.[6] Perhaps most important, the I.T.O. was empowered to

---

[1] George Bronz before Commission A (9 July 1947), PC/T/A/PV. 29, p. 16.
[2] The non-discrimination clause of the London Draft.
[3] M. Baraduc, before Commission A (9 July 1947), PC/T/A/PV. 28, p. 25.
[4] Geneva Draft, Article 23, 1 (b).
[5] Article 23, 1 (b) (ii). Other criteria were that the prices of goods so imported should not be 'substantially higher' than those prevailing for comparable goods available from other members and that the discrimination should not cause 'unnecessary damage' to the interests of other members. Article 23, 1 (b) (i) and (iii).
[6] Article 23, 1 (a) and (b).

request the removal of discriminatory restrictions after 1 March 1952.[1]

At the Havana Conference Britain and other countries sought a further loosening of the rules of non-discrimination. When the Conference began in the autumn of 1947 there were few countries besides the United States who were willing to accept non-discrimination even at the end of a transition period. Some countries wanted to return to the London formula with its reference to the transitional provisions of the Fund. Perhaps they proposed this on the theory that there was now little prospect that the Fund would achieve the early elimination of transitional restrictions! But the London formula was still unacceptable to the United Kingdom. Thus a labyrinthian set of provisions had to be worked out whereby countries could choose either the Geneva formula or the London formula as adopted with modifications at Havana.[2] The United Kingdom also wanted to liberalize the Geneva formula itself. Once again it sought to eliminate the provision for a review date. Once again the United States objected. The review date was retained.[3] Despite British objections, the final version of the I.T.O. Charter at least embodied the principle that discrimination was only a transitional device.

Months of negotiation at Geneva and Havana on the discriminatory use of quantitative restrictions had brought the Preparatory Commission substantially back to its London formula. But now the articles on non-discrimination were a good deal more complicated. They contained something to please—but also to offend—nearly everybody. On the one hand, they paid tribute to the principle of non-discrimination and provided for review of departures from that principle after 1 March 1952. On the other hand, they allowed wide scope for discrimination during the transition period—with no assurance that the transition period would ever end. It had been hoped that these provisions might provide a framework in which discrimination could be harmoniously discussed. Unfortunately they were more likely to cause widespread antagonism without offering any workable standards for the guidance of national policy.

Exceptions for economic development

So far we have discussed the drafting of the I.T.O. Charter only in terms of the Anglo-American issues. This has meant the omission

---

[1] Article 23, 3 (c).
[2] Havana Charter, Article 23 and Annex K.   [3] Article 23, 1 (g).

of many important subjects covered in the Charter but not strictly within the scope of the present study. One of these must now engage our attention, for it did much to determine the fate of the Charter in the United States—the special exceptions to multilateralism inserted in the name of economic development.

Up to the time of the London Conference the subject of economic development had played a comparatively minor role in Anglo-American planning. Neither Government had taken very serious account of the ambitious programmes of industrialization announced by the under-developed countries and the implications of such programmes for financial or commercial policy. No attempt had been made to establish an institution providing aid in the amounts and on the credit terms required to speed development in some of the backward areas.[1] But once it was decided to seek the adherence of the under-developed countries to a code of multilateral principles in the field of commercial policy their demands could no longer be ignored.

At London the under-developed countries, led by Australia, India, Brazil, and Chile, had made a broad attack on the Anglo-American principles. In their view the 'Proposals' and the 'Suggested Charter' took inadequate account of development problems. They fought successfully to insert a special section in the Draft Charter proclaiming that economic development was a primary objective of the I.T.O. and that its promotion was the responsibility of the industrially advanced countries as well as the under-developed countries themselves. Now, at Geneva and Havana, the under-developed countries advanced a number of specific exceptions to the commercial policy rules to safeguard their national plans for economic development. The United States and Britain joined forces in opposing these exceptions. The resulting controversy threatened to destroy the whole project for commercial collaboration.

One of the principal exceptions, ironically, was provoked by the United States itself. The chapter on economic development inserted at London contained vague references to the rights and obligations of capital-exporting and capital-importing countries, but no specific provisions about standards of treatment of private investment. American business groups complained about this omission. Accord-

---

[1] The International Bank might have been made to serve this purpose, but in the months preceding the Bretton Woods Conference the British and American Governments were disposed to restrict rather than expand its functions. See Chapter VII, *supra*.

ingly, with some misgivings, the United States delegation came to Geneva with a new draft article on foreign investment. The result was the very opposite of what was hoped would be achieved. The under-developed countries filled the article with broad exceptions assert-ing the right to place all kinds of restrictions on foreign investment, even the right to expropriate particular investments without paying compensation for the full value of the investments and without com-pensating the foreign owners in convertible currency or in the currency of their respective countries.[1] To the American delegates it seemed as if the Geneva Draft on investment, 'instead of promising to stimulate the flow of private capital, threatened to check it'.[2] At Havana the entire subject had to be reopened. Although some objectionable parts of the Geneva version were removed, the final provisions at Havana still did more to affirm the right of under-developed countries to interfere with investments than it did to affirm the rights of the investors themselves.[3]

The investment provisions were not the only source of difficulty. The under-developed countries also sought to achieve a sweeping ex-ception to the provisions on tariff preferences. They sought a special authorization for regional preferences to promote economic develop-ment. Their arguments for such preferences were aided not a little by the broad exceptions already allowed for existing preferences of the more mature countries, such as the Imperial Preference system. At Geneva the under-developed countries succeeded in inserting an entirely new article permitting new regional preferences subject to the prior approval of two-thirds of the members of the I.T.O.[4] At Havana even the safeguard of prior approval was substantially weakened. In its final form the article provided for automatic approval by the Organization upon a finding that a regional agreement conformed to certain standards about the size of the preferences created, the

[1] Geneva Draft, Article 12, para. 2 (a) (iv) and (b). An interpretative note to this Article explained that 'just compensation' would be judged 'from the point of view both of the payer and the receiver, and . . . compensation would not be payable where, because of a violation of a law in force, property has been forfeited or taken under public management or occupation whether by executive action in accordance with pre-existing law or as a penalty under judicial procedure'. It was also stated that the obligation of a member to pay 'just compensation' was 'essentially an obligation to make payment in the local currency of that member'.

[2] Clair Wilcox, *A Charter for World Trade* (New York, 1949), p. 146.

[3] Without prejudice to existing international agreements, a capital-importing coun-try retained the right, *inter alia*, (1) to 'prescribe and give effect on just terms to requirements as to the ownership of existing and future investments' and (2) to 'determine whether and to what extent and upon what terms it will allow future foreign investment . . .'. Havana Charter, Article 12, 1 (c) (ii) and (iii).

[4] Geneva Draft, Article 15. This was, of course, an exception to the 'no new prefer-ence' rule which the United States regarded as vitally important.

duration of the agreement, and notice and negotiation with countries affected by the agreement.[1]

The third and most serious controversy arose over the demands of the under-developed countries for quantitative restrictions. At London they had gained permission to employ special quantitative restrictions to promote economic development. With respect to restrictions imposed upon commodities covered by trade agreements, however, they were obliged to negotiate with countries having rights under those agreements. With respect to restrictions imposed upon commodities not covered by trade agreements, they were obliged to ask the approval of the affected members or of the Organization itself.[2] The Geneva Draft now introduced the principle of automatic approval for restrictions of the latter type upon a finding that such restrictions were unlikely to be more restrictive of trade than any other reasonable or practical alternatives and were suited to the economic needs of the industry and the member concerned.[3] It also granted authority for the immediate imposition of quantitative restrictions to prevent a rush of imports pending decision by the I.T.O.[4]

At Havana the under-developed countries asked still greater authority to impose quantitative restrictions. Some argued for complete freedom to exclude luxuries and products competitive with the products of their new industries. This pressed the American delegation to the breaking point. Clair Wilcox, its Vice-Chairman, employed the bluntest language yet used by an American delegate in the I.T.O. negotiations:

> The debate in this committee seems to have proceeded on the assumption that the smaller countries and the weaker countries will be accorded complete freedom to employ QR[5] while the larger and the stronger ones will voluntarily forego its use. This, I fear, is the sheerest fantasy. . . . If we are to arm the nations of the world with this 'weapon' of QR and send them into economic battle, the advantages will not be with the smaller and the weaker adversaries. It will be with the big and the strong. . . .
>
> My Government offered, in the proposals which it published in December of 1945, to enter into an international agreement under which it would surrender its freedom to use QR for protective purposes. It maintained this offer at London. It maintained it at Geneva. It will maintain it at Havana. If this offer is accepted, no nation need fear that the United States will ever employ QR in ways that would be harmful to them. But if the offer is rejected, what then?

[1] Havana Charter, Article 15.   [2] London Draft, Article 13 (3).
[3] Geneva Draft, Article 13, 4 (b).   [4] Id., Article 13, 4 (c).
[5] Quantitative restrictions.

If the offer were rejected, I assure you that my Government would do everything within its power to prevent the general employment of QR by the United States. But I cannot assure you that it would succeed. For as QR spreads around the world, and as one group after another in the United States came to feel its effects, there would be angry reactions and insistent demands for retaliation. If QR were everywhere accepted in principle and widely employed in practice, it is less than likely that these demands could be resisted. If the United States, however reluctantly and however tardily, were to join in the procession that marched behind the banner of QR, how would this affect the welfare of the other countries of the world?[1]

These words helped curb the more extreme proposals for greater freedom in the use of quantitative restrictions. But they could not work a miracle. The Havana Charter ended up with all the leeway for quantitative restrictions on behalf of development that had been incorporated in the Geneva Draft. It even contained some additional freedom. With respect to restrictions on commodities not covered by trade agreements the I.T.O. was now required to give its automatic approval if any of a number of specified conditions was fulfilled—among them that the industry in question was established between 1939 and 1948.[2] This would permit the use of restrictions to protect uneconomic industries started during the war or early post-war period. It was a major compromise of the multilateral conceptions shared by Britain and the United States.

In Havana, on 23 March 1948, Will Clayton delivered a speech at the final signing of the I.T.O. Charter:

This is a day for history. There have been other conferences on international affairs, but none of them has undertaken a task so difficult as the one that is completed here today. None of them has come to an arrangement concerning so many vital economic interests of so many states. None of them has produced a document so comprehensive as the Havana Charter for World Trade. Few, if any, of them have attained so notable a measure of success.[3]

It remained to be seen whether the work of Havana would be so well regarded in Britain and the United States.

[1] Quoted in U.S. Congress, Committee on Foreign Affairs, *International Trade Organization—An Appraisal of the Havana Charter in Relation to United States Foreign Policy* (Report by Congressmen James G. Fulton and Jacob K. Javits), 80th Cong., 2nd sess. (Washington, 1948), p. 51.

[2] Havana Charter, Article 13, 7 (a) (i).

[3] Press Release ITP/194, United Nations Conference at Havana (23 Mar. 1948), p. 1.

PLATE 7

Above: Will Clayton signs the I.T.O. Charter for the U.S. as Clair Wilcox looks on. *Below*: The proceedings at Havana are watched by American representatives: (*left to right*) Congressman James Fulton, Congressman Jere Cooper, Wilcox, and Clayton

THE END OF THE I.T.O.

The British debate

It looked as if the British Government would finally have to make a final choice one way or the other on the question of multilateralism in commercial policy. But the time for decision had not quite arrived. The Government indicated that the I.T.O. Charter would not be presented for Parliamentary approval until action had been taken by the United States.[1] In the meantime a preliminary debate took place in political and academic circles on both the I.T.O. and the General Agreement on Tariffs and Trade.

As might have been expected, this debate followed the same general pattern as earlier discussions on commercial policy. The critics were particularly outspoken on two familiar grounds. First, they charged that Britain had been forced to agree to harmful principles of commercial policy in return for American aid. The British negotiators, they contended, had not been free agents during the I.T.O. discussions. No less an authority than Sir Hubert Henderson complained that in the preparation of the I.T.O. Britain had been hampered by a desire to avoid the 'impropriety' of seeming to challenge principles to which it had already been committed.[2] Less responsible commentators ignored the history of the Anglo-American negotiations and repeated the old misconception that the I.T.O. Charter 'was of American origin and therefore embodied American views as to the conduct of international trade'.[3]

As their second major ground for attack the critics chose the subject of Imperial Preference. Much was made of the ban on new or increased preferences contained in the I.T.O. Charter and the G.A.T.T., and of the commitment to negotiate for the elimination of existing preferences contained in the I.T.O. The intensity of the outcry on these points seemed out of all proportion to their practical importance. Thanks to the increasing use of quantitative restrictions and state-trading, there was little need to rely on preferences as instruments for discrimination in favour of Commonwealth trade.[4]

---

[1] See the statement of Harold Wilson, 449 H.C. Deb. 1583 (19 Apr. 1948).

[2] 'A Criticism of the Havana Charter', *Am. Ec. Rev.*, xxxix (1949), p. 608.

[3] W. A. Wells, *The Havana Charter, G.A.T.T., and the I.T.O.*, Empire Industries Association and British Empire League (London, 1950), p. 7.

[4] This fact was stated frankly by the Government in its defence of the tariff-preference settlement. Harold Wilson pointed out, for example, that although the preference in favour of Rhodesian tobacco had been reduced by one-third, the new long-term agreement to purchase two-thirds of Rhodesian tobacco exports for five years would

Moreover, as the Geneva negotiations had clearly shown, the elimination of existing preferences remained very much within the control of the British Government. Nevertheless, the Preference issue continued to dominate public discussion of commercial policy. The Conservative Party even resolved, at its annual conference in 1948, to oppose both the I.T.O. and G.A.T.T. until such time as their limitations on Imperial Preference were removed.

But such traditional grounds for opposition to the I.T.O. were now eclipsed by a new factor. This was the drastic deterioration in Britain's external economic position. Many now saw the 'dollar shortage' as a long-term problem whose solution required not simply American financial aid but a system of planned discrimination against dollar goods. The I.T.O. Charter, it was true, permitted departures from multilateralism in exceptional cases. But was it not still ill-advised, as Henderson contended, to accept general principles which were 'fundamentally unsuited to the conditions and problems of the modern world'?[1] The United States itself, in granting Marshall Aid, was encouraging closer economic links between the European countries. Was there not a contradiction between this regional approach, now endorsed fully by the United Kingdom, and the universal system of non-discrimination that remained the aim of the I.T.O.? As one Member of Parliament complained: 'Here we have a Government which on Thursday and Friday of last week asked us to think in terms of a western union and on the following Thursday asks us to ratify an agreement which destroys the whole basis of a western union and the conception on which their foreign policy is to be based.'[2]

Government spokesmen had a defence against criticisms of this kind, but it was not a defence designed to arouse enthusiasm for multilateral principles. In the words of Harold Wilson, now President of the Board of Trade:

> There has been particular criticism that we are tied down prematurely to obligations on non-discrimination and that nothing is being done to restore the fundamental imbalance of world payments. *I do not disagree with that point of view. However, this is essentially a long-term scheme.*[3]

Wilson, in short, did not deny that multilateralism might be incompatible with Britain's immediate needs. He could hardly do this, in

raise Britain's imports of Rhodesian tobacco to twice the pre-war figure. 446 H.C. Deb. 1330 (29 Jan. 1948).   [1] Op. cit., p. 616.
   [2] R. W. G. Mackay, 446 H.C. Deb. 1254 (29 Jan. 1948).
   [3] Italics supplied. 446 H.C. Deb. 1321 (29 Jan. 1948).

view of the bilateral and discriminatory trade agreements that the Government was now negotiating in the wake of the 1947 crisis.[1] Wilson denied only that multilateralism would be required now by the I.T.O.:

So I leave this question to be judged on facts and not on theory— whether the Geneva Agreement is in fact preventing us from having Empire development, the bilateral trade agreements, co-operation with Western Europe, *which this country has set as its programme for the immediate future.*[2]

To put the matter bluntly, it was no longer good politics to make a strong case for multilateral trade. Judging from the Parliamentary debate there seemed to be unqualified support for the I.T.O. and G.A.T.T. only among the handful of Liberal members. Indeed, the leader of the Liberal Party was virtually alone in recalling the spirit which had animated Anglo-American collaboration in the earliest days of the war. He cast a defiant challenge in the teeth of the critics:

Who are they deriding? Not merely the past, not merely the men who used to be in this House, who professed a belief in these doctrines and carried them out, but they are actually deriding more recent people, such as the right Hon. Gentleman for Woodford [Mr. Churchill] and the late President of the United States of America. After all, these principles, about which it is today said, 'Thank Heavens, they are dead and we have departed from them, for they belong to the eighteenth century and have nothing to do with the modern world,' were in paragraphs 4 and 5 of the famous Atlantic Declaration which thrilled the world and brought all democracies together to fight for an ideology.[3]

These were brave words, but they evoked very little response. It was doubtful that Britain would ratify the I.T.O., even if the United States should choose to do so. And events across the Atlantic were now tending against the latter possibility.

The American debate

When the American delegates returned from Havana in the spring of 1948 their most difficult struggle was still ahead of them. Somewhere in the course of the three lengthy conferences domestic support for the I.T.O. had begun to fade. To some extent, Clayton and his advisers were aware of the danger. Nevertheless, they remained

---

[1] 'Mr. Wilson can point to his own policies if the House accuses him of throwing away his weapons in the name of premature non-discrimination. No British Government has ever practised discrimination so widely.' 'A Trade Policy for Europe', *The Economist*, cliv (1948), p. 212.   [2] Italics supplied. 446 H.C. Deb. 1321 (29 Jan. 1948).
[3] Id., col. 1906.

optimistic about the eventual outcome. After all, they assured themselves, Bretton Woods and the British loan had been passed in the face of serious obstacles. It required only another campaign for multilateralism to arouse the necessary Congressional and public support.

And so, once again, the Administration called upon the familiar arguments. The I.T.O. would establish the rule of law in international economic relations.[1] It would mean nearly universal acceptance of America's economic philosophy.[2] It would eliminate foreign trade practices harmful to American export interests.[3] Conversely, failure to accept the I.T.O. would 'jeopardize every effort that has been made to organize the world for peace'.[4] It would be

a tragedy . . . every country in the world would feel that it was again on its own, that it was compelled to rely on unilateral action, in short that it had no other recourse except to return to the practices of the international economic jungle—everyone for himself and the devil catch the hindmost. Bilateralism, import quotas, export quotas, exchange controls, cartels, subsidies, discriminations, retaliations . . . would again become standard procedure throughout the world.[5]

But these arguments, it soon became clear, were no longer enough. The campaign for the I.T.O. had to contend with political and economic circumstances much less favourable than those which existed during previous campaigns on behalf of multilateral trade. In the case of the Bretton Woods institutions, approval had been facilitated by the war-time hopes for a better world; in the case of the British loan, by the need for an ally against Soviet expansion. For reasons that will shortly appear, neither of these factors was now available to assist the I.T.O.

[1] Acheson, 'Economic Policy and the ITO Charter', *Dept. State Bull.*, xx (1949), p. 626.

[2] Winthrop G. Brown, 'Why Private Business Should Support the ITO', *Dept. State Bull.*, xxii (1950), p. 132. Brown described the I.T.O. as an 'amazing and unprecedented achievement' because it 'secured agreement between the representatives of 54 nations, representing every stage of economic development and a wide variety of political philosophies, on a code of rules to guide their international trade *which embodies fundamentally the United States philosophy of the maximum amount of competition and the minimum amount of government control*'. Italics supplied. Id., pp. 134–5.

[3] Acheson, Memorandum for the President on the Charter for an ITO, April 27, 1949, in U.S. Congress, House, Committee on Foreign Affairs, *Membership and Participation by the United States in the International Trade Organization*, Hearings on H.J. Res. 236, 81st Cong., 2nd sess. (Apr.–May 1950), p. 7.

[4] Wilcox, 'Why the International Trade Organization?', *Annals of the Am. Ac. of Pol. and Soc. Sci.*, ccclxiv (1949), p. 69.

[5] Will Clayton, 'Why and How We Came to Find Ourselves at the Havana Conference', *Dept. State Bull.*, xviii (1948), pp. 825–7.

There had been, to begin with, a general disenchantment with the Administration's major war-time assumptions. The American people were now somewhat disillusioned with the Bretton Woods institutions and even with the United Nations itself. It was no longer possible to count on a large body of support for international organization *per se*. To make matters worse, the world was now divided into two hostile coalitions—for reasons that had little to do with the conduct of international trade. Thus it was increasingly difficult to link the achievement of multilateralism with the achievement of world peace. Finally, the unhappy experience of the British crisis had undermined the idea that the elaboration and enforcement of formal principles would always promote the orderly settlement of national differences.

The anti-Soviet argument was also proving of doubtful assistance. It was easy enough to see how financial aid to Britain would shore up western defences; it was less easy to see how the adoption of the I.T.O. Charter would do so. Even experts in the field—to say nothing of the general public—were no longer sure that the capacity of European countries to resist Communism would be enhanced by the immediate enforcement of multilateral principles. And even if multilateralism was still important, could it not be promoted well enough by the G.A.T.T. alone? Why add the expensive paraphernalia of another international secretariat? There appeared to be more direct and effective ways of countering the Soviet challenge. As these received increasing attention there was less and less time left for consideration of the I.T.O. When the Havana Conference ended in the spring of 1948, Congress was busy with the Marshall Plan. In 1949 it was preoccupied with N.A.T.O. Not until 1950 did Congress begin to hold hearings on the Charter. These had scarcely begun when the Communists invaded South Korea and the 'cold war' turned 'hot'.

But it was not only international developments that threatened the I.T.O.; there were grave obstacles on the domestic front as well. The renewal of the strengthened Reciprocal Trade Agreements Act in 1945 turned out to be the high-water mark of liberal trade sentiment in the United States. Had the I.T.O., as originally intended, been presented to Congress in 1948, it would have faced a Republican majority and a coalition of conservatives from both parties bent on restoring a considerable amount of protection. This Congress passed the 'peril point' amendment to the Reciprocal Trade Agreements Act providing for the very kind of advance limitation on tariff concessions that the Administration had rejected the year before.[1] Although the Democrats were back in control the following year, they brought no secure majority for freer trade. By now the tariff cuts made at Geneva were beginning to hurt domestic producers. Protectionist pressure was stronger than at any time since before the war.[2]

One particularly disturbing aspect of this protectionist revival deserves special comment. This was the trend in American agricultural policy. We noted earlier the conflict between the State Department's espousal of multilateral principles and the Department of Agriculture's programmes of price support for agricultural products. We observed that Section 22 of the Agricultural Adjustment Act authorized the application of quantitative restrictions to imports which threatened to interfere with certain domestic agricultural programmes. The final provisions of the G.A.T.T. and the I.T.O. Charter followed the 'Proposals' of 1945 in seeking to resolve the dilemma which such legislation posed for American policy. They permitted members to impose quantitative restrictions on agricultural or fisheries products if like domestic products were subject to equally restrictive production or marketing limitations. When these provisions were drafted the Administration expected that future domestic price support programmes would be accompanied, as they usually had been in the past, by some form of production control. Thus there appeared to be every likelihood that the quantitative restrictions employed under Section 22 would conform to the requirements of the I.T.O. and G.A.T.T. To ensure such conformity the Administration even succeeded in getting Congress to amend Section 22 with the following provision: 'No proclamation under this section shall be enforced in contravention of any treaty or other international agreement to which the United States is or hereafter becomes a party.'[3]

Unfortunately, Congress did not prove willing to observe the I.T.O. and G.A.T.T. limitations in actual practice. It renewed and broadened existing price support legislation and amended Section 22 in such a way that virtually all agricultural commodities became subject to possible import control. As a result the United States was soon applying quotas on the importation of a number of agricultural commodities which were not subject to equally restrictive domestic

---

[1] See p. 352, *supra*.

[2] For the protectionist attack on the I.T.O., see the testimony of the American Tariff League, the National Labour-Management Council on Foreign Trade Policy, and representatives of chemical, textile, and other import-competing industries, in the House I.T.O. hearings.   [3] Agricultural Adjustment Act of 1948.

production or marketing limitations. Eventually the Congress was moved to assert its complete independence from the G.A.T.T. obligations. It removed the self-denying ordinance it had placed in Section 22 and passed a new amendment providing: 'No trade agreement or other international agreement heretofore or hereafter entered into by the United States shall be applied in a manner inconsistent with the requirements of this section.'[1] It also made the more general declaration that the renewal of the Reciprocal Trade Agreements Act should 'not be construed to determine or indicate the approval or disapproval by the Congress of the Executive Agreement known as the General Agreement on Tariffs and Trade'.[2]

Too much emphasis, however, should not be placed on these symptoms of a protectionist revival. The I.T.O. might still have been saved had it not been for the defection of that critical portion of the American business community whose co-operation had made possible the passage of the Bretton Woods and British Loan agreements. By the time the American Congress finally began to hold hearings on the Havana Charter all the business groups who appeared to have the greatest interest in foreign trade were arrayed in opposition—the National Association of Manufacturers, the National Foreign Trade Council, the U.S. Chamber of Commerce, and the U.S. Council of the International Chamber of Commerce. In view of the fact that their members were supposed to be the main beneficiaries of the project, the stand taken by these organizations greatly diminished the prospects for Congressional approval.[3]

Among the most disagreeable features of the I.T.O. from the viewpoint of the American business community were the very provisions which the British delegation had helped to insert at the London Conference. The first was the saving clause forbidding the I.T.O. to ask a member to remove quantitative restrictions on the ground that this would be made possible by a change in that member's domestic policies.[4] The critics argued that this provision alone was sufficient ground for rejecting the entire project, since members of

---

[1] Trade Agreements Extension Act of 1951, Section 8 (b).   [2] Id., Section 10.

[3] Official statements of position by these business groups (except the U.S. Council of the International Chamber of Commerce) are contained in the House I.T.O. Hearings. For the Council's position, see Executive Committee of the United States Council of the International Chamber of Commerce, *Statement of Position on the Havana Charter for an International Trade Organization* (9 May 1950). For vigorous statements of the business case against the I.T.O., see Michael Heilperin, 'How the U.S. Lost the ITO Conference', *Fortune* (Sept. 1949), pp. 80–82; and Philip Cortney, *The Economic Munich* (New York, 1949).

[4] Havana Charter, Article 21, 4 (b) (i).

the I.T.O. would be permitted to pursue inflationary domestic policies and maintain quantitative restrictions against American exports for an indefinite period.[1] The second disagreeable feature lay in the affirmative provisions on full employment. While proclaiming their support of measures to achieve high income and employment in the United States, the critics balked at the suggestion[2] that the maintenance of full employment was a responsibility the United States owed to other countries. They expressed anxiety lest membership in the I.T.O. might commit the American Government to undesirable domestic or international action in pursuit of that objective.[3] They attacked the provision which appeared to place upon the United States the primary responsibility for correcting a persistent surplus in its balance of payments,[4] and that which offered to other countries the possibility of escape from their commercial policy obligations in the event of an American slump.[5] Taken together, the National Foreign Trade Council declared, the employment provisions 'would operate inexorably to transform the free enterprise system of this country into a system of planned economy, with consequent initiative-destroying regimentation, reduction in productive output and standards of living, and threat to the free institutions and liberties of the American people'.[6]

In general, the business groups opposed the Charter on the grounds that it was inconsistent with the very multilateral objectives for which the American Government had fought so hard. A note of disappointment ran through their criticism: Tariff preferences were to have been removed. Instead, the largest existing preferential system still remained. Foreign investment was to have been made more secure. Instead, it was given less protection that it had previously enjoyed. Quantitative restrictions were to have been proscribed. Instead, they were given widespread sanction on balance of payments grounds. In the exceptional cases where quantitative restrictions were to have been allowed, they were to have been non-discriminatory. Now discrimination against American goods was given a wide measure of freedom. In short, it seemed that American trade was to be the object of more restrictions and discriminations than ever before. Thus, the business groups complained, American participation in the Charter would be a step away from, not toward, the goal of multilateral trade:

---

[1] See Cortney, op. cit.   [2] In Article 2, 1.
[3] Under Articles 2 and 3.   [4] Article 4, 1.   [5] Article 6.
[6] *Position of the National Foreign Trade Council on the I.T.O. Charter* (New York, 1950), p. 32.

It is a dangerous document because it accepts practically all of the policies of economic nationalism; because it jeopardizes the free enterprise system by giving priority to centralized national governmental planning of foreign trade; because it leaves a wide scope to discrimination, accepts the principle of economic insulation and in effect commits all members of the I.T.O. to state planning for full employment. From the point of view of the United States, it has the further very grave defect of placing this country in a position where it must accept discrimination against itself while extending the Most-Favored-Nation treatment to all members of the Organization. It places the United States in a permanent minority position owing to its one vote-one country voting procedure. Because of that, membership in the I.T.O. based on this Charter would make it impossible for the United States to engage in an independent course of policy in favor of multilateral trade.[1]

This was a disappointing contrast to the Charter the business community had been led to expect. Was this contrast due to the ineptitude of the Administration—or to the bad faith of foreign governments? One business observer blamed the latter, at least in part, when he complained that during the negotiations the British 'so much and so consistently lined themselves up in opposition to the position taken by the United States'.[2] He expressed doubts that either Britain or the other countries had ever desired multilateralism in the first place. After all, he pointed out, they had agreed to work for that objective only in return for American financial aid:

One would have to be naïve indeed not to connect these benefits with their professed agreement with the purposes of the proposed trade organization. Nor need one be cynical to suggest that the United States was paying a very substantial price to get what it now appears was largely lip service to certain objectives. Illustrative of this statement is the concurrence in the view that there should be elimination of all forms of discriminatory treatment in international commerce, payments, and investments. That was an objective. It still remains only an objective, for when we get to the point of implementation, these nations go along only if there are exceptions permitting their non-compliance with the objectives.[3]

For Clayton and his dwindling band of followers, this was Armageddon. There was not much hope of disguising the Charter's lapses from their very own doctrines of multilateral trade. Nothing now

---

[1] U.S. Council of the International Chamber of Commerce, op. cit., pp. 2–3.

[2] Testimony of Elvin H. Kilheffer, House I.T.O. Hearings, p. 606. Kilheffer represented the U.S. Chamber of Commerce at the Havana conference.

[3] Excerpt from A Rejoinder by Elvin H. Kilheffer to the Report by Congressmen James G. Fulton of Pennsylvania and Jacob K. Javits of New York on the Havana Conference for an I.T.O, id., p. 607.

remained but retreat from the full rigour of those doctrines. Clayton himself, waging a desperate personal campaign to convert some influential business figures at the last moment, was actually pressed to this extremity. In answer to the charge that the Charter had compromised with the evil of tariff preferences, he now declared that the elimination of Preference was 'never contemplated' by the American Government.[1] 'In this connection', he said, 'we should not overlook, when damning the British for their preferential system, that we also have substantial preferences in our trade with Cuba and the Philippines. As a matter of fact, if we want to be honest with ourselves, we will find that many of the sins that we freely criticize other countries for practising have their counterpart in the United States.'[2]

This was a commendable, but rather belated, admission. A decade of indoctrination had done its work. The Administration had already lost the I.T.O. debate by standards of its own making. On 6 December 1950, it quietly issued a press release:

[T]he interested agencies have recommended, and the President has agreed, that, *while the proposed Charter for an International Trade Organization should not be resubmitted to the Congress*, Congress be asked to consider legislation which will make American participation in the General Agreement more effective. . . .[3]

Thus was removed the third great instrument for the reconstruction of multilateral trade.

CONCLUSION

The third major instrument of multilateralism—the International Trade Organization—enjoyed no more success than the other two. Indeed, its fate was rather more ignominious. It did not have a chance to die: it was simply still-born. When a decision was finally required, neither Britain nor the United States was anxious to approve the project. In the end, the latter specifically declined to do so.

What were the reasons for this dramatic failure? The present study has suggested a number of likely causes. One was the failure to get

---

[1] Memorandum of Clayton to Members of the Research and Advisory Board, Committee for Economic Development, in reply to comments of Henry P. Bristol concerning the Committee's proposed policy statement 'Reconstruction of World Trade', *Clayton Papers*. [2] Ibid.
[3] Italics supplied. *Dept. of State Bull.*, xxiii (1950), p. 977. A short time later the British Government noted this statement and announced it would not ask for ratification of the I.T.O. 483 H.C. Deb. 232–3 (Written Answers) (8 Feb. 1951). It also gave an undertaking 'that opportunity would be afforded for debate in Parliament before any decision by His Majesty's Government to ratify the General Agreement would be implemented . . .'. Id., col. 233.

the project started, like the Fund and Bank, in the full flush of wartime enthusiasm. Another was the failure to devote more attention at the very outset to the economic needs of the under-developed countries. A third was the failure to make a timely attack on the transitional problem. Like the Bretton Woods organizations and the Anglo-American Financial Agreement, the Charter was designed for a very different world than the one which emerged in 1947. If bolder measures had been undertaken on behalf of reconstruction, the I.T.O. might possibly have been saved from its unhappy fate.

To these three failures we must add another that is somewhat more difficult to define. The two major sponsors of the I.T.O. sought to incorporate in the Charter a detailed statement of their favourite economic doctrines. The United States pressed formal undertakings for the elimination of Imperial Preference, quantitative restrictions, and discrimination of all kinds. The United Kingdom pressed equally detailed undertakings to protect domestic policies of full employment. The result was an elaborate set of rules and counter-rules that offered imperfect standards for national policy. These rules and counter-rules satisfied nobody and alienated nearly everybody. They grew into such a mountain of complexity that the I.T.O. finally collapsed of its own weight.

The end of the I.T.O., of course, was by no means the end of collaboration in commercial policy. Both the United States and Britain had signed the Protocol of Provisional Application of the General Agreement on Tariffs and Trade. This not only committed them to the result of the Geneva tariff bargaining but also to the most important obligations of the I.T.O. Charter dealing with tariffs, preferences, quantitative restrictions, and other impediments to trade. The representatives of the two countries, along with the other Contracting Parties, continued to meet periodically to adjust their differences under the Agreement and to negotiate new tariff concessions. And the very informality of the G.A.T.T. procedures compared to those of the I.T.O. was probably a significant gain.

Nevertheless, the situation left by the abandonment of the I.T.O. was not entirely satisfactory. The G.A.T.T. was a slender reed on which to base progress toward a multilateral régime. It lacked adequate administrative machinery to deal with problems arising between the periodic meetings of the Contracting Parties. Without provision for a permanent secretariat, it was handicapped in the size and scope of its operations. Its signatories were bound to give effect to most of its trade rules only to the extent not inconsistent with their existing legislation. Finally, even with respect to future legislation, developments in both Britain and the United States cast doubt upon the extent to which either country felt bound to observe the G.A.T.T. obligations. In short, the G.A.T.T. was permeated by an atmosphere of impermanence. Some day it would have to be put on a more solid basis. In the meantime the effort of Britain and the United States to create an organization for commercial collaboration had fallen well short of its primary objective.

CHAPTER XVIII

CONCLUSION

ONE of the most difficult problems in historical writing is finding an appropriate place to end. The wheel of fortune turns round and round; in the life of a man, a nation, or an idea, the failures are followed by successes and the successes in turn by failures. In writing a history of some subjects one cannot wait until the revolutions cease; yet to stop the account at any given point in a cycle is to risk premature and perhaps erroneous judgement. Wilson's conception of world order, to take one example, reached a low ebb in the nineteen-thirties; it was revived with enthusiasm in the Second World War; it has receded once again. We cannot know how it will fare in the next generation or how it will be judged by some future historian.

The same must be said of the effort to reconstruct a system of multilateral trade after the Second World War. We closed our history at a given point. But the effort still goes on. The years that have followed the end of this narrative have, in some respects, provided new hope of eventual success. There has been a steady expansion of world trade, in which Britain has been a leading beneficiary. The British balance of payments, while not entirely secure, has become satisfactory enough to permit tentative steps toward a multilateral régime. At the same time the United States, in its campaign for multilateralism, has become more sympathetic to the practical political and economic difficulties faced by its partners in the free world.

Even in the shorter perspective of the period we chose to review, the record is by no means unfavourable. This is particularly true when comparisons are made with previous periods. The peacemakers after the Second World War at least avoided the grave mistakes of the earlier post-war decade. The United States did not return to isolation. There were none of the wild currency disorders or violent fluctuations of the trade cycle. After some hesitation, a programme of sustained recovery was begun. Due credit for these achievements must be given to the British and American Governments and to some of the central figures in the present study.

Histories, nevertheless, must have an end, and their conclusions may properly recall the circumstances of their beginnings. The major objective set forth at the outset of this narrative was the reconstruction of multilateral trade. That objective was not achieved. We must try now, in a tentative way, to suggest some of the principal reasons for the failure.

Perhaps the best way to do this is to recall the main conditions of multilateralism discussed in the course of the present study. The first was the achievement of a tolerable state of political equilibrium. The multilateral system projected by the post-war planners could not exist in the midst of political instability and the threat of war. The serious differences between the Soviet Union and the West which emerged in the post-war period destroyed all hope of reconstructing multilateralism on a universal basis. Multilateralism could not be revived even within the Western camp until its members were made reasonably secure against Soviet aggression. A major political and military effort was required to achieve this security. Inevitably it involved modification and even postponement of some parts of the multilateral programme.

A second condition of multilateralism discussed in this study was the attainment of a reasonable state of economic equilibrium. The multilateral system could not be achieved unless individual nations were in approximate balance with the rest of the world as a whole. Unfortunately the post-war planners did not foresee the full extent of the measures necessary to achieve such balance after the destruction and dislocation of the Second World War. They underestimated Britain's balance of payments problem and the difficulty of restoring equilibrium between the rest of the world and the United States. The institutions they built for the achievement of multilateralism were not designed to withstand the unfavourable pressures of the post-war transition period.

The third condition of multilateralism was the adoption of appropriate internal and external policies by creditor and debtor nations. No multilateral system could long endure unless countries in surplus and deficit positions adopted corrective measures designed to restore equilibrium in their balance of payments. This meant, for surplus countries, the reduction of obstacles to imports and the maintenance of a reasonable state of full employment; for deficit countries, control of domestic inflation to keep imports at a tolerable level and release sufficient exports for world markets. The post-war planners did not face up to the full implications of these facts for the policies of their own countries. The institutions they devised frequently contained no adequate recognition of the need for creditor-debtor adjustments, and, even when they did so, provided no adequate mechanism to ensure that such adjustments would in fact be made.

The failure of these three conditions, to be sure, cannot be charged entirely to errors of national policy. The reconstruction of multi-lateralism after the Second World War would have caused difficulty in the face of the most enlightened and far-sighted British and American policies. Nevertheless, the difficulties actually encountered in the fulfilment of the conditions were greater than they need have been. This was due, in turn, to the three basic errors of post-war planning described at the outset of the present study.

The first error we called, for want of a better name, the error of Economism. This was the idea that economic policy could be made in a political vacuum and that the principal approach to world peace lay through co-operation in the economic field. Such a philosophy failed to appreciate the intimate relation between economic and non-economic factors. It substantially delayed the creation of that political equilibrium which was the first condition of multilateral trade.

The second error noted at the outset of our study was the error of Universalism. This was the idea that the post-war order could be created on a universal basis without alliances or any special arrangements between individual members of the world community. The resulting concentration on universal institutions led to neglect of the central problem of British reconstruction and of the special relationship between Britain and the United States as the two key countries of the world economy.

The third error we cited was that of Legalism. This was a tendency to think that outstanding international problems could be resolved by drafting detailed codes of formal principles. Legal forms and documentary trappings became a substitute for collaboration. Anglo-American agreements frequently gave a false appearance of security without embodying a genuine consensus on the way they were to be carried out. They were not flexible enough to be adapted in the face of future contingencies. Adherence to them, in some cases, appeared to be purchased by financial aid. This inevitably destroyed the necessary disposition to co-operate which had to be present if any agreement was to work.

At this point it may be well to add a word of warning. There has been a tendency in recent years to depreciate the role of law in the conduct of international affairs. We are not here following this line.

Law does and must play a major part in the settlement of differences, whether national or international, political or economic. Critics who maintain the contrary view make the mistake of regarding law as a frozen cake of doctrine rather than as a system of useful arrangements for the orderly solution of human problems.

When we look at the matter in this way we can see that many of the difficulties described in our history resulted from an inadequate, not an excessive, attention to law. The post-war planners, it is true, devoted a great deal of time to the elaboration of substantive rules; but they paid less attention to the specific procedures by which those rules could be made effective. They failed to recognize that the promulgation of formal codes may be a less effective method of international collaboration than the establishment of informal working relationships. With what degree of precision, they might have asked themselves, should multilateral principles be elaborated? By what mechanism should they be interpreted? How can they be rendered flexible enough in the face of changing conditions? What methods are most likely to induce desirable changes in national policies? It was the failure to deal successfully with these questions that contributed to the downfall of the ambitious programme for multilateral trade.

This failure to devise a suitable institutional framework for multilateralism leads us to one final point. It is axiomatic that without a flexibility of mind, a sympathy for the other fellow's difficulties, no institutions, however perfect, can be made to work. Yet Anglo-American economic collaboration in the period we have described was constantly impeded by doctrinaire attitudes on both sides of the Atlantic. The United States pressed for non-discrimination both in and out of season and adopted an unbecoming evangelism in its assault on the sterling area and Imperial Preference. British opinion, in turn, yielded to an overweening insistence on the sanctity of these institutions and of ambitious programmes of domestic expansion. The resulting controversies inflamed public opinion and impeded essential adjustments in national policy. They led eventually to immoderate and inflexible positions not founded in the genuine interests of the two countries.

In this final criticism we may well be faced with the charge of perfectionism. Doctrines are necessary, it may be argued, to simplify and organize a complex environment. Hyperbole may be required to arouse the enthusiasm of a democratic electorate. There is some merit in these objections. Still, if doctrinaire statements must be made, they should be made with due regard for the consequences. It is particularly fatal when they are taken too literally by their own authors. As Keynes once observed: 'Words ought to be a little wild, for they are an assault of thought upon the unthinking. But when the seats of power and authority have been attained, there should be no more poetic licence. . . . When a doctrinaire proceeds to action, he must, so to speak, forget his doctrine. For those who in action remember the letter will probably lose what they are seeking.'[1]

[1] 'National Self-Sufficiency', *Yale Review*, xxii (1933), p. 755.

APPENDIX

FINANCIAL AGREEMENT BETWEEN THE GOVERNMENTS OF THE UNITED STATES AND THE UNITED KINGDOM

It is hereby agreed between the Government of the United States of America and the Government of the United Kingdom of Great Britain and Northern Ireland as follows:—

1. *Effective date of the Agreement*

The effective date of this Agreement shall be the date on which the Government of the United States notifies the Government of the United Kingdom that the Congress of the United States has made available the funds necessary to extend to the Government of the United Kingdom the line of credit in accordance with the provisions of this Agreement.

2. *Line of Credit*

The Government of the United States will extend to the Government of the United Kingdom a line of credit of $3,750,000,000 which may be drawn upon at any time between the effective date of this Agreement and 31st December, 1951, inclusive.

3. *Purpose of the Line of Credit*

The purpose of the line of credit is to facilitate purchases by the United Kingdom of goods and services in the United States, to assist the United Kingdom to meet transitional post-war deficits in its current balance of payments, to help the United Kingdom to maintain adequate reserves of gold and dollars and to assist the Government of the United Kingdom to assume the obligations of multilateral trade, as defined in this and other agreements.

4. *Amortisation and Interest*

(i) The amount of the line of credit drawn by 31st December, 1951, shall be repaid in 50 annual instalments beginning on 31st December, 1951, with interest at the rate of 2 per cent. per annum.

Interest for the year 1951 shall be computed on the amount outstanding on 31st December, 1951, and for each year thereafter interest shall be computed on the amount outstanding on 1st January of each such year.

49 annual instalments of principal repayments and interest shall be equal, calculated at the rate of $31,823,000 for each $1,000,000,000 of the line of

credit drawn by 31st December, 1951, and the fiftieth annual instalment shall be at the rate of $31,840,736·65 for each such $1,000,000,000.

Each instalment shall consist of the full amount of the interest due and the remainder of the instalment shall be the principal to be repaid in that year. Payments required by this section are subject to the provisions of Section 5.

(ii) The Government of the United Kingdom may accelerate repayment of the amount drawn under this line of credit.

5. *Waiver of Interest Payments*

In any year in which the Government of the United Kingdom requests the Government of the United States to waive the amount of the interest due in the instalment of that year, the Government of the United States will grant the waiver if:—

(a) the Government of the United Kingdom finds that a waiver is necessary in view of the present and prospective conditions of international exchange and the level of its gold and foreign exchange reserves, *and*

(b) the International Monetary Fund certifies that the income of the United Kingdom from home-produced exports plus its net income from invisible current transactions in its balance of payments was on the average over the five preceding calendar years less than the average annual amount of United Kingdom imports during 1936–8 fixed at £866,000,000, as such figure may be adjusted for changes in the price level of these imports. Any amount in excess of £43,750,000 released or paid in any year on account of sterling balances accumulated to the credit of overseas governments, monetary authorities and banks before the effective date of this Agreement shall be regarded as a capital transaction and therefore shall not be included in the above calculation of the net income from invisible current transactions for that year. If waiver is requested for an interest payment prior to that due in 1955, the average income shall be computed for the calendar years from 1950 through the year preceding that in which the request is made.

6. *Relation of this line of credit to other obligations*

(i) It is understood that any amounts required to discharge obligations of the United Kingdom to third countries outstanding on the effective date of this agreement will be found from resources other than this line of credit.

(ii) The Government of the United Kingdom will not arrange any long term loans from Governments within the British Commonwealth after 6th December, 1945 and before the end of 1951 on terms more favourable to the lender than the terms of this line of credit.

(iii) Waiver of interest will not be requested or allowed under Section 5 in any year unless the aggregate of the releases or payments in that year of sterling balances accumulated to the credit of overseas governments, monetary authorities and banks (except in the case of colonial dependencies) before the effective date of this agreement, is reduced proportionately, and unless interest payments due in that year on loans referred to in (ii) above are waived. The proportionate reduction of the releases or payments of sterling balances shall be calculated in relation to the aggregate released and paid in the most recent year in which waiver of interest was not requested.

(iv) The application of the principles set forth in this section shall be the subject of full consultation between the two Governments as occasion may arise.

7. *Sterling Area Exchange Arrangements*

The Government of the United Kingdom will complete arrangements as early as practicable and in any case not later than one year after the effective date of this agreement, unless in exceptional cases a later date is agreed upon after consultation, under which immediately after the completion of such arrangements the sterling receipts from current transactions of all sterling area countries (apart from any receipts arising out of military expenditure by the Government of the United Kingdom prior to 31st December, 1948, to the extent to which they are treated by agreement with the countries concerned on the same basis as the balances accumulated during the war) will be freely available for current transactions in any currency area without discrimination with the result that any discrimination arising from the so-called sterling area dollar pool will be entirely removed and that each member of the sterling area will have its current sterling and dollar receipts at its free disposition for current transactions anywhere.

8. *Other Exchange Arrangements*

(i) The Government of the United Kingdom agrees that after the effective date of this agreement it will not apply exchange controls in such a manner as to restrict

(*a*) payments or transfers in respect of products of the United States permitted to be imported into the United Kingdom or other current transactions between the two countries or

(*b*) the use of sterling balances to the credit of residents of the United States arising out of current transactions.

Nothing in this paragraph (i) shall affect the provisions of Article VII of the Articles of Agreement of the International Monetary Fund when those Articles have come into force.

(ii) The Governments of the United States and the United Kingdom agree that not later than one year after the effective date of this agreement, unless in exceptional cases a later date is agreed upon after consultation, they will impose no restrictions on payments and transfers for current transactions. The obligations of this paragraph (ii) shall not apply

(*a*) to balances of third countries and their nationals accumulated before this paragraph (ii) becomes effective; or

(*b*) to restrictions imposed in conformity with the Articles of Agreement of the International Monetary Fund, provided that the Governments of the United Kingdom and the United States will not continue to invoke the provisions of Article XIV Section 2 of those Articles after this paragraph (ii) becomes effective unless in exceptional cases after consultation they agree otherwise; or

(*c*) to restrictions imposed in connection with measures designed to uncover and dispose of assets of Germany and Japan.

(iii) This Section and Section 9 which are in anticipation of more comprehensive arrangements by multilateral agreement shall operate until 31st December, 1951.

9. *Import Arrangements*

If either the Government of the United States or the Government of the United Kingdom imposes or maintains quantitative import restrictions, such restrictions shall be administered on a basis which does not discriminate against imports from the other country in respect of any product; provided that this undertaking shall not apply in cases in which

(*a*) its application would have the effect of preventing the country imposing such restrictions from utilizing, for the purchase of needed imports, inconvertible currencies accumulated up to 31st December, 1946; or

(*b*) there may be special necessity for the country imposing such restrictions to assist, by measures not involving a substantial departure from the general rule of non-discrimination, a country whose economy has been disrupted by war; or

(*c*) either Government imposes quantitative restrictions having equivalent effect to any exchange restrictions which that Government is authorised to impose in conformity with Article VII of the Articles of Agreement of the International Monetary Fund.

The provisions of this Section shall become effective as soon as practicable, but not later than 31st December, 1946.

10. *Accumulated Sterling Balances*

(i) The Government of the United Kingdom intends to make agreements with the countries concerned, varying according to the circumstances of each case, for an early settlement covering the sterling balances accumulated by sterling area and other countries, prior to such settlement (together with any future receipts arising out of military expenditure by the Government of the United Kingdom to the extent to which they are treated on the same basis by agreement with the countries concerned). The settlements with the sterling area countries will be on the basis of dividing these accumulated balances into three categories:

(a) balances to be released at once and convertible into any currency for current transactions;

(b) balances to be similarly released by instalments over a period of years beginning in 1951; and

(c) balances to be adjusted as a contribution to the settlement of war and post-war indebtedness and in recognition of the benefits which the countries concerned might be expected to gain from such a settlement.

The Government of the United Kingdom will make every endeavour to secure the early completion of these arrangements.

(ii) In consideration of the fact that an important purpose of the present line of credit is to promote the development of multilateral trade and facilitate its early resumption on a non-discriminatory basis, the Government of the United Kingdom agrees that any sterling balances released or otherwise available for current payments will, not later than one year after the effective date of this agreement, unless in special cases a later date is agreed upon after consultation, be freely available for current transactions in any currency area without discrimination.

11. *Definitions*

For the purposes of this agreement:

(i) The term 'current transactions' shall have the meaning prescribed in article XIX (i) of the Articles of Agreement of the International Monetary Fund.

(ii) The term 'sterling area' means the United Kingdom and the other territories declared by the Defence (Finance) (Definition of Sterling Area) (No. 2) Order, 1944, to be included in the sterling area, namely 'the following Territories excluding Canada and Newfoundland, that is to say:

(a) any Dominion,

(b) any other part of His Majesty's dominions,

(c) any territory in respect of which a mandate on behalf of the League of Nations has been accepted by His Majesty and is being exercised by his Majesty's Government in the United Kingdom, or in any Dominion,

(d) any British Protectorate or Protected State,

(e) Egypt, the Anglo-Egyptian Sudan and Iraq,

(f) Iceland and the Faroe Islands.'

12. *Consultation on Agreement*

Either Government shall be entitled to approach the other for a reconsideration of any of the provisions of this agreement, if in its opinion the prevailing conditions of international exchange justify such reconsideration with a view to agreeing upon modifications for presentation to their respective Legislatures.

Signed in duplicate at Washington, District of Columbia, this 6th day of December, 1945.

For the Government of the United States of America:
FRED M. VINSON,
Secretary of the Treasury of the United States of America.

For the Government of the United Kingdom of Great Britain and Northern Ireland:
HALIFAX,
His Majesty's Ambassador Extraordinary and Plenipotentiary at Washington.

BIBLIOGRAPHY

THIS bibliography contains a list of the principal documents which form the basis of the present study. It does not pretend to be exhaustive, but is designed rather as a basic collection of source materials.

Much of the author's material has necessarily been drawn from unpublished sources, including interviews with participants in the Anglo-American negotiations as well as certain documents concerning those negotiations which have not yet been made generally available. Because of their confidential nature, such sources are cited neither in footnotes nor bibliography.

The author has also made use of two important manuscript collections, each of which requires separate comment. The first of these has been cited as *The Private Papers of Harry Dexter White*. This is a large collection of documents accumulated by White during his official tenure in the United States Treasury Department. It includes unpublished drafts of the Fund and Bank plans, written exchanges between the British and American Governments, and memoranda written by officials in various agencies of the U.S. Government. Upon the death of White the collection was taken from his office and presented to the Firestone Library of Princeton University.

The second manuscript collection, *The Private Papers of Will Clayton*, consists of selected documents given by Clayton to the Clayton Center for International Economic Affairs of the Fletcher School of Law and Diplomacy, Medford, Massachusetts. This collection also contains memoranda of U.S. Government officials, as well as correspondence between Clayton and members of the American business and financial community. Mr. Clayton wishes the author to state that the collection is not generally available to researchers.

In addition to the materials specifically listed below the author has drawn on the files of newspaper clippings maintained by the Royal Institute of International Affairs. These files made possible the numerous references to newspaper comment in Britain and the United States.

The preparation of this book also entailed extensive reading in the *Congressional Record, Hansard*, and *The Economist*. The author has cited below only the most important leading articles and debates.

An important source for official statements of British and American leaders during the war period was Louise W. and Hajo Holborn (eds.), *War and Peace Aims of the United Nations* (Boston, 1943, 1948, 2 vols.). The primary sources for such statements have been cited only when the statements were not found in this volume.

The bibliography is divided for convenience into two main sections. The General Bibliography consists of materials which proved useful throughout the entire book or in a considerable number of its parts. The

Special Bibliography consists of materials of special relevance to a particular chapter or group of chapters.

1. GENERAL BIBLIOGRAPHY

Official documents

Bank for International Settlements, *The Sterling Area* (Basle, 1953).
European Co-operation Administration Special Mission to the United Kingdom, *The Sterling Area* (London, 1951).
League of Nations, *Commercial Policy in the Inter-war Period* (Geneva, 1942).
—— *Commercial Policy in the Post-War World* (Geneva, 1945).
—— *The Network of World Trade* (Geneva, 1942).
U.S. Commission on Foreign Economic Policy (Randall Commission), *Staff Papers* (Washington, 1954).
U.S. Congress, Senate, Committee on Foreign Relations, *A Decade of American Foreign Policy: Basic Documents 1941–49*, S. Doc. 123, 81st Cong., 1st sess. (Washington, 1950).
U.S. Department of Commerce, *The United States in the World Economy*, Economic Series No. 23 (Washington, 1943).

Other sources

ALLEN, H. C., *Great Britain and the United States. A History of Anglo-American Relations 1783–1952* (London, 1954).
ALMOND, GABRIEL A., *The American People and Foreign Policy* (New York, 1950).
American Economic Association, *Readings in the Theory of International Trade* (London, 1950).
BALOGH, THOMAS, *The Dollar Crisis* (Oxford, 1949).
—— 'Britain's Foreign Trade Problem: A Comment', *Ec. Jour.*, lviii (1948), pp. 74–85.
—— 'The United States and International Economic Equilibrium', in Harris, S. E. (ed.), *Foreign Economic Policy for the United States* (Cambridge, U.S.A., 1948), pp. 446–80.
BAREAU, PAUL, *The Sterling Area—What It Is and How It Works* (2nd ed., London, 1950).
—— 'Is It Good-Bye to Bretton Woods?', *Three Banks Review*, No. 13 (1952), pp. 3–18.
BEHRMAN, JACK N., *Foreign Aid as a Technique in Attaining U.S. International Economic Objectives* (Dissertation Presented to the Faculty of Princeton University in Candidacy for the Degree of Doctor of Philosophy, May 1951).
BERNSTEIN, EDWARD M., 'British Policy and a World Economy', *Am. Ec. Rev.*, xxxv (1945), pp. 891–908.
BEVAN, ANEURIN, *In Place of Fear* (London, 1952).
BEYEN, J. W., *Money in a Maelstrom* (New York, 1949).
BRIERLY, J. L., *The Outlook for International Law* (Oxford, 1945).
BRINTON, CRANE, *The United States and Britain* (2nd ed., Cambridge, U.S.A., 1948).

Brookings Institution, *Anglo-American Economic Relations* (Washington, 1950).
—— *Rearmament and Anglo-American Economic Relations* (Washington, 1952).
CLAY, SIR HENRY, 'Britain's Declining Role in World Trade', *For. Aff.*, xxiv (1946), pp. 411–28.
Committee for Economic Development, Research and Policy Committee, *Britain's Economic Problem and Its Meaning for America* (New York, 1953).
CONAN, A. R., *The Sterling Area* (London, 1952).
CONDLIFFE, John B., *The Reconstruction of World Trade* (New York, 1940).
CORBETT, PERCY E., *Britain: Partner for Peace* (New York, 1946).
DESPRÈS, ÉMILE, and KINDLEBERGER, CHARLES P., 'The Mechanism for Adjustment in International Payments—The Lessons of Post-war Experience', *Am. Ec. Rev.*, xlii (Supp., 1952), pp. 332–44.
ELLIOTT, WILLIAM Y., *et al.*, *United States Foreign Policy* (New York, 1952).
ELLIS, HOWARD S., *Bilateralism and the Future of International Trade*, Essays in International Finance No. 5 (Princeton, 1945).
ELLSWORTH, PAUL T., *The International Economy* (New York, 1950).
FEIS, HERBERT, *The Sinews of Peace* (New York, 1944).
—— 'Keynes in Retrospect', *For. Aff.*, xxix (1951), pp. 564–77.
—— 'On Our Economic Relations with Britain', *For. Aff.*, xxi (1943), pp. 462–75.
—— 'The Future of British Imperial Preferences', *For. Aff.*, xxiv (1946), pp. 661–74.
FISHER, A. G. B., *International Implications of Full Employment in Great Britain* (London, 1946).
—— 'The Future of International Economic Institutions', *Yearbook of World Affairs*, i (1947), pp. 178–201.
GLICKMAN, D. L., 'The British Imperial Preference System', *Quart. Jour. Ec.*, lxi (1947), pp. 439–70.
GORDON, MARGARET S., 'International Aspects of American Agricultural Policy', *Am. Ec. Rev.*, xxxvi (1946), pp. 596–612.
HABERLER, GOTTFRIED, *The Theory of International Trade* (London, 1950).
—— 'Concluding Remarks to Discussion on the Problem of Long-Term International Balance', *Int. Soc. Sci. Bull.*, iii (1951), pp. 91–99.
—— 'Dollar Shortage?', in Harris, S. E. (ed.), *Foreign Economic Policy for the United States* (Cambridge, U.S.A., 1948), pp. 426–45.
—— 'Some Factors Affecting the Future of International Trade and International Economic Policy', in Harris, S. E. (ed.), *Economic Reconstruction* (New York, 1945), pp. 319–35.
HARRIS, SEYMOUR E. (ed.), *Foreign Economic Policy for the United States* (Cambridge, U.S.A., 1948).
—— *The New Economics* (New York, 1947).
—— *Postwar Economic Problems* (New York, 1943).
HARROD, ROY F., *The Dollar* (New York, 1953).
—— *The Life of John Maynard Keynes* (London, 1951).
—— *The Pound Sterling*, Essays in International Finance No. 13 (Princeton, 1952).
—— 'Hands and Fists Across the Sea', *For. Aff.*, xxx (1951), pp. 63–76.
HEILPERIN, MICHAEL A., *The Trade of Nations* (London, 1946).
HELMORE, SIR JAMES R. C., and HOLMES, STEPHEN L., 'British Commercial Policy', in *The Cotton Industry in a Changing World* (Papers prepared for the Cotton Board Conference at Harrogate, England, 21–23 October 1949).

HILGERDT, FOLKE, 'The Case for Multilateral Trade', *Am. Ec. Rev.*, xxxiii (Supp., 1943), pp. 393–407.

HINSHAW, RANDALL, 'Keynesian Commercial Policy', in Harris, S. E. (ed.), *The New Economics* (New York, 1948), pp. 315–22.

HOLBORN, LOUISE W. and HAJO (eds.), *War and Peace Aims of the United Nations* (Boston, 1943, 1948, 2 vols.).

HOOVER, CALVIN B., *International Trade and Domestic Employment* (New York, 1945).

HULL, CORDELL, *The Memoirs of Cordell Hull* (New York, 1948, 2 vols.).

Institute of Bankers, *The Sterling Area* (London, 1949).

JOHNSON, D. GALE, *Trade and Agriculture* (New York, 1950).

KEIRSTEAD, B. S., 'The Conditions of Multilateral Trade', *Int. Soc. Sci. Bull.*, iii (1951), pp. 17–22.

KENNAN, GEORGE F., *American Diplomacy 1900–1950* (London, 1952).

KEYNES, JOHN MAYNARD, *The Economic Consequences of the Peace* (New York, 1920).

—— *Essays in Biography* (2nd ed., London, 1951).

—— *Essays in Persuasion* (London, 1952).

—— *The General Theory of Employment, Interest and Money* (London, 1951).

—— 'National Self-Sufficiency', *Yale Review*, xxii (1933), pp. 755–69.

KINDLEBERGER, CHARLES P., *The Dollar Shortage* (New York, 1950).

KREIDER, KARL, *The Anglo-American Trade Agreement* (Princeton, 1943).

LASSWELL, HAROLD D., *The Political Writings of Harold D. Lasswell* (Glencoe, Ill., 1951).

LIPPMANN, WALTER, *U.S. Foreign Policy* (Boston, 1943).

—— *U.S. War Aims* (Boston, 1944).

MACDOUGALL, G. D. A., 'Britain's Bargaining Power', *Ec. Jour.*, lvi (1946), pp. 27–37.

—— 'Britain's Foreign Trade Problem', *Ec. Jour.*, lvii (1947), pp. 69–113.

—— 'Britain's Foreign Trade Problem: A Reply', *Ec. Jour.*, lviii (1948), pp. 86–98.

MARSH, DONALD B., *World Trade and Investment* (New York, 1951).

MASON, EDWARD, *Controlling World Trade* (New York, 1946).

MCDOUGAL, MYRES S., 'Law and Power', *Am. Jour. Int. Law*, xlvi (1952), pp. 102–14.

MEADE, JAMES, 'Bretton Woods, G.A.T.T., and the Balance of Payments—A Second Round?', *The Three Banks Review*, No. 16 (December 1952).

—— 'Bretton Woods, Havana, and the United Kingdom Balance of Payments', *Lloyds Bank Review*, New Series No. 7 (January 1948), pp. 1–18.

METZLER, LLOYD, A., 'The Theory of International Trade', in *Survey of Contemporary Economics* (Philadelphia, 1948, vol. i), pp. 210–54.

MIKESELL, RAYMOND F., *Foreign Exchange in the Postwar World* (New York, 1954).

—— *United States Economic Policy and International Relations* (New York, 1952).

—— 'The Role of the International Monetary Agreements in a World of Planned Economies', *Jour. of Pol. Ec.*, lv (1947), pp. 497–512.

MORGENTHAU, HANS J., *In Defense of the National Interest* (New York, 1951).

—— *Politics Among Nations* (New York, 1950).

National Institute of Economic and Social Research, *Trade Regulations and Commercial Policy of the United Kingdom* (Cambridge, 1943).

NURKSE, RAGNAR, *Conditions of International Monetary Equilibrium*, Essays in International Finance No. 4 (Princeton, 1945).

PARKS, WALLACE, *United States Administration of its International Economic Affairs* (Baltimore, 1951).

PENROSE, E. F., *Economic Planning for Peace* (Princeton, 1953).

Political and Economic Planning, *Britain and World Trade* (London, 1947).

RASMINSKY, LOUIS, 'Anglo-American Trade Prospects: A Canadian View', *Ec. Jour.*, lv (1945), pp. 161–78.

ROBBINS, LIONEL, 'The Sterling Problem', *Lloyds Bank Review*, No. 14 (1949), pp. 1–31.

—— 'Towards an Atlantic Community', *Lloyds Bank Review*, No. 17 (1950), pp. 1–24.

ROBERTS, HENRY L., and WILSON, PAUL A., *Britain and the United States: Problems in Co-operation* (London, 1953).

ROBERTSON, SIR DENNIS, *Britain in the World Economy* (London, 1954).

ROBINSON, E. A. G., 'John Maynard Keynes, 1883–1946', *Ec. Jour.*, lvii (1947), pp. 1–68.

ROSTOW, EUGENE V., 'American Security and Foreign Economic Policy', *Yale Review*, xxxiv (1944–5), pp. 495–523.

RUSSELL, RICHARD, *Imperial Preference* (London, 1947).

SMITH, ADAM, *The Wealth of Nations* (New York, 1937).

SMITHIES, ARTHUR, 'Multilateral Trade and Employment', *Am. Ec. Rev.*, xxxvii (Supp., 1947), pp. 560–8.

—— 'Reflections on the Work and Influence of John Maynard Keynes', *Quart. Jour. Ec.*, lv (1951), pp. 578–601.

SOULE, GEORGE, *America's Stake in Britain's Future* (London, 1946).

TEW, BRIAN, *International Monetary Co-operation 1945–1952* (London, 1952).

TRIFFIN, ROBERT, 'Discussion on International Trade in the Post-war World', *Am. Ec. Rev.*, xlii (Supp., 1952), pp. 362–8.

VARGA, E., 'Anglo-American Rivalry and Partnership: A Marxist View', *For. Aff.*, xxv (1947), pp. 583–95.

VINER, JACOB, *International Economics* (Glencoe, Ill., 1951).

—— *International Trade and Economic Development* (Oxford, 1952).

—— *The Customs Union Issue* (New York, 1950).

—— *Anglo-American Post-War Economic Relations* (unpublished typescript of address delivered at the Royal Institute of International Affairs, London, 6 June 1946).

WARD, BARBARA, *The West at Bay* (New York, 1948).

WEBSTER, SIR CHARLES; JACOB, MAJOR-GENERAL SIR IAN; and ROBINSON, E. A. G.; *United Kingdom Policy—Foreign, Strategic, Economic* (London, 1950).

WHIDDEN, HOWARD P., *Preferences and Discriminations in International Trade* (New York, 1945).

WILLIAMS, JOHN H., *Economic Stability in a Changing World* (New York, 1953).

—— *Economic Stability in the Modern World* (London, 1952).

—— *Postwar Monetary Plans* (3rd ed., Oxford, 1949).

WILSON, HAROLD, *In Place of Dollars* (London, 1952).

World Peace Foundation, *Documents on American Foreign Relations* (Boston, Annual, 1941–9).

WORSWICK, G. D. N., and ADY, P. H., *The British Economy, 1945–1950* (Oxford, 1953).

2. SPECIAL BIBLIOGRAPHY

CHAPTER I

The American Challenge

Official documents

U.S. Congress, House, Committee on Ways and Means, *Hearings on Extension of the Reciprocal Trade Agreements Act*, 76th Cong., 1st sess. (Washington, 1940, vol. i).

—— —— Committee on Un-American Activities, *Soviet Espionage Within the United States Government*, 80th Cong., 2nd sess. (Washington, 1948).

U.S. Tariff Commission, *Colonial Tariff Policies* (Washington, 1922).

—— *Reciprocity and Commercial Treaties* (Washington, 1922).

Other sources

ALLEN, WILLIAM R., 'The International Trade Philosophy of Cordell Hull, 1907–1933', *Am. Ec. Rev.*, xliii (1953), pp. 101–16.

ANONYMOUS, 'The Principles of Trade', *The Economist*, cxli (1941), pp. 553–4.

—— 'The New Frontier', *The Economist*, cxlii (1942), pp. 824–5.

—— 'The American Challenge', *The Economist*, cxliii (1942), pp. 66–67.

CULBERTSON, WILLIAM S., *International Economic Policies* (New York, 1945).

—— *Reciprocity* (New York, 1937).

GAYER, ARTHUR D., and SCHMIDT, CARL T., *American Economic Foreign Policy* (New York, 1939).

HULL, CORDELL, *Economic Barriers to Peace* (New York, 1937).

ICKES, HAROLD L., *The Secret Diary of Harold L. Ickes* (New York, 1953, 1954, 3 vols.).

ISTEL, ANDRÉ, 'Equal Access to Raw Materials', *For. Aff.*, xx (1942), pp. 450–65.

LUBELL, SAMUEL, *The Future of American Politics* (New York, 1952).

MALLERY, OTTO T., *Economic Union and Durable Peace* (New York, 1943).

NEVINS, ALLEN, *The New Deal and World Affairs* (New Haven, 1950).

PASVOLSKY, LEO, *et al.*, 'Round Table on Bases of International Economic Relations', *Am. Ec. Rev.*, xxxiii (Supp., 1943), pp. 455–65.

SAYRE, FRANCIS B., *America Must Act* (New York, 1936).

SCHACHT, HJALMAR, 'Germany's Colonial Demands', *For. Aff.*, xv (1937), pp. 223–4.

SCHATTSCHNEIDER, ELMER, *Politics, Pressures and the Tariff* (New York, 1942).

STALEY, EUGENE, *Raw Materials in Peace and War* (New York, 1937).

TASCA, HENRY J., *The Reciprocal Trade Policy of the United States* (Philadelphia, 1938).

TUGWELL, REXFORD G., 'The Progressive Orthodoxy of Franklin D. Roosevelt', *Ethics*, lxiv (1953), pp. 1–23.

WELLES, SUMNER, *Seven Decisions that Shaped History* (New York, 1950).

YOUNG, JOHN PARKE, 'Problems of International Economic Policy for the United States', *Am. Ec. Rev.*, xxxii (Supp., 1942), pp. 182–94.

CHAPTER II

The British Response

Official documents

U.K. Government, *Report of the Committee on Finance and Industry* (MacMillan Report), Cmd. 3897 (London, 1931).

—— *Imperial Conference at Ottawa 1932, Summary of Proceedings and Copies of Trade Agreements*, Cmd. 4174 (London, 1932).

—— *Imperial Conference at Ottawa 1932, Appendices to the Summary of Proceedings*, Cmd. 4175 (London, 1932).

—— *Trade Agreement Between the United Kingdom and the United States of America*, Cmd. 5882 (London, 1938).

Other sources

ANONYMOUS, 'The American View', *The Banker*, lx (1941), pp. 187–93.

—— 'Ten Years Off Gold', *The Economist*, cxli (1941), pp. 346–7.

—— 'Ten Years of Protection', *The Economist*, cxlii (1942), pp. 276–8.

—— 'The Post-War Exchange Regime', *The Banker*, lviii (1942), pp. 8–19.

Association of the British Chambers of Commerce, *Report of the Special Committee on Post-War Industrial Reconstruction* (London, 1942).

BALOGH, THOMAS, 'Foreign Exchange and Export Trade Policy', *Ec. Jour.*, l (1940), pp. 1–26.

BENHAM, FREDERIC, *Great Britain Under Protection* (New York, 1941).

BEVERIDGE, Sir WILLIAM, *et al.*, *Tariffs—The Case Examined* (London, 1932).

—— *Social Insurance and Allied Services* (New York, 1942).

CARR, EDWARD, H., *The Conditions of Peace* (New York, 1942).

CROWTHER, GEOFFREY, 'Anglo-American Pitfalls', *For. Aff.*, xx (1941), pp. 1–17.

—— 'Discussion on International Economic Relations', *Am. Ec. Rev.*, xxxii (Supp., 1943), pp. 332–4.

Federation of British Industries, *Reconstruction: A Report by the Federation of British Industries* (London, 1942).

FRY, RICHARD, 'The Rebirth of International Trade', *The Banker*, lx (1941), pp. 193–9.

HENDERSON, SIR HUBERT (HENRY CLAY., ed.), *A Selection from the Writings of Hubert Douglas Henderson* (Oxford, 1954).

KAHN, ALFRED E., *Great Britain in the World Economy* (New York, 1946).

Labour Party, *The International Post-War Settlement* (London, 1944).

—— *The Old World and the New Society* (London, 1942).

Liberal National Party, *A Basis for Britain's Post-War Policy* (London, 1941).

London Chamber of Commerce, *Report on General Principles of a Post-War Economy* (London, 1942).

LORWIN, LEWIS L., *Postwar Plans of the United Nations* (New York, 1943).

LOWE, MARVIN E., *The British Tariff Movement* (New York, 1942).

MEADE, JAMES, *The Economic Basis of a Durable Peace* (London, 1940).

National Institute of Economic Research (D. N. Chester, ed.), *Lessons of the British War Economy* (Cambridge, 1951).

OPIE, REDVERS, 'A British View of Postwar Trade', *Am. Ec. Rev.*, xxxiii (Supp., 1943), pp. 322–31.

RICHARDSON, J. HENRY, *British Economic Foreign Policy* (New York, 1936).
ROBBINS, LIONEL, *Economic Planning and International Order* (London, 1938).
SCHWARZENBERGER, G., 'The Most-Favoured-Nation Principle in British State Practise', *Br. Y. Int. Law*, xxii (1945), pp. 96–121.
TASCA, HENRY J., *World Trading Systems* (Paris, 1939).

CHAPTER III

The Atlantic Charter

Official documents

U.K. Parliament, House of Commons, 'War Situation', 374 H.C. Deb. 67–156 (9 Sept. 1941).
U.S. Congress, Senate, 'Conference Between the President and Members of Congress', 87 *Cong. Rec.* 7204–12 (19 Aug. 1941).
U.S. Department of State, 'Joint Declaration of the President of the United States and the Prime Minister of Great Britain', *Dept. State Bull.*, v (1941), pp. 125–6.
—— 'Message of the President to the Congress, Regarding Conference at Sea With British Prime Minister', *Dept. State Bull.*, v (1941), p. 147.

Other sources

ANONYMOUS, 'The Freedom to Trade', *The Economist*, cxli (1941), pp. 220–2.
CHURCHILL, WINSTON S., *The Grand Alliance* (London, 1950).
EDITOR, 'An End to Economic Nationalism', *The Banker*, lx (1941), pp. 174–81.
LANGER, WILLIAM L., and GLEASON, S. EVERETT, *The Undeclared War* (New York, 1953).
LINDLEY, ERNEST K., and DAVIS, FORREST, *How War Came* (New York, 1942).
STONE, JULIUS, *The Atlantic Charter* (London, 1942).
SHERWOOD, ROBERT E., *Roosevelt and Hopkins* (New York, 1948, vol. ii).
WELLES, SUMNER, *The Time for Decision* (New York, 1944).
—— *Where Are We Heading?* (London, 1947).

CHAPTER IV

Article Seven

Official documents

U.S. Congress, House, Committee on Foreign Affairs, *Extension of Lend-Lease*, Hearings on H.R. 1501, 78th Cong., 1st sess. (Washington, 1943).
——— *Report on the Extension of Lend-Lease*, House Rept. No. 188, 78th Cong., 1st sess. (Washington, 1943).
U.S. Department of State, 'Mutual Aid Agreement with Great Britain', *Dept. State Bull.*, vi (1942), pp. 190–2.

Other sources

ANONYMOUS, 'Lend-Lease Terms', *The Economist*, cxlii (1942), p. 281.
EDMINSTER, LYNN R., 'International Trade and Postwar Reconstruction', *Am. Ec. Rev.*, xxxiii (Supp.), Mar. 1943), pp. 303–4.
MALLERY, OTTO T., 'A Practical Approach to a World Trade Board', *Annals of the Am. Acad. of Pol. and Soc. Sci.*, ccxxxiv (1944), pp. 84–90.

CHAPTERS V AND VII

Planning for Financial Collaboration

The Compromise on Financial Collaboration

Official documents

ACHESON, DEAN, 'Statement on Postwar International Economic Problems to a Sub-committee of the Committee on Postwar Economic Policy and Planning of the House of Representatives', *Dept. State Bull.*, xi (1944), pp. 656–62.

U.K. Parliament, House of Commons, 'Economic Policy', 386 H.C. Deb. 770–848, 916–96 (2 and 3 Feb. 1943).

—— —— 'Post-war International Currency', 389 H.C. Deb. 645–745 (12 May 1943).

—— —— 'Monetary Policy', 399 H.C. Deb. 1935–2046 (10 May 1944).

—— House of Lords, 'International Clearing Union', 127 H.L. Deb. 521–63 (18 May 1943).

—— House of Lords, 'International Monetary Fund', 131 H.L. Deb. 834–83 (23 May 1944).

U.K. Government, *Proposal for an International Clearing Union*, Cmd. 6437 (London, 1943).

—— *United States Proposal for a United and Associated Nations Stabilization Fund* (London, 1943).

—— *Joint Statement by Experts on the Establishment of an International Monetary Fund*, Cmd. 6519 (London, 1944).

—— *United Nations Monetary and Financial Conference: Final Act*, Cmd. 6546 (London, 1944).

U.S. Congress, House, Committee on Banking and Currency, *Bretton Woods Agreements Act*, Hearings on H.R. 2211, 79th Cong., 1st sess., Parts I and II (Washington, 1945).

—— —— —— *Participation of the United States in the International Monetary Fund and the International Bank for Reconstruction and Development*, Report to Accompany H.R. 3314, 79th Cong., 1st sess., H. Rept. 171 (Washington, 1945).

—— —— Committee on Un-American Activities, *Hearings Regarding Communist Espionage in the U.S. Government*, 80th Cong., 2nd sess. (Washington, 1948).

—— Senate, 'Bretton Woods Agreements—International Monetary Fund and International Bank', 91 Cong. Rec. 7557–84, 7597–626, 7666–90 (16–18 July 1945).

—— —— Committee on Banking and Currency, *Bretton Woods Agreements Act*, Hearings on H.R. 3314, 79th Cong., 1st sess. (Washington, 1945).

—— —— —— *Participation of the United States in the International Monetary Fund and the International Bank for Reconstruction and Development*, Report to Accompany H.R. 3314, 79th Cong., 1st sess., S. Rept. 452, Parts I and II (Washington, 1945).

U.S. Department of State, *Proceedings and Documents of the United Nations Monetary and Financial Conference, Bretton Woods, New Hampshire, July 1–22, 1944* (Washington, 1948, 2 vols.).

U.S. Treasury, *Preliminary Draft Outline of an International Stabilization Fund of the United and Associated Nations* (Washington, 1943).

—— *Preliminary Draft Outline of a Proposal for a Bank for Reconstruction and Development of the United and Associated Nations* (Washington, 1943).

—— *The Bretton Woods Proposals* (Washington, 1945).

—— *Questions and Answers on the Fund and Bank* (Washington, 1945).

YOUNG, JOHN PARKE, 'Developing Plans for an International Monetary Fund and a World Bank', *Dept. State Bull.*, xxiii (1950), pp. 778–90.

Other sources

ALDRICH, WINTHROP W., *Some Aspects of American Foreign Economic Policy* (New York, 1944).

American Bankers Association, *Practical International Financial Organization* (New York, 1945).

—— Economic Policy Committee, *The Place of the United States in the Post-War Economy* (New York, 1943).

ANDERSON, BENJAMIN, *The Postwar Stabilization of Foreign Exchange* (New York, 1943).

—— *International Currency Gold Versus Bancor or Unitas* (New York, 1944).

ANONYMOUS, 'The Future of Gold', *The Economist*, cxliii (1942), pp. 655–6.

—— 'The Future of the Exchanges', *The Economist*, cxliv (1943), pp. 3–5.

—— 'Economic Equipoise', *The Economist*, cxliv (1943), pp. 452–3.

—— 'The Currency Plans', *The Economist*, cxliv (1943), pp. 556–8.

—— 'Post-War Currency', *The Economist*, cxlv (1943), pp. 261–2.

—— 'The Principles of Trade', *The Economist*, cxlvi (1944), pp. 4–5, 32–34, 64–65, 94–95, 136–7, 169–70, 204–5, 232–3.

—— 'Bretton Woods', *The Economist*, cxlix (1945), pp. 75–76, 109–11, 151–2, 182–3, 220–1, 252–3.

—— 'Plans for World Currency Stabilization', *The Guaranty Survey*, xxiii (1943), pp. 1–4.

BERNSTEIN, E. M., 'A Practical International Monetary Policy', *Am. Ec. Rev.*, xxxiv (1944), pp. 771–84.

—— 'Scarce Currency and the International Monetary Fund', *Jour. Pol. Ec.*, liii (1945), pp. 1–14.

BOURNEUF, ALICE E., 'Professor Williams and the Fund', *Am. Ec. Rev.*, xxxiv (1944), pp. 840–7.

—— 'Lending Operations of the International Monetary Fund', *Rev. Ec. Stat.*, xxviii (1946), pp. 237–47.

Chamber of Commerce of the United States, Finance Department Committee, *Bretton Woods Program* (Washington, 1945).

—— *The Bretton Woods Proposals* (Washington, 1945).

CHARLES, EDWARD, 'Labour and Bretton Woods', *The Banker*, lxxv (1945), pp. 139–41.

COLE, G. D. H., *Money* (2nd ed., London, 1945).

EINZIG, PAUL, 'A Challenge to Mr. Harrod', *The Banker*, lxxvii (1946), pp. 87–92.

Federation of British Industries, *Interim Report on the Final Act of the United Nations Monetary and Financial Conference* (London, 1944).

—— *Second Report on the Final Act of the United Nations Monetary and Financial Conference* (London, 1945).

FEIS, HERBERT, 'Restoring Trade After the War', *For. Aff.*, xx (1942), pp. 282–92.

FELLNER, WILLIAM, 'The Commercial Policy Implications of the Fund and Bank', *Am. Ec. Rev.*, xxxv (Supp., 1945), pp. 262–71.

GARDNER, WALTER R., 'The Future International Position of the United States as Affected by the Fund and Bank', *Am. Ec. Rev.*, xxv (Supp., 1945), pp. 272–88.

HALM, GEORGE N., *International Monetary Cooperation* (Chapel Hill, N.C., 1945).

HANSEN, ALVIN H., *America's Role in the World Economy* (New York, 1945).

—— World Institutions for Stability and Expansion, *For. Aff.*, xxii (1944), pp. 248–55.

—— and KINDLEBERGER, CHARLES P., 'The Economic Tasks of the Postwar World', *For. Aff.*, xx (1942), pp. 466–76.

HARROD, ROY, 'Anglo-American Co-operation', *The Banker*, lxxvii (1946), pp. 139–43.

HAWTREY, R. G., *Bretton Woods* (London, 1945).

KEYNES, JOHN MAYNARD, *Letter to Jacob Viner, June 9, 1943*.

—— *Letter to Jacob Viner, October 17, 1943*.

KINDLEBERGER, CHARLES P., 'International Monetary Stabilization', in Harris, Seymour (ed.), *Postwar Economic Problems* (New York, 1943), pp. 375–95.

—— 'Planning for Foreign Investment', *Am. Ec. Rev.*, xxxiii (Supp., 1943), pp. 347–54.

London Chamber of Commerce, *Report on the Final Act of the United Nations Monetary and Financial Conference* (London, 1944).

LUTZ, F. A., *International Monetary Mechanisms: The Keynes and White Proposals*, Essays in International Finance No. 1 (Princeton, 1943).

MIKESELL, RAYMOND R., 'The Key Currency Proposal', *Quart. Jour. of Econ.*, lix (1945), pp. 563–76.

MORGENTHAU, HENRY Jr., 'Bretton Woods and International Co-operation', *For. Aff.*, xxiii (1945), pp. 182–94.

PEHLE, JOHN, 'The Bretton Woods Institutions', *Yale Law Journal*, lv (1946), pp. 1127–39.

RASMINSKY, LOUIS, 'International Credit and Currency Plans', *For. Aff.*, xxii, (1944), pp. 589–603.

ROBERTSON, D. H., 'The Post-War Monetary Plans', *Ec. Jour.*, lii (1943), pp. 352–60.

ROBINSON, JOAN, 'The International Currency Proposals', *Ec. Jour.*, li (1943), pp. 161–75.

SCHUMACHER, E. F., *et al.*, 'New Plans for International Trade', *O.I.S.B.*, v (Supp. No. 5, 1943), pp. 3–39.

DE VEGH, I., 'The International Clearing Union', *Am. Ec. Rev.*, xxxiii (1943), pp. 534–56.

—— 'Peace Aims, Capital Requirements, and International Lending', *Am. Ec. Rev.*, xxxv (Supp., 1945), pp. 253–61.

VINER, JACOB, 'Two Plans for International Monetary Stabilization', *Yale Review*, xxiii (1943), pp. 77–107.

WHITE, HARRY D., 'Postwar Currency Stabilization', *Am. Ec. Rev.*, xxxiii (Supp., 1943), pp. 382–7.

—— 'The Monetary Fund: Some Criticisms Examined', *For. Aff.*, xxiii (1945), pp. 195–210.

WILLIAMS, JOHN H., 'Currency Stabilization: The Keynes and White Plans', *For. Aff.*, xxi (1943), pp. 645–58.

WILLIAMS, JOHN H., 'Currency Stabilization: American and British Attitudes', *For. Aff.*, xxii (1944), pp. 233–47.
—— 'International Monetary Plans: After Bretton Woods', *For. Aff.*, xxiii (1945), pp. 38–56.

CHAPTERS VI AND VIII

Planning for Commercial Collaboration

The Compromise on Commercial Collaboration

Official documents

NOTTER, HARLEY A., *Postwar Foreign Policy Preparation 1939–1945*, Dept. State Pub. 3580 (Washington, 1949).

U.K. Government, 'Employment Policy', Cmd. 6527 (London, 1944).

U.K. House of Commons, 'Empire and Commonwealth Unity', 399 H.C. Deb. 390–486, 498–586 (20 and 21 Apr. 1944).

U.S. Congress, House, Committee on Ways and Means, *Extension of Reciprocal Trade Agreements Act*, Hearings on H.R. 111, 78th Cong., 1st sess. (Washington, 1943).

—— —— —— *1945 Extension of the Reciprocal Trade Agreements Act*, Hearings on H.R. 2652 Superseded by H.R. 3240, 79th Cong., 1st sess. (Washington, 1945).

—— —— —— *Foreign Trade Agreements*, Report to Accompany H.R. 3240, H. Rep. 594, 79th Cong., 1st sess. (Washington, 1945).

—— ——, Special Committee on Postwar Economic Policy and Planning, *Sixth Report*, H. Rept. 541, 79th Cong., 1st sess. (Washington, 1945).

—— Senate, Committee on Finance, *1945 Extension of the Reciprocal Trade Agreements Act*, Hearings on H.R. 3240, 79th Cong., 1st sess. (Washington 1945).

U.S. Department of State, *Proposals for the Expansion of World Trade and Employment* (Washington, 1945).

Other sources

ANONYMOUS, 'The Trade Proposals', *The Economist*, cxlix (1945), pp. 853–7.

BALOGH, THOMAS, 'The International Aspects of Full Employment', in Oxford University Institute of Statistics, *Economics of Full Employment* (Oxford, 1947), pp. 126–81.

BIDWELL, PERCY W., 'A Postwar Commercial Policy for the United States', *Am. Ec. Rev.*, xxxiv (Supp., 1944), pp. 340–53.

CHURCHILL, WINSTON S., *Mr. Churchill's Declaration of Policy to the Electors* (London, 1945).

EDMINSTER, LYNN R., 'International Trade and Postwar Reconstruction', *Am. Ec. Rev.*, xxxiii (Supp., 1943), pp. 303–21.

Federation of British Industries, *International Trade Policy*, Report of the F.B.I. International Trade Policy Committee (London, 1944).

HANCOCK, W. K., *Empire in the Changing World* (New York, 1943).

HOSELITZ, BERT F., *British Trade Policy and the United States: A Survey of Recent Discussion in Great Britain on Post-War Commercial Policy* (New Haven, 1943).

SCHUMACHER, E. F., *Export Policy and Full Employment*, Fabian Research Ser. No. 77 (London, 1944).

CHAPTER IX

The Rise and Fall of War-time Collaboration

Official documents

U.K. Parliament, House of Commons, 'Lend-Lease Contracts (Cancellation)', 410 H.C. Deb. 955–58 (24 Aug. 1945).

U.K. Treasury, *Statistical Material Presented During the Washington Negotiations*, Cmd. 6707 (London, 1945).

U.S. Congress, House, 'Extension of Lend-Lease', 91 *Cong. Rec.* 2120–52 (13 Mar. 1945).

—— Senate, 'Extension of Lend-Lease Act', 90 *Cong. Rec.* 4092–106 (8 May 1944).

—— —— Committee on Foreign Relations, *Extension of Lend-Lease*, Hearings on H.R. 2013, 79th Cong., 1st sess. (Washington, 1945).

U.S. President, *Fifth Report to Congress on Lend-Lease Operations* (June 1942).

Other sources

ANONYMOUS, 'Transatlantic Transactions', *The Economist*, cxli (1941), pp. 344–6.

—— 'Painless Prosperity?', *The Economist*, cxliii (1942), pp. 131–2.

—— 'The End of Isolation', *The Economist*, cxliii (1942), pp. 665–6.

BERLE, ADOLPH, 'The Realist Base of American Foreign Policy', *Dept. State Bull.*, vii (1942), pp. 831–5.

BROWN, WILLIAM A., JR., and OPIE, REDVERS, *American Foreign Assistance* (Washington, 1953).

CHURCHILL, WINSTON S., *Closing the Ring* (London, 1952).

—— 'Address to the Alumni of Harvard University', in British Information Services, *British Speeches of the Day*, No. 7 (1943).

HANCOCK, W. K., and GOWING, M. M., *British War Economy* (London, 1949).

LEAHY, WILLIAM D., *I Was There* (New York, 1950).

ROSENMAN, SAMUEL I., *Working With Roosevelt* (New York, 1952).

STALEY, EUGENE, 'The Economic Implications of Lend-Lease', *Am. Ec. Rev.*, xxxiii (Supp., 1943), pp. 362–76.

STIMSON, HENRY L., and BUNDY, MCGEORGE, *On Active Service in Peace and War* (New York, 1947).

CHAPTERS X–XII

Negotiating the Loan

The Loan Agreement as an Instrument of Multilateralism

Passing the Loan

Official documents

BYRNES, JAMES, 'U.S.-U.K. Economic and Financial Agreements', *Dept. State Bull.*, xiv (1946), pp. 267–71.

CLAYTON, WILL, 'The Implications of International Economic Relations to World Peace', *Dept. State Bull.*, xiv (1946), pp. 678–81.

TRUMAN, HARRY S., 'Message Transmitting Anglo-American Financial Agreement', 92 *Cong. Rec.* 586–7 (30 Jan. 1946).

U.K. Government, *Financial Agreement between the Governments of the United States and the United Kingdom*, Cmd. 6708 (London, 1945).

U.K. Parliament, House of Commons, 'Anglo-American Financial and Economic Discussions', 417 H.C. Deb. 422–558, 661–747 (12 and 13 Dec. 1945).

—— House of Lords, 'Anglo-American Financial Arrangements', 138 H.L. Deb. 677–775, 777–898 (17 and 18 Dec. 1945).

U.S. Congress, House, 'Anglo-American Financial Agreement', 92 *Cong. Rec.* 8823–82, 8913–57 (12 and 13 July 1946).

—— —— Committee on Banking and Currency, *Anglo-American Financial Agreement*, Hearings on H.R. Res. 311, 79th Cong., 2nd sess. (Washington, 1946).

—— Special Committee on Postwar Economic Policy and Planning, *Economic Reconstruction in Europe*, H. Rept. 1205, 79th Cong., 1st sess. (Washington, 1945).

—— Senate, 'Proposed Loan to Great Britain', 92 *Cong. Rec.* 4084–91, 4104–26 (22 and 24 Apr. 1946).

—— —— Committee on Banking and Currency, *Anglo-American Financial Agreement*, Hearings on S.J. Res. 138, 79th Cong., 2nd sess. (Washington, 1946).

—— —— —— *Implementation of the Financial Agreement Between the United States and the United Kingdom*, S. Rept. 1144 (Washington, 1946).

U.S. Department of State, *Anglo-American Financial and Commercial Agreements*, Dept. of State Pub. 2439 (Washington, 1945).

U.S. National Advisory Council on International Monetary and Financial Policy, *The Foreign Loan Policy of the United States*, House Doc. 489, 79th Cong., 2nd sess. (Washington, 1946).

U.S. Treasury, *Questions and Answers on the Anglo-American Financial Agreement* (Washington, 1946).

Other sources

AMERY, L. S., *The Washington Loan Agreements* (London, 1946).

—— *The American Loan Conditions: The British Case*. A Speech delivered by the Rt. Hon. L. S. Amery before the American Chamber of Commerce in London on March 19, 1946 (London, 1946).

ANONYMOUS, 'The Dollar Loan', *The Economist*, cxlix (1945), pp. 820–1.

—— 'Second Thoughts', *The Economist*, cxlix (1945), pp. 849–50.

—— 'The Two and the One', *The Economist*, cl (1946), pp. 360–1.

—— 'The Loan Hearings', *The Economist*, cl (1946), p. 455.

—— 'The Loan in Congress', *The Economist*, cl (1946), p. 743.

—— 'Warning from the West', *The Economist*, cli (1946), pp. 1–2.

COTTRELL, LEONARD S., and EBERHARDT, SYLVIA, *American Opinion on World Affairs* (Princeton, 1948).

EDITOR, 'Towards an Expanding World Economy', *The Banker*, lxxvii (1946), pp. 5–9.

EINZIG, PAUL, 'Economic Peace in Our Time?', *The Banker*, lxxvii (1946), pp. 13–17.

Empire Industries Association, *Statement of the Executive Committee* (London, 1945).

HARROD, R. F., *A Page of British Folly* (London, 1946).

HENDERSON, SIR HUBERT, 'The Anglo-American Financial Agreement', *O.I.S.B.*, viii (1946), pp. 1–13.

KEYNES, JOHN MAYNARD, *Letter to Jacob Viner, January 4, 1946.*

POLK, JUDD, and PATTERSON, GARDNER, 'The British Loan', *For. Aff.*, xxiv (1946), pp. 429–40.

VANDENBERG, ARTHUR H., Jr. (ed.), *The Private Papers of Senator Vandenberg* (Boston, 1952).

WILCOX, CLAIR, *What Do We Get?*, Speech to the Pennsylvania Chamber of Commerce (unpublished typescript 7 May 1946).

CHAPTERS XIII AND XV

Savannah: Two Conceptions of Financial Collaboration
The End of Bretton Woods

Official documents

ACHESON, DEAN, 'The Requirements of Reconstruction', *Dept. State Bull.*, xvi (1947), pp. 991–4.

ANONYMOUS, 'International Transactions of the United States in the First Post-war Years', *Fed. Res. Bull.*, xxxii (1946), pp. 1321–34.

International Bank for Reconstruction and Development, *Annual Report* (Washington, 1947–9).

International Monetary Fund, *Annual Report* (Washington, 1947–9).

—— *First Annual Meeting of the Board of Governors, Report of the Executive Directors, and Summary Proceedings* (Washington, 1946).

—— *Selected Documents—Board of Governors Inaugural Meeting* (Washington, 1946).

—— *World Fund and Bank Inaugural Meeting*, Fund. Doc. 27 (Washington 1946).

MARSHALL, GEORGE C., 'European Initiative Essential to Economic Recovery' *Dept. State Bull.*, xvi (1947), pp. 1159–60.

United Nations, Economic Commission for Europe, *A Survey of the Economic Situation and Prospects of Europe* (Geneva, 1948).

—— —— *Economic Survey of Europe in 1948* (Geneva, 1949).

—— —— *Economic Survey of Europe Since the War* (Geneva, 1953).

U.S. Congress, House, Committee on Foreign Affairs, *Hearings on a Bill to Amend the Economic Cooperation Act of 1948, as Amended*, 81st Cong., 2nd sess., Part I (Washington, 1950).

—— Senate, Committee on Foreign Relations, *European Recovery Program*, Hearings on United States Assistance to European Recovery, 80th Cong., 2nd sess., Parts I–III (Washington, 1948).

U.S. Delegation to the U.N., *Press Release No. 78* (14 Nov. 1946).

U.S. Department of State, 'Aid to Greece and Turkey', *Dept. State Bull.*, xvi (Supp., 4 May 1947).

U.S. National Advisory Council on International Monetary and Financial Problems, *Report on Activities*, House Doc. 497, 79th Cong., 2nd sess. (Washington, 1946).

—— *First Special Report on the Operations and Policies of the International Monetary Fund and the International Bank for Reconstruction and Development*, House Doc. No. 656, 80th Cong., 2nd sess. (Washington, 1948).

U.S. National Advisory Council on International Monetary and Financial Problems, *Report on Activities from October 1, 1947 to March 31, 1948*, House Doc. No. 737, 80th Cong., 2nd sess. (Washington, 1948).

—— *Report on Activities from April 1, 1948 to September 30, 1948*, House Doc. No. 120, 81st Cong., 1st sess. (Washington, 1948).

Other sources

ANONYMOUS, 'Dollars for Europe', *The Economist*, cliii (1947), pp. 833–5.

—— 'Mr. Marshall's Challenge', *The Economist*, cliii (1947), pp. 921–3.

BAREAU, PAUL, 'Two Conceptions of the International Monetary Fund', *Journal of the Institute of Bankers* (1946), pp. 1–10.

BASCH, ANTONIN, 'International Bank for Reconstruction and Development 1944–1949: A Review', *International Conciliation*, cccclv (1949), pp. 791–827.

BRATTER, HERBERT M., 'Fund and Bank: The First Full Year', *The Banker*, lxxxiii (1947), pp. 147–52.

CAMPBELL, JOHN C., *The United States in World Affairs 1945–47* (New York, 1947).

DIEBOLD, WILLIAM, Jr., *Trade and Payments in Western Europe* (New York, 1952).

ELLIS, HOWARD S., *The Economics of Freedom* (New York, 1950).

GUTT, CAMILLE, 'The International Monetary Fund and Its Functions', *Proc. Am. Ac. of Pol. and Soc. Sci.*, xxii (1947), pp. 152–8.

KEYNES, JOHN MAYNARD, *Letter to E. M. Bernstein, May 29, 1945.*

—— 'The Balance of Payments of the United States', *Ec. Jour.*, lvi (1946), pp. 172–87.

KNORR, KLAUS, 'The Bretton Woods Institutions in Transition', *Int. Org.*, ii (1948), pp. 19–38.

MIKESELL, RAYMOND F., 'The International Monetary Fund 1944–1949', *International Conciliation*, cccclv (1949), pp. 828–74.

STIMSON, HENRY L., 'The Challenge to Americans', *For. Aff.*, xxvi (1947), pp. 5–14.

VINSON, FRED. M., 'After the Savannah Conference', *For. Aff.*, xxiv (1946), pp. 622–32.

WHITE, HARRY D., 'The International Monetary Fund: The First Year', *Annals Am. Ac. Pol. and Soc. Sci.*, cclii (1947), pp. 21–9.

CHAPTERS XIV AND XVII

London: Two Conceptions of Commercial Collaboration
The End of the I.T.O.

Official documents

ACHESON, DEAN, 'Economic Policy and the I.T.O. Charter', *Dept. State Bull.*, xx (1949), pp. 623–7.

BROWN, WINTHROP G., 'Why Private Business Should Support the I.T.O.', *Dept. State Bull.*, xxii (1950), pp. 132–5.

CLAYTON, WILL, 'Why and How We Came to Find Ourselves at the I.T.O. Conference', *Dept. State Bull.*, xviii (1948), pp. 825–7.

U.K. Board of Trade, *Report on the Geneva Tariff Negotiations*, Cmd. 7258 (London, 1947).

U.K. Parliament, House of Commons, 'Export and Import Trade', 435 H.C. Deb. 865–99 (24 Mar. 1947).

U.K. Parliament, House of Commons, 'Geneva Tariff Agreement', 446 H.C. Deb. 1210–1334 (29 Jan. 1948).

United Nations, Economic and Social Council, *Report of the First Session of the Preparatory Committee of the Conference on Trade and Employment*, E/PC/T/33 (London, 1946).

—— —— *Report of the Second Session of the Preparatory Committee of the United Nations Conference on Trade and Employment*, E/PC/T/186 (Geneva, 1947).

—— —— Preparatory Committee of the United Nations Conference on Trade and Employment, First and Second Sessions, Plenary Meetings, *Verbatim Records*, E/PC/T/PV.1–PV.6, E/PC/T/PV.2/1–PV.2/7 (London and Geneva, 1946–7).

—— —— First Session of the Preparatory Committee of the United Nations Conference on Trade and Employment, Committee I (Employment and Economic Activity), *Verbatim Records and Working Papers*, E/PC/T/C.I/PV. 1–PV. 4, and W. 1–W. 4 (London, 1946).

—— —— —— Committee II (General Commercial Policy Committee), *Verbatim Records*, E/PC/T/C.II/PV. 1–PV.13 (London, 1946).

—— —— —— Sub-committee on Quantitative Restrictions and Exchange Control of Committee II (General Commercial Policy), *Verbatim Records*, E/PC/T/C.II/QR/PV.1–PV.6 (London, 1946).

—— —— —— Procedures Sub-Committee, *Verbatim Records*, E/PC/T/C.II/ PRO/PV.1–PV.15 (London, 1946).

—— —— Second Session of the Preparatory Committee of the United Nations Conference on Trade and Employment, Tariff Agreement Committee, *Verbatim Records*, E/PC/T/TAC/PV.1–PV.28 (Geneva, 1947).

—— —— —— Commission A, *Verbatim Records*, E/PC/T/A/PV.1–PV.43 (Geneva, 1947).

U.S. Congress, House, Committee on Foreign Affairs, *The International Trade Organization*, Report by Hon. James G. Fulton and Hon. Jacob K. Javits (Washington, 1948).

—— —— —— *Membership and Participation by the United States in the International Trade Organization*, Hearings on H.J. Res. 236, 81st Cong., 2nd sess. (Apr.–May, 1950).

—— Senate, Committee on Finance, *Extension of the Reciprocal Trade Agreements Act*, Hearings on H.R. 1211, 81st Cong., 1st sess. (Washington, 1949).

—— —— —— *International Trade Organization*, Hearings on Trade Agreements System and Proposed International Trade Organization Charter, 80th Cong., 1st sess., Parts I and II (Washington, 1947).

U.S. Department of State, *Analysis of the General Agreement on Tariffs and Trade*, Dept. State Pub. 2983 (Washington, 1947).

—— *Peace, Freedom, and World Trade—Address by the President*, Dept. State Publ. 2789 (Washington, 1947).

—— *Havana Charter for an International Trade Organization*, Dept. of State Pub. 3206 (Washington, 1948).

—— *The General Agreement on Tariffs and Trade and Texts of Related Documents*, Dept. of State Pub. 3758 (Washington, 1950).

Other sources

ANONYMOUS, 'The Republicans Return', *The Economist*, cli (1946), pp. 737–8.
—— 'Trade Make Believe', *The Economist*, cli (1946), pp. 859–60.

ANONYMOUS, 'The Vandenberg Tariff', *The Economist*, clii (1947), pp. 376–7.
—— 'Prelude to Geneva', *The Economist*, clii (1947), pp. 444–5.
—— 'Interim Report on Geneva', *The Economist*, clii (1947), pp. 941–2.
—— 'A Trade Policy for Europe', *The Economist*, cliv (1948), pp. 212–13.
—— 'Goodbye to All G.A.T.T.', *The Economist*, clx (1951), pp. 901–2.
BALOGH, THOMAS, 'The Charter of the International Trade Organization and the Preparatory Committee of the United Nations Conference on Trade and Employment', *O.I.S.B.*, ix (1947), pp. 104–28.
—— 'Britain and The Geneva Tariff Agreements', *O.I.S.B.*, ix (1947), pp. 417–29.
BEVERIDGE, SIR WILLIAM, *Full Employment in a Free Society* (London, 1945).
BROWN, WILLIAM A., *The United States and the Restoration of World Trade* (Washington, 1950).
Clearing Committee for Organizations Supporting Reciprocal Trade, *Grass Roots Opinion on International Trade* (Washington, 1947).
Committee for Economic Development, Research and Policy Committee, *The International Trade Organization and the Reconstruction of World Trade* (New York, 1949).
Conservative Party, *Imperial Policy* (London, 1949).
CORTNEY, PHILIP, *The Economic Munich* (New York, 1949).
DIEBOLD, WILLIAM, Jr., *The End of the I.T.O.*, Essays in International Finance No. 16 (Princeton, 1952).
Empire Industries Association and British Empire League, *The Geneva Trade Agreement*, Monthly Bull. No. 81 (London, 1947).
—— (Wells, W. A., ed.), *The Havana Charter, G.A.T.T., and the I.T.O.* (London, 1950).
FEIS, HERBERT, 'The Conflict Over Trade Ideologies', *For. Aff.*, xxv (1947), pp. 217–28.
—— 'The Geneva Proposals for an International Trade Charter', *Int. Org.*, ii (1948), pp. 39–52.
FRISCH, RAGNAR, 'On the Need for Forecasting a Multilateral Balance of Payments', *Am. Ec. Rev.*, xxxvii (1947), pp. 535–51.
FURTH, J. HERBERT, 'Short-Run Escape Clauses of the Havana Charter', *Am. Ec. Rev.*, xxxix (Supp., 1949), pp. 252–60.
GORDON, MARGARET S., 'The Character and Significance of the General Commitments That Nations Will Make Under the ITO Charter', *Am. Ec. Rev.*, xxxix (Supp., 1949), pp. 241–50.
HAWKINS, HARRY C., 'Problems Raised by the International Trade Organization', in Harris, S. E. (ed.), *Foreign Economic Policy for the United States* (Cambridge, U.S.A., 1948), pp. 271–88.
HEILPERIN, MICHAEL A., 'How the U.S. Lost the I.T.O. Conference', *Fortune* (Sept. 1949), pp. 80–82.
HENDERSON, SIR HUBERT, 'A Criticism of the Havana Charter', *Am. Ec. Rev.*, xxxix (1949), pp. 605–17.
KILHEFFER, 'I.T.O.—Illusion or Reality?', *Annals of the Am. Acad. of Pol. and Soc. Sci.*, cclxiv (1949), pp. 75–86.
KNORR, K. E., 'The Functions of an International Trade Organization: Possibilities and Limitations', *Am. Ec. Rev.*, xxxvii (Supp., 1947), pp. 542–59.
LOFTUS, JOHN A., 'Permanent Exceptions to the Commercial Policy Provisions of the ITO Charter', *Am. Ec. Rev.*, xxxix (Supp., 1949), pp. 261–8.

National Association of Manufacturers, *The Havana Charter for an International Trade Organization* (New York, 1950).

National Foreign Trade Council, *Position With Respect to the Havana Charter for an International Trade Organization* (New York, 1950).

United States Council of the International Chamber of Commerce, *G.A.T.T.—An Analysis and Appraisal of the General Agreement on Tariffs and Trade* (New York, 1955).

—— Executive Committee, *Statement of Position on the Havana Charter for An International Trade Organization* (New York, 1950).

VINER, JACOB, 'Conflicts of Principle in Drafting a Trade Charter', *For. Aff.*, xxv (1947), pp. 612–28.

WILCOX, CLAIR, *A Charter for World Trade* (New York, 1949).

—— 'The London Draft Charter for an International Trade Organization', *Am. Ec. Rev.*, xxxvii (Supp., 1947), pp. 529–41.

—— 'The Promise of the World Trade Charter', *For. Aff.*, xxvii (1949), pp. 486–96.

—— 'Why the International Trade Organization?', *Annals of the Am. Ac. of Pol. and Soc. Sci.*, cclxiv (1949), pp. 69–74.

WILGRESS, EDWARD D., *A New Attempt at Internationalism* (thesis presented to the University of Geneva for Docteur en Sciences Politiques, Univ. of Geneva Thèse No. 62, 1949).

CHAPTER XVI

The End of the Loan Agreement

Official documents

ANONYMOUS, 'The British Crisis', *Fed. Res. Bull.*, xxxiii (1947), pp. 1071–82.

KNAPP, J. BURKE, and TAMAGNA, F. M., 'Sterling in Multilateral Trade', *Fed. Res. Bull.*, xxxiii (1947), pp. 1083–1090.

U.K. Government, *Economic Survey for 1947*, Cmd. 7046 (London, 1947).

—— *United Kingdom Balance of Payments 1946 to 1950*, Cmd. 8065 (London, 1950).

U.K. Parliament, House of Commons, 'Import Programme', 439 H.C. Deb. 2041–157 (8 July 1947).

—— —— 'State of the Nation', 441 H.C. Deb. 1473–1595, 1654–1770 (6 and 7 Aug. 1947).

—— —— 'Debate on the Address', 443 H.C. Deb. 384–469 (24 Oct. 1947).

U.S. Congress, House, Select Committee on Foreign Aid, *Report on the United Kingdom* (Washington, 1948).

U.S. National Advisory Council on International Monetary and Financial Problems, *Report on Activities from April 1, 1947 to September 30, 1947*, 80th Cong., 1st sess. (Washington, 1947).

Other sources

ANONYMOUS, 'The Dollar Gap', *The Banker*, lxxxiii (1947), pp. 7–11.

—— 'Inquest on the Dollars', *The Banker*, lxxxiii (1947), pp. 15–20.

—— 'The Twelfth Hour', *The Banker*, lxxxiii (1947), pp. 65–70.

—— 'The Dollar Drain', *The Banker*, lxxxiii (1947), pp. 143–6.

—— 'Sterling After July 15th', *The Economist*, clii (1947), pp. 1032–3.

—— 'After July 15th', *The Economist*, cliii (1947), pp. 117–18.

412 *Bibliography*

ANONYMOUS, 'The Lash of Adversity', *The Economist*, cliii (1947), pp. 225–6.
—— 'Articles Seven to Ten', *The Economist*, cliii (1947), pp. 228–30.
—— 'Post-Mortem on Dollars', *The Economist*, cliii (1947), pp. 288–9.
—— 'Inconvertible Again', *The Economist*, cliii (1947), pp. 305–6.
—— 'Sterling's Future Role', *The Economist*, cliii (1947), pp. 331–3.
—— 'A Curse on the Tinker', *The Economist*, cliii (1947), pp. 345–6.
BYRNES, JAMES M., *Speaking Frankly* (New York, 1947).
CASSELS, JOHN M., 'Anglo-American Economic Relations', in Harris, Seymour (ed.), *Foreign Economic Policy for the United States*, pp. 57–78.
EINZIG, PAUL, 'The Case for Bilateralism', *The Banker*, lxxxiv (1947), 27–31.
FITZSIMMONS, M. A., *The Foreign Policy of the British Labour Government: 1945–1951* (Notre Dame, Ind., 1953).
HARROD, ROY, *Are These Hardships Necessary?* (London, 1947).
—— *And So It Goes On* (London, 1951).
—— 'The Dollar Problem', *The Banker*, lxxxiv (1947), pp. 151–62.
MORGAN, E. VICTOR, 'Multilateralism Eventually . . .', *The Banker*, lxxxiv (1947) pp. 21–26.
ROBBINS, LIONEL, 'Inquest on the Crisis', *Lloyds Bank Review*, New Series No. 6 (1947), pp. 1–27.
ROBERTSON, D. H., 'The Economic Outlook', *Ec. Jour.*, lvii (1947), pp. 421–37.
TETHER, GORDON C., 'Bretton Woods and the Crisis', *The Banker*, lxxxiv (1947), pp. 32–35.
VINER, JACOB, 'An American View of the British Crisis', *Lloyds Bank Review*, New Series No. 6 (1947), pp. 28–38.
WILLIAMS, JOHN H., 'Economic Lessons of Two World Wars', *For. Aff.*, xxvi (1947), pp. 134–54.

INDEX

Acheson, Dean, United States Secretary of State, 299; and post-war planning, 58, 67, 104, 135; and U.N.R.R.A., 296; and aid to Western Europe, 301, 302.

Advisory Economic Staff for United Nations, 106.

Agriculture (Great Britain): influence of protection and Imperial Preference on, 36; influence of, on right-wing opposition to multilateralism, 33–34.

— (U.S.A.): 3–4, 20–21; Agricultural Adjustment Act, 21, 149, 374; import quotas on agricultural commodities, 149, 150; programme of price supports for American agricultural products, 374.

Aldrich, Winthrop, 132, 197.

American Bankers Association, 98.

— Stabilization Fund, 73.

Amery, L. S., Secretary of State for India, 33; criticizes Anglo-American commercial collaboration, 145; chairman of Empire Industries Association, 33; and Imperial Preference, 33.

Anderson, Sir John: and American aid to Great Britain, 189; Chancellor of the Exchequer, 65–66; supports Anglo-American commercial collaboration, 145; criticizes Loan Agreement, 227, 230; Lord President of the Council, 25.

Anglo-American Commercial Collaboration: Anglo-American Financial Agreement, an impediment to, 346, 347; birth of the I.T.O., 101–3; compromise on, 145–60; doctrinaire attitudes to, 384; employment issue, 104–6, 146–8; planning for, 101–9; quantitative restrictions issue, 106–7, 148–50; 'seminar' on, 103–9; tariff-preference issue, 107–9, 150–3; war-time collaboration, 165–87; see also International Trade Organization.

— Financial Agreement: British debate on, 225–36; convertibility of sterling under, 217, 218; and 1947 crisis, 306, 312, 318, 337; and dollar pool, 330; failure of, 347; interest payment on the Loan, 211; line of credit in, 210–23; multilateral obligations of, 213–21, 346; non-discrimination clause of, 331, 332; quantitative trade controls under, 216; scarce-currency provisions of, 331; signed (Dec. 1945), 208; sterling balances provisions of, 218, 219, 220; waiver clause in, 212, 213.

Anglo-American Financial Collaboration: adjustment issue, 88–95, 114–17; American debate on, 129–43; British debate on, 121–9; compromise on, 110–21; Keynes's plan for, 77–80; liquidity issue, 86–88, 112–14; planning for, 71–100; transitional issue, 80–86, 117–21; White plan for, 71–77.

— war aims (1941), 41.

Argentina, 317, 320; Anglo-Argentine payments agreement (1947), 313, 320.

Article Nine of American Loan Agreement, 333, 334, 335.

— Seven of Mutual Aid Agreement, 54–68, 71, 107–9, 128; and elimination of Imperial Preference, 152, 156, 349, 351; see also Lend-Lease.

Atlantic Charter, 40–53; Anglo-American opinion of, 47–52; Atlantic Conference, 40–42, 52–53; first definition of multilateralism in, 42–47.

Attlee, Clement, Lord Privy Seal, 26; and non-discrimination, 332; and post-war planning, 25, 26; Prime Minister, 184.

Australia, 273, 327.

Axis powers: trade agreements with U.S.A., 9, 10; trade discrimination by, 19, 45.

Balogh, Thomas, quotation from *International Aspects of Full Employment*, 122.

'Bancor', 79, 89.

PRINTED IN
GREAT BRITAIN
AT THE
UNIVERSITY PRESS
OXFORD
BY
CHARLES BATEY
PRINTER
TO THE
UNIVERSITY